The Institutions of the European Union

Second Edition

Edited by

John Peterson
and
Michael Shackleton

OXFORD
UNIVERSITY PRESS

OXFORD

UNIVERSITY PRESS

Great Clarendon Street, Oxford OX2 6DP

Oxford University Press is a department of the University of Oxford.
It furthers the University's objective of excellence in research, scholarship,
and education by publishing worldwide in

Oxford New York

Auckland Cape Town Dar es Salaam Hong Kong Karachi
Kuala Lumpur Madrid Melbourne Mexico City Nairobi
New Delhi Shanghai Taipei Toronto

With offices in

Argentina Austria Brazil Chile Czech Republic France Greece
Guatemala Hungary Italy Japan Poland Portugal Singapore
South Korea Switzerland Thailand Turkey Ukraine Vietnam

Oxford is a registered trademark of Oxford University Press
in the UK and in certain other countries

Published in the United States
by Oxford University Press Inc., New York

First published 2002

British Library Cataloguing in Publication Data

Data available

Library of Congress Cataloging in Publication Data
The institutions of the European Union / edited by John Peterson and Michael
Shackleton.—2nd ed.
p. cm.—(The new European Union series)
Includes bibliographical references and index.
ISBN-13: 978-0-19-927900-5
1. European Union. 2. European Union countries—Politics and government.
I. Peterson, John, 1958- II. Shackleton, Michael, 1949- III. Series.
JN30.I578 2006 341.242'2—dc22 2006010946

Typeset by Laserwords Private Limited, Chennai, India
Printed in Great Britain
on acid-free paper by
Ashford Colour Press Limited, Gosport, Hampshire

ISBN 978-0-19-927900-5

3 5 7 9 10 8 6 4

Outline contents

Detailed Contents

Preface

The first edition of this book was only the second to appear in the Oxford University Press 'New European Union' series, after Helen and William Wallace's milestone in the EU literature, *Policy-Making in the European Union*. The shelf on which these two books once sat alone now groans under the weight of no fewer than five other volumes, including a new (2005), fifth version of *Policy-Making*. Whereas we once faced 'only' the (already daunting) task of living up to the high standards set by Wallace and Wallace (recently joined by Mark A. Pollack), we now find ourselves having to be good enough to avoid letting down a stable of other authors and editors who together have made the 'New European Union' series an essential set of works for any student of European integration. Quite a lot of the blame for putting us under so much pressure lies with Professor Helen Wallace, the series co-editor, whose energy, enthusiasm, razor sharp mind, and all-around good citizenship never cease to amaze us.

We owe a large debt to our colleagues at Oxford University Press for helping to keep the project on track. Miranda Vernon's professionalism in seeing the book through the production process was exemplary. Ruth Anderson has worked hard to ensure that this book, along with others in the series, finds the audiences it deserves. John Peterson wishes to make it clear that the past efforts of Ruth's predecessors, Sue Dempsey and Angela Griffin, have not been forgotten. Michael Shackleton wishes to make clear that the views expressed in chapters he has authored are purely personal and do not necessarily reflect the position of the European Parliament.

Our authors have almost invariably worked to a high standard, while patiently coping with our active editorship and constant urgings to respect the next deadline. We have learned much from them and are enormously grateful to each for the part they played in making this project a success. We also are in debt to Craig Stewart, Natasa Zambelli, and Kath Francis for their crucial help in preparing the final text.

Our final expression of thanks is to our families: Elizabeth, Miles, and Calum in Edinburgh and Katie, Lucy, and Jan in Brussels. They have now put up with literally years of the two of us neglecting them while we conferred, debated, and cajoled each other and our authors about this project. Their support was especially appreciated in 2005 after French and Dutch voters kicked us (along with their own governments) in the shins by voting down the Constitutional Treaty just as we thought this book was done. We dedicate the final product to them.

JP, MS

List of Exhibits

List of Figures

List of Tables

List of Abbreviations

Here we list the abbreviations for European Parliament party groups in the 2004–09 Parliament only. See Chapter 15 for details of groups that existed beforehand, of European political parties and of national political parties.

ABM	activity-based management
ACP	African, Caribbean and Pacific countries
ADAR	Audit Developments and Reports
AFSJ	area of freedom, security and justice
ALDE	Alliance of Liberals and Democrats for Europe
AMP	annual management programme
APA	Administrative Procedure Act (United States)
APS	annual policy strategy
BSE	bovine spongiform encephalopathy (mad cow disease)
CAP	common agricultural policy
CATS	Comité de l'article trente-six (operating in JHA field)
CCP	common commercial policy
CEECs	central and eastern European countries
CFI	Court of First Instance
CFP	common fisheries policy
CFSP	common foreign and security policy
CHMP	Committee for Medicinal Products for Human Use
CIREA	Centre for Information, Discussion, and Exchange on Asylum
CIREFI	Centre for Information, Discussion, and Exchange on the crossing of Frontiers and Immigration
COA	Court of Auditors
COCOR	Commission de Coordination du Conseil des Ministres
COMP	Committee for Orphan Medicinal Products
CoR	Committee of the Regions
Coreper	Committee of Permanent Representatives
Coreu	Correspondant Européen (EPC communications network)
CPMP	Committee for Proprietary Medicinal Products
CPVO	Community Plant Variety Office
CSCE	Conference for Security and Cooperation in Europe
CST	Civil Service Tribunal

CVMP	Committee for Veterinary Medicines
DG	Directorate-General (in European institutions)
EAGGF	European Agricultural Guidance and Guarantee Fund
EASA	European Aviation Safety Agency
EBRD	European Bank for Reconstruction and Development
EC	European Community
ECA	European Court of Auditors
ECB	European Central Bank
ECHO	European Community Humanitarian Office
ECJ	European Court of Justice
Ecofin	(Council of) Economic and Finance Ministers
Ecosoc	Economic and Social Committee
ECSC	European Coal and Steel Community
EDC	European Defence Community
EDP	excessive deficit procedure
EDU	European Drugs Unit
EEA	European Environment Agency
EEC	European Economic Community
EFC	Economic and Financial Committee
EFSA	European Food Safety Authority
EFTA	European Free Trade Association
EIB	European Investment Bank
EIF	European Investment Fund
EJN	European Judicial Network
EMEA	European Agency for the Evaluation of Medicinal Products
EMI	European Monetary Institute
EMSA	European Maritime Safety Agency
EMU	economic and monetary union
ENISA	European Network and Information Security Agency
EP	European Parliament
EPC	European political cooperation (or European Political Community)
EPP	European Public Prosecutor
EPP-ED	European People's Party and European Democrats
ERDF	European Regional Development Fund
ESCB	European System of Central Banks
ESDP	European security and defence policy
ESS	European security strategy

EU	European Union
EUL/NGL	European United Left/Nordic Green Left
EU-OSHA	European Agency for Safety and Health at Work
EURATOM	European Atomic Energy Community
Eurojust	European Union Judicial Cooperation Unit
Europol	European Police Office
Eurostat	EU statistical office
G8	Group of eight industrialized nations
GAC	General Affairs Council
GAERC	General Affairs and External Relations Council
GATT	General Agreement on Trade and Tariffs
GDP	gross domestic product
G/EFA	Greens/European Free Alliance
GNP	gross national product
HMPC	Committee on Herbal Medicinal Products
HR/CFSP	High Representative for common foreign and security policy
IND/DEM	Independence and Democracy
IGC	intergovernmental conference
IMF	International Monetary Fund
IO	international organization
JHA	justice and home affairs
LI	liberal intergovernmentalism
MEP	member of the European Parliament
MFA	minister for foreign affairs (under Constitutional Treaty provisions)
NATO	North Atlantic Treaty Organization
NI	new institutionalism
NPM	new public management
OHIM	Office for Harmonization in the Internal Market (Trade Marks and Designs)
OJ	Official Journal of the European Communities
OLAF	Office européen de la lutte antifraude (fraud prevention office)
OMC	open method of coordination
OSCE	Organization for Security and Cooperation in Europe (formerly CSCE)
PES	Party of European Socialists
PSC	Political and Security Committee (also known as COPS)
QMV	qualified majority voting
RRF	rapid reaction force
SCA	Special Committee on Agriculture

SEA	Single European Act
SGCI	Secrétariat général du Comité interministériel pour les questions de coopération économique européenne
SGP	Stability and Growth Pact
SOA	statement of assurance (also known as DAS)
SRO	self-regulatory organization
TEC	Treaty of the European Community
TEU	Treaty on European Union
UCLAF	Unité de coordination de la lutte antifraude (anti-fraud unit)
UEN	Union for Europe of the Nations
UK	United Kingdom
UN	United Nations
US	United States
WEU	Western European Union
WTO	World Trade Organization

List of Contributors

Sir Brian Crowe *Royal Institute for International Affairs*

Philippe de Schoutheete, *University of Louvain*

Renaud Dehousse, *Institut d'Etudes Politiques (Paris)*

Fiona Hayes-Renshaw, *College of Europe (Bruges)*

Liesbet Hooghe, *University of North Carolina (Chapel Hill)*

Charlie Jeffery, *University of Edinburgh*

Tom Kennedy *European Court of Auditors*

Theodora Kostakopoulou, *University of Manchester*

Brigid Laffan, *University College, Dublin*

Jeffrey Lewis, *Cleveland State University*

Kathleen R. McNamara, *Georgetown University*

Paul Magnette, *Free University of Brussels*

Giandomenico Majone, *University of Pittsburgh*

Neill Nugent, *Manchester Metropolitan University*

John Peterson, *University of Edinburgh*

Tapio Raunio, *University of Helsinki*

Michael Shackleton, *Secretariat, European Parliament*

Michael E. Smith, *University of St. Andrews*

Table of Cases

(Names in brackets refer to abbreviations used in Chapter 7.)

Editors' Note

We have had to make decisions on a number of presentational issues and adopted the following conventions:

- the book follows the numbering of the Treaty articles that emerged from the Treaty of Amsterdam and was maintained in the Treaty of Nice;
- we use the initials 'TEU' to refer to articles in the Treaty on European Union, or those which lie outside the scope of the European Community Treaty (notably the provisions on a common foreign and security policy—and more recently the European security and defence policy—as well as police and judicial cooperation in criminal matters, the so-called second and third pillars). The initials 'TEC' are used to refer to first-pillar articles within the Treaty establishing the European Community;
- the book refers consistently to the 'Constitutional Treaty' rather than the 'Constitution'. The former title seems to us to correspond more correctly to the nature of what member state governments agreed to in 2004. Irrespective of its fate, the Treaty remains an important part of the analysis in most chapters. References are made to the different articles in the three main parts of the Constitutional Treaty's text, distinguished by 'I', 'II', or 'III' before the number of the article.
- shortly before publication we learned that from May 2006 the website addresses of all of the institutions will be changed (to take account of the adoption of the .eu domain). Each institution will have a new address based on that of the main portal *www.europa.eu*. The European Parliament's site, for example, will be re-named *www.europarl.europa.eu*. Internet users will, however, be redirected automatically from the addresses found throughout this book.

Chapter 1

The EU's Institutions

An Overview

John Peterson and Michael Shackleton

Contents

Summary

The European Union (EU) straddles accepted categories of political organization. It is neither a state nor an 'ordinary' international organization. What sets the EU apart, above all, is its unique institutions: they resemble no other bodies found at the national or international levels. Now, perhaps more than ever, Europe's institutions *are* Europe's politics. The point was illustrated dramatically in 2005 by the political crisis over the EU's Constitutional Treaty, designed to reform the Union's institutions to cope with the Union's enlargement, following its rejection in two referendums in France and the Netherlands. This chapter introduces contending definitions of 'institution' and approaches to studying them. It argues that understanding politics always begins with understanding institutions, not least in the EU.

Introduction

The EU remains one of the most elusive of all subjects of study in the social sciences. It is neither a state nor an 'ordinary' international organization (see Peterson 2001; W. Wallace 2005). Rather, it is a unique experiment embedding the national in the

European and the European in the national (Laffan *et al.* 2000). What distinguishes the EU above all is its institutions: they have no close analogues at either the national or international levels.

The EU exists to provide collective goods—such as an internal market, a single currency, and international power—which the Union's Member States cannot deliver (or not as well) on their own. The EU's institutional system is both the central mechanism for achieving those goals and the locus of disagreement about the future development of the Union, as was illustrated dramatically by the crisis that followed rejection of the EU's 'Constitutional Treaty' in referendums held in France and The Netherlands in 2005. Now, perhaps even more than when Ludlow (1992) first made the argument, Europe's institutions *are* Europe's politics: battles over the political direction of the EU are inevitably clashes about how its institutional system can and should work. For example, the Constitutional Treaty—a traditional Treaty between EU member states but meant to be more permanent than its predecessors—was portrayed by its supporters as simply a pragmatic attempt to rationalise the EU system to cope with its radical enlargement. Yet, it became a lightning rod for Eurosceptics opposed to closer European integration.

Most academic work on European integration highlights the highly variable capacity of the EU to govern effectively in the different phases of its development. The standard version of that development suggests that Europe integrated surprisingly rapidly in the 1950s and early 1960s. Then, in the 1970s and early 1980s, the Community became immobilized by economic crisis and a set of rules that made effective decision-making almost impossible. During this period of so-called Eurosclerosis, it seemed the Community could accomplish nothing very important. Then, dramatically, European integration was given fresh impetus by the so-called single market project, which sought to transform (then) twelve national economies into a single, seamless European one. Before the project's 1992 target date for completion, even more dramatic changes were unleashed by the collapse of the Warsaw Pact and Soviet Union in 1989–91. West European governments responded by agreeing the Maastricht Treaty, which contained bold commitments to economic and monetary union, a 'common' European foreign and security policy, and a political union. Suddenly, it seemed the EU could accomplish *anything* (Laffan *et al.* 2000: 4). Twelve years after Maastricht was ratified, the turmoil surrounding the Constitutional Treaty raised questions about whether the EU would again become immobilized, and perhaps as never before.

These perceptions of total breakdown and dramatic advance are both products of failed imagination: lack of it during the Eurosclerosis period, overactivity in the 1990s, and a failure to imagine that the EU might, as it always had in the past, eventually recover from its constitutional crisis of 2005. The EU has always been somewhere between inert and ideal. In the past decade, it has successfully introduced the euro, thus reinforcing the identity of the Union in the minds of millions of Europeans (if not always positively[1]). It has also negotiated the entry of ten new member states, thus exporting its liberal democratic habits to Europe's east and south. At the same time, it has made few strides towards the goal it set itself in Lisbon in 2000 to make the Union the most dynamic economy in the world. It was entirely unable to agree a common European response to the 2003 war in Iraq.

What spans the EU's successes and failures, its potential and shortcomings, its state-centrism and European-ness, is its institutions. There is no one single, uncontroversial definition of 'institution' but rather a variety of contending ones. Article 7 of the EU's Treaties follows the European tradition of defining institutions as organizations which enjoy special legal status, and designates five: the European Parliament (EP); the Council of Ministers; the European Commission; the European Court of Justice (ECJ); and the Court of Auditors. Article I-19 of the Constitutional Treaty also lists five but substitutes the European Council for the Court of Auditors. If we used either of these definitions, this book would be much shorter and narrower in focus than it is.

Yet, institutions are often defined in a far broader sense in the study of politics, as 'extending beyond the formal organs of government to include standard operating procedures, so-called soft law, norms and conventions of behaviour' (Bulmer 1994: 355). According to this perspective, 'institutions do not think, have preferences or act, but are sets of commonly accepted formal and informal norms that constrain political actors' (Marks 1996: 22). In this sense, virtually anything that is accepted as 'normal' could be considered institutionalized. Coverage of all that fits under this definition in the EU would result in a book far longer than this one.

This book takes a sort of middle way. First, we conceive of institutions as arenas where power and influence are exercised, regardless of the precise legal status of the organizations that preside over them. Second, we invite our readers to think of institutions not just in terms of specific people and premises but also as rules and practices.

We begin by explaining why the study of institutions has been brought 'back in' to the study of politics in recent years. We then develop the argument that the EU's institutions provide an essential and revealing window into Europe's politics (see Exhibit 1.1). Our next task is to consider how and why the Union's institutions have changed yet endured over time. Finally, we set out some of the book's major themes, and conclude with advice on how this book might be read.

Exhibit 1.1 Perceptions of the EU's institutions[2]

Each man begins the world afresh. Only institutions grow wiser. They store up collective experience . . . From this experience and wisdom, men subject to the same laws will gradually find . . . not that their natures change . . . but that their behaviour does.

Source: Jean Monnet (1950)

The fusion of interests in the European Community is being achieved through a new mechanism of institutions which it is only slight exaggeration to call a constitutional framework.

Source: Walter Hallstein (1962)

What a model our institutions, which allow every country irrespective of its size to have its say and make a contribution, offer the nations of Eastern Europe.

Source: Jacques Delors (1989)

continues

Exhibit 1.1 continued

Supranational institutions — above all, the European Commission, the European Court, and the European Parliament — have independent influence in policy-making that cannot be derived from their role as agents of state executives.

Source: Gary Marks, Liesbet Hooghe, and Kermit Blank (1992)

All along [the] road, the European institutions — the Council, the European Parliament, the Commission, and the Court of Justice — have provided sterling service, to which we must pay tribute. At the same time ... the process of European union is showing signs of flagging.

Source: Valéry Giscard d'Estaing (2002)

Like other reformers, political leaders in the EU try to make institutions more rational and efficient, more humane, representative, responsive, transparent and accountable ... The motivations of EU reformers are complex and shifting. They want many, different and not necessarily consistent things.

Source: Johan Olsen (2003)

Why study institutions?

The social sciences came of age in the early twentieth century by focusing intensely, often exclusively, on institutions. In political science, the overwhelming emphasis was on formal structures of government and systems of law-making. Political analysis began — and often ended — by describing institutions in great detail. Methodology was generally not a matter for debate nor was the behaviour of political leaders, officials or citizens. As Rhodes (1995: 42) suggests, 'the focus on institutions was a matter of common sense, an obvious starting point ... and therefore there was no need to justify it'.[3]

Everything changed in the 1950s and early 1960s. First, the so-called behavioural revolution was unleashed (see Sanders 1995). Behaviouralists condemned the traditional emphasis on institutions as too narrow, unscientific, and atheoretical. Traditional institutionalist analysis not only failed to explain policy or power. It also suffered from 'hyperfactualism': reverence for 'facts' amounted to theoretical malnutrition (Easton 1971).

For behaviouralists, institutions were relatively uninteresting compared to the *behaviour* of political actors. Institutions had no political interests or personalities of their own. In a sense, behaviouralism assumed that an institution was just a car waiting for a driver. What was far more interesting than studying the car was studying the behaviour of the agents — political leaders, parties, voters — competing to seize power, control institutions, or drive the car. Behaviouralists sought to make political science a true science, often through the use of statistics and quantitative analysis. Institutions — leaving aside some notable exceptions (see Allison 1971) — more or less disappeared from the radar screens of most political scientists.

The second big change was a shift in the study of international relations. Traditionally, scholarship had focused mostly on competition (especially military) between sovereign states in what was assumed to be a Hobbesian and anarchic international system (see Morgenthau 1948). However, the post-war creation of the United Nations (UN) and the Bretton Woods institutions (the General Agreement on Tariffs and Trade, the World Bank, and the International Monetary Fund, or IMF) led to a blossoming of scholarship on international cooperation. In time, Europe became the primary focus of this scholarship as the continent embarked on ambitious experiments in (especially economic) integration. 'Neofunctionalists' theorized that modest steps towards cooperation would lead to more ambitious moves in a process that was, in many ways, self-sustaining (see Haas 1958; Lindberg 1963).

Yet, the dawning of the so-called Second Cold War (Halliday 1983), a period of heightened international tension in the early 1980s, made most international organizations (IOs)—including the apparently Eurosclerotic Community—seem too weak to foster much meaningful cooperation. The focus shifted towards explaining renewed conflict, especially between the United States and Soviet Union (see Waltz 1979). Europe was politically and—along with institutionalism—academically marginalized.

Then, beginning in the mid-1980s, institutions began to be rediscovered. A groundswell of academic momentum developed behind the idea that institutions were important but neglected, and it was time to bring them 'back in' to the study of politics (see Skocpol 1985; March and Olsen 1989). In some respects, the 'new institutionalism' was a rebellion against behaviouralism. Neoinstitutionalists insisted that political behaviour was determined in fundamental ways by the nature of political institutions, how they are constructed and how power is distributed between them.

The basic neoinstitutionalist argument is that institutions matter. They define group loyalties in any political system and help determine how political debates are structured. They are *not* just cars waiting for drivers. In particular, institutions, even ones that are formally apolitical, can develop their own interests, agendas and priorities and act with considerable autonomy despite being formally controlled by political actors, such as governments. Actual policy outcomes can reflect the *agency*—the determined pursuit of favoured choices—of institutions more than of the preferences of governments. One reason why is that the policy priorities of governments are often disputed or vaguely defined, thus allowing scope for formally apolitical institutions to set the agenda.

The new institutionalism is more a *perspective* on politics than a fully developed theory. Still, neoinstitutionalism has emerged as a leading, even (arguably) dominant perspective on European integration and politics (Pollack 2004; Cowles and Curtis 2004). If nothing else, it is accepted as a viable alternative to state-centric or intergovernmental approaches derived from the study of international relations (see Grieco 1995; Moravcsik 1998). The latter assume, reasonably, that the EU has a strong intergovernmental backbone and that policy debates are mostly debates between national actors pursuing national interests. Yet, battles over EU policy are mostly fought out far from national capitals and governments. Nearly all actors in EU politics have multiple identities and mixed loyalties, to their member state, political party, or the interests of the policy sector in which they work. Institutional affiliations thus give actors a sort of anchor or orientation that may override others. Neoinstitutionalist treatments argue that EU politics have to be understood in terms of institutional competition (and cooperation) between, above all, the Council of Ministers, the European Commission, the European Parliament (EP), and the European Court of Justice (ECJ), and not just in terms of *intergovernmental* competition (and cooperation).

There are at least three main variants of institutionalism (see Hall and Taylor 1996; Peters 1999; Pollack 2004). Historical institutionalists focus on how EU governance has evolved over time (Bulmer 1994; Armstrong and Bulmer 1998; Lindner and Rittberger 2003). This work highlights the importance of emergent institutional norms, such as the Council's engrained habit of seeking unanimity on any measure regardless of whether qualified-majority voting (QMV) applies (see also Golub 1999). Such norms can constrain political decision-making and produce 'path dependence'—a concept central to all variants of institutionalism—because 'initial policy choices may restrict subsequent [policy] evolution' (Armstrong and Bulmer 1998: 55). Path dependence is particularly powerful when consensus is required to *change* an existing policy or institution. Historical institutionalists, as neofunctionalists before them, insist that European integration must be studied as a historical process, in which actors often apply a high 'discount rate' to the future. Thus, today's decisions often are taken with little regard for tomorrow's consequences. In these circumstances, member governments can become 'locked in' to policy paths on which they have set the Union, with its institutions becoming guardians of long-established policies and 'not simply passive tools of the member states' (Pierson 1996: 132; see also Pierson 2004).

A second, sociological variant of institutionalism shares with the historical version a preoccupation with the Union's 'uneven institutional history' (Fligstein and McNichol 1998: 88; see also Fligstein and Brantley 1995; Fligstein 1997). Yet, sociological institutionalists assign even greater weight to norms, conventions, and ideas. For example, Parsons (2003: 1) argues that the EU 'stands out as the major exception in the thinly institutionalized world of international politics' because certain ideas about how solutions could be connected to problems became institutionalized in postwar Europe. The political effects have been powerful, since the 'institutionalization of certain ideas gradually reconstructs the interests of powerful actors' (Parsons 2003: 6). Sociological institutionalists share important analytical assumptions with constructivists, who insist that preferences in EU policy debates are 'constructed' through the social interaction of actors in Brussels and Strasbourg as much (or more) than they are determined prior to such interactions (see Christiansen *et al.* 2001). More generally, sociological institutionalism holds that institutions matter because they determine what is considered appropriate behaviour by actors, which itself has powerful implications for political and policy outcomes.

A third variant of institutionalism builds on rational choice theory (see Farrell and Héritier 2005). Rational choice institutionalists argue that institutions matter most when they become subject to what economists call 'increasing returns': that is, they generate sufficient benefits that member governments, who themselves rationally calculate their own interests, face disincentives to abandon or reformulate them. Thus, the European Court of Justice has been able to pursue legal integration even beyond the collective preferences of member governments because of the high costs to member states of seeking to overrule it or failing to comply with its judgments (Garrett 1995). Rational choice institutionalism sometimes draws on principal–agent theory, which seeks to explain how and why governments, or 'principals', solve collective action problems by delegating functions to international institutions which then act as their 'agents', although usually with a variety of mechanisms put in place to control or monitor their behaviour (see Majone 2000; Pollack 2003).[4]

The point here is not that neoinstitutionalism, in one or more of it variants, is the only, or even best, way to study the EU's institutions. In fact, the contributors to this volume deploy a range of different theoretical approaches. The point is rather that institutions are worth studying because, as is now widely acknowledged across all the social sciences, institutions matter.

Why study the EU's institutions?

If institutions matter, they may matter even more in the European Union than in other political systems. Why? We can think of at least eight reasons.

First, the EU is probably the most powerful non-state actor in the contemporary international world (see Josselin and Wallace 2001). Its institutions generate a wide array of policies that impact directly upon EU states and their citizens (as well as many beyond Europe) and in ways that are unmatched by any other international organization. Every day, EU citizens in 12 states use the currency that was adopted as a result of a series of decisions taken by EU leaders meeting in the European Council. Air passengers in Europe whose flights end up being cancelled are now often entitled to generous compensation mostly due to the stubborn insistence of the European Parliament (EP) that they should be. One of the largest proposed corporate mergers in history, between the *American* firms General Electric and Honeywell, was scuppered by a decision of the European Commission. In short, the European Union is enormously powerful, and not *only* because it combines the power of twenty-five (as of 2006) European states, including several major powers. Much of the EU's power is vested in its institutions.

Second, the EU's institutional structure has uniquely blended continuity and change. The institutions established in the 1950s (see Table 1.1) have retained many of their essential characteristics, revealing how deeply engrained established institutional norms and cultures have become. In most policy areas, the Commission retains to this day a monopoly right to present legislative proposals, a power it has held since the origins of the European Economic Community. For its part, the European Parliament has evolved from a mostly toothless body to an effective co-legislator with the Council in many areas. Meanwhile, there has been a remarkable burgeoning of new bodies starting with the European Council and European Court of Auditors in the 1970s and continuing with a seemingly endless array of decentralised agencies that have sprung up in the last decade (see Table 1.1).

Third, the EU's institutions matter because they are the vehicles used by the Union's member governments to enforce the terms of the bargains they make with each other (see Moravcsik 1998). But they are more than just passive instruments, or cars waiting for drivers. The powers they have accrued over time—arising from the *acquis communautaire*, or the full set of rights and obligations deriving from EU

Table 1.1   An institutional timeline

Start of activities	Title of institution	Location
1950		
1952	**Council of Ministers**	Brussels/Luxembourg
1952	**ECSC High Authority**	Luxembourg
1952	**European Court of Justice**	Luxembourg
1952	**ECSC Parliamentary Assembly**	Strasbourg/Luxembourg
1958	**European Commission**	Brussels/Luxembourg
1958	**Economic and Social Committee**	Brussels
1958	**European Investment Bank**	Luxembourg
1958	**Committee of Permanent Representatives (Coreper)**	Brussels/Luxembourg
1960		
1962	European Parliamentary Assembly changes its name to **European Parliament**	Strasbourg/Luxembourg/ Brussels
1965	Merger Treaties create a single **Commission**	Brussels/Luxembourg
1970		
1974	**European Council** (formally established by Paris Summit)	
1975	European Centre for the Development of Vocational Training	Berlin (since 1995 Thessaloniki)
1975	European Foundation for the Improvement of Living and Working Conditions	Dublin
1977	**European Court of Auditors**	Luxembourg
1980		
1989	**Court of First Instance**	Luxembourg
1990		
1994	European Environment Agency	Copenhagen
1994	**Committee of Regions**	Brussels
1994	Office for Harmonization in the Internal Market	Alicante
1994	Translation Centre for the Bodies of the European Union	Luxembourg
1995	**European Ombudsman**	Strasbourg
1995	European Training Foundation	Turin
1995	Community Plant Variety Office	Angers
1995	European Agency for Safety and Health at Work	Bilbao
1995	European Medicines Agency (EMEA)	London
1995	European Monitoring Centre for Drugs and Drug Addiction	Lisbon
1998	European Monitoring Centre on Racism and Xenophobia	Vienna
1998	**European Central Bank**	Frankfurt
1999	European Anti-Fraud Office (OLAF)	Brussels
1999	Europol	The Hague
2000		
2000	European Police College (CEPOL)	Bramshill
2000	European Agency for Reconstruction	Thessaloniki
2001	European Data Protection Supervisor	Brussels
2002	Eurojust	The Hague
2002	European Maritime Safety Agency	Lisbon (since 2004)

continues

Table 1.1 continued

Start of Activities	Title of Institution	Location
2002	European Aviation Safety Agency	Cologne (since 2004)
2002	European Food Safety Authority	Parma (since 2004)
2002	European Institute for Security Studies	Paris
2002	European Union Satellite Centre	Torrejon de Ardoz
2003	European Communities Personnel Selection Office (EPSO)	Brussels
2004	European Network and Information Security Agency	Heraklion
to be established	European Railway Agency	Lille, Valenciennes
	European Centre for Disease Prevention and Control	Sweden
	European Chemicals Agency	Spain
	Community Fisheries Control Agency	Helsinki

Note: (Institutions in bold are designated in the Treaties as 'EU institutions'.)

treaties, laws and regulations—give the Union's institutions substantial autonomy. For example, the ECJ has had an intensely powerful impact on the shape and direction of European integration both through its own judgements and its integration of national courts into a single system of judicial review (Weiler 1999; Alter 2001). More generally, the EU's institutions are an important reason why European states continue to respond to their interdependence by cooperating (while competing, sometimes fiercely, over the details).

Fourth, the Union's institutions not only manage but also provide direction. More than the international secretariats of any other IO, the EU's institutions possess rational-legal authority to make rules. They also create social knowledge in less formal ways: defining shared European tasks, creating new categories of actors (such as refugees or 'EU citizens'), forming new interests for actors or reshaping old ones, and transferring new models of political and administrative organization across Europe (see Barnett and Finnemore 1999). Of course, political direction comes mostly from member governments and is channelled via the European Council and Council of Ministers. But there is scope for agency by the Commission and Parliament, each of which has its own political agenda and priorities which cannot be reduced to the sum total of those of the EU's member governments.

Moreover, the Commission, Parliament and other EU institutions also act to integrate interests, including those of actors who either oppose or act independently of their 'home' government. Certainly, it is easy to overestimate the EU as a Brussels-based system of politics in which national interests or institutions are marginalized or blended together. As Helen Wallace (2000: 7) argues:

> much of EU policy is prepared and carried out by national policy-makers and agents who do not spend much, if any, time in Brussels. Rather what they do is consider how EU regimes might help or hinder their regular activities, and apply the results of EU agreements on the ground in their normal daily work. If we could calculate the proportions, we might

well find that in practice something like 80 per cent of that normal daily life was framed
by domestic preoccupations and constraints.

At the same time, the EU has given rise to a multi-level polity in which the boundary
between politics in national capitals and Brussels has become blurred. The Union's
institutions have aided and abetted this blurring by providing opportunities for
interests, including ones that lack influence at the national level, to join their counterparts across Europe in pursuing common objectives. Many truly pan-European interests have been nurtured, sometimes manufactured, by the Union's institutions.
Some lobbies have been energised by their perceived need to respond to agency
on the part of the EU's institutions. Witness, for example, the resolute lobbying effort of the European chemicals industry in response to the Commission's proposed
REACH (Registration, Authorization, and Restriction of Chemicals) Directive, which
threatened the industry with significant new costs.

Fifth, the EU's institutions are worth studying because they are powerful yet often
unloved or misunderstood by European citizens. Arguably, popular disillusion with
the EU's institutions is no more severe — some evidence suggests less — than is disillusion with national institutions and politics.[5] Still, the EU's institutions are clearly not
as accepted or respected as national institutions are by European citizens. Average
voter turn-out in EP elections has fallen with each successive poll. After the French
and Dutch voted against the Constitutional Treaty by surprisingly large margins in
the 2005 referenda, one seasoned observer detected a 'collapse of self confidence and
general morale in the EU institutions', and especially in the Commission which was
'close to an institutional nervous breakdown' (Palmer 2005; see also Tsakatika 2005).
However, its President, José Manuel Barroso, fought back by urging member governments to break their habit of blaming all of Europe's ills on the EU: 'If you attack
Brussels six days of the week, can you really expect citizens to support it on Sunday?'[6]

Sixth, the EU's institutions not only link Brussels to national EU capitals. They also
link Europe to the wider world of international politics and, particularly, an extensive network of IOs. As the world's largest trading power, the EU is a crucial player in
the World Trade Organization (WTO). The creation of a European Security and Defence Policy (ESDP) has required extensive interaction with the North Atlantic Treaty
Organization (NATO). As the Iraq war illustrated, the EU continues to disappoint
those who wish to see it become, in Tony Blair's memorable phrase, 'a superpower,
not a super-state'. Yet, the Constitutional Treaty foresaw the transformation of the
post held by Javier Solana, of 'High Representative' for the Common Foreign and
Security Policy (CFSP), into an outright EU Minister for Foreign Affairs. Whatever
the move's future prospects, political agreement on it by twenty-five member governments illustrated a remarkable depth of will in Europe to make the EU a more
effective global actor.

More generally, the Union's institutions are increasingly more powerful actors in
the so-called 'international community', a world once almost exclusively dominated
by sovereign states. One effect is to allow Europe (sometimes, at least) to wield its formidable, collective power. Ironically, in an era when the US often seems unrivalled
in international politics (Ikenberry 2002), and with the EU apparently at its weak-
est given the crisis over the Constitutional Treaty, a surfeit of works has piled up

predicting that the twenty-first century will be one of European dominance (Kupchan 2003; Haseler 2004; Reid 2004; Rifkind 2004; Leonard 2005).

Seventh and somewhat paradoxically, EU politics are largely a product of competition between its institutions, but the Union's institutions are inescapably interdependent. The EU's decision rules are designed to foster collective responsibility for the Union's policies. Little of importance may be agreed without the joint consent of the Commission, EP and Council—with appeal to the ECJ always likely when such consensus is *not* achieved. Regardless of its fate, the Constitutional Treaty spells out far more explicitly than ever before aims that *all* of the EU's institutions share collectively: to advance the EU's objectives, promote its values, serve the interests of the Union, its citizens and member states, and ensure the consistency, effectiveness and continuity of its policies. It explicitly states that all EU institutions should work in 'full mutual cooperation'.

Thus, our understanding of the Union runs up against hard limits when we study them as separate and autonomous entities. In practice, they form a series of networks, differing in structure and membership in different policy sectors, with each bound together by both formal and informal rules (see Keohane and Hoffmann 1991). Even an institution that is formally designated as independent, such as the European Central Bank (ECB), cannot be understood without reference to the decisions taken by the European Council and the Council of (Economic and Finance) Ministers at its inception. In line with institutionalist assumptions, these decisions have heavily structured the kind of decisions the ECB can now take.

Institutional interdependence is clearly uneven across policy sectors. For example, the EP has little power to determine the CFSP. The Commission acts with considerable independence in competition policy. There exists no single mode of EU policy-making (see H. Wallace 2005), and the traditional Community method—which gives distinct and exclusive powers to the Commission, EP and Council—has often been found inappropriate for new policy tasks, such as freeing labour markets or creating the European Security and Defence Policy (ESDP). These and other objectives have been pursued via some variant of the so-called Open Method of Coordination (OMC), which usually involves peer review of national policies as a way to disseminate best practices, with policy change occurring voluntarily (as opposed to being imposed by new EU rules) when it occurs at all.

The early record of the OMC was, at best, mixed. More generally, it was easy to conclude that the EU is suffering from 'a crisis of governance' (Eberlein and Kerwer 2004: 135), given its radical enlargement, attempts to tackle problems that were not readily soluble by traditional methods, and the turmoil surrounding the Constitutional Treaty. Whether or not new policy modes such as the OMC are just stages on the way towards the embrace of the tried and true Communitarian model (see Wessels 2001), the trend is towards finding new, non-traditional ways to encourage collective action on the part of multiple EU institutions. Good examples include the EU Minister of Foreign Affairs who (if the post were ever created) would be a European Commissioner yet chair the Council when EU foreign ministers met, or the European data protection supervisor, who both oversees how the institutions apply the EU's own privacy rules and coordinates a network of data protection officers appointed by each EU institution.

Last but not least, the Union's institutions are worth studying because they are a testing ground: they will go far towards determining history's verdict on the EU's success in managing enlargement. Since the first edition of this book was published, 10 new states have joined the EU, bringing with them nine new official languages and increasing the number of language combinations from 110 to 380. No other IO has ever had to face this kind of challenge on this scale. To illustrate the point, trade officials stressed the gravity of China's accession to the World Trade Organization in 2001. Yet, even admitting a state with a market of 1.3 billion consumers whose language was not an official WTO working language did not come close to posing the challenges posed by the EU's 2004 expansion: mathematically, the WTO would have to have admitted around 90 new states alongside China to stand comparison to what the EU did on 1 May 2004. The possible institutional effects of EU enlargement are a central theme of this volume.

'Frustration without disintegration' — the persistence of the EU system

We have argued that the EU's institutions are both important and essential to understanding the European Union. It also must be acknowledged that the EU is home to considerable institutional weakness and dysfunction. By no means is the Union alone amongst international organizations in having institutions that sometimes appear obsessed with their own internal rules or neglectful of their missions (Barnett and Finnemore 1999). Yet, European citizens who express stronger support for a united Europe in the abstract than for the EU in practice[7] exhibit a sort of collective, common sense. It is perfectly plausible to be pro-European but to believe that the EU's institutional system does not work very well: apparently, the European Union flag was widely displayed at many 'non' rallies during the 2005 French referendum campaign on the Constitutional Treaty (Palmer 2005).

Part of the problem may be historical. Many of the EU's institutions were created for a Community of six states, not a Union of twenty-five plus. Even in the original EEC, very different ideas about what kind of polity the EU should be created scope for weak compromises and institutions that were dysfunctional almost from the moment of their creation (see Lindner and Rittberger 2003). In these circumstances, it could be argued that the EU's institutions have adapted remarkably well to successive enlargements. Yet, the 2004 enlargement clearly marked a step-level change. The Constitutional Treaty was intended to be a quasi-permanent solution to the problem of modernizing the EU's institutional system so that it could cope with enlargement. The Treaty's rejection by French and Dutch voters revealed that Europe remains far from a consensus about what kind of polity the EU should become. Arguably, it has relied for far too long on an institutional system that is long past its sell-by date.

Another part of the problem is political. Without a government (or opposition), the Union often seems unable to steer the European project. For one thing, the project has always depended for its sustenance on appearing to be apolitical, consensual, or uncontroversial. For another thing, the capacity of the EU's institutions—with the arguable exception of the European Council—to give political impulses to the Union are strictly limited. For all of the capacity of the EU's institutions for agency, political leadership of Europe must inevitably come mostly from national capitals.

A third and related problem is managerial. The 1980s saw the Commission under the Presidency of Jacques Delors show (unusually) genuine political leadership. However, Delors and his college of Commissioners took little interest in efficient management. Amidst charges of mismanagement and nepotism, the collective resignation of the Commission under Delors' successor, Jacques Santer, in March 1999 was a low point in the institutional history of the EU. It illustrated that the EU's lack of hierarchy and reliance on informal networks had serious costs. For students of public management, it was axiomatic that 'pluralistic policy networks are undermanaged because the constituent organisations do not invest in the capacities needed to manage their mutual interdependence' (Metcalfe 2000: 13). For students of the EU, it was hard to resist Metcalfe's (2000: 13) conclusion that 'the substandard performance of the system is everyone's problem and no-one's responsibility'.

Yet, there was little question that the Commission was far better managed (if not necessarily better led) by the end of Romano Prodi's Presidency in 2004. Prodi's Vice-President and Commissioner for Administrative Reform, Neil Kinnock, piloted an ambitious programme of reforms (see Spence 2000; Kassim 2004). Meanwhile, the Council was taking its own steps to better manage its agenda and make itself more transparent. The Court was revamping itself to cut down on its backlog of cases.

One view of these developments is that they reflect the steady maturation of the EU's institutions into modern, high-performance bodies as the Union itself slowly but steadily comes of age politically. This view focuses more on long-term process than short-term crises. It assumes that no Constitutional Treaty was ever going to be greeted with universal enthusiasm. It also reminds us that, after all, the version rejected by the French and Dutch in 2005 had been agreed within a broadly inclusive constitutional convention that produced the most transparent and readable European treaty in modern history (see Norman 2003). Implicitly, this view assumes that political consensus on institutional reforms, as reflected in the Constitutional Treaty, means that most of its provisions that advance or consolidate the position of the EU's main institutions will eventually be implemented. For example, the rotating Council Presidency system (a source of discontinuity in the work of the Council) will be abandoned. The Commission will keep its monopoly right of legislative initiative. One day, perhaps sooner rather than later, the European Council will have a sitting President.

These two portraits that we have painted—of institutional weakness and fresh dynamism—are less incompatible than they appear. First, consider how one of the primary functions of the EU's institutions, integrating political interests, has often *not* been abetted and sometimes has been actively resisted by member governments. Naturally, perhaps, EU governments wish to retain their own, favoured, primary relationships with voters and interest groups. The result is that the EP and Commission lack their own, independent sources of authority and support. They also lack resources. The EP has nothing approaching the resources of say, the US Congress (with its large Congressional Research Service, General Accounting Office, and so on). The Commission has one official per 10,000 EU citizens, while national civil services average 300 per 10,000 (Leonard 2005: 15). There are clear limits to the willingness of the Union's member governments to delegate control of the European project.

Second, the EU almost never makes a hard decision today that can be put off until tomorrow. Barroso was explicit in stating that making a success of the so-called Lisbon process of economic reform would be one of the priorities of his Commission. Yet, its fate clearly would be overwhelmingly determined by difficult decisions that had to be taken at the national level, most of which had been avoided thus far (see EU 2004).

Third and finally, it is impossible to banish path dependency from EU governance. Even after attempts to constitutionalize the EU seemed to go so badly wrong in the mid-2000s (Skach 2005), 'frustration without disintegration' remained an apt description for how the EU's institutional system remained sub-optimal but never stopped working (Scharpf 1999). The desire amongst European governments to make the Union work better, but to avoid a genuine process of state-building, were both time-honoured impulses, however contradictory they sometimes seemed to be.

The EU's institutions have always, from their earliest origins, operated in a highly contested environment. There is no universal agreement about what the European Union is or ought to be, and never has been. Is it a particularly elaborate IO that enables states to achieve certain goals more efficiently than they could otherwise do? Or does it now transcend the state, in some areas emerging as more than the sum of its parts? Since academics as well as practitioners (see Exhibit 1.1) give different answers to these questions, they inevitably disagree as to what the Union's institutions—individually and collectively—exist to do.

One thing should be clear from our analysis thus far: the EU's institutions cannot simply be seen as a purely functional set of bodies designed to achieve certain common purposes. If they were, they could be judged purely on the basis of efficiency. Yet, the EU's institutional system no longer rests 'on a single principle of legitimacy, but several' (Lord and Magnette 2004: 199). European integration has become a highly political exercise, and the EU's institutions have evolved into highly political animals. Arguments about how to make the EU more efficient often ignore widespread doubts about the legitimacy of the Union as a whole.

Thus, we encourage our readers to look beyond debates about what each institution should do. Can the EU withstand new demands to be more open and transparent even as it digests radical enlargement? Is the EU a model for the world or a one-off? Are its best days behind it? Answering each of these questions begins, inevitably, by understanding its institutions.

Conclusion

Most leading texts on the EU offer a straight review of what the Treaty designates as institutions, with one chapter each on the Council, Commission, EP, and so on. Less weighty institutions, such as the Court of Auditors and Committee of the Regions, are covered in a composite, 'lest we forget' chapter. This book does not present a simple, standard, one-institution-per-chapter dash across the EU's institutional landscape. Instead, after an overview (in Chapter 2) of the EU's, tortured attempts at institutional reform, we offer three grouped sections of chapters that examine how different institutions provide political direction, manage the Union, and integrate interests. Each of these chapters begins with an analysis of the origins and development of the institution specified, followed by an overview of its structure and functions. Each author then reflects on 'their' institution's powers, before considering how it fits into the EU's wider institutional system. All consider which theories of European integration and EU governance help us best to understand the institution. None ignores the crucial questions of how their institution is likely to be changed by enlargement or by the debate surrounding the Constitutional Treaty.

Some EU institutions—particularly the Commission, Council and EP—perform more than one function, and thus analysis of them is spread across more than one chapter. The reader who wants to understand the institutions 'one by one' (or teacher who wants to teach them that way) should not hesitate from reading, say, Chapter 5 on the college of Commissioners together with Chapter 8 on the Commission's services. But we encourage the reading of chapters together in the sections into which they are grouped. The effect, we hope, is to help our readers to come to grips with the intensity of both inter-institutional cooperation *and* competition in the performance of the Union's three core functions, and thus to come to grips with the politics of European integration.

Notes

1 One third of Dutch 'no' voters in the June 2005 referendum cited the euro as a reason for rejecting the Constitutional Treaty. See *Financial Times*, 2 June 2005, p. 6.

2 Years indicated are those of delivery (of speeches) or publication. References to each quote (several taken from excerpts reproduced in 'readers') in the order they appear in the exhibit are as follows: Duchêne 1994: 401; Weigall and Stirk 1992: 125; Nelson and Stubb 1998: 60–1, 197; Giscard d'Estaing 2002; Olsen 2003: 50.

3 The story of the social sciences that we present here is one that fits the English-speaking world better than the European continent, where intellectual trajectories have been rather different (see Jorgensen 2000).

4 Arguably (and certainly in strict legal terms), it is incorrect to describe the EU's institutions as 'agents' as they have been attributed wide discretion—not only executive power—and their powers cannot be clawed back by governments, short of closing down the EU altogether. We are grateful to Kieran Bradley for making this point to us.

5 To illustrate the point, the annual Eurobarometer poll of European public opinion in 2005 indicated that levels of trust in the EU's institutions were measurably higher than for national governments or parliaments (with an even wider gap, in favour of the EU, between levels of 'mistrust'). See standard Eurobarometer 63 (based on fieldwork undertaken in Spring 2005) available on *http://europa.eu.int/comm/public_opinion/index_en.htm*

6 Quoted in *Financial Times*, 9 June 2005.

7 Consistent majorities of European citizens express precisely this view in biannual Eurobarometer surveys (available on *http://europa.eu.int*) of public opinion.

Further reading

For alternative perspectives on the EU's institutions, see Warleigh (2002), Doutriaux and Lequesne (2002), and Wallace (2005). The best and most comprehensive coverage of the institutions given in any basic EU text is Nugent (2006). Good overviews of the neoinstitutionalist literature—in which March and Olsen (1989) remains seminal—are Hall and Taylor (1996) and Peters (1999). Essential applications of neoinstitutionalism to the EU are Pierson (1996), Armstrong and Bulmer (1998), and Pollack (2003). Börzel (2005) is an interesting 'revisitation' of neofunctionalism from a variety of angles.

Armstrong, K., and Bulmer, S. (1998), *The Governance of the Single European Market* (Manchester: Manchester University Press).

Börzel, T. A. (2005) (ed.), 'The Disparity of European Integration: Revisiting Neofunctionalism in Honour of Ernst Haas', special issue of *Journal of European Public Policy*, 12 (2).

Doutriaux, Y., and Lequesne, C. (2002), *Les Institutions de l'Union Européenne* (Paris, La Documentation Française, collection Réflexe Europe), 4ième édition.

Hall, P. A., and Taylor, R. C. R. (1996), 'Political Science and the Three New Institutionalisms', *Political Studies*, 44 (5): 936–57.

March, J., and Olsen, J. (1989), *Rediscovering Institutions* (New York: The Free Press).

Nugent, N. (2006), *The Government and Politics of the European Union*, 5th edn. (Basingstoke and New York: Palgrave).

Peters, B. G. (1996), *Institutional Theory in Political Science* (London and New York: Continuum)

Pierson, P. (1999), 'The Path to European Integration: A Historical Institutionalist Analysis', *Comparative Political Studies* 29, 2: 123–63.

Pollack, M. (2003), *The Engines of European Integration: Delegation, Agency, and Agenda Setting in the EU* (Oxford and New York: Oxford University Press).

Wallace, H. (2005), 'An Institutional Anatomy and Five Policy Modes', in H. Wallace, W. Wallace, and M. A. Pollack (eds.), *Policy-Making in the European Union* 5th edn. (Oxford and New York: Oxford University Press).

Warleigh, A. (2002), *Understanding European Union Institutions* (London and New York: Routledge).

Web links

The European Commission's website (traditionally *http://europa.eu.int*) is the place to start any search for basic information on the EU's institutions, as it contains links to all of the websites of the Union's other institutions. The European Research Papers Archive (ERPA) is a valuable research tool, offering access to papers posted on the websites of several leading EU research institutes (including the European University Institute in Florence, Italy and the Harvard Law School), and reliably containing work in the neoinstitutionalist vein: *http://eiop.or.at/erpa*.

Chapter 2
Institutional Change in the EU

Renaud Dehousse and Paul Magnette

Contents

Summary

EU institutions have been reformed frequently since the origins of what is now the European Union, and particularly so in the last twenty years. This chapter explains why and how this quasi-constant change has taken place. It first identifies four phases in this history: the founding, consolidation, adaptation, and rationalization of the institutional system. It then assesses the respective weight of state interests, ideas and institutions in this process. With hindsight, institutional change in the EU appears to have followed a functionalist logic, leading to complex compromises which, in turn, prompt regular calls for 'simplification' and democratization.

Introduction

It is widely recognized that the dynamics of European integration owe much to the originality of its institutional structure, in which the delegation of powers to supranational institutions has been more intensive than in 'classical' international organizations. But European institutions themselves have changed significantly since the creation of the European Coal and Steel Community in 1951. Today's European Union, with a membership of twenty-five countries, includes about 450 million people. Several treaty changes have taken place, and new institutions have been created. The EU deals with a much wider range of issues than its forerunners of fifty-odd years ago. New problems, such as the need to democratize the European political system, have emerged.

The aim of this chapter is to understand how the institutional setting has evolved. To this end, we will start by reviewing the main changes that have taken place, covering not only the grand 'constitutional moments', that is the intergovernmental conferences (IGCs) that have marked the history of European integration, but also the changes that have taken place in the meantime. We will then dwell for some time on the European Convention, to determine the extent to which this new way of approaching treaty reform really differed from earlier episodes. Finally, we will discuss the main factors that have affected the dynamics of institutional change.

The four phases of institutional development

The institutional system of the European Union has constantly evolved since its creation in the 1950s. The intergovernmental conferences concluded by the signature of the Treaties of Paris (1951) and Rome (1957) were but the first of a long series of interstate negotiations. Moreover, many institutional adaptations took place without treaty reform in the periods between IGCs. In retrospect, institutional change in the EU can be seen as a quasi-permanent process.

The EU's institutional history can be divided into four phases. These are not, to be sure, clearly identified and precisely delimited 'stages'. But each period has its own peculiarities, and consequently its own dynamics of change.

The foundations

Contrary to many other polities, the EU's institutional system was not brought about by a dramatic revolution inspired by a clear doctrine. With hindsight, the long decade between the end of the Second World War and the signature of the Treaty of Rome in 1957 appears as a period of trial and error, which gave birth to an unprecedented system via the accumulation of partial compromises. What is now called the 'Community model' was not born overnight, through a sudden conversion of the European elites to Jean Monnet's plans, contrary to what the official historiography would lead us to believe. Between 1948 and 1957, European leaders were actually torn between competing visions of Europe's future, which each reflected a particular institutional model.

For one thing, the 'constitutional avenue' was a widespread aspiration in the founding years. At the Congress of Europe held in The Hague in May 1948—a private initiative gathering dozens of European movements that had mushroomed in the two preceding years—many voices supported the idea that a European constitutional assembly should be convened to define the basic rules governing relations among European countries. The institutional conceptions of these federalist movements were in large part inspired by the American model. The idea that Europe should have its own 'Philadelphia'[1] was their *leitmotiv*. In the following months, however, a neat opposition between governments supporting a federal vision and those who imagined Europe's future in more classical intergovernmental terms, echoing the debates of the inter-war period, showed that Europe was not ready to adopt anything like the 1787 US Constitution. Ten European governments finally managed to sign the treaty establishing the Council of Europe in May 1949. Yet, even before its signing, it was clear for most of its members that the consensus on which it was based was so narrow that it would end in deadlock.

The Schuman Declaration of May 1950 launching the idea of a more modest European Coal and Steel Community, signalled a change of strategy: the states most interested in European cooperation shifted to a functionalist approach. Though very classical in some respects—confining cooperation to a limited field is a standard practice in international organizations—this approach was underpinned by an original institutional philosophy. The cornerstone of ECSC institutional architecture was the delegation of powers to an international High Authority, the independence of which was guaranteed against state interference, and to a court with much wider powers than other international jurisdictions. In addition, the governments gathered in the Council of Ministers could renounce the classic international practice of unanimity in favour of qualified-majority voting (QMV). By virtue of these 'supranational' elements (a word used both in the Schuman declaration and in the ECSC Treaty), the 'Community model' was much more constraining than other international organizations. Still it fell short of a federal model, given among other things the absence of a direct link to the people (though there was a provision in the Treaty for member states to create such a link; see Chapter 6).

A hybrid institutional system always gives rise to competing interpretations, and the Community model was no exception. Many supporters of the functionalist approach hoped that integration would be a dynamic process: thanks to issue linkages and spill-over effects, cooperation would extend to other fields so that, ultimately, the functionalist approach could lead to the adoption of a real constitution. In the months following the signing of the Paris Treaty, the dynamics of European integration seemed indeed to accelerate. In an international context marked by the intensification of the Cold War, the six member states of the ECSC agreed to try to extend their cooperation to the military field, and negotiated a new treaty establishing a European Defence Community (EDC). In the framework of these negotiations, the governments of the Six also agreed to set up a 'constitutional assembly' (prudently called an *ad hoc* assembly) to define a broader institutional framework inspired by federal principles, so as to gather the various forms of cooperation under a single constitutional umbrella, which came to be known as the European Political Community (EPC). The assembly chaired by Paul-Henri Spaak adopted a draft constitution inspired by federalist principles in March 1953 (Griffith 2001). However, this constitutional phase was short lived. One year later the EDC treaty was rejected by the French National Assembly, after a lively public campaign, and the EPC sank with it. The rejection of the EDC Treaty led to a revival of the functionalist approach. The relaunch at the Messina Conference, and the subsequent creation of the European Economic Community (EEC) in March 1957, were in part a reaction to this failure.

The negotiations that gave rise to the Treaties of Paris and Rome were but the first in a long series of diplomatic bargains between the member states. They took the classic form of 'intergovernmental conferences', rather than 'constitutional assemblies'. Formally, the governments never departed from the canons of international practice. The outcome, worked out in discrete and complex negotiations, was a treaty agreed upon by 'the High contracting parties', not a constitution. As such, it could only enter into force after having been ratified by all the member states. In these conferences, where each country was represented by a delegation of government officials, mixing diplomats and experts drawn from economic ministries, everything had to be agreed by consensus. National experts gathered in working groups examined the details of the arrangements, while the heads of delegation—usually senior diplomats—met regularly to assess the progress of the negotiations and settle the most sensitive issues in close consultation with Foreign Ministers. In parallel, the heads of state and governments met bilaterally or multilaterally to provide the political impetus and address the most contentious issues. Mindful of the political crisis generated by the ratification of the EDC Treaty, the national delegations worked in closer contact with national parliamentarians, party leaders and interest groups during the Brussels IGC of 1956–57. But the conference remained classically intergovernmental. Its deliberations took place behind closed doors and were almost entirely invisible to ordinary citizens, with the Community institutions merely acting as outside advisers.

In retrospect, this founding decade appears as a constant oscillation between a 'constitutional way' and a functionalist approach. In the end, the repeated failures of the constitutional approach consolidated the latter (Magnette 2005a). The governments of the member states had accepted some limitations of their sovereignty in order to improve the efficiency of their cooperation. They nevertheless intended to retain control of the process of institutional change.

The consolidation of the Community model

The first decade after the foundation was a period of sharp contrasts among the Six, which paradoxically strengthened the European Community (EC)'s institutional system. Whereas several governments still hoped to expand the scope of their cooperation and to strengthen the Community institutions, France under President Charles de Gaulle was concerned to prevent encroachments on its sovereignty. In these circumstances, the Community model was subjected both to centripetal and centrifugal forces.

In the early 1960s, two well-known episodes of the European saga, the rejection of the Fouchet Plans and the crisis of the 'empty chair', showed that any attempt to alter the balance between intergovernmentalism and supranationality in the Community model would be opposed by at least one member state. In 1961–62, de Gaulle thought he could reassert French hegemony by creating a Political Community based on pure intergovernmental cooperation. The Fouchet plans, named after de Gaulle's special envoy to European capitals, contemplated an extension of the scope of European cooperation to military issues, as well as the creation of an administrative secretariat, which was largely seen as a potential rival for the supranational European

Commission. These plans were, however, thwarted by the opposition of the Benelux countries (Belgium, The Netherlands, and Luxembourg). Although they had initially feared the supranational High Authority, which they saw as a Trojan Horse of French influence, the three small states now realized that a strictly intergovernmental Community would weaken them. In the absence of a supranational agenda-setter and independent monitoring of treaty implementation, it would be harder to resist French dominance.

Advocates of supranationalism were no more successful, however. In 1964, believing he could force France to accept more supranationality in exchange for a consolidation of the common agricultural policy (CAP), the ambitious Commission President Walter Hallstein proposed to strengthen the Commission and the European assembly's powers. But he had underestimated de Gaulle's capacity of resistance: France deserted Council meetings for six months, before imposing on its partners the so-called 'Luxembourg compromise', a declaration which made the use of qualified majority voting practically impossible, thereby significantly reducing the Commission's margin of manœuvre (see Chapter 5).

Similarly, the European Court's foundational case law, which gave the Community legal order a quasi-constitutional authority, was paralleled by a strengthening of intergovernmental influence over decision-making. In a series of landmark cases, the Court, despite the opposition of several governments, ruled that European law could be invoked directly by private plaintiffs (*direct effect*) even where this was not explicitly contemplated by the treaties, and that it should enjoy *supremacy* in case of conflict with national law (see Chapter 7). This jurisprudence enhanced the pressure on national governments, who now realized that their decisions could be more constraining than they had expected. In this new legal context, the Commission's prerogatives took on a new dimension: its powers to set the agenda upstream and to monitor the implementation of EU decisions by the national administrations downstream seemed less innocuous (Stein 1981). Moreover, during the same period, a number of ECJ rulings enabled integration to proceed irrespective of deadlocks in the Council (Dehousse 1998). These developments in the legal sphere were however compensated for by the evolution of policy-making structures. The creation of the Committee of Permanent Representatives (Coreper) and the gradual extension of its tasks enabled governments to control the Commission's power of initiative. Their influence in the executive phase was made possible by another *ad hoc* development: the establishment of an ever denser network of committees composed of national civil servants to 'assist' the Commission, a phenomenon known as 'comitology' in Eurospeak (Joerges and Vos 1998; Pedler and Schaefer 1996). Like the Luxembourg compromise, these developments confirmed the Community's partly intergovernmental character in the face of an ever stronger legal supranationalism (Weiler 1981).

In terms of institutional development, the 1960s were thus a paradoxical period. Divergences between member states did not allow formal amendment of the treaty, except for the decision, taken in 1965, to merge the institutions of the three European communities (the ECSC, the EEC, and Euratom) without altering their powers. Nonetheless, crucial developments took place within the same period: the 'constitutionalization' of the Community legal order compensated for the member governments' stronger grip over the policy process. Ultimately, these tensions ended up strengthening the original matrix: by resisting any attempt to strengthen either its intergovernmentalism or its supranationality, the Community model demonstrated its stability.

The 'relaunch': institutional change through task extension

The two decades that followed were a period of considerable expansion for the EC. Three consecutive enlargements doubled the number of its members, making decision-making more difficult, but also creating demands for new policies.

The 1970s were perceived as a period of relative stagnation, due to a severe economic crisis and the institutional strains created by the first enlargement. Yet, the resignation of General de Gaulle created a political climate more favourable to change. The Treaty revision agreed at Luxembourg in 1970 endowed the EC with its own financial resources, thereby ensuring the financing of the CAP. It also saw an increase—the first in a long series—in the powers of the European Parliament, which was given a significant role in the adoption of the EC budget. At the Paris Summit of 1972, heads of state and government decided to 'relaunch' the integration process by developing policies more in tune with citizens' expectations, such as environmental and consumer protection, or regional development. That decision served to justify the development of a series of policies which went beyond economic integration.

While reflections on the institutional development of the Community were not entirely absent, they failed to trigger any real momentum. At Monnet's instigation, the meetings of heads of state and government were institutionalized, giving birth amid some controversy to the European Council. A 1976 decision foresaw the direct election of members of the European parliament, realizing an idea first mooted three decades earlier at the Hague Congress. The first directly elected Parliament rapidly started pressing for bolder reforms: in 1984, it presented a 'Draft Treaty on European Union' that was clearly inspired by federal ideas. While several of the ideas contained in that project inspired future reforms, it was not even discussed by most national parliaments, to which it had been sent for consideration.

The Parliament's pressure in favour of institutional reform was, however, exploited by another actor. As soon as Jacques Delors was nominated to become President of the Commission from 1985, he began searching for a new strategic concept capable of imparting a fresh dynamic to the integration process. Many of the options contemplated at the time—monetary union, a joint defence, or institutional reform—seemed out of reach, as each was opposed in some national capitals. Delors (2004) and his aides therefore settled for a seemingly more modest plan: the completion of the internal market by the end of 1992. As much of the preparatory work had already been done by the previous Commission, a road map detailing a long series of directives to be adopted to do away with obstacles to free movement could be presented to the European Council within a few months. The strength of this approach was that it did not appear to require any major transfer of legal competence or budgetary resources to the European level. Moreover, the emphasis laid on the concept of mutual recognition of national standards, developed by the European Court of Justice in its famous *Cassis de Dijon* ruling (1979), gave the programme a de-regulatory flavour which appealed to the Conservative government of the United Kingdom (UK) headed by Margaret Thatcher, which strongly opposed further transfers of power to the Community (Dehousse 1988).

Having secured the member states' support for its 1992 programme, the Commission was then in a good position to obtain treaty changes that were needed to facilitate its implementation. A large majority of governments supported the Commission agenda in a vote (the first ever) in the Milan European Council in June 1985, where it was decided to convene an intergovernmental conference. Despite the initial furore of the countries who opposed such a move (the UK, Denmark and Greece), their fears were soon allayed by the pragmatic character of the proposals tabled by the Commission, which mostly aimed at making it possible to implement the 1992 programme (De Ruyt 1987). The 1985 IGC was short, and largely structured by the Commission's proposals, two features that did not reappear in the IGCs that were to follow (Moravcsik 1998). The Single European Act (SEA), which it elaborated, contained mostly incremental changes: new tasks for the Community (environmental, research and regional development policies), a closer association of the European Parliament with law-making through the establishment of the so-called cooperation procedure (see Chapter 6) and, above all, the shift to qualified majority voting for much of the 1992 legislation. The harvest seemed meagre to the pro-integration camp (Pescatore 1987). Yet it sufficed to inject a new dynamic to the EC which, thanks in part to the open texture of several new legal bases, enabled a number of new policy areas to develop and conveyed to the populace the feeling that Europe could influence their daily lives.

This episode suggests that when the Commission, acting as a 'policy entrepreneur', is able to 'soften up' the relevant policy community by getting it used to new ideas, it may then exploit the opportunities that arise to push forward its preferred reform proposals (Kingdon 1984). This was confirmed by the path leading to economic and monetary union (EMU). When it appeared that the single market was making substantial progress, the Commission started arguing that it needed to be supplemented by greater coordination of macro-economic policies. Otherwise, the liberalization of capital movements would lead to major disruption (Padoa-Schioppa 1987). Delors realized that this prospect had little chance to materialize without the support of central bankers. Thus, he convinced the European Council to create a working party, composed of central banks governors, to discuss the establishment of EMU. This committee, chaired by Delors himself, largely endorsed the Commission's view and began a gradual move towards a single currency (Committee for the Study of Economic and Monetary Union 1989). The Committee's plans were endorsed by the European Council in June 1989, despite British reservations (compare Chapter 3, Exhibit 3.8).

The IGC that led to the Maastricht Treaty (1991) largely followed the Delors Committee's blueprint on EMU, with the establishment of a European Central Bank, the autonomy of which was protected by the Treaty, and a process of economic policy convergence that was regarded as indispensable prior to the creation of a single currency. But it did not stop there. In the meantime, the collapse of communism in Eastern Europe and the rapid move towards German unification completely modified the context in which the integration process was taking place. Eager to anchor Germany firmly to Europe, French President Mitterrand and German Chancellor Kohl suggested convening a second IGC to deal with the creation of a 'political union'; that is, non-economic policies and institutional questions. Achievements in that framework were less spectacular. Incremental changes were made to the Community's institutional structure: more majority voting, the opening of new areas to Community intervention and the improvement of the legislative prerogatives of the Parliament, notably through the creation of a co-decision procedure (see Chapter 6). In addition, the EP was granted the right to approve the appointment of the Commission, a power that went largely unnoticed at the time, but subsequently proved to be of great importance. In contrast, the member states did not consent to any delegation of power in relation to issues of 'high politics', such as foreign policy or immigration policy. The newly created European Union was therefore given a complex structure, the EC being supplemented by two intergovernmental 'pillars', in which the role of supranational institutions was strictly limited. In the view of the masters of the treaty, 'political decisions' were therefore to remain primarily in the hands of national governments.

This mixed result confirmed the experience of the previous decades: transfers of sovereignty are more readily accepted when they are approached in a functional manner, the emphasis being on substantive issues. In contrast, when institutional issues are handled separately, negotiations are likely to end up with some kind of lowest common denominator, as the following IGCs were to confirm.

Adjusting the institutional system

After the monumental changes decided in Maastricht, and the intense debates which followed, one could have expected a period of relative institutional stability. Actually, the opposite happened: two IGCs took place in the second half of the 1990s, leading to the Treaties of Amsterdam (1997) and Nice (2000). Even before the latter was ratified, pressure for further reforms led to the convening of a European Convention, which drafted a 'treaty establishing a Constitution for Europe', signed in Rome in October 2004. How can one account for this acceleration of the pace of change?

Contrary to the previous phase, this period was not characterized by major new projects, leaving aside the concern to improve the effectiveness of European action in the areas opened to EU intervention by the Maastricht Treaty, specifically foreign policy and justice and home affairs. The difficult ratification of that treaty had revealed widespread dissatisfaction within the European public and generated a 'spirit of subsidiarity', with many European leaders arguing that the EU should resist the temptation to regulate all matters from Brussels and leave more discretion to national authorities. Instead, institutional change was motivated by two concerns: the willingness to respond to the criticisms of the EU's 'democratic deficit' by bringing EU institutional architecture closer to European democratic standards, and the need to prepare for the enlargement to Central and Eastern European countries (CEECs).

Meeting these two challenges proved tricky, given the considerable heterogeneity of member states' preferences. Divergences between them largely explain the rhythm of treaty changes (Moravcsik and Nicolaïdis 1999). The 1996 IGC had been foreseen in the Maastricht Treaty: forced to accept the 'pillar' structure by a minority of their peers, several pro-integration governments had obtained the guarantee that the institutional setting would be revisited four years later. This scenario was

repeated at Amsterdam in 1997 and in Nice in 2000: unable to reach a comprehensive agreement, but unwilling to abandon their claims, a group of governments made
sure that the process of institutional revision carried on.

The main difficulty was not democratic concerns. As will be seen in the last part
of this chapter, governments share a vision of democracy in which the parliamentary element plays a key role and this makes compromises easier. From the Single
European Act to the 2004 IGC, the most stable trend of institutional change has
indeed been the increase in the powers of the European Parliament. The reforms
aimed at adjusting the EU to its new membership proved much more controversial. The problem was unprecedented: whereas earlier enlargements were about
adding a maximum of three countries at a time and did not alter the initial balance between large and small states, the 2004 one involved ten countries, of which
nine were small states. Mechanical adjustments were therefore not sufficient: they
would have led to an excessive enlargement of the size of both Commission and the
EP, and given too much influence to the small states in the Council. Strategic dis-
agreements made a compromise difficult. Since unanimity was required for treaty
changes, the pro-integration camp, which found strong support in the Commission
and the Parliament, argued that consolidating the institutional structure was a necessary pre-condition of enlargement. In contrast, the CEECs, having recently recovered
their sovereignty, were concerned not to dilute it in the EU, while some countries,
like Britain, Denmark and Sweden, hoped the enlargement would counterbalance
the integration that had taken place in the previous decade.

The problem was addressed unsuccessfully during the Amsterdam negotiations.
The Nice IGC in 2000 confirmed the sensitivity of the issues. The large countries tried
to reassert their influence to avoid being bound by coalitions of smaller states, while
the latter resisted attempts to reduce their weight in the EU institutions. The classic
federal dilemma between equality of states and equality of population became tenser
than ever. As the EU regime is based on a complex balance of state representation in
the three poles of the institutional triangle, changes made at the level of one institution rendered adaptations indispensable in the others, as well as in the balance of
power among the institutions. The large states were willing to abandon their second
commissioner, but only to the extent that this loss was compensated by a strengthening of their position in the two other institutions. This crucial issue could not be
solved in Nice. A complex compromise, including a redistribution of seats in the EP,
the eventual downsizing of the Commission and a re-weighing of votes in the Council, was reached after protracted bickering, but it was the focus of intense criticism.
As such these issues re-emerged as one of the central contentions of the treaty reform
negotiated in the years that followed.

What would the Constitutional Treaty have changed?

The Berlin speech of the German Minister for Foreign Affairs Joschka Fischer on 9
May 2000, calling for the adoption of a European constitution, triggered a grand

debate on the institutional future of the EU. In the ensuing months, the leaders of most of the member states made public their own views.

Those who advocated transforming the procedure of treaty change made a dual argument. In terms of substance, the EU's institutional system had to undergo thorough reforms before the next enlargement (Dehaene Report 1999). In terms of process, the Nice Summit had demonstrated the limits of the IGC process; more inclusive and more transparent methods were required (Duhamel Report 2000). The precedent of the first Convention—set up in 1999 to draft a Charter of Fundamental Rights—offered an alternative model consistent with a 'constitutional' perspective on the issues at stake, since it comprised European and national parliamentarians and operated in public. The assumption underlying this argument was that a new process would produce a new outcome. Half a century after its foundation, the EU appeared ready to resume the constitutional work abandoned after the abortive attempts of the 1950s. One year after the bitter compromise reached in Nice, the governments of the member states seemed to confirm this shift when they agreed to create a new body to prepare a blueprint for the next intergovernmental conference and to reflect, among other things, on the constitutionalization of the EU.

Two years later, the Convention had adopted its 'Draft Treaty Establishing a Constitution for Europe', and the governments signed the 'Constitutional Treaty' in Rome on 24 October 2004. Was the Convention able to overcome the deadlocks that had characterized earlier intergovernmental bargains, and to pre-empt the IGC's negotiation? Or was it forced to anticipate potential vetoes? In other words, to what extent did the transformation of the process shape the eventual outcome?

To be sure, supporters of the convention model had a vested interest in this process. The European Parliament and the Commission which, until then, were deprived of a formal role in treaty reforms,[2] expected to benefit from a process where their representatives would be associated as full and equal partners with governments. Likewise, the representatives of the smaller member states had found out in previous IGCs that their capacity to shape the final outcome of the negotiations was limited (Moravcsik and Nicolaïdis 1999). Resorting to their veto power, while possible in theory, was extremely costly. Within the framework of the Convention, composed of more than a hundred members, and where the representatives of the governments would have to negotiate with MEPs, commissioners and national parliamentarians, they hoped that large countries' influence would be lessened, while the range of opportunities to forge alternative coalitions—with MEPs notably—would be broadened. Obviously, expectations of this kind were strongest among those governments who wanted to go beyond the *status quo*—namely, the Benelux countries, Portugal, Greece and Finland.

On the other side of the fence, governments from bigger member states (with the exception of Germany) were less prone to change the rules of the game. They nevertheless accepted opening the discussion on this new process as they were all aware of the limits of the IGC method. The eventual compromise was that the setting up of the Convention was accompanied by safeguards enabling governments, acting collectively and individually, to remain in control of future developments. First, the Convention would only be a preparatory body, all decisions remaining with the IGC. Second, national representatives would make up three quarters of the membership. Finally, the Convention's President was to be appointed by, and would report to, the European Council. The convention was thus a half-way compromise between the intergovernmental tradition and the constitutional avenue supported by the federalist movements since the 1950s.

It was always reasonable to believe that the Convention would be more flexible than the IGCs. It comprised a broader range of actors, a number of whom were independent from national governments (the two Commissioners, most of the MEPs and the MPs drawn from the domestic opposition, or about one third of the members), making the emergence of new coalitions possible. Moreover, the Convention was free to organize its own work, and it had to deliberate in public—a factor which, according to students of constitution-making, renders the crude expression of naked interests more difficult (Elster 1998). On the other hand, the conventioneers knew that their text would be but a draft, and that it could be altered by the IGC.

In the end, the intergovernmental safeguards proved very powerful. True, the Convention's autonomy was not directly put into question by the governments. The chairman of the Convention, former French President Valéry Giscard d'Estaing, dwelled on the originality of this experience, from his inaugural speech up until the conclusion of the Convention eighteen months later. He insisted on the necessity *not* to reproduce the patterns of former IGCs, which he defined as 'for diplomatic negotiations between member states in which each party sought legitimately to maximize its gains without regard for the overall picture'. Instead, he tried to convey what he called a 'Convention spirit': 'If your contributions genuinely seek to prepare a consensus, and if you take account of the proposals and comments made by the other members of the Convention, then the content of the final consensus can be worked out step by step here within the Convention' (Giscard d'Estaing 2002). To some extent, this strategy was successful, at least in the first part of the Convention's work. The majority of the conventioneers shared Giscard's ambitions, and looked for a comprehensive compromise. They took the time to deliberate on each and every issue in plenary sessions, and to examine the most technical issues in more detail within smaller working groups. In their work, they were helped by a rather flexible Presidium which coordinated their work without imposing its own vision, and by an efficient Secretariat which provided them with detailed notes on the state of the EU. The flexibility of their organization, the absence of obvious pressures from the governments, the collective willingness of most of the members to reach an ambitious outcome, alongside the 'constitutional ethos' surrounding their work, combined to make compromises possible on several issues that former IGCs had been unable to settle: the abolition of the pillars, the consolidation of the treaties, the EU's legal personality, the simplification of decision-making procedures, and the incorporation of the Charter on Fundamental Rights in the draft Constitution. All these points were agreed without contention at an early stage of the Convention's work (Magnette 2005b). True, none of these elements were totally new and original, and the legal clarity of the text was often disputable (Jacqué 2004). But the Convention nevertheless succeeded where the three previous IGCs had failed.

Still, by the Fall of 2002, when discussions on institutional issues were initiated, the pendulum moved back to classic forms of diplomatic bargaining. Most government representatives started openly to defend their brief, build coalitions among themselves and use in veiled language the threat of vetoes in the IGC. All Convention members were well aware of that threat. Neither political parties, nor the institutional representatives were able to develop coherent visions and positions, except in a few specific instances. Instead, two classic cleavages dominated the debates in the Convention as well as the parallel debates taking place at the national levels (Magnette and Nicolaïdis 2004): the traditional 'federalist' versus 'intergovernmentalist' cleavage, as well as the opposition between big and small countries. With the exception of Germany, the large states sought to strengthen the role of the European Council, and thereby the role of the governments in the decision-making process. Meanwhile most small states defended supranational institutions and the rotating presidency of the Council. A Franco–German compromise made public in January 2003 sought to reconcile the two views by combining the French demand for an EU Council President with the German desire to see the Commission President elected by the Parliament. A coalition of small states opposed this prospect, while the British Government, backed by Denmark and Spain, remained reluctant to strengthen the EP–Commission pair. The final compromise—reached through very typical intergovernmental bargains, with the MEPs kept on the sidelines—reflected the Franco–German proposal. Granted, some governments had to make concessions in the course of the negotiation—as they had during previous IGCs. When a government was isolated on points that could not easily be presented as 'red lines', and unable to build a coalition against a reform supported by a very large majority (as was Britain on the incorporation of the Charter of Fundamental Rights), it was generally forced to make unilateral concessions.

The Presidium played an important role in shaping the final outcome. On the one hand, like presidencies in IGCs (Tallberg 2004), it acted as organizer and as mediator with the support of the Convention's Secretariat, seeking to forge a compromise on a step-by-step basis. But it chose to do so not by leaving options open until a last-minute package deal but rather by submitting a single negotiating text which became the reference or the *status quo*, with the burden of proof being put on the dissenters. Since, on the other hand, the Presidium was a collective organ rather than a single presiding member state, it could present its viewpoints as 'the best possible compromise'. In this context, potential vetoes were forestalled and actual ones ignored, such as the Spanish and Polish opposition to the idea of a double majority (50 per cent of states, 60 per cent of population) that would replace the system of weighting votes agreed at Nice. These tactics succeeded in bringing about a 'consensus' which might have eluded a traditional IGC. But they also left a definite bitter taste among many delegates, which in the end, might have deprived the Presidium proposal of the kind of legitimacy that a more negotiated text would have had. Unsurprisingly, the governments of Poland and Spain, whose objections had been ignored, subsequently played a major role in the failure of the Brussels Summit in December 2003. The IGC was not a mere rubber-stamping exercise. First, it had to settle these contentious issues. Second, the governments took their role seriously and re-examined each and every aspect of the draft treaty, rejecting some of the Convention's novelties and adding new ones.

Even though the reference to a Constitution suggests a radical break with the past, continuity was the main theme of the new document. Not only did it require ratification by all member countries before it could come into force, but intergovernmental negotiations and unanimous ratification were also deemed necessary for future modifications. Many of the innovations contained in the text were actually discussed in previous IGCs, and the elements that consolidate the supranational institutions are similar to those of earlier interstate bargains, particularly more QMV and more co-decision. Above all, several of the changes introduced, from the full-time President of the European Council to the status of the double-hatted Foreign Minister, who will be at the same time a member of the Commission and accountable to the European Council, show a clear reluctance to allow the development of a strong executive at European level. In many respects, the draft Constitutional Treaty displayed the same ambivalence as earlier arrangements: the contention that 'all institutions have been strengthened' showed an inability to choose between a supranational and an intergovernmental avenue. Given the Constitutional Treaty's uncertain future, following its rejection in the 2005 French and Dutch referenda, it is unlikely in the short term that EU governments will find it any easier than it has been in the past to choose which of these avenues to take.

The dynamics of institutional change

The history of institutional change in the European Union shows that its motivations and dynamics vary widely over time. It is nevertheless possible to identify three permanent factors of change, whose respective weight varies, and to identify the conditions under which they may influence the negotiation. The classical trilogy of interests, institutions and ideas (Hall 1997) may serve here as a helpful guide.

The weight of interests

That institutional change has largely been shaped by state interests should not come as a surprise. After all, the creation of the EU took the form of an interstate agreement which, like most treaties, could only be modified with the assent of all parties. Economic interests played a key role in the process, as the states saw the construction of Europe as a means to re-assert their influence in an ever more interdependent world (Milward 1992). Domestic concerns clearly impinged upon governments' attitudes whenever reforms were contemplated. France's farming interests, Germany's industries, and the need to foster free trade for export-oriented Benelux countries featured prominently in the European agenda of their respective governments. The most important stages of the integration process have therefore been associated with key interests of the member states (Moravcsik 1998). Institutional changes generally have responded to an instrumental logic rather than to some kind of grand design. In a functional organization, the governments 'define a series of underlying objectives or preferences, bargain to substantive agreements concerning cooperation, and finally select appropriate international institutions in which to embed them' (Moravcsik 1998: 5).

States' willingness to retain some control of the process also shaped the contours of institutional evolution. Intergovernmental bodies were given a central role. The position of the Council of Ministers in decision-making was consolidated by structures such as Coreper, the web of intergovernmental committees or the European

Council. More recent developments, such as the Maastricht pillar system or the creation of the High Representative for foreign policy, were clearly inspired by reluctance to relinquish power in sensitive areas. Representative concerns are apparent in the design of every European institution, including the supranational ones: nationals of all member countries sit in the Commission and on the Court's bench. Balance among states has indeed been a key point in most institutional negotiations. From the outset, QMV within the Council of Ministers was based on a system of weighted votes balancing state equality and demographic size. The three biggest states made sure that they would only need one ally to block a decision, while preventing the three small ones from forming a blocking minority. Fifty years later, these strategic concerns have anything but disappeared, as shown by the drafting of the Constitutional Treaty. The debates on the composition of the Commission (should it include one national of each member state or should its size be reduced?), on the presidency of the Union (should the system of rotation among member states be maintained, or should it be replaced by a permanent chair?) and on the reform of QMV (should the system of weighing votes revised at Nice be maintained or should it be replaced by a more proportional double majority?) were clearly dominated by the governments' ambition to maximize their weight in the EU's decision-making bodies.

While the emphasis on states' interests has occupied a central place in the analysis of European integration, it should not blind us to the importance of other factors. On several occasions, states have decided that their interests were better served by mechanisms that could facilitate their negotiations (the Commission's monopoly of initiative), reduce transaction costs (majority voting in the Council), or ensure that joint decisions would be implemented fairly by their partners (the enforcement powers of the Commission and the Court). Furthermore, supranational actors have often used their (formal or informal) powers to foster their own interests as an institution, as discussed below. Because of its very complexity, the process of institutional change responds to logics of various kinds.

The role of institutions

Understood in their broadest sense, as the rules that structure political relationships (Steinmo 2004), institutions have also considerably influenced the dynamics of change. This point is quite clear in the case of formal rules: the requirement of unanimity for any amendment to the treaties means that governments must take the final crucial steps in the negotiations. They can also use the threat of a non-ratification by their legislature to obtain concessions from their partners. Likewise, the change in the rules of the game reflected in the setting up of the Convention allowed the development of a new dynamic which largely explains why the convention could reach an agreement on issues where previous IGCs had failed. There also exist informal rules affecting the way in which actors behave. Smaller countries know that the veto power they enjoy can only be used sparingly, and preferably not without allies when a major reform is at stake. This explains why Belgium at Nice, or even Poland at the 2004 IGC, ended up accepting agreements which they had forcefully opposed.[3]

While these principles are valid in many international regimes, the weight of institutions is of particular relevance at EU level, because of the political clout enjoyed by its supranational organs. They are endowed with a substantial degree of autonomy, and thus are naturally inclined to promote interests of their own. As was seen earlier, through its rulings on direct effect and supremacy, the European Court of Justice has conferred a federal structure on the European legal order. In so doing, however, it has considerably increased its own role in the integration process (Dehousse 1998). The Parliament's stubborn insistence on the necessity to address the 'democratic deficit' was of course underpinned by its eagerness to improve its own institutional position.[4] Likewise, we have seen that even if it is deprived of any formal role in IGCs, the Commission, acting as a policy entrepreneur or as a mediator between national preferences, can at times shape the contours of the final agreement. The Single European Act is the best illustration of this kind of dynamic. One year before the conclusion of that treaty, three member states had opposed any extension of majority voting in the so-called Dooge Committee. It was the Commission that developed the idea which enabled a breakthrough to be made, and it did so by drawing inspiration from principles worked out in the path-breaking *Cassis de Dijon* case law of the ECJ (1979). Even if one accepts the centrality of interstate bargains in the cumbersome process of institutional change, one must recognize that state preferences are not static and can be influenced by the action of supranational institutions. Any study of the dynamics of institutional change should therefore take their role into consideration (Dehousse and Majone 1994), though research still needs to be done to assess the impact of this factor more precisely.

When do ideas matter?

Beside state interests and institutional constraints, ideas can at times contribute to shaping the EU's institutional system. All the actors of the EU political system have their own view of what the system should look like. In some cases, those views derive from the actors' broader perceptions of the nature of the EU. Since its origins, two competing interpretations of the 'meaning' of European integration have proved very influential. On the one hand, the federalist doctrine remains influential in some circles, particularly in the founding member states. But the EU is also seen by others as a functional organization, designed to maximize economic state interests in an ever more interdependent world economy—a view underlying British leaders' perceptions of the EU and which is also widespread in Nordic and Central European countries. These two 'models' are, in key respects, the poles of the debate: they structure, positively or negatively, the continuing discussion on the EU's *raison d'être*, very much like the 'federalist' and 'anti-federalist' doctrines dominated constitutional debates in the US for decades, and they bear their own institutional patterns. In some cases, governments can support an institutional reform that defies their own short term interests—as when the Benelux countries defend the extension of the EP's prerogatives, although they are less over-represented in this institution than in the Council—because it is part of their broader vision of the EU.

Very often, a country's institutional conceptions will also reflect its own national political culture. When German leaders support the parliamentarization of the EU's regime they tend, explicitly or not, to project the constitutional balance of the Federal Republic (Kohler-Koch 2000). On their side, French politicians tend to perceive

the European Council as a collective 'head of state', and to understand the Commission–European Council duopoly as a European equivalent of the Fifth Republic's
dualist executive (Quermonne 1999). The Nordic insistence on the mechanisms enhancing the transparency of the EU system (the ombudsman, parliamentary scrutiny,
and the publicity of the Council's deliberations) is another example of seeking to import national traditions into the EU (Gronbech-Jensen 1998).

Although some of these ideas have found their way into the EU treaties, they remain secondary factors of change. In most cases, the governments' positions depend
on their perception of their interests. But when the long-term implications of an institutional decision are unclear, ideas may bear a certain weight. This may notably
explain one of the most original elements of EU institutional evolution, namely the
gradual consolidation of the European Parliament's powers, although the latter could
undermine the member states' influence. Some governments were prompted by an
ideological bias in favour of parliamentary democracy (Dehousse 1995); others made
what they considered symbolic concessions with no foreseeable impact on their interests (Pollack 1997; Moravcsik 1998; Rittberger 2001). Needless to say, governments'
expectations can at times prove wrong: one of the 'minor' concessions made to parliamentary orthodoxy in the Maastricht Treaty, the conferral on the EP of the right
to approve the appointment of the Commission, allowed the assembly to gain significant leverage over the European executive (Magnette 2001).

More generally, 'federalist ideology is still required to account for the general institutional structure of the EC' and particularly 'its quasi-constitutional form' (Moravcsik 1998: 153). This should not be a surprise: as a legal theorist puts it, 'A good deal of
legal development (and this includes constitutional development) is autonomous. . . .
The decision actually taken is chosen out of habit, or out of respect for the constitutional practices and traditions' (Raz 2002: 156). When they think of the EU's overall
institutional order, the governments tend to reason, like the lawyers of the EU institutions, in conceptual terms with which they are familiar. Hence the reforms of
the EU that aim to 'simplify' its institutional and legal order by making it more compatible with classic constitutional canons. Like most other polities, the EU oscillates
between institutional complexity prompted by pragmatic concerns to accommodate
divergent interests, and institutional rationalization driven by the leaders' will to clarify the rules of the game (Olsen 2002). Bearing this in mind may help one to understand why EU leaders collectively decided, at the turn of the century, to dwell on the
'constitutional' dimension of the EU.

Conclusion

The institutional history of the European Union can be read in several ways. On the
one hand, the system has substantially evolved. The Union has enlarged and the missions devolved upon it have considerably increased, creating regular pressures for
adaptation. On the other, it has demonstrated a remarkable stability. The EU has not
become a centralised superstate, nor have the member states done away with the
atypical powers enjoyed by the European Commission, such as its right to initiate

legislation. On several occasions, attempts to consolidate the powers of the supranational institutions have been balanced by the governments' eagerness to see their role in the system preserved.

Institutional change has been mostly incremental. Even the Constitutional Treaty signed in 2004, for all the surrounding rhetoric, could really not be seen as marking a rupture in the history of European construction, as it largely built on the innovations introduced at earlier stages. IGCs have been the key moments in this evolution, but they cannot be understood apart from the rest of the process. Their successes have owed much to the institutional adjustments that have taken place between conferences. Their failures have paved the way for continuing tensions.

This gradualism is largely the result of a process in which governments retain the central role, as they have to agree to all formal changes. For the same reason, functionalism has been the main force in this evolution. Governments had to agree on joint objectives prior to any major transfer of powers to the European level. This, however, is but one part of the story. The complexity of the system has generated pressures for simplification and legitimation according to a process in which ideational factors play an important role. The European Commission has at times succeeded in influencing the preferences and negotiation strategies of the member states. The co-existence of these contrasting forces largely accounts for the schizophrenic character of an institutional evolution characterized at the same time by a consolidation of intergovernmentalism and the conferral of ever-larger powers on the European Parliament. In all likelihood, the same structural factors will impinge upon future changes and prevent a radical simplification of European institutional architecture.

Notes

1 The American Constitution was drafted by delegates of the thirteen states gathered in Philadelphia in 1787.

2 Although two members of the EP had been nominated as members of the Westendorp group that prepared the negotiation of the 1996–97 IGC, the MEPs themselves acknowledged that this minimal form of participation did not give them the opportunity to influence the outcome significantly, since this group only identified 'questions' and 'options' and all decisions were left to the IGC. In 1994, before the enlargement that took place the following year, some MEPs had also suggested the EP should threaten to refuse its 'assent' to the treaty changes to force the governments to adopt the reforms they advocated (Bourlanges-Dury Report 1994), but they could not form a majority within the Parliament. Their threats were thus far from credible.

3 At Nice, Belgium was asked to accept as part of the new Treaty having fewer votes under QMV than the Netherlands, with which it had always had numerical parity in the past (despite Belgium's population being only about two-thirds of that of the Netherlands). Poland had to accept a new QMV system in the Constitutional Treaty that was far less favourable to it numerically than the system in the Treaty of Nice.

4 This does not mean that the EP proved able to impose its views upon the governments. In only two cases can it be considered that the EP was really able to

compel governments. The first concerns the Commission's appointment. After the 1992 Maastricht Treaty gave the European Parliament the power to approve the candidate for Commission President nominated by member governments, the MEPs were able to use the threat of refusing this approval to press their case for being consulted on the college's appointment as a whole. The second case concerns their influence in the co-decision procedure, also created by the Maastricht Treaty. The MEPs managed to get the 'third reading'—a procedure meant to give the Council the last word—abolished by systematically rejecting the agreements confirmed by the Council against the MEPs' wishes. At Amsterdam in 1997, governments brought these practices, established by the Parliament, into alignment with the Treaty (Hix 2002a). But these are exceptions which cannot be generalized. In many other cases, the claims supported by the majority in the Parliament (approval of appointment to the ECJ, generalization of co-decision, consolidating budgetary power, etc.) were not followed up by the governments (Costa 2001).

Further reading

There is no systematic overview of institutional change in the EU available in the current literature. In-depth historical accounts can be found in Moravcsik (1998), and for more recent periods Moravcsik and Nicolaïdis (1999) and Magnette and Nicolaïdis (2004). Analyses of individual institutions can be found in Nugent (2001) for the European Commission, Costa (2001, in French) and Kreppel (2002) for the EP, Wallace and Hayes-Renshaw (2006) for the Council and Dehousse (1998) for the Court. The classic presentation of the liberal intergovernmentalist interpretation is Moravcsik (1998). On the role of ideas in the founding period Persons (2002) is a stimulating view, as is Rittberger (2001) for an institutionalist reading. (While many websites followed the negotiations on the Constitutional Treaty, we found none that seemed certain to endure on institutional change.)

Costa, O. (2001), *Le Parlement européen, assemblée délibérante* (Brussels: Editions de l'Université de Bruxelles).

Dehousse, R. (1998), *The European Court of Justice: the Politics of Judicial Integration* (Basingstoke and New York: Palgrave).

Hayes-Renshaw, F., and Wallace, H. (2006), *The Council of Ministers*, 2nd edn. (Basingstoke and New York: Palgrave).

Kreppel, A. (2002), *The European Parliament and Supranational Party System: a Study in Institutional Development* (Oxford and New York: Oxford University Press).

Magnette, P., and Nicolaïdis, K. (2004), 'The European Convention: Bargaining under the Shadow of Rhetoric', *West European Politics*, 27/3: 381–404.

Moravcsik, A. (1998), *The Choice for Europe, Social Purpose and State Power from Messina to Maastricht* (Ithaca NY: Cornell University Press).

Moravcsik, A., and Nicolaïdis, K. (1999), 'Explaining the Treaty of Amsterdam: Interests, Influence, Institutions', *Journal of Common Market Studies*, 37/1: 59–85.

Persons, C. (2002), 'Sharing Ideas as Causes: the Origins of the European Union', *International Organization*, 56/1: 47–84.

Rittberger, R. (2001), 'Which Institutions for Post-war Europe? Explaining the Institutional Design of Europe's First Community', *Journal of European Public Policy*, 8/5: 673–708.

Part I

Providing Direction

Chapter 3

The European Council

Philippe de Schoutheete

Contents

Summary

Since its creation in 1974, the European Council has played a fundamental role in the development of European integration. It gives political guidance and impetus to the Union, takes the most important decisions, guides the open method of coordination, gives high visibility to external policy positions and declarations, and plays a major role in amending the treaties. Its composition gives it an intergovernmental character yet successive decisions at this level have increased the supranational character of the Union. The European Council has been, over a quarter of a century, a formidable locus of power, and the Constitutional Treaty would give it a clear institutional status. But it has its weaknesses and cannot, by itself, solve all present and future problems of European governance.

Introduction

The European Council brings together Heads of State or Government (a formula designed to cover the situation of the French and Finnish Presidents, who are both heads of state and chief executives) and the President of the Commission. They are assisted by the ministers for foreign affairs and a member of the Commission. When the European Council deals with questions linked to economic and monetary union, finance ministers are invited.[1] They either replace or sit alongside foreign ministers (both cases have been known to occur). Apart from a very small number of civil servants, nobody else is allowed in the meeting. This is the essence of the European Council: a limited number of political figures, headed by the chief executives of all member states, meeting in a closed room with no assistants.

The treaty specifies that the European Council 'shall provide the Union with the necessary impetus for its development and shall define the general political guidelines thereof'. That is a very inadequate description of reality but there is no other task description of the European Council in the present treaty.

As a result, and until such time as the Constitutional Treaty or equivalent provisions enter into force, the only points which can be made with some legal certainty about the European Council are negative in nature:

- the European Council is not an institution of the Union (not mentioned in Article 5 TEU which encompasses all EU institutions);

- nor is it a specific form of the Union institution known as the Council (the composition is different because the President of the Commission is a member); and

- the description of its task in Article 4 TEU does not correspond to what, in fact, it has been doing, for many years, as a major decision-maker.

The Constitutional Treaty would bring significant changes to the nature, composition, competences, decision-making process, and presidency of the European Council. These potential new elements are considered in this chapter.

Rules adopted by the European Council at Seville in June 2002 specify that it shall meet in principle four times a year with the possibility of extraordinary meetings in exceptional circumstances. Whereas in former years European Council meetings would usually take place in the country of the presidency, they are now held in Brussels.[2] The European Council meets in the Justus Lipsius building, which houses the Council, but it decided in March 2004 to move its meetings to an adjacent building (Residence Palace) as soon as it has been refurbished.

Two further preliminary comments need to be made:

- The Treaty occasionally requires heads of government to meet as a formation of the Council: notably to appoint the president of the Commission, or to adopt the single currency. Moreover, participants in a European Council fulfil the description of the Council as given by Article 203 TEC: 'a representative of each member state at ministerial level'. It has, therefore, generally been acknowledged that it could, if it so wished, exercise the powers vested in the Council by the Treaties, and should then respect Council procedures. In fact it has refrained from doing so.

- When adopting treaty changes, in Maastricht, Amsterdam, Nice or more recently in Brussels in June 2004, the participants meet not as a European Council but as an Intergovernmental Conferences at the level of Heads of State or Government (Art. 48 TEU).

These legal distinctions are not generally understood by public opinion, and are frequently unknown even to participants.

Origins

Heads of government have always played an important role in the development of European integration. The legendary Belgian Foreign Minister, Paul-Henri Spaak (1969: 95) described a meeting in Paris in February 1957, on the eve of the signature of the Treaty of Rome, where heads of government had to settle the last politically sensitive issues: 'It went on day and night. I had to run from one to the other, pleading, looking for compromises. Finally at dawn on 20 February a solution was found.' This sounds no different from some present-day European Councils!

In 1969 a summit held at The Hague opened the way for British accession and initiated an effort at foreign policy coordination called 'European Political Cooperation' (see Chapter 13). Other summits were held in Paris in 1972 and Copenhagen in 1973. But it was at Paris in December 1974 that it was decided to have regular meetings of what was to become the 'European Council' (see Exhibit 3.1). The first such meeting was held in Dublin in March 1975. Two to four meetings have been held every year since then: up to the end of 2004, Heads of Government had met more than 90 times in this format.

Exhibit 3.1 The origins of the European Council, Paris, December 1974

Recognizing the need for an overall approach to the internal problems involved in achieving European unity and the external problems facing Europe, the Heads of Government consider it essential to ensure progress and overall consistency in the activities of the Communities and in the work on political co-operation.

The Heads of Government have therefore decided to meet, accompanied by the Ministers of Foreign Affairs, three times a year, whenever necessary, in the Council of the Communities and in the context of political cooperation. The administrative Secretariat will be provided for in an appropriate manner with due regard for existing practices and procedures.

In order to ensure consistency in Community activities and continuity of work, the Ministers of Foreign Affairs, meeting in the Council of the Community, will act as initiators and coordinators. They may hold political co-operation meetings at the same time.

Source: Bulletin of the European Communities, 1974, n° 2

Two basic reasons can be put forward as justifications for the Paris Summit decision:

- Community institutions were felt not to be working as well as they should, especially since the Luxembourg compromise of 1965 was in practice blocking majority voting. The first enlargement of the Community to include Britain, Ireland and Denmark was likely to make decision-making more ponderous. The creation of a regular (as opposed to an occasional) source of strategic direction and political impulse made sense in this context.

- Foreign ministers were (already!) finding it difficult to coordinate the activities of a growing number of Council formations. Moreover, European political cooperation (EPC) posed a problem. Some member states, France in particular, were insisting that Community institutions should have no authority whatsoever over this new activity. Clearly, some form of overall coordination would be needed if the 'European Union', as it was beginning to be called, was to develop in a coherent manner. Introducing the heads of government as the ultimate source of authority, with foreign ministers at their side, was felt to be the only way, or the least controversial way, to ensure coordination and consistency.

As is frequently the case for important decisions, personalities also played a role in the creation of the European Council. Valéry Giscard d'Estaing, newly elected President of the French Republic, wanted to continue playing a significant role in European affairs (see Giscard d'Estaing 1988) and convinced the new West German Chancellor, Helmut Schmidt. Jean Monnet, whose influence in all Community countries was considerable, came to the conclusion that regular meetings of Heads of Government were needed. His views were instrumental in securing the agreement of the smaller member states.

In any institutional framework the regularity of meetings makes a fundamental difference. Before 1974 summit meetings were important occasions where significant decisions were taken, but with little or no lasting impact on the working of Community institutions. Since then, and increasingly as time has gone by, European Council meetings have come to mark the rhythm of EU activities. Commission papers are put forward, Council reports approved, parliamentary resolutions voted in view of this or that European Council. It plays a leading role in the European integration process.

Composition

The restricted composition of the European Council has already been mentioned. There is, however, a small amount of flexibility: when a foreign minister is absent a junior minister (even, in rare cases, a Permanent Representative) may take his seat. The Prime Minister of France sometimes replaces, and sometimes assists, the President of the Republic. Over the years a limited number of officials from the Presidency, the Council Secretariat or the Commission have gained a seat in the room, or even, in the case of the Secretary-General of the Council, at the table. (See Fig. 3.1.)

Figure 3.1 Seating arrangements at European Councils

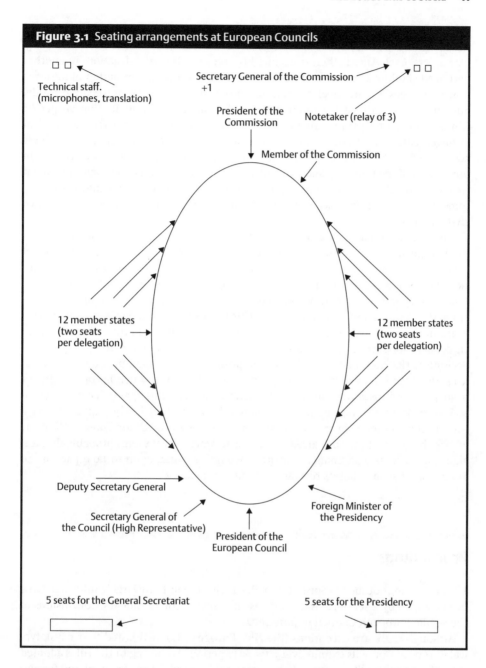

On these matters, as in others, the Presidency has a certain margin of appreciation. Two delegates per delegation are issued red badges, which allow them to enter the meeting, in order to submit a note or whisper a message, but they may not stay.

The debate in the European Council is relayed to the outside world by a system of note takers. An official from the Council Secretariat sits in the room and takes notes. Every quarter of an hour he is replaced, and goes out to brief orally the Antici group (personal assistants of the Permanent Representatives) who are sitting in an adjacent room, in the red zone where other members of national delegations do not have regular access. Each Antici[3] then transmits his notes to his own delegation, in another part of the building known as the blue zone. This indirect dissemination of information guarantees that national delegations know something of the proceedings inside, but with considerable delay and in a way which makes direct attribution of specific words to any participant nearly impossible. Peter Ludlow has compared the physical arrangements at a European Council 'to a vast temple in some oriental rite' (Ludlow 2000: 15) where high priests officiate in seclusion, while lesser participants remain in other parts of the building. Such an extraordinary system would not have survived if Heads of Government were not happy with the result, namely that they operate at some distance, both in space and time, from the views and comments of their own civil servants.

The Constitutional Treaty would bring significant change to the composition of the European Council. It states that the European Council consists of the heads of state or government together with its President and the President of the Commission. The Union Foreign Minister takes part in its work. Members of the European Council may (but need not) be assisted by a minister or, in the case of the President of the Commission, a commissioner. This means that foreign ministers who have been, since the beginning and up to now, *de jure* participants in the European Council deliberations would lose that capacity. The justification generally given for that decision is that in an enlarged Union the presence of two members per delegation leads to a meeting of sixty or more people round the table which becomes difficult to manage and loses that intimate character to which participants have always attached great importance. It should be noted, however, that foreign ministers get a sort of proxy presence in the European Council through the Union Foreign Minister, who is chairman of the Foreign Affairs Council. Moreover, it seems probable that foreign ministers, as also finance ministers, would be called upon to take part in the discussion of agenda points relevant to their competence.

Proceedings

The proceedings of the European Council, which were initially largely informal, have been codified by a set of rules adopted as an annex to the Presidency Conclusions of the Seville European Council in June 2002.

Although there are exceptions (the Nice European Council lasted four days), typical European Councils extend over a two-day period. According to the rules adopted at Seville it begins with a dinner held separately for heads of government and foreign ministers. Foreign ministers will normally discuss a few specific points of international relations. Prime ministers may have a freewheeling discussion on European affairs, recalling the fireside chats of the early European Councils or have a preliminary exchange on politically sensitive issues such as nominations. The next day, after a family photograph, the meeting begins with an address by the President of the European Parliament. This custom, introduced in the late 1980s, has high symbolic value for the Parliament and sometimes leads to a short debate. For the rest of the day, the full European Council meets to debate the different points on the agenda and approve the draft conclusions.

It is up to the Presidency 'to ensure that business is conducted smoothly'. If the discussion gets bogged down, the Presidency may well interrupt the meeting and hold bilateral conversations (known as 'confessionals') with each delegation. The President can also encourage two or more delegations to get together to solve a specific problem. Any procedural suggestion which seems likely to get results is usually accepted, at least on an experimental basis.

Conclusions reached are encapsulated in a final document. Traditionally, these texts are known as 'Presidency Conclusions' but the time spent on them shows that everyone is aware of their importance for the daily working of the Union. In one exceptional case (Athens in 1983) disagreement was such that no conclusions could be drafted.[4]

The Seville rules brought major change to the drafting of Presidency Conclusions. Draft conclusions are now submitted to Coreper weeks before the European Council and discussed first at that level, and then at the General Affairs Council. This means that by far the largest part of the conclusions is approved before the European Council meets. Only those politically sensitive points on which Heads of Government must decide themselves remain open. This has cut short the lengthy, divisive, and frustrating exercises in drafting which used to be the unnatural task of Heads of Government on the second day of European Councils. As a result, the meetings have become shorter. An additional advantage is that Coreper and the General Affairs Council now manage to eliminate the lengthy contributions, documents, reports, and action plans, coming from various Council formations or the Commission, which used to be automatically attached to the Presidency Conclusions without in fact having at any moment received the attention of the heads of government. These changes have undoubtedly been beneficial and have increased the efficiency of the European Council as a decision-making body.

Political guidance remains in the hands of the President of the European Council himself. Together with the Council Secretary-General, the President normally makes a tour of capitals in the weeks preceding the meeting to clarify positions, test possible solutions, or suggest a form of words. On this basis he or she fixes the agenda and communicates it to his colleagues in a letter sent a few days before the meeting. This agenda is not absolutely binding, because there is no way of preventing a head of government from raising a subject he or she wants to raise. But in general terms the authority of the President is respected.

As a rule, decisions are taken in the European Council by consensus. However, rules of procedure are adopted by a simple majority as is the decision to call an intergovernmental conference. Some major appointments, such as the President of the Commission, require qualified majority. Unanimity applies to common defence. More cases where a vote can be taken would be introduced by the Constitutional Treaty (see Exhibit 3.7; p. 54). Neither the President of the Commission nor a future President of the European Council takes or would take part in votes.

In the course of accession negotiations it is customary to invite Heads of Government from candidate countries for lunch and/or a brief session on the second day. This applies also to special guests such as Kofi Annan, UN Secretary-General, who came to Brussels for a European Council meeting in December 2004 or Iyad Allawi, the Iraqi Prime Minister who came in November of the same year

The last, but certainly not least important, act of a European Council is to give press conferences. Frequently, each national delegation gives its own press conference to a number of journalists who commute from one delegation to another. By comparing notes on sometimes contradictory statements experienced hands can often get a clear picture of the actual debate. This led Roy Jenkins (1989: 75), President of the Commission from 1977 to 1981, to call European Councils 'a restricted meeting with full subsequent publicity'.

In the days that follow, the President of the European Council, accompanied by the President of the Commission, reports to the European Parliament on the meeting. Although this exercise tends to repeat information already available in the press, it has contributed to a better understanding between the institutions, thereby diminishing the sense of frustration that the European Parliament initially entertained *vis à vis* the European Council, on whose activities it exerted no control and little influence.

The Constitutional Treaty would introduce an important new element in the role of the President as the driving force of a European Council. Article I-22 provides that it would be chaired by a president elected for a two-and-a-half-year period. The president would make use of the Council secretariat, an arrangement designed to avoid the creation of a new bureaucracy. In the heated debates which took place in the Convention on this issue, one of the arguments in favour of the new system was that in an enlarged Union the workload of the President would reach a point where it would become incompatible with the national obligations of a head of government. Most of the smaller member states opposed it because they feared it would increase the weight and influence of the bigger participants. Some doubted whether an elected president, who will no longer be the chief executive of a member state, could in fact have the necessary authority on the apparatus of the Union and on the European Council itself. Others foresaw potential conflicts with the President of the Commission and the Foreign Minister, in cases where respective competences might overlap. Time will tell whether these fears were justified or not.

Special meetings

- **Extraordinary meetings**: The Seville rules specifically mention the possibility of holding extraordinary meetings of the European Council in exceptional circumstances. Extraordinary European Councils were held in Brussels after the 9/11 terrorist attacks on the United States (21 September 2001) and at a crucial moment in the Iraq crisis (17 February 2003).

- **Informal meetings**: The first informal meeting was called by the Spanish presidency at Formentor (Mallorca) in September 1995 to discuss the issues of the ongoing IGC. The purpose of informal meetings is to allow for the sort of confidential exchange of views and brainstorming which a growing workload has gradually eliminated from regular meetings. Informal meetings are usually shorter than formal meetings. Foreign ministers are not always present. As a rule, there are no presidency conclusions though, in recent cases, official declarations have been issued.

- **Thematic meetings**: In recent years there has been a tendency to call meetings on a specific subject such as justice and home affairs (JHA) (Tampere, October 1999) or economic and social affairs (Lisbon, March 2000). Spring meetings of the European Council are supposed to be devoted mainly to the implementation of the Lisbon agenda on the economic, social and environmental situation of the Union. In fact, heads of government cannot avoid dealing with issues of immediate relevance: in March 2004 the issue of terrorism came to the forefront as a result of the bombings in the Atocha railway station in Madrid. In practice, thematic meetings differ only slightly from the normal ones.

Legal nature and characteristics

Under the provisions of the Constitutional Treaty, the legal nature of the European Council would be clear: it would be an institution of the Union, just like the Parliament, the Commission or the Court. But for the time being, the legal nature of the European Council remains the object of much academic debate (see Taulègne 1993: 92–100). Part of the problem derives from the fact that for the first twelve years of its existence (1974–86), the European Council met, and exercised significant power, without any legal basis in the treaties. In a highly structured legal system, such as the Community, this was indeed a strange phenomenon. The Single European Act specified the composition of the European Council but deliberately abstained from defining its role (De Ruyt 1987: 108–9). The Treaty of Maastricht, slightly modified in Amsterdam, offered some description of its role,[5] but, as we shall see, this description is largely inadequate.

In a limited number of cases the Treaty specifies that decisions must be taken by the Council meeting at the level of heads of state or government. In those cases the legal status of the meeting is clear. In all other cases the situation remains ambiguous.

Perhaps the best way to visualize the European Council for the time being is to consider it not as an institution, in legal terms, but as a locus of power. This makes it easier to explain its main characteristics: its authority, its informality, its flexibility, the special relationship between participants including the impact of seniority, and finally its ambivalence.

- **Authority**: The European Council brings together political personalities who, in their national capacity, are ultimate decision-takers. Collectively they consider themselves, in the European context, as having a similar task. Essentially they come together to take decisions, and expect these decisions to be respected. Hence the specific nature of European Council conclusions. Strictly speaking they are not legally binding, but in fact they constitute a form of *soft law* which European

---

Exhibit 3.2 Flexible rules for European Councils

An informal meeting was called at Ghent on 19 October 2001. Foreign ministers were not invited. Normal rules implied that no conclusions would be drafted, no statements issued. However, heads of government decided that they wanted to issue declarations on terrorism, the economic situation, and the introduction of the euro. These declarations are entitled 'Declarations by the Heads of Government and the President of the Commission', a formulation which acknowledges the fact that the composition of the meeting is not in conformity with Article 4 TEU (no foreign minister) and that therefore *it is not* legally a European Council. However in the text of these declarations it is the European Council that 'states, confirms, takes note, is determined, will continue, invites member states etc'. In other words, although the meeting should not issue declarations it does do so, and although it is not a European Council it takes positions and issues instructions as if it were one ... And nobody complains!

---

institutions (Council, Commission, and Parliament) have to take into account and respect.

- **Informality**: The European Council has always attached the highest importance to the informality of its meetings. It works on the basis of restricted sessions where heads of government and foreign ministers sit alone, face to face, frequently addressing each other by their first names. In the seventies the Chancellor of West Germany, Willy Brandt, wanted summit meetings to be like a fireside chat (*Kamingespräch*). Roy Jenkins considered the European Council as 'a surprisingly satisfactory body, mainly because it is intimate' (Jenkins 1989: 74). With time, and as a result of enlargement, meetings have tended to become more structured and more formal. Specific papers are, in practice, actively debated. But the principle of privacy and direct contact, quite frequently confrontational, remains.

- **Flexibility**: Rules of procedure have been gradually adopted over the years, but the fact is that they remain highly flexible. European Councils do not hesitate to depart from rules they have themselves formulated, as indicated in Exhibit 3.2.

- **Unequal relationships**: In the abstract all heads of government are equal, just as their states have equal status in international law. But because the European Council is a locus of power, the fact that some participants have in fact more power (because they represent a bigger country) is immediately apparent and implicitly understood by all. Put simply, 'the intergovernmental nature of the European Council is more marked than that of the sectoral Councils' (Hayes-Renshaw 1999: 25).

- **Seniority**: Because participants are relatively few in number and personal relations important, the balance of power in the European Council is influenced by seniority. Newcomers will not be able to pull their full weight at first meetings. Heads of government of smaller member states can expect to exert more influence after several years of being present, particularly after they have led a successful Presidency. The case of Jean Claude Juncker, Prime Minister of Luxembourg since 1995, is an example of the representative of a small member state exercising considerable influence, certainly due to his personal qualities but also because of his seniority.

- **Ambivalence**: Finally, viewing the European Council as a locus of power helps explain its ambivalence in institutional terms. Without the Constitutional Treaty its powers, procedures, and decision-making process are not determined by legal texts. It deals with whatever problem it wants to deal with, in the manner it judges most appropriate. Nowhere is its role clearly defined, yet that role is fundamental to the life of the Union. It can live with that ambivalence because it is bent on the exercise of power *de facto* and not on legally binding decision-making.

Because the European Council stood apart from the institutional framework of the Union it has generally been considered strictly intergovernmental, except when it acts formally as a Council. However, it has been known to vote (in Milan in 1985 to call the intergovernmental conference that was to lead to the Single European Act, with Britain, Denmark and Greece opposing). Moreover, the President of the Commission is *de jure* a member of the European Council and highly important decisions concerning the Community are taken at that level.

Perhaps because of this ambivalence, theories of European integration have some difficulty in accommodating the role of the European Council. Its composition and the power it wields would seem at first sight to confirm liberal intergovernmentalist (LI) theory, best developed by Andrew Moravcsik. LI explains European integration as a succession of bargains between the bigger member states, based on national interests, domestic politics, and the constraints of the world environment. According to this view, 'the creation of the European Council was explicitly designed to narrow rather than to broaden the scope for autonomous action by supranational actors' (Moravcsik 1998: 488). 'Its major consequence was to transfer policy initiative away from the more rule governed Commission and Parliament' (Moravcsik 1998: 310). 'Bargaining outcomes reflect the relative power of states rather than supranational entrepreneurship' (Moravcsik 1998: 485).

One may indeed consider, with Moravcsik, successive intergovernmental conferences as 'bargains' concluded by member states at the highest level. However the fact is that the Union has obviously more supranational elements today than it did in 1974. If supranational actors 'have only a rare and secondary impact' on negotiations (Moravcsik 1998: 485), how is this transfer of power to be explained?

Historical institutionalism, on the other hand, considers that institutions, by themselves, 'structure political situations and leave their own imprint on political outcomes' (Thelen and Steinmo 1992: 9). According to this view, actors are assumed not to be entirely aware of, or concerned about, the long term institutional consequences of the decisions they take. To explain in this way the integrative impact of the European Council over a quarter of a century presupposes, however, a lasting degree of political naiveté not normally associated with Heads of Government. The European Council, unlike other institutions, is not bound by strict rules and procedures. It is master of its own agenda and can quite easily change one of its own decisions if unforeseen consequences become apparent

The fact is that theoretical models have difficulty reconciling the different and sometimes contradictory aspects of the European Council. That difficulty might be settled by the Constitutional Treaty, if it came into force, as it includes the European Council in the institutional framework of the Union, thereby putting an end to thirty years of ambiguity.

Functions

According to the existing Treaty, the role of the European Council is defined as follows: 'it shall provide the Union with the necessary impetus for its development and shall define the general political guidelines thereof'. It has a specific role in foreign and security policy, and in the definition of broad economic guidelines. The treaty reserves to the heads of government certain specific decisions in the field of economic and monetary union[6] and the appointment of the President of the Commission. These texts are partly based on a document adopted as a 'Solemn Declaration' (therefore not legally binding) at Stuttgart in 1983 (see Exhibit 3.3) which is, historically, the first tentative description of the role of the European Council.

The Constitutional Treaty would bring some clarification by saying that the European Council shall provide the Union with the necessary impetus for its development and shall define its general political directions and priorities. The formulation is certainly closer to political reality than the present one, but it still does not adequately reflect the role of ultimate negotiator and at times detailed decision-maker which is so frequently that of the European Council.

The fact is that functions of the European Council go well beyond the official texts. They are described hereafter under the following headings:[7]

Exhibit 3.3 Functions of the European Council, Stuttgart, June 1983

2.1.2 In the perspective of European Union, the European Council

- provides a general political impetus to the construction of Europe;
- defines approaches to further the construction of Europe and issues general political guidelines for the European Communities and European Political Cooperation;
- deliberates upon matters concerning European Union in its different aspects with due regard to consistency among them;
- initiates cooperation in new areas of activity;
- solemnly expresses the common position in questions of external relations.

2.1.3 When the European Council acts in matters within the scope of the European Communities, it does so in its capacity as the Council within the meaning of the treaties

Source: Bulletin of the European Communities, 1983 n° 6

- strategic guidelines;
- decision-making;
- open method of coordination;
- foreign policy;
- amending the treaties;
- simplified treaty revision.

Strategic guidelines

The most traditional function of the European Council is to provide political guidance and impetus across the whole spectrum of Union activities. This was indeed the main reason given for its creation. It is mentioned both by the Tindemans Report[8] (1976) and by the Stuttgart Declaration (1983) and is the sole function clearly described in the Treaty. In the early texts the accent was put on ensuring consistency between Community affairs and other forms of European activity. At a time (before the Treaty of Maastricht) when these branches were completely separated, the European Council was indeed the only place where some form of consistency could be ensured.

This task implies the right to launch new fields of activities. In Rome, in December 1975, the European Council decided to initiate cooperation in the fight against terrorism and organized crime. In Hanover in June 1988 it appointed a group to look into economic and monetary union. At Lisbon in March 2000 it opened up a new field of action in social affairs and economic policy. Gradually it has acquired a sort of monopoly in this respect: 'Nothing decisive can be proposed or undertaken without its authority' (Taulègne 1993: 481).

Basically, the European Council fixes the agenda of the European Union and is the place where strategic orientations are given. This is true for all fields of activity. It is the European Council which approves common strategies in the framework of CFSP, as it has done *vis à vis* Russia and Ukraine. As far as the Community is concerned, orientations leading to the completion of the internal market and to monetary union were defined at that level. One example of political guidance can be seen in the enlargement process. Momentous decisions were taken at Copenhagen in December 1993 on Central and Eastern European countries and in Brussels in December 2004 on Turkey (see Exhibit 3.4). They could not have been taken at any other level.

Exhibit 3.4 Political guidance of the European Council on enlargement to Turkey, Brussels, December 2004.

. . . The European Council welcomed the adoption of the six pieces of legislation identified by the Commission. It decided that, in the light of the above and of the Commission report and recommendation, Turkey sufficiently fulfils the Copenhagen political criteria to open accession negotiations provided that it brings into force these specific pieces of legislation. It invited the Commission to present to the Council a proposal for a framework for negotiations with Turkey, on the basis set out in paragraph 23. It requested the Council to agree on that framework with a view to opening negotiations on 3 October 2005.

Source: European Council, Presidency Conclusions, Point 22

Decision-making

It was certainly not the initial intention of the member states that the European Council should serve as ultimate decision-taker, a court of appeal for settling problems too complex, or too politically sensitive to be resolved at the Council level. Quite the contrary: both the Tindemans Report on European Union (1976) and the Dooge Report[9] on institutional reform (1985) stated that this should *not* be the case. Official texts, such as the Stuttgart Declaration (1993), steer clear of giving to the European Council a decision-making capacity. But in fact, over the years, that is exactly what it has acquired and exercised.

Examples abound. Successive European Councils wrestled in the early 1980s with the intractable British budgetary problem until a solution was finally found at Fontainebleau in June 1984. 'Virtually every decision that affected the development of the internal market since the early 1980s was taken by the European Council' (Sbragia 1991: 63). The 'packages' around the financial perspectives of the Union (Delors I, Delors II, Agenda 2000), which involve an element of distributive bargaining between member states, have always been settled at the top level (see Exhibit 3.5). The same is true of decisions concerning the seat of European institutions: Edinburgh

---

Exhibit 3.5 Decision-making in the European Council, Berlin, March 1999

The Berlin European Council settled the financial perspectives (Agenda 2000) for the period 2000–06. The following table (one of several) is indicative of the detailed decisions such an exercise implies.

11. An indicative financial framework for EU-21 as set out in Table B attached should accompany the financial perspective. It should include additional own resources resulting from the accession of 6 new Member States, and set out in an additional heading 8 (enlargement) the total cost of enlargement for each of the years 2002–2006, expressed as maximum amounts in appropriations for commitments for agriculture, structural operations, internal policies and administration, as follows:

Heading 8 (Enlargement) (appropriations for commitments) (Million £1999 prices)					
	2002	2003	2004	2005	2006
Heading 8 (Enlargement)	6.45	9.03	11.61	14.20	16.78
Agriculture	1.600	2.03	2.450	2.930	3.400
Structural op.	3.750	5.83	7.920	10.00	12.08
Internal policies	730	760	790	820	850
Administration	370	410	450	450	450

Source: Berlin European Council. Presidency conclusions, Part I

in December 1992; Brussels in October 1993; and December 2003. It also applies to the appointment of the President of the Commission.

The reason generally given for this evolution is the incapacity of the General Affairs Council to coordinate the activities of other Councils. This failure compels the European Council to step in as arbiter. However, it is also the case that heads of government, though accepting in principle that their role should be one of mere guidance, have not in practice refused to deal in substance with the growing number of problems coming on to their agenda. After all, decision-making is a sign of power, and power is not something successful politicians tend to eschew.

Open method of coordination

This process was established by the European Council at Lisbon in March 2000 (and is generally known as the 'Lisbon process'). In essence it aims at generating agreement among governments to move together towards tackling a range of socio–economic challenges, where the policy powers remain located at the level of national or sub-national government in the member states, and where the scope for agreement depends on soft prescriptions rather than hard law. The approach adopted lies somewhere between classical intergovernmental cooperation and the Community method, and provides for a central role of the European Council. It has been called intensive transgovernmentalism in which 'the primary actors are leading national policy-makers, operating in highly interactive mode and developing new forms of commitment and mutual engagement' (H. Wallace 2002: 341). As far as questions of economic reform are concerned, the European Council should become a forum, even a kind of 'seminar', for comparing different national experiences and experiments, with the detailed work to be taken forward over the year. It should make use of guidelines, timetables, indicators, benchmarks, periodic monitoring, and peer review to exercise a strong guiding and coordinating role.

The process is not limited to activities at the highest level: it implies significant work at Council and committee levels. Nevertheless the centrepiece is the Spring meeting of the European Council which, as indicated above, should (but does not always) concentrate on the Lisbon process. There is no doubt that the European Council has thereby deliberately undertaken a new responsibility and that it is in fact exercising a new role, if not a new type of competence. Appreciation of the results of the Lisbon process lies outside the institutional framework of this book but it is worth mentioning that doubts persist as to the ability of the Union to reach, through this new process, the ambitious goals defined at Lisbon.

Foreign policy

Formulation of foreign policy has always been one of the primary tasks of the European Council. Its very first meeting in Dublin in March 1975, approved a declaration on Cyprus and one on the Conference for Security and Cooperation in Europe (CSCE). The present Treaty says that the European Council shall define the principles of and general guidelines for the common and foreign and security policy including for matters with defence implications. This is rephrased in the Constitutional Treaty: the European Council shall identify the Union's strategic interests and determine the objectives of its common foreign and security policy and the President of the European Council shall ensure, at his or her level, the external representation of the Union in the field of CFSP.

Over the years European Councils have approved a great number of statements on foreign policy, covering events in all parts of the world and developments in all fields of diplomacy. Some of these statements are made at a time of existing or impending crisis, such as the one made in Berlin in March 1999 on the eve of NATO air strikes in Yugoslavia. Similarly, invitations addressed to high-ranking personalities for a meeting in the margins of a European Council underline the importance attached to a specific international issue : President Trajkovski of Macedonia (Stockholm, March 2001) and, as mentioned above, Prime Minister Iyad Allawi of Iraq and UN Secretary-General Kofi Annan attended European Councils in 2004.

It can be argued that some Presidency Conclusions contain an excessive number of foreign policy declarations and that this proliferation diminishes the impact of such statements. There is no doubt however that member states have used the European Council effectively as a means of expressing forcefully common positions on international affairs. It is clear, for example, that the message demanding that the siege of Sarajevo be lifted, sent by the Cannes European Council in June 1995, would be taken seriously precisely because it was sent, in no uncertain terms, at the level of authority which might, if necessary, decide the use of force (see Exhibit 3.6).

When acting in this external capacity the European Council operates in fact like a 'collective head of state' and this has been used as an argument in favour of a semi-permanent presidency of that body, to avoid the disadvantages of a six month rotation. As indicated above, that argument prevailed in the Convention. The President of the European Council would have an important foreign policy role according to the Constitutional Treaty.

Amending the treaties

As we have seen, heads of government have always played some role in treaty negotiations, including in the negotiation of the Treaty of Rome. But over time that role has become predominant: the European Council has become 'the key forum for determining treaty reforms' (Wallace and Wallace 2000: 20).

In the negotiation of the Single European Act (1985–86) the input of heads of government was limited. The main top level decision was that the Act would indeed be 'single', that it would incorporate in one document articles relating to political co-operation *and* Community activities, which had been negotiated separately. This was an important decision in terms of political symbolism, and it was appropriate that it should be taken by heads of government. But the texts themselves had been negotiated and largely finalized at the level of officials or foreign ministers.

In the Maastricht negotiations (1990–91) several important points of substance were only decided at the highest level and at the last minute. The contribution of heads of government was therefore more significant than had previously been the case. Nevertheless a large amount of work had been done both by finance ministers, on the articles on monetary union, and by foreign ministers, notably on the second pillar relating to CFSP.

> **Exhibit 3.6** Foreign policy statement by the European Council, Cannes, June 1995.
>
> Meeting in Cannes on 26 and 27 June 1995, the European Council sends the following message to the leaders and peoples of former Yugoslavia:
>
> ... The European Union strongly advises all the parties in the conflict to refrain from placing obstacles in the way of the freedom of movement and action of UNPROFOR and of the humanitarian organizations bringing aid to the civilian population. It warns them that the peace forces are determined to overcome such obstacles. The siege of Sarajevo must be lifted. The European Union demands freedom of access to Sarajevo, its enclaves and the safe areas.
>
> *Source:* Cannes European Council, Presidency Conclusions

In the Amsterdam negotiations (1996–97), and again in the negotiations leading to the Treaty of Nice, foreign ministers had little impact. Practically all the problems not resolved at the level of personal representatives went to the European Council. Its direct contribution was not limited to basic issues: it included points such as the status of public credit institutions in Germany or crisis meetings of the Political Committee.

The Intergovernmental Conference leading to the Constitutional Treaty gives us a more balanced example. It is true that important modifications were made to the draft treaty submitted by the Convention on issues such as majority voting, reinforced cooperation or defence, and that these modifications were largely decided at head of government level. Nevertheless by far the largest part of the Constitutional Treaty is to be found in the Convention draft.

Simplified Treaty revision

The Constitutional Treaty would give the European Council a new and potentially important competence in allowing it, in certain cases and following certain procedures, to modify treaty articles without going through the process of an intergovernmental conference (see Exhibit 3.7). Article IV-444 would allow the European Council to modify the decision-making procedure (qualified majority instead of unanimity) or the legislative procedure (ordinary procedure instead of special procedure). The proposal would first have to be communicated to national Parliaments, each one of which would have six months to veto it. In the absence of such a veto, the decision could be taken by unanimous decision of the European Council and would enter into force if it received the consent of the European Parliament given by a majority of its component members. Specific clauses for foreign policy decisions and the multiannual financial framework would allow modifications of the decision-making procedure without having to refer to national parliaments or the European Parliament. The European Council, acting by unanimity, would also be able to modify the provisions concerning the internal policies and actions of the Union (Title III of Part III) but in that case amendments would have to be approved by member states according to their respective constitutional procedures.[10]

Clauses of a similar nature, known as *passerelles* in Community jargon, have existed in various forms since the Treaty of Maastricht, but have never been used. The widening of their scope in the new text reflects the conviction, widely shared by members

---

Exhibit 3.7 European Council decision-making according to the Constitutional Treaty

Art. I-20 §2: composition European Parliament *
Art. I-24 §4: configurations of the Council * *
Art. I-24 §7: rotation of presidencies * *
Art. I-26 §6: composition of the Commission *
Art. I-27 §1 and 2: proposal for President and appointment of the Commission * *
Art. I-28 §1: appointment of the Minister for Foreign Affairs * *
Art. I-40 §6: CFSP decisions (see also III-295 §1) *
Art. I-40 §7: *passerelle* clause for CFSP (see also III-300 §3) *
Art. I-55 §4: *passerelle* clause for multiannual financial framework *
Art. I-59 §2: persistent breach of Union values *
Art. III-136 §2: emergency brake for social security
Art. III-258: strategic guidelines for the area of freedom and justice
Art. III-270 §3 and 271 §3: emergency brakes for judicial cooperation in criminal matters.
Art. III-274 §4: powers of the Public Prosecutor's Office. *
Art. III-293 §1: strategic objectives and interests of the Union *
Art. III-295 §1: general guidelines for CFSP.
Art. III-341 §3: rules of procedure of the European Council * * *
Art. III-382-2: appointment of the board of the Central Bank * *
Art. IV-440 §7: amending the status of overseas territories *.
Art. IV-443 §2: convening a Convention or an intergovernmental conference * * *
Art. IV-444 §1 and 2: general *passerelle* clause (simplified revision procedure). *
Art. IV-445 §2: simplified revision procedure for internal policies and actions *

Protocol on the statute of the European Central Bank—Art. 40 §2: amending the voting rules of the Governing Council of the Bank. *

(References: * means unanimity, * * means qualified majority, * * * means simple majority. Where no procedure is indicated, Art. I-21 §4 applies, i.e. consensus)

---

of the Convention, that future treaty revisions will become increasingly difficult because of enlargement. The fact that Part III of the Treaty was examined only very cursorily by the Convention because of lack of time also played a role. It remains to be seen whether these procedures, which are not as simple as the title of the articles suggests, will in fact be used.

Strengths and weaknesses

For over a quarter of a century the European Council has been the guiding force of the European integration process: 'the primary source of history making decisions' (Peterson and Bomberg 1999: 33). Time and time again, the most difficult problems have been debated, and solutions have been found, at that level. The European Union would not be what it is if heads of government had not been systematically involved in major decisions.

But top-level decision-making has of course its limits and its dangers. Dangers relate to the irretrievable character of mistakes; limits to the nature and the quantity of decisions to be taken. Negotiation at the highest level is risky: miscalculations or tactical errors occur and cannot, in most cases, be corrected. It is clear, for instance, that in Rome in December 1990 Mrs Thatcher's insistence on having a separate paragraph for Britain in the Presidency Conclusions enabled the other member states to define monetary union as they wished, which was not her intention (see Exhibit 3.8).[11]

When considering the limits of the decision-making capacity of the European Council, two points are significant:

- **The number of meetings**: It is reasonable to assume that, in view of their other obligations, it would be impossible for heads of government to meet more frequently than four or five times a year on a regular basis. But on the other hand it is far from clear that such a limited number of meetings, however intense, are sufficient to deal effectively with the governance of an increasingly complex multinational entity. European Councils are frequently short of time.

- **Consensus**: Some modifications have been introduced but decision-making in the European Council remains, in general, based on consensus, that is on a relatively inefficient procedure. European Councils frequently fail to reach decisions, creating 'left overs' which means postponing decisions to a future date.

In practical terms, the limits of the European Council are particularly apparent when it is amending the treaties. The important point, not always well understood even by participants, is that the work of the European Council as treaty negotiator is different in nature from its other functions. When it gives political guidance or impetus, when it makes foreign policy statements or debates economic policy, decisions are political, not legal. When necessary, these political decisions receive legal form *ex post*, by a Council directive or regulation (such as for the structural funds) or by an interinstitutional agreement (for financial perspectives). 'The input of the European Council, which takes the form of a political decision, only has legal force once it has been adopted by the Council according to the relevant legislative procedures' (Hayes-Renshaw and Wallace 1997: 164). But when it acts as negotiator, the European Council is directly modifying the Treaty, the basic law of the Community. It is in fact legislating. That is a completely different task.

The structure and the *modus operandi* of the European Council are well adapted to collective bargaining, to the definition of general guidelines, even to the drafting of political statements. It is not well adapted to a legislative function. Hectic night sessions with no assistants in the room, multilingual debate on texts which appear and disappear from the negotiating table without having been studied in depth, and across-the-board compromises on unrelated issues at the break of dawn cannot lead to clear legal texts. The complexity and confusion of the treaties (with numerous protocols and declarations annexed to the Final Act of each Intergovernmental Conference) must be partly attributed to the way in which they are negotiated. It regularly takes legal and linguistic experts, under the guidance of Coreper, several weeks to establish in legal terms what has been decided. The fact is that no civilized nation legislates in such an uncoordinated and risky way. As Tony Blair famously remarked at the end of the Nice European Council: 'We cannot go on working like this.'

Although this, and other weaknesses, have been apparent for a number of years, there had been, until quite recently, very little criticism of the functioning of the European Council. At Helsinki in December 1999 heads of government approved welcome and substantial changes in the working methods of the Council but barely mentioned the European Council. Two years later, the Laeken Declaration included

---

Exhibit 3.8 A tactical error, Rome, October 1990

The main point on the agenda was the state of preparation of the IGC and in particular monetary union. A major point in the debate was whether the future currency (then called the ECU) should be:

- A common currency, that is a currency circulating in parallel with, but not supplanting, national currencies (pounds, francs, marks and so on);
- A single currency, that is a currency taking the place of national currencies.

On this fundamental point no agreement was reached on the first day of the European Council. The draft Presidency Conclusions, circulated early on the second day, were based on the principle of a *common* currency. When questioned before the meeting started, the Presidency answered that it had reluctantly come to the conclusion that the British Prime Minister would in no circumstance accept conclusions based on a *single* currency. Given the previous day's discussions, it was difficult to question that judgement.

At the beginning of the meeting Mrs Thatcher declared that the Presidency Draft Conclusions on monetary union were unacceptable, the United Kingdom would not be party to conclusions based on that draft, and would need a separate paragraph in which the British point of view would be described.

This changed the deal completely. Frantic activity was noted in the corridors, with several delegations putting pressure on the Presidency. The Italian Prime Minister, Giulio Andreotti, who was in the chair, stated in the course of discussion that the Presidency had changed its mind and would propose conclusions based on the principle of a *single* currency. When Mrs Thatcher protested, he answered (with a Sicilian smile) that since the UK would not be party to that part of the conclusions, and would have a paragraph of its own, it could hardly expect to influence the formulation preferred by other member states.

The European Council conclusions were as follows: 'The Community will have a single currency which will be an expression of its identity and unity.' A separate paragraph notes British dissent. If, as seems to be the case, the strategic objective of the British Government at the time was to prevent the birth of a single currency, Mrs Thatcher made a serious tactical error. At this level tactical errors are irretrievable. Today, the euro is a single currency.

---

a variety of institutional points for consideration by the subsequent Convention but was silent on the European Council. It was not before 2002 that critical voices began to be heard, in the Convention, in academic circles[12] but also in the institution itself. In March of that year the Barcelona European Council heard strong words from the Secretary-General of the Council. Solana considered that for some years the European Council had been sidetracked from its original purpose, it spent too much time on low level drafting work and its meetings had been reduced to 'report-approval sessions or inappropriate exercises in self congratulation'. This led to the rules of procedure adopted at Seville in June 2002, described above, and which have had a substantial positive effect.

The Convention and the Constitutional Treaty proposed several measures which would further strengthen the European Council: recognizing it as a full fledged institution, reducing the number of participants, giving it a semi-permanent Presidency, bringing some clarification to its competences and its decision-making process. Moreover treaty modifications would henceforth be amended by way of a

Convention, which, on the basis of our single experience, seems to reduce the number of issues that need to be addressed at the top level.

Conclusion

In many ways 'the whole European Union system revolves round the European Council' (Ludlow 2000: 15). The dates of its meetings, announced well in advance, mark the rhythm of the Union's various activities in the way religious feast days marked the rhythm of daily life in medieval Christendom. Foreign governments, the press, and business organizations study Presidency Conclusions to gauge the health, the dynamics, future orientations, and potential actions of the Union.

In successive meetings over the years, the European Council has largely fashioned the Union as we know it today. And the fact is that, even if the European Council is basically intergovernmental in nature, the system it has so largely contributed to is not mainly intergovernmental. At the beginning of a new century the Union is much larger, much more integrated and more supranational than it was in 1974. With hindsight it is clear, therefore, that Monnet was justified in advocating its creation. Those who feared, at the time, that it would lead to an intergovernmental system dominated by a *directoire* of major partners were proven wrong. 'The European Council worked its way into the Community decision making process without deeply undermining the institutional balance' (Werts 1992: 295).

What are the underlying reasons which have led to this result? For most of the time since 1974, France and Germany have been governed by leaders strongly committed to their mutual cooperation and to furthering European integration. They found enough support for this ambition in the Benelux, in Italy, sometimes in Spain and Portugal, more recently in Finland, to push the Union forward, even in the face of winds of scepticism blowing from Britain or Scandinavia. Monetary Union is a typical example. Moreover, for a long time, from 1985 to 1995, the Commission was chaired by Jacques Delors, a man who had developed a real talent for harnessing the power of the European Council to further the dynamics of integration (see Chapter 5). In the absence of any of these conditions the results would have been very different.

Efforts have been made, both by the European Council itself and through the Convention, to adapt to an enlarged Union. Time will tell whether those adaptations can be adopted and will be sufficient. There is no doubt that an increased number of participants weighs on the working of the European Council as it does on the other institutions of the Union. The informality, direct contact, and personal confidence, characteristic of the institution, are difficult to maintain in a larger body. Unofficial preparatory caucuses or other forms of *directoire* may become more tempting, and cause dismay.

Two conclusions seem appropriate:

- management of the Union could not be assured without a top-level institution of this type: the European Council has played a fundamental role in European integration and will continue to do so;

- top-level meetings have their limits and are not a panacea: they will certainly play a significant role in resolving the problems of European governance. But they will only be a part of the solution to that most difficult problem.

Notes

1 This results from declaration 4 annexed to the Final Act of the Maastricht Treaty.

2 This results from declaration 22 annexed to the Final Act of the Nice Treaty: 'When the Union comprises 18 members, all European Council meetings will be held in Brussels.'

3 This group, which plays an important role in the coordination of Coreper II activities, is named after Massimo Antici, an Italian diplomat who was, in 1975, its first chairman.

4 It is worth noting that European Council deliberations are in fact recorded, but only the Secretary-General of the Council has access to the recording. In exceptional cases he will verify a specific point at the request of one or more delegations. This is particularly important when there is wide disagreement as to what was agreed at a European Council, as was the case after the meeting in Nice in December 2000.

5 See Arts. 4 and 13 TEU.

6 Arts. 112, 121, and 122 TEC.

7 These distinctions are somewhat arbitrary and they frequently tend to overlap. Some authors identify no less than nine different functions (Bulmer and Wessels 1987: 76–80). Elsewhere they are counted as three (Dinan 2000: 190), six (Nugent 1999: 201) or even twelve (Werts 1992: 120–2). This variety is, of course, a consequence of the absence of clear legal texts but basically the ground covered is the same.

8 Leo Tindemans was Prime Minister of Belgium in December 1974 when he was asked by the Paris Summit to draft a report on European Union, which he presented in early 1976.

9 James Dooge, a former Irish Foreign Minister, was asked by the Fontainebleau European Council in June 1984 to chair a group to draft a report on institutional reform. The report, presented in 1985, prepared the negotiation of the Single European Act.

10 See Arts. I.40 §7 (and III.300 §3), I.55 §4, and IV.445 of the Constitutional Treaty.

11 Information is provided mainly by a series of interviews conducted in 1997 by the British Broadcasting Corporation (BBC) for the preparation of a documentary on monetary union called 'The Money Makers'.

12 See, for instance, Grant (2002) and de Schoutheete and Wallace (2002).

Further reading

Peter Ludlow (2002; 2004) has set himself the task of making a book-length commentary on every formal meeting of the European Council. His analyses have created a better understanding of the role and importance of an institution which had been neglected by academic research. De Schoutheete and Wallace (2002) makes a critical analysis of the functioning of the European Council at the beginning of the Convention. Older publications are now dated because of recent change in the working of this institution. The debate in the Convention is described in de Schoutheete (2003) and Norman (2003).

Ludlow, P. (2002), *The Laeken Council* (Brussels: EuroComment).

Ludlow, P. (2004), *The Making of the New Europe: The European Councils in Brussels*

and Copenhagen 2002 (Brussels: EuroComment).

de Schoutheete, P. (2003), *Die Debatte des Konvents über den Europäischen Rat* (Berlin) Integration Nr 4/03.

de Schoutheete, P., and Wallace, H. (2002), *The European Council* (Paris: Notre Europe), available on *http://www.notre-europe.asso.fr*

Norman, P. (2003), *The Accidental Constitution: the Story of the European Convention* (Brussels: Eurocomment).

Web links

The Commission website 'Europa' (*http://europa.eu.int*) gives in all Community languages the full text of Presidency Conclusions since the Corfu meeting in 1994.

Chapter 4
The Council of Ministers

Fiona Hayes-Renshaw

Contents

Summary

In the Council, national interests are articulated, defended, and aggregated by ministerial representatives of the member governments, who then adopt European Union (EU) legislation, increasingly in tandem with the European Parliament (EP). Each member state exercises the Presidency of the Council in turn, supported by an international secretariat at the Council's headquarters in Brussels. Most decisions are taken by consensus. But when the Council votes by qualified majority, the larger member states are just as likely as the smaller ones to be out-voted. Enlargement has provided the impetus for changes to the Council's organization and working methods. Further changes contained in the Constitutional Treaty regarding the Council's Presidency and voting rules are on hold following negative referendum results.

Introduction

The builders are at work in the Brussels headquarters of the Council of Ministers. They have added new meeting rooms and adapted old ones in the Council's Justus Lipsius building to cater for increased numbers of national delegates. They are covering over the central courtyard at the front of the building to provide additional space for journalists covering European Council meetings in a wing of the adjacent Résidence Palace building, once it too has been adapted. Further along the street they are constructing an entirely new edifice, the Lex Building, with additional meeting rooms and office space for translators. The Council is expanding along with the EU, and the extension and adaptation of its buildings is the most obvious outward manifestation of this trend.

This chapter examines the inhabitants of, and some of the visitors to, the Council's Justus Lipsius building. First, the present-day Council is traced back to its origins in the 1951 Treaty of Paris. Second, the structure of the institution is explored, in order to identify those individuals who together constitute the various layers of the Council hierarchy. As this volume contains separate chapters on the European Council (Chapter 3) and the Committee of Permanent Representatives or Coreper (Chapter 14), this chapter will concentrate on the remaining layers of the Council hierarchy—the ministerial Council, the preparatory bodies (the working parties and senior committees apart from Coreper), the Presidency and the Council Secretariat. The third section describes the formal and informal powers of the Council and its members, the ways in which its work is coordinated and the means available to its members to exert influence and affect its output. The Council's relationships with the Commission and the EP are examined in the next section, as is the frequently vexed question of the Council's accountability. In the final section, the Council's role in the context of the EU as a whole is analysed, as are the challenges posed to the Council by enlargement. Changes affecting the Council contained in the Constitutional Treaty are mentioned in the relevant sections of the chapter.

The origins of the Council

The Council of the European Union can trace its origins back directly to the (Special) Council of Ministers provided for in the 1951 Treaty of Paris, which established the European Coal and Steel Community (ECSC). The creation of a body representing the governments of the member states was a direct and rather obvious attempt to temper the powers of the ECSC's innovative supranational High Authority (later the European Commission). When the founding treaties of the two new European Communities were negotiated and adopted six years later, a slightly altered version of the ECSC blueprint was agreed, and the Council of the European Communities was born.

Despite the shared name, the powers of the old and new Councils could not have been more different. The ECSC's Special Council was required merely to exchange information with and consult the High Authority, while the 1957 Treaties of Rome provided that their Council should 'ensure coordination of the general economic policies of the member states and have power to take decisions'.

This enhanced role derived from the increased assertiveness of member governments *vis-à-vis* the more supranational elements of the European Communities, a confidence that has become still more marked in recent years. It is reflected not only in the additional formal and informal powers acquired by the Council but also in the changes that have been made to its structure and working methods (documented in successive treaties and in the Council's internal rules of procedure).

The Council hierarchy

The Council may be envisaged as a layered triangle, composed of the European Council at the top, followed by the ministers, then by Coreper and a number of other senior preparatory bodies and, at the base, a large number of working parties. Heading each of these levels is the Presidency, and the entire hierarchy is underpinned by a General Secretariat. As mentioned above, this chapter will deal directly with all levels except the European Council and Coreper.

The ministers

Although we speak of 'the' Council of Ministers, in practice it meets in a number of different configurations, each dealing with a distinct policy area (see Exhibit 4.1). Every Council is composed of the relevant minister(s) from each of the member states, and is chaired by a representative of the member state currently holding the Presidency. The Commission is invited to attend, and is represented by one or more Commissioners. Officials from the member states, the Commission services, and the Council Secretariat accompany the ministers, the Commissioners, and the Presidency to advise and assist them in their deliberations.

About 75 formal Council meetings are convened every year, usually in the Council's Brussels headquarters. However, in April, June, and October every year they are held in Luxembourg, the grossly inefficient result of a 1965 political agreement on the seat of the institutions, and most recently confirmed in the 1997 Treaty of Amsterdam. Each Presidency is also entitled to schedule five informal ministerial meetings, which normally take place in the Presidency member state.

The preparatory bodies

Council meetings are prepared by committees and working parties, composed of officials from each of the member states and a representative of the Commission. Coreper, the most senior of these committees, is formally responsible for preparing

---

Exhibit 4.1 Council configurations and frequency of meetings, 2004

The Council currently meets in nine configurations. In practice, the General Affairs and External Relations Council (GAERC) and the Economic and Financial Affairs Council (Ecofin) both meet in two distinct parts, while the agenda items of the others may be grouped according to policy sector, thereby enabling ministers with distinct portfolios to attend separate parts of the session.

Configurations	No. of meetings in 2004
General affairs and external relations (GAERC) (including European security and defence policy and development cooperation)	26
Economic and financial affairs (Ecofin) (including the budget)	11
Agriculture and fisheries (AgFish)	10
Justice and home affairs (JHA) (including civil protection)	9
Transport, telecommunications, and energy (TTE)	5
Employment, social policy, health, and consumer affairs (EPSCO)	4
Competitiveness (Comp) **(Internal market, industry, and research)** (including tourism)	4
Environment (Env)	4
Education, youth, and culture (EYC) (including audiovisual affairs)	3
TOTAL 2004	76

Source: Council Secretariat

---

the work of the entire Council and fulfils an important horizontal coordination function (see Chapter 14). Other senior bodies coordinate work in particular policy areas, such as the Economic and Financial Committee (EFC), the Special Committee on Agriculture (SCA), the Political and Security Committee (COPS—*Comité politique et de sécurité*) and the Article 36 Committee (CATS—*Comité article trente-six,*—which operates in the field of justice and home affairs (JHA)).

Officials from the national ministries represent their governments in the 160 or so specialized working parties and 100 or so sub-groups that constitute the base of the Council hierarchy. Some of these officials are based in Brussels in their national permanent representations (see Chapter 14), while others travel to Brussels from their national capitals for meetings. All are experts in their policy field, operating on the basis of instructions from their home ministries. The Commission is represented by officials from the relevant Directorate-General (DG) in the 4,000 or so working party meetings that take place every year.

The Presidency

The Presidency of the Council rotates every six months among the member states according to a pre-established order, which also determines the place their representatives occupy at the table in meetings throughout the Council hierarchy (see Fig. 4.1). A new order of rotation comes into effect on 1 January 2007 (see Exhibit 4.2).

Taking on the Council Presidency directly affects large numbers of civil servants from the member state in question. A chairperson and a national spokesperson must be provided for every meeting at each level of the Council, a particular challenge for smaller member states with limited personnel. A coordinating unit is normally created in the Presidency capital that, with the Council Secretariat, is responsible for ensuring coherence and consistency across the entire range of issues being discussed in the Council hierarchy. The national permanent representation in Brussels becomes the operations centre for all Brussels-based activity during that member state's Presidency.

Figure 4.1 Seating arrangements in the Council of Ministers, 2006

Bulgaria and Romania were granted observer status in the Council and its preparatory bodies following the signature of their Accession Treaty on 25 April 2005. At the same time, seating arrangements were modified to reflect the new order of Presidency rotation due to commence on 1 January 2007. While observers, Romania and Bulgaria occupy the seats immediately to the left of the Presidency. Following their accession, they will take their designated seats according to the agreed order of rotation (see Exhibit 4.2). All delegations move one place to the left at the beginning of a new presidential term (on 1 January and 1 July every year).

January–June 2006 Presidency (Austria)		July–December 2006 Presidency (Finland)	
Austria	Romania	Finland	Romania
Finland	Bulgaria	Germany	Bulgaria
Germany	Estonia	Portugal	Austria
Portugal	UK	Slovenia	Estonia
Slovenia	Malta	France	UK
France	Slovakia	Czech Republic	Malta
Czech Republic	Netherlands	Sweden	Slovakia
Sweden	Luxembourg	Spain	Netherlands
Spain	Latvia	Belgium	Luxembourg
Belgium	Italy	Hungary	Latvia
Hungary	Greece	Poland	Italy
Poland	Lithuania	Denmark	Greece
Denmark	Ireland	Cyprus	Lithuania
Cyprus		Ireland	
Commission		Commission	

Exhibit 4.2 Order of Presidency rotation, 2007–20

The Constitutional Treaty provided for a system of team presidencies, whereby groups of three member states would exercise the Presidency over a period of eighteen months, each one chairing meetings for a period of six months and offering material support to its team colleagues during their turn in the chair. The new order of rotation (agreed in December 2004) provides for such teams by dividing the member states into groups of three, intended to reflect a balance of geographical situation, economic weight and 'old' and 'new' members. Since the idea does not require treaty change to be implemented, an embryonic version of team presidencies is likely to emerge from 2007 onwards.

Germany	January–June	2007
Portugal	July–December	2007
Slovenia	January–June	2008
France	July–December	2008
Czech Republic	January–June	2009
Sweden	July–December	2009
Spain	January–June	2010
Belgium	July–December	2010
Hungary	January–June	2011
Poland	July–December	2011
Denmark	January–June	2012
Cyprus	July–December	2012
Ireland	January–June	2013
Lithuania	July–December	2013
Greece	January–June	2014
Italy	July–December	2014
Latvia	January–June	2015
Luxembourg	July–December	2015
Netherlands	January–June	2016
Slovakia	July–December	2016
Malta	January–June	2017
United Kingdom	July–December	2017
Estonia	January–June	2018
Bulgaria	July–December	2018
Austria	January–June	2019
Romania	July–December	2019
Finland	January–June	2020

The Council Secretariat

The General Secretariat of the Council (to give it its official title) is a relatively small and ostensibly politically neutral body. It has undergone a period of profound change over the past decade. Enlargement has provided the necessary impetus for implementing reforms to the Secretariat's structure and working methods, the avowed aim being to create a slim-line secretariat capable of taking on the extra tasks resulting from increased numbers and extensions to the Council's (and the Secretariat's) scope of activities.

The Council Secretariat is headed by a Secretary-General who (a novelty under the 1997 Treaty of Amsterdam) combines this role with that of the High Representative for the common foreign and security policy (HR/CFSP). A Deputy Secretary-General (a role also introduced by the Treaty of Amsterdam) is responsible for the day-to-day running of the Secretariat. Both the Secretary-General and the Deputy Secretary-General are appointed by agreement of the Council. The current incumbents (Javier Solana and Pierre de Boissieu respectively) were first appointed in 1999, and both had their mandates renewed for another five years in 2004.

The main body of the Secretariat is divided into eight DGs, the largest of which is responsible for personnel and administration. Six DGs are organized on a functional basis, according to the Councils they serve, and the eighth is responsible for press, information, and protocol. A horizontal Legal Service serves all levels of the Council hierarchy, and a number of specialized units, including military personnel, are directly answerable to the Secretary-General and/or his Deputy.

The Secretariat is staffed by independent, international civil servants (some 2,800 in 2005), recruited by open competition from among the nationals of the member states. In addition, a number of national officials, experts and military personnel are seconded to the Secretariat from the member states (about 210 in 2005). The Secretariat has virtually doubled in size since the early 1980s, a direct result of extensions in the scope of the Council's activities and successive enlargements.

What does the Council do?

The Council is responsible for decision-making and coordination. As such, it:

- passes laws, legislating jointly with the EP under co-decision;
- coordinates the broad economic policies of the member states;
- constitutes, together with the EP, the authority that agrees the Community's budget;
- defines and implements the CFSP and the related European security and defence policy (ESDP), based on guidelines set by the European Council;
- coordinates the actions of the member states and adopts measures in the area of police and judicial cooperation in criminal matters; and
- concludes international agreements on behalf of the Community or the EU with one or more third states or international organizations.

The Council fulfils these functions mainly by reference to formal rules laid down in the treaties and in its internal rules of procedure. These formal rules have been supplemented over the years by informal conventions and rules of the game that govern the work of the Council, the Presidency, and the Secretariat, as well as their relations with the Commission and the EP.

Formal and informal powers

The ministers and preparatory bodies

The Council is the EU's principal legislative and policy-making institution, being formally charged with decision-making across the three pillars that constitute the Union. Specific decision-making procedures and voting rules apply to the different areas of Council activity, entailing a greater or lesser role for the EP, and unanimity or some form of majority voting in the Council itself.

In fulfilling its decision-making functions, the Council as a body represents and attempts to aggregate the interests of all the member governments. The reconciliation of conflicting interests within the Council is achieved through a continuous process of negotiation, in the course of which the Commission proposal on the table is discussed in detail, national positions are articulated and defended, coalitions are formed and compromises advanced. In addition to these internal deliberations, the Council must also negotiate with the other institutions involved in the legislative process, in particular the EP (see Chapter 6).

The ministers' deliberations are prepared first by one or more working parties of national officials and finally by Coreper or another senior committee. At their meetings, the ministers adopt without discussion those items on the agenda that have been the object of agreement at Coreper or working party level (the so-called 'A points'), and engage in detailed discussions on those still requiring agreement (the so-called 'B points'). Following discussion in the Council, an agenda item may be adopted, referred back down to a senior committee or a working party for further discussion, or sent up to the European Council for a higher-level political input.

Legally speaking, there is only one Council. In effect, this means that any grouping of ministers may legally take a decision on any issue coming within the scope of the Council as a whole. Thus, the Fisheries Council of 21–22 December agreed the fishing quotas for 2005, but also approved without discussion a large number of items regarding external relations, ESDP, development cooperation, JHA, trade policy, and economic and financial affairs. Generally speaking, though, each Council configuration discusses issues within its own field of competence, and has its own idiosyncratic ways of conducting its business (see Westlake and Galloway 2004).

Most of the detailed negotiation and much of the actual agreement tends to occur at various levels below that of the ministerial Council itself. Insiders estimate that, in some Council configurations, the ministers actively discuss only between 10 and 15 per cent of all the items on their agendas. Implicit indicative voting may occur in senior preparatory bodies or even in some working parties, but it is the ministers themselves who take (and they alone who are legally authorized to take) the final decision in the name of the Council, whether by consensus or by actual voting.

Ministers vote in the Council on the basis of simple majority, qualified majority or unanimity, depending on the rules governing the issue in question laid down in the treaties. Under simple majority voting, which is normally used for procedural issues, each member state has a single vote, and thirteen votes in favour are required to adopt a measure in the EU of 25. (The Commission representative and the Council President do not vote.) Unanimity is required in some specific policy areas (such as taxation) and for most questions concerned with the CFSP and JHA. Under unanimity voting rules, an unhappy member state can exercise a veto by voting against, or can choose to abstain from voting without preventing agreement by the others (an abstention, in effect, counts as a 'yes').

Qualified-majority voting (QMV) is fast becoming the most usual voting rule in the Council, accounting for some 70 per cent of all its definitive legislative decisions. Under QMV, each member state is allocated a set number of votes in approximate relation to its size, and specific thresholds have to be attained in order to adopt or block a measure (see Table 4.1). A member state has the right to abstain from voting, thereby making the construction of a qualified majority or a blocking minority more difficult to achieve.

The threshold for the achievement of a qualified majority has always been set at about 70 per cent of the total number of votes, implicitly also requiring a majority of the member states. The 2001 Treaty of Nice added a possible third requirement, namely that the member states constituting the qualified majority should represent at least 62 per cent of the total population of the EU. Official population figures are agreed on an annual basis in order to facilitate the calculation of this latter figure. This requirement was deemed likely to increase the leverage of the larger member states in general and Germany in particular. The Constitutional Treaty, on the other hand, provides that a qualified majority would be made up of at least 55 per cent of the member states representing at least 65 per cent of the total population of the EU.

Much time and effort has been expended over the years on the details of the Council's voting rules, and the implications for individual member states' voting strength and possible winning coalitions. Yet voting in the Council does not always occur (even under QMV), and does not often take the form of a show of hands. Instead, the President may allow all delegations to have their say on the point under discussion, then sum up and conclude the debate by asking whether any delegation is opposed to the decision reached. If no one objects, the measure is deemed to have been adopted in line with the President's conclusions.

Since the late 1990s, the Council has been obliged under new transparency rules to publish the results of any votes taken, and to identify those Council members that contest them. Consequently, a growing body of firm data is available against which to test hypotheses and anecdotal evidence. It is now possible to demonstrate, for example, that less than one in five agreed decisions is contested, that only about one-fifth of decisions technically subject to QMV are explicitly contested at ministerial level, and that even when decisions are contested, the number of 'no-sayers' normally falls far short of a blocking minority (see Hayes-Renshaw and Wallace, 2006, forthcoming).

The Presidency

Exercising the Presidency of the Council has always been an important task, but the list of duties has increased in recent years, in line with the Council's expanded scope of activities (see Exhibit 4.3). In addition, more member states mean that negotiations have become more time-consuming and can be very much more conflictual. Exercising the Presidency today can therefore be a rather daunting prospect, particularly for small or new member states.

Table 4.1 Qualified-majority voting in the Council, EU-25

Member state	Votes under QMV
Germany	29
France	29
Italy	29
United Kingdom	29
Spain	27
Poland	27
Netherlands	13
Belgium	12
Czech Republic	12
Greece	12
Hungary	12
Portugal	12
Austria	10
Sweden	10
Denmark	7
Ireland	7
Lithuania	7
Slovakia	7
Finland	7
Cyprus	4
Estonia	4
Latvia	4
Luxembourg	4
Slovenia	4
Malta	3
Total	**321**
Qualified majority	232
Blocking minority	90

Exhibit 4.3 Duties of the Presidency

The main formal task of the presidency is the management of the Council's business over the duration of its six-month period in office. This involves a number of different duties:

- convening formal and informal meetings at ministerial and official levels;
- providing chairpersons for all meetings held at all levels of the Council hierarchy;
- ensuring the businesslike conduct of discussions at all meetings;
- hosting one or more European Council meetings;
- acting as spokesperson for the Council within and outside the Union;
- acting as the main point of contact for the Commission, European Parliament, and other bodies involved in decision-making;
- speaking on behalf of the Council in the trialogues and conciliation meetings scheduled under the co-decision procedure;
- managing the CFSP in close association with the High Representative;
- ensuring that all the Council's legislative and other obligations are met;
- aiding the reaching of agreement in negotiations within the Council (with the help of Coreper, the Council Secretariat, and the Commission).

In fulfilling all these tasks, the Presidency is assisted by the Council Secretariat, and works closely with the Commission services.

Arguably, the main task of the Presidency is to be (and, more importantly, to be seen to be) neutral. Specifically, this is achieved by the Presidency member state fielding two delegations for each meeting: one to chair and manage the meeting, the other to articulate and defend the national position. This can place a heavy burden on national resources, particularly when a small member state is in the chair. The introduction of 'compromises from the chair' (often with substantive input from the Council Secretariat) when negotiations get bogged down is further evidence of the neutrality of the Presidency, as is the fact that the President does not vote.

The Presidency can and does play a critical role in shaping the Council's agenda (Talberg 2003), but its ability to impose its own interests on the rest of the EU is limited by the fact that Council activities are now programmed on a multi-annual basis, in close cooperation with preceding and succeeding presidencies. A Presidency member state needs to tread carefully in attempting to highlight certain issues, since its colleagues will not look kindly on a Presidency which appears to use (or abuse) the office too flagrantly for its own ends. The French Presidency in the second half of 2000, for example, was widely criticized for manifestly pushing the interests of the larger member states in discussions on institutional reform (Talberg 2004: 1013–19).

It has become a point of pride for outgoing office-holders to be viewed by their colleagues as having conducted a 'good' presidency. Such judgements are obviously subjective, but a number of objective criteria can be employed as measuring devices. For example, it is possible to gauge whether Council business was dealt with efficiently and impartially; whether the main objectives outlined in the Presidency programme (presented to the EP at the beginning of the six-month period) were achieved; whether European Council meetings (particularly the 'rounding-off' one at the end) were well managed and productive; and whether unpredictable events were dealt with calmly, efficiently, and effectively.

Anecdotes abound to support the suggestion that smaller member states tend to run more effective Presidencies. The smaller member states are generally perceived (rightly or wrongly) as having fewer interests to pursue than their larger partners, and stronger incentives to seek consensus—a good trait in a Presidency! There is general agreement that the most successful Presidencies in recent years have been small state ones, the Danish Presidency in the second half of 2002 and the Irish Presidency in the first half of 2004 being good examples.

The Council Secretariat

The changing role of the Council Secretariat is evident in the description of its basic formal functions contained in the earliest and most recent versions of the Council's rules of procedure. Originally charged with 'assisting' the Council, it is now required to be 'closely and continually involved in organizing, coordinating and ensuring the coherence of the Council's work and implementation of its annual programme. Under the responsibility and guidance of the Presidency, it shall assist the latter in seeking solutions'.

Some 85 per cent of the Secretariat's staff is engaged in the technical and logistical organization of the Council's work. This involves convening meetings, preparing meeting rooms, and producing and distributing documents (including their translation, photocopying, and archiving). The remainder of the Secretariat's staff is engaged in the substantive preparation of the Council's work—drawing up agendas, preparing briefing notes for the Presidency, advising the Presidency on questions of substance, procedure and legality, helping to draft amendments, and producing reports, minutes or press releases regarding meetings held within the Council hierarchy. In addition, a small number of Secretariat officials have taken on a new (for the Secretariat) executive role in the planning and organization of military and civilian crisis management operations. In fulfilling all of these functions, the Secretariat is at the service of the Presidency, but is independent both of it and of the member governments.

Coordinating the work of the Council

From the outset, the General Affairs Council (GAC), composed of the national ministers for foreign affairs, was given overall responsibility for coordinating the work of the Council as a whole—a relatively easy task when the number of policy areas (and member states) involved was small. However, the gradual expansion in the scope of the European Communities and then the EU resulted in the creation of a large number of specialized Council configurations and an increasing fragmentation of Council activity.

Some of these specialist Councils took on the leading role in important policy discussions, thereby undermining the central coordinating function of the GAC and its position as the most 'senior' of the Council formations. The most notable example is the Economic and Financial Affairs Council (Ecofin), whose powerful national ministers have come to play a central role in discussions (and rather meaty decisions) on such important issues as economic and monetary union (EMU) and taxation.

The GAC was also responsible for foreign affairs, and this part of its agenda expanded rapidly, particularly in the 1990s following the formalization of the CFSP and the greater representational role *vis-à-vis* third countries attributed to the GAC by the 1992 Treaty on European Union (TEU). The foreign ministers were less inclined to spend time on coordinating the work of a growing number of technical Councils, preferring instead to focus on the foreign policy questions on which they were better qualified to speak. Consequently, the European Council frequently found itself debating issues that, in an ideal world, would have been settled by the foreign ministers. It was also the European Council that increasingly set the EU's agenda, with the GAC frequently being reduced to the position of a senior organ of execution for the decisions of the heads of state or government.

Over the years, the need to ensure proper coordination of the work of the various Council configurations became more obvious and pressing. This was merely one aspect of a more general discussion on Council reform that took place at various levels between the Helsinki European Council of December 1999 and the Seville European Council of June 2002. The Seville conclusions attempted to facilitate coordination by, *inter alia*:

- creating a General Affairs and External Relations Council (GAERC), which would hold separate meetings, possibly on different dates, with separate agendas, in order to distinguish its coordinating from its foreign policy responsibilities;
- explicitly making the general affairs formation of the GAERC responsible for preparing and ensuring the follow-up of meetings of the European Council (including the coordinating activities necessary to that end); and
- reducing the number of Council configurations from sixteen to nine.

The effect of the Seville reforms as regards the preparation of European Council meetings is generally viewed as positive. But more general coordination by the GAC of the work of the other Council configurations is still criticized, and described by some insiders as 'rather ritualistic'.

Exerting influence in the Council

The Council's central position in the EU in general and in EU decision-making in particular endows it with a large degree of influence over other institutions and authorities. But the Council is not a monolithic body. It is composed of the representatives of twenty-five very different governments, whose member states differ according to size, economic weight, length of EU membership, administrative culture, negotiating style, and attitude to European integration (*inter alia*). Despite these differences, they continue to reach agreement. So who wields influence within the Council, and what form does this influence take?

Where unanimity is the rule, influence is shared equally among the Council members. Any national representative can block agreement, so the interests of all have to be taken into account. Under QMV, numbers matter, and those member governments with the largest number of votes could be expected to wield the largest amount of influence. However, safeguards have been built into the system to ensure that the smaller member states, working together, have as much chance as the larger ones to exert influence over the final outcome. Indeed, the big member states are frequently out-voted in the Council, as Table 4.2 demonstrates.

A detailed analysis of Council voting records since 1993 (Hayes-Renshaw and Wallace, 2006) supports the institutionalist view of the EU, which maintains that the rules of the game are devised to ensure that it is not only the big member states that win. The analysis confirms that there is no enduring solidarity between the larger member states (or, for that matter, the smaller ones), or between the northern member states or the southern member states. Nor is there any systematic evidence of old or new members voting together consistently. Rather, coalitions in the Council emerge as constantly shifting, and tending to be issue driven rather than power driven, with consensus and compromise being, by and large, the name of the game. Certain member governments may have common or complementary goals or aspirations which may drive the Union for a period of time, but attempts to create and sustain a type of *directoire* at the heart of the Union fail to endure when they attempt to move from questions of the overall direction of EU policy to the minutiae of the policies themselves (or *vice versa*).

Influence can be exerted by large and small member states alike in more informal (and less easily quantifiable) ways, by putting forward compromise proposals acceptable to a majority of the member governments, by forming coalitions with like-minded states, and by making their point of view known to the Commission, the Presidency, and the Council Secretariat. Yet, the number of votes attributed to a member state continues to matter, as the rather unedifying scramble for votes at Nice in December 2000 amply demonstrated. The decisions on QMV that emerged from the Nice summit did so only after some of the most heated and bitter exchanges ever witnessed in the EU, fuelled by real concerns on the part of the individual member governments about future influence in an enlarged Council. The long-term effects of enlargement on voting behaviour in the Council remain to be discerned, but it is unlikely that decades of commitment to consensus will be ditched overnight. Indeed, one year into enlargement, there was no evidence of increased contestation. However, new dynamics affecting relative weight and influence in the Council can be expected to emerge in time.

Dealing with the other institutions

The Council and EP

The Council–EP relationship is based on the natural rivalry or tension that exists between all executives and legislatures, even though neither institution closely resembles the European national model of such bodies. A large part of the inter-institutional tension in the EU setting is a result of the EP's unremitting and largely successful campaign to wrest increasing amounts of legislative and budgetary power from the reluctant grasp of the Council. Following years of divisive disputes, the

Table 4.2 Losing the vote in the Council of EU-15.

Legislative acts adopted by qualified-majority voting (QMV) with abstentions and votes against, 1996–2003

Member states	Abstentions									Votes against								
	1996	1997	1998	1999	2000	2001	2002	2003	Total	Total	1996	1997	1998	1999	2000	2001	2002	2003
Austria	1	1	0	0	0	4	0	2	8	17	2	2	3	1	2	1	1	5
Belgium	1	1	3	0	5	1	1	3	15	14	5	0	4	2	1	2	0	0
Denmark	0	1	1	0	2	1	3	2	10	33	2	6	7	4	3	3	2	6
Finland	0	0	0	0	1	0	2	0	3	10	1	4	0	0	1	1	2	1
France	1	3	2	0	0	3	6	1	16	19	3	3	3	3	1	3	0	3
Germany	4	2	7	1	0	5	3	1	23	50	14	9	11	2	4	3	2	5
Greece	0	0	2	0	0	0	0	1	3	17	2	4	2	1	3	1	2	2
Ireland	0	1	0	0	0	0	0	1	2	10	2	1	2	1	0	1	0	3
Italy	1	1	5	1	3	3	0	2	16	36	6	6	8	8	1	2	2	3
Luxembourg	2	1	2	0	0	2	1	1	9	7	0	1	0	2	0	0	1	3
Netherlands	2	0	1	1	1	1	1	1	8	28	2	2	12	4	2	1	5	0
Portugal	2	2	4	1	0	1	3	0	13	13	1	2	2	1	0	0	1	6
Spain	0	1	7	2	0	2	1	2	15	17	4	2	1	1	0	3	1	5
Sweden	0	0	0	0	0	0	4	3	7	31	4	7	3	0	2	4	6	5
United Kingdom	0	3	0	3	1	2	4	5	18	25	7	7	2	0	2	2	1	4
Total	14	17	34	9	13	25	29	25	166	327	55	56	60	30	22	27	26	51

Source: Statistics supplied by the Council Secretariat

Council–EP relationship in the budgetary field is now 'more predictable, consensual and rule-bound' (Laffan 2000: 733), thanks mainly to successive inter-institutional agreements (IIAs) on budgetary discipline, and the introduction of multi-annual financial packages.

In contrast, the EP had to fight harder and longer for legislative powers, which it won in increments via court cases, IIAs, and treaty reform. The introduction and simplification of the co-decision procedure in the 1990s transformed the Council–EP relationship from one of permanent confrontation to one of both formal and informal cooperation. The EP is now a real co-legislative authority with the Council on a large number of issues, even if the cooperation between the two institutions is subject to complicated procedures that can result in tensions between them. The fact that these tensions rarely flare up into full-scale inter-institutional battles is a testament to the new spirit of interdependence that prevails between them. It is perceptible in the increased contacts between the two institutions at all levels, not least the very visible presence of Council officials in the EP's corridors and committees.

If it is to operate smoothly and efficiently, the co-decision procedure requires constant contact between the main protagonists. Initially, the Council concentrated its resources and attention on the final, conciliation phase of the process, but following changes in the co-decision procedure introduced by the Treaty of Amsterdam, the Council's attention shifted to the earlier stages of the process. Its strategy now is to reach agreement as swiftly as possible whenever feasible, thereby reducing the number of issues that end up in formal conciliation (currently less than 20 per cent of co-decision dossiers). Great efforts are now made to ensure that the work of both institutions proceeds in parallel, and much informal negotiation goes on behind the scenes in advance of trialogue meetings, bringing together representatives of the Council, Commission, and Parliament at presidential and official levels (see Chapter 6). The effect on decision-making speed has been positive: EP officials have calculated that, whereas the average length of a co-decision procedure was 23.3 months in the period from November 1993 to April 1999, it fell to 20.3 months during the period from May 1999 to April 2004.

Despite a small number of sometimes spectacular failures, there is now a growing and rather positive balance-sheet of agreements reached between the Council and the EP under the co-decision procedure, proof of the greater cooperative spirit that now underpins their entire relationship. This should not be interpreted as evidence of the Council and the Parliament being hand in glove on all issues, however; rather it is a case of the Parliament choosing its battles more judiciously than in the past. There is still some resistance within the Council to EP-inspired suggestions for greater collaboration, often entailing increased availability of the Presidency (as the representative of the Council) at EP plenary sessions and committee meetings. This resistance is a direct result of the private reservations of some member governments regarding the EP's current and future role and powers.

The Council and Commission

Council–Commission relations have always been typified by a complex mixture of cooperation and competition. Observers who view the EU as a unique supranational experiment tend to talk up Council–Commission skirmishes, presenting them as battles for dominance. Others point to the very reduced role played by the Commission in the areas of CFSP and JHA (arguably the areas of greatest and most innovative activity in the Union today). Some member governments, for whom 'keeping the Commission in its place' is a deliberate if not always explicitly articulated policy, have taken comfort from the perception that the Commission has yet to recover fully from the debilitating effects of the resignation of the Santer Commission in 1999.

The day-to-day reality of Council–Commission relations is much more mundane and reassuring, bearing in mind that the relationship differs between policy arenas and between the three pillars. One area of structural tension is the external representation of EU policies, with policy competence sometimes being clearly attributed to the EU level (and therefore the Commission) and sometimes shared between the Commission and the member states. The result of this fluidity and complexity is a tricky division of labour, necessitating constant liaison between the Commission, on the one hand, and the Council Secretariat and Presidency on the other. This is the case, for example, as regards external trade negotiating mandates and representation *vis-à-vis* third countries or other international bodies, and also on the important negotiations with candidates for accession.

As regards issues subject to the so-called 'Community method', the two institutions are required to cooperate because they are so clearly interdependent. Thanks to its right of initiative, the Commission is responsible for producing the proposals on which most Council debates are based, but it is reliant on the Council (increasingly in tandem with the Parliament) to adopt the measures it has proposed. Accordingly, it attends meetings at all levels of the Council hierarchy in effect as the 26th delegation, acting both as protagonist and mediator in an attempt to have its proposals adopted. As one of the potential architects of compromise between conflicting positions in the Council, the Commission delegation is frequently regarded by beleaguered member governments in the Council as their greatest ally on particular issues under discussion.

There is a direct correlation between the desire of the member governments to engage in greater integration and the degree of influence wielded by the Commission, in the sense that the latter's hands are tied if one or more member governments are determined to block a legislative proposal. This is clearly the case where unanimity is required, but given the consensual instinct that informs decision-making in the Council, the Commission can be more influential in shaping the policy process when QMV applies. Like a pair of horses pulling a carriage, both institutions need each other in order to fulfil their respective functions properly.

The altered Council–EP relationship under the co-decision procedure has had a knock-on effect on the Commission's dealings with both institutions. The EP can now approach the Council directly rather than being dependent on the Commission as its interlocutor with the member governments. However, this should not be interpreted as the Parliament no longer needing the Commission (even if the EP sometimes behaves as if this were the case). Indeed, the support of the Commission can be helpful for both the Parliament and the Council in their dealings with each other, and the Commission is well placed to play a brokerage role between them.

At least two of the institutional provisions in the Constitutional Treaty would require new types of Council–Commission cooperation. The proposed EU Foreign Minister is intended to be both a member (indeed, a Vice-President) of the

Commission and the President of the Foreign Affairs Council. He or she would be assisted by a European External Action Service, composed of permanent officials from the Commission and the Council Secretariat and seconded officials from the national foreign ministries. The future of both of these experiments in merged institutional roles is now uncertain.

The Council and accountability

The democratic accountability of the Council has always been an issue of concern to both proponents and detractors of European integration. Whereas the members of the EP are directly elected, the members of the Council take their seats *ex officio* in their capacity as national ministers, elected on issues often unrelated to those they discuss and decide upon in the Council. While the Commission can be voted out of office by the EP, the Council as a body has permanent tenure, although the individuals who make it up may (and frequently do) change following elections or cabinet reshuffles in their national capitals.

The Presidency, on behalf of the Council, is accountable to the EP. Presidency representatives attend the EP's plenary sessions during their term of office, where they answer questions put to them by members of the European Parliament (MEPs). The member state in question, represented by its prime minister or foreign minister, presents its Presidency programme to the EP in advance of taking office, and sums up its achievements to the Parliament when it hands on the mantle to the next incumbent. Between plenary sessions, MEPs may address written questions to the Council via the Presidency, and ministers and officials from the Presidency state sometimes attend EP committee meetings, where they inform the MEPs about ongoing negotiations in the Council. The EP would prefer such appearances to be much more regular and the discussions to be more in depth.

The Council is regularly charged with being an over-secretive body, operating far from the public gaze. Arguably, this is a central reason for its success, but there is general agreement that more needs to be done to increase the institution's transparency. Some measures were introduced in the early 1990s, but many were subsequently criticized for merely paying lip service to the notion of transparency.

One area where a good deal of progress has been made, however, is on public access to the Council's documents. Interested outsiders can download the majority of the documents on the Council's register from its website (*www.consilium.eu.int*), and can apply to the Secretariat in writing regarding those not directly available. In most of the latter cases, full or partial access is granted (see Exhibit 4.4).

The Council in context

The Council and the larger 'EU system'

In this chapter, the Council has been presented as a club of member governments, and as the locus of persistent competition among them for relative influence. The

Exhibit 4.4 Public access to Council documents

A higher percentage of EU documents was supplied to those who requested them from 2001 onwards, after a decision taken at the end of that year to allow partial access to some documents. In effect, this meant that documents could be released with certain sections deleted, or with the names of delegations (and any content that would make it possible to identify them) blocked out. The percentage of documents released wholly in 2002, 2003, and 2004 was 76.1 per cent, 76.2 per cent, and 81.3 per cent respectively.

	1997	1998	1999	2000	2001	2002	2003	2004
Number of requests	282	338	889	1,294	1,234	2,394	2,830	2,160
Number of documents reviewed	2,431	3,984	6,747	7,032	8,090	8,942	12,565	12,937
Percentage of documents supplied	78.3	82.4	83.7	83.9	88.2	88.8	87.3	85.3

Source: Council Secretariat

Council is regarded as the central body by those who stress the importance of national interest as the factor explaining outcomes in the EU. Indeed, the Council as it exists and operates today may be viewed as the living symbol of the continuing power of the member states in the EU, and of the desire of the national governments to remain at the centre of the process of European integration. Since it is also representatives of the member governments who constitute the intergovernmental conferences (IGCs) that initiate constitutional reform in the EU, we can expect the Council to endure and to continue to play a central role in the larger EU.

Despite being the EU's intergovernmental institution *par excellence*, however, this chapter has also attempted to show that, in reality, the Council is a unique blend of the intergovernmental and the supranational. It represents member state interests that are aggregated under conditions frequently owing more to supranationality than to intergovernmentalism, and it is not necessarily the interests of the larger member states that determine the final outcomes. The Council as an institution works closely with the Commission and the EP, both of whose views inform its work and impinge in important ways on its output.

Coping with enlargement

Enlargement is no novelty for the EU, or indeed for the Council which, by 2005, had had to adapt to new members on five separate occasions. An increase in numbers has always necessitated adjustment in the Council and elsewhere, both in terms of socialization (of old and new members alike), and in terms of adaptation of working methods, systems, and structures. The prospect of the 2004 enlargement had given

rise to some disquiet and much discussion regarding the capacity of the Council physically to deal with such an unprecedented number of new arrivals. Consequently, the
Seville reforms agreed in 2002 were supplemented by a code of conduct on working
methods in an enlarged Council, agreed in March 2003 and now incorporated into
the Council's rules of procedure (as Annex IV).

In early 2005, most insiders were of the opinion that the full impact of enlargement had yet to be experienced in the Council. The task of instructing a large number
of new recruits about the Council's formal (and perhaps more importantly, informal)
procedures had been facilitated by the participation of representatives of the new
member states as observers throughout the Council hierarchy for more than a year
in advance of their accession. However, some negative effects of enlargement were
already evident in the Council. Discussion and negotiation were hampered by a lack
of full interpretation and translation facilities, informal gatherings were larger resulting in a change in the *esprit* in certain long-standing groupings, and the workload
was greater because of the need to take an increased number of positions and interests into account. That said, there was an acknowledgement that the newcomers
were adapting well, and showing a growing understanding of the 'rules of the game'
governing Council activity. Where problems arose, it was felt that they were normally a consequence of poor coordination in the national system rather than a lack
of socialization on the part of participants in Brussels.

Theorizing the Council

Spanning as it does the supranational and intergovernmental camps, the Council embodies the enduring tension between the two approaches as explanatory tools for understanding the construction of the EU. The behaviour of the ministerial and official
representatives who comprise the Council may be better explained by sociology and
anthropology than by regional integration theory, but the outcome of their conduct
is a testimony to 'collective purpose, collective commitment and collective ideas'
(Hayes-Renshaw and Wallace 1997:2).

Yet realist observers such as Hoffmann (1966) and more recently the liberal intergovernmentalist (Moravcsik 1993) school could neatly put paid to this cosy picture by
pointing to the 2000 Nice Summit as an instance where national governments, when
the chips are down, continue to rely on 'state interests' to inform their negotiating
preferences. Indeed, it remains to be seen whether the Nice Summit will, in retrospect, prove to have been merely the first, overt skirmish in a much larger battle
for both intergovernmental and inter-institutional dominance in an enlarged EU. It
is possible that, in future, the skills of sociologists and anthropologists rather than
regional integration theorists will be required to predict possible outcomes.

Two opposing suggestions for the Council linger in the debate over EU institutional
reform. One advocates that it should become an explicitly representative and legislative rather than an executive institution. The other asserts that the Council should be
made even more explicitly dominant, as the core of executive power within the EU.
The Constitutional Treaty did not resolve this argument, and its rejection by referenda in 2005 did nothing to clarify the situation. In the continued absence of agreement in the tussle between supranationalism and intergovernmentalism, it is likely
that the Council will have to continue to serve both camps: that is, to constitute the

vehicle through which member governments exercise leverage on the uncertain process of collective governance, both representational and executive, with the constitutional and operational ambiguities that this implies. Much is therefore left to be played for and much to be settled by evolving practice, not least in the context of an EU enlarged in membership from fifteen to twenty-five, twenty-seven, or even more member states.

Further reading

There are two recently updated books on the Council: Hayes-Renshaw and Wallace (2006) and Westlake and Galloway (2005). Sherrington (2000), which analyses different Council configurations, is now somewhat dated but contains useful historical information. The Presidency's powers are addressed in Talberg (2003; 2004), while Norman (2005) and Milton and Keller-Noëllet (2005) have detailed descriptions of the discussions on Council reform that took place during the negotiation of the Constitutional Treaty.

Hayes-Renshaw, F., and Wallace, H. (2006), *The Council of Ministers* (Basingstoke and New York: Palgrave).

Milton, G., and Keller-Noëllet, J. (2005), *The European Constitution: its origins, negotiation and meaning* (London: John Harper).

Norman, P. (2005), *The Accidental Constitution*, 2nd edn. (Brussels: Eurocomment).

Sherrington, P. (2000), *The Council of Ministers: Political Authority in the European Union* (London: Pinter).

Talberg. J. (2003), 'The Agenda-Shaping Powers of the EU Council Presidency', *Journal of European Public Policy*, 10/1: 1–19

Talberg, J. (2004), 'The Power of the Presidency: Brokerage, Efficiency and Distribution in EU Negotiations', *Journal of Common Market Studies*, 42/5: 999–1022.

Westlake, M., and Galloway, D. (2004), *The Council of the European Union*, 3rd edn. (London: John Harper Publishing).

Web links

The Council's website (*www.consilium.eu.int*) contains a wealth of information on its structure, output, and day-to-day activities, including direct access to most of its documents. It also contains a link to the website of the current Council Presidency.

Chapter 5

The College of Commissioners

John Peterson

Contents

Summary

No other institution closely resembles the European Commission. It is a distinct hybrid: the EU's largest administration and main policy manager, but also a source of political and policy direction. This chapter focuses on the Commission's most 'political' level: its college of Commissioners. Yet, Commissioners are unelected, independent (in theory) of member governments, and often portrayed as unaccountable technocrats. The Commission seemed to be in a permanent state of decline after 1999, after being headed by Presidents who were perceived as weak, ineffective, or both. The appointment of José Manuel Barroso as President in 2004 at least spurred debates about whether and how the Commission could be revived. However, the rejection of the Constitutional Treaty in the 2005 referenda, alongside bruising political rows over the EU's budget and economic policy direction, revealed how the Commission's fate remained largely determined by factors over which it had little or no control.

Introduction

The European Commission may be the strangest administration ever created. Despite brave attempts to compare it to other bureaucracies (Page 1997), the Commission is in many respects a *sui generis* institution. Legally, the Commission is a single entity. In practice, it is a unique hybrid. It is given direction by a political arm, or college, of Commissioners. But the College is unelected. Its members act independently of the states that appoint them (at least in theory) and even swear an 'oath of independence' when appointed. The College exists alongside a permanent, formally apolitical administration, made up of what are known as the Commission's services or Directorates-General (DGs). This book squarely confronts the Commission's duality by focusing here on the college and devoting a separate chapter (Chapter 8) to the services.

Even if they are unelected, Commissioners 'are appointed via a highly politicised process ... are almost invariably national politicians of senior status, and are expected to provide the Commission's political direction' (Nugent 2001: 3). At times, the College—the President, Commissioners, and their advisers—has provided political direction to European integration, particularly during the earliest days of the EEC and again in the 1980s. More recently, it has become almost accepted wisdom that 'the decline of the Commission ... has continued ... and there seems little possibility that the situation will be reversed' (Kassim and Menon 2004: 102; see also de Schoutheete and Wallace 2002; Hill and Smith 2005b: 399). The Commission has always been powerful as a designer and manager of EU policy. But its role has never been uncontested (Lequesne 1996; Spence 2005). The central theme of this chapter is that the Commission and most of what it does is highly politicized, despite its ambitions to be an 'honest broker' and independent guardian of the EU's treaties.

The origins and history of the College

The forerunner of today's European Commission was the High Authority of the European Coal and Steel Community (ECSC). Its first President was the legendary Jean Monnet (1978; see also Duchêne 1994). Provisions in the 1951 Treaty of Paris that gave the High Authority significant independent powers to regulate markets for coal and steel bore Monnet's own fingerprints. The ECSC thus established that common European policies would be managed, and European integration given political impulse, by a non-partisan, central authority.

The High Authority was headed by nine senior officials—two from France (one of whom was Monnet) and West Germany and one from all other Member States (plus a co-opted ninth member). Thus, a precedent was set for national representation in what was meant to be a supranational administration. Over time, the High Authority became much less nimble and more bureaucratic than Monnet wanted it to be (Nugent 2001: 21–2). Partly in protest, Monnet resigned before the end of his term.

The design of common institutions for the new European Economic Community was one of the most difficult issues in negotiations on the Treaty of Rome. A Dutch proposal sought to give the EEC a supranational administration that would be even more independent of member governments than the ECSC's High Authority. However, it ran into opposition, particularly from France, and ended up being 'almost the reverse of what was finally decided' (Milward 1992: 217–18). Compared to the High Authority, the new European Commission (the label 'High Authority' was discarded as too grandiose) was subject to considerably tighter political control by a Council of (national) Ministers.

The Treaty assigned three basic functions to the Commission: overseeing the implementation of policies, representing the Community in external trade negotiations, and—most importantly—proposing new policies. The Commission's monopoly on the right to initiate policies, along with its prerogative to 'formulate recommendations or deliver opinions on matters dealt with in this Treaty' gave it licence to act as a sort of 'engine of integration', or a source of ideas on new directions the Community might take. Alongside the European Court of Justice (ECJ), the Commission was also designated as a guardian of the Treaty, and tasked with ensuring that its rules and injunctions were respected.

The early Commissions were small (nine members) and united by a 'dominating sense of team spirit' (Narjes 1998: 114). Between 1958 and 1967, only fourteen different men[1] served as Commissioners, supported by two *cabinet* advisers (with four advising the President). Walter Hallstein, Foreign Policy Adviser to the first West German Chancellor, Konrad Adenauer, became the Commission's first President. Hallstein was both a political heavyweight and a forceful leader, repeatedly referring to himself as the equivalent of a 'European Prime Minister'. The Commission achieved considerable policy success during this period, laying the foundations for the Common Agricultural Policy (mere agreement on the CAP was considered a 'success'), representing the Community in the successful Kennedy Round of world trade talks, and convincing member governments to accelerate the timetable for establishing the EEC's customs union.

A watershed in the history of the Commission was reached in 1965. A year away from a scheduled extension of qualified-majority voting (QMV) as a decision rule in the Council, the Hallstein Commission proposed a new system of financing the CAP through 'own resources', or revenue directly channelled to the Community rather than cobbled together from national contributions. The plan proposed to give new budgetary powers both to the Commission and the European Parliament (EP). It became a pretext for the French President, Charles de Gaulle, to pull France out of nearly all EEC negotiations for more than six months. De Gaulle's hostility to Hallstein's federalist rhetoric and actions, which included receiving foreign ambassadors to the EEC with a red carpet, was highly personal but also reflected deep-seated French anxiety about a resurgent Germany (see de Gaulle 1970: 195–6).

The so-called 'empty chair' crisis ended and France returned to EEC negotiations after the Luxembourg compromise was agreed in 1966 (with Luxembourg holding the Council Presidency). The agreement, made public only in the form of a press release, stated that 'where very important interests are at stake the discussion must be continued until unanimous agreement is reached'. Any member government could invoke the compromise in any negotiation if it felt its 'very important interests' were

Table 5.1 The Presidents of the Commission

Presidents (nationality*)	Period of tenure
Walter Hallstein (D)	1958–67
Jean Rey (B)	1967–70
Franco Maria Malfatti (I)	1970–72
Sicco Mansholt (N)	1972–73
François Xavier-Ortoli (F)	1973–77
Roy Jenkins (UK)	1977–81
Gaston Thorn (L)	1981–85
Jacques Delors (F)	1985–95
Jacques Santer (L)	1995–99
Romano Prodi (I)	1999–2004
José Manuel Barroso (P)	2004–present

* Note that the Presidency has been held by a non-national of one of the original EEC-6 only twice.

at risk. The upshot was to give political blessing to unanimous decision-making in the Council, and generally to hobble the Commission.[2]

De Gaulle insisted that Hallstein be replaced as President of the Commission, which itself became a single, integrated administration for all three previously distinct 'Communities'—the EEC, the ECSC, and the European Atomic Energy Community—in 1967. Headed by the low-key Belgian, Jean Rey, the new Commission initially contained fourteen members (reduced to nine in 1970). The next decade was a lean time for the Commission, both because of weak Presidential leadership (see Table 5.1) and the EEC's more general lack of dynamism. In retrospect, the Community may have actually achieved more in the 1970s than it appeared at the time (see Nugent 2001: 35–8). Still, Western Europe suffered through a series of economic crises, and the Community itself was widely seen as dilapidated.

By the late 1970s, a critical mass of member governments was persuaded that the Commission should be led by a political figure, or one who was a potential Prime Minister in their own country. Thus, Roy Jenkins, a senior member of the United Kingdom's governing Labour Party, was appointed as President in 1977. Jenkins was the first President to be nominated in advance of the college as a whole, thus giving him scope to influence the composition of his team.

Jenkins' record was ambiguous. On one hand, member governments frequently disregarded his advice. There is little dispute that he 'was not a great success at running or reforming the Brussels machine' (Campbell 1983: 195). On the other, Jenkins raised the external policy profile of the Commission by insisting (against

French resistance) that the Commission President should attend Group of Seven economic summits. Jenkins also worked tirelessly with the German Chancellor, Helmut Schmidt, and French President, Valéry Giscard-d'Estaing, to build a consensus behind the European Monetary System (EMS). The EMS helped keep European currency values stable in the 1980s after enormous exchange rate turbulence in the 1970s. It was an important forerunner both to the 'freeing' of the Community's internal market and, later, monetary union.

Before the 1979 election of Margaret Thatcher as UK Prime Minister, Jenkins seemed a candidate to be the first Commission President since Hallstein to be reappointed to a second four-year term.[3] However, reappointing Jenkins became politically untenable when Thatcher doggedly pursued the so-called 'British budgetary question' (arising from the size of its net EU budgetary contribution), which preoccupied the Community for no fewer than five years. It cast a dark cloud over the Commission Presidency of the former Luxembourg Prime Minister, Gaston Thorn, whose tenure marked a retreat in the direction of the lacklustre, post-Hallstein Commissions.

Thorn was replaced in 1985 by the former French Finance Minister, Jacques Delors. Thatcher accepted the nomination of Delors, a French Socialist, on the strength of his role in France's economic policy U-turn of the early 1980s, when it abandoned protectionism and increased public expenditure in favour of market liberalism. Delors carefully reflected on how the Community could be relaunched via a headline-grabbing political project. Working closely with the former British Trade Minister and Commissioner for the 'internal market', Lord (Arthur) Cockfield, Delors opted for an integrated programme to dismantle most barriers to internal EU trade by the end of 1992. Seizing on converging preferences among the EU's largest member states for economic liberalization (Moravcsik 1991), as well as the strong support of the European business community, the 1992 project gave European integration renewed momentum (see Cockfield 1994). A substantive overhaul of the Community's founding Treaties was agreed in the 1986 Single European Act, which gave the Commission significant new powers, notably by extending the use of QMV in the Council.

Delors then convinced European leaders, despite the scepticism of many, to allow him to chair a high-level committee of (mostly) central bankers and relaunch long-dormant plans for economic and monetary union (EMU). Progress towards EMU was uninterrupted by the geopolitical earthquakes that shook the European continent in late 1989. German unification was handled with skill and speed by the Delors Commission (Spence 1991; Ross 1995), which also stepped forward to coordinate Western economic aid to the former Warsaw Pact states. By Spring 1990, with a round of Treaty revisions to create EMU on course, the French President, François Mitterrand, and German Chancellor, Helmut Kohl, threw their combined political weight behind the idea of a separate, parallel set of negotiations to create a 'political union'. By this point Delors was accepted by Kohl, Mitterrand, and even Thatcher as a political equal in the European Council.

The second half of Delors' ten-year reign was a far less happy time for the Commission. Member governments agreed mostly intergovernmental mechanisms for making new internal security and foreign policies via the (Maastricht) Treaty on European Union, denying the Commission its traditional Community prerogatives in these areas. Delors also shouldered some of the blame for the 1992 Danish rejection of the new Treaty, after suggesting that the power of small states would inevitably be weaker in a future EU (Nugent 2001: 46–7). By the time Delors left Brussels in 1995, a critical mass of member governments wanted a less visionary successor.

After a tortured selection process,[4] Jacques Santer, the Prime Minister of Luxembourg, was chosen to replace Delors. Santer promised that his Commission would 'do less but do it better'. Yet, it inherited a full agenda, including the launch of the Euro, eastern enlargement, another round of Treaty reforms, and negotiations on the Union's multi-annual budget and structural funds for regional development. The Santer Commission generally handled these issues well. Its stewardship of the launch of EMU in particular seemed 'enough to earn any Commission President a proud legacy' (Peterson 1999: 61).

In fact, Santer's legacy was hardly a proud one. For all of the dynamism of the Delors era, the Commission had become far more focused on policy initiation than on effective management. Presiding over an administration which had become inefficient and sometimes chaotic, the Santer era culminated in the dramatic mass resignation of the college in March 1999 after the publication of a report of a Committee of Independent Experts (1999), convened by the EP, on charges of fraud, mismanagement and nepotism (see Exhibit 5.1).

Exhibit 5.1 The fall of the Santer Commission

Jacques Santer's troubles began in earnest in late 1998 after the publication of a damning Court of Auditors' report, which suggested that large amounts of EU funding had gone missing. Around the same time, press reports appeared alleging that the Research Commissioner (and former French Prime Minister), Edith Cresson, had given plum advisers' jobs in the services to unqualified personal cronies. Characteristically, Cresson dismissed them as part of an Anglo–German 'conspiracy'. A motion of censure tabled under the EP's Treaty powers to sack the entire Commission was defeated (by 293 votes to 232) after Santer accepted that a Committee of Independent Experts would investigate charges of fraud and mismanagement within the Commission. At this point, according to Leon Brittan (2000: 10), a veteran of the Delors and Santer Commissions, the Commission began 'to sleepwalk towards its own destruction'. Santer told the EP that the college would implement the recommendations of the Experts' report, regardless of what they were, in a clear sign of the Commission's political weakness.

The Experts had exactly five weeks to investigate the Commission, yet produced a report that was painstaking in detail. Its most serious charges — leaving aside those against Cresson — concerned improprieties that had occurred during the Delors years. Bitter animosity between Delors and the Experts' chair, the former head of the Court of Auditors, André Middlehoek, was palpable in the report, which drew conclusions that seemed to go well beyond the evidence it contained. The report built to a crescendo with the devastating charge that it was 'becoming difficult to find anyone who has even the slightest sense of responsibility' for the work of the Commission (Committee of Independent Experts 1999: 144). The EP's largest political group, the Socialists, announced that it would vote to sack all twenty Commissioners, thus making the outcome of any vote all but inevitable.

A series of efforts were mounted by individual Commissioners to isolate Cresson, including a bid by Santer to convince the French President and Prime Minister, Jacques Chirac and

continues

Exhibit 5.1 continued

Lionel Jospin, respectively, to ask her to step down. None succeeded. Thus, Santer insisted that the entire Commission, as a collegial body, had to resign. The President was defiant in a subsequent press conference, claiming that the Experts' report was 'wholly unjustified in tone'.[5] Whether or not Santer's combativeness was ill judged, his fate was sealed by a stroke of bad luck: an English interpreter mistakenly communicated Santer's claim (in French) that he was *blanchi*, or exonerated, from personal charges against him in the Experts' report, to the non-French press as a claim that he was 'whiter than white'. It became widely seen as a political necessity that Santer had to go, and quickly.

Ironically, the Commission under Santer had undertaken a series of reforms that made it—on balance—better managed than it had been under Delors (see Peterson 1999; Cram 1999; Metcalfe 2000; Nugent 2000: 49–50). But the efforts were far from enough to cure the Commission of pathologies that had festered under Delors. The Experts' report exposed the Commission as everyone's favourite scapegoat in Brussels. More generally, the fall of the Santer Commission showed, in the words of one of its members, that 'in economic and monetary terms Europe is a giant in the world. But politically we are very young'.[6]

Santer's resignation in Spring 1999 came at a particularly difficult moment. The Berlin Summit, at which a series of major decisions needed to be made on the EU's seven-year budget, structural funds, and agricultural reform, was about a week away. A political crisis over Kosovo was deepening. The German Council Presidency thus undertook a whirlwind tour of national EU capitals to seek a swift decision on replacing Santer. In Berlin, after ten minutes of discussion, the European Council agreed that the new Commission President should be the former Italian Prime Minister, Romano Prodi.

Prodi was by no means free to choose his own College. Nevertheless, armed with new powers granted to the Commission President by the Amsterdam Treaty (see below), Prodi had more influence over its composition than had most of his predecessors over theirs. He ended up with a less charismatic College than Santer's, but one in which expertise was matched to portfolio to an extent unseen in the Commission's history.

One EU ambassador spoke for many in Brussels in claiming that Prodi's economic team was 'collectively the best the Commission has ever had'.[7] One of two Vice-Presidents, Neil Kinnock, was charged with implementing an ambitious series of internal reforms of the Commission (Kassim 2005). Prodi himself helped shift the debate on eastern enlargement to the point where EU governments—at the 1999 Helsinki Summit—decided to open accession talks with no fewer than twelve applicant states on a more or less equal basis.

Yet, Prodi's weakness as a political communicator was probably his Commission's most glaring liability (Peterson 2004). Kinnock's administrative reform programme encountered bitter resistance in the services, where morale seemed to sink ever lower. The Commission was marginalized first in the negotiations that yielded the Treaty of Nice and then in the Convention on the Future of Europe that drafted a new Constitutional Treaty (Exhibit 5.2). The most charitable comments that could be made about Prodi himself were that he mostly avoided interference in the work of a highly competent College.

Exhibit 5.2 The Commission and the Convention on the Future of Europe

Most accounts of negotiations on the 2000 Treaty of Nice concur that the Commission had little impact on the outcome (see Gray and Stubb 2001; Peterson 2002: 81). At the Nice Summit itself, Prodi was bullied mercilessly by the summit's Chair, Jacques Chirac, revealing how low the Commission President's standing in the European Council had sunk. Two participant-observers concluded that Nice marked the end of a decade when the Commission never managed to agree a unified position on its own composition in four different rounds of debate (Gray and Stubb 2001: 19).

A rather different version of events starts with the observation that the Commission—leaving aside Delors' influence on the Single European Act and blueprint for EMU—never contributed much before to what were, after all, revisions of Treaties between member states (not EU institutions). The Treaty of Nice was not unkind to the Commission, giving future Presidents more authority to reshuffle portfolios, ask for resignations, and 'ensure that [the college] acts consistently, efficiently and on the basis of collective responsibility'. One seasoned observer insisted that Nice showed that European leaders 'agree[d] that a more efficient Commission, including in particular a more powerful President, is highly desirable' (Ludlow 2001: 18).

Still, deep dissatisfaction with the Treaty of Nice was revealed in the Laeken Declaration, agreed only a year later and which put the EU on the road to its grandiosely-titled Convention on the Future of Europe. Decision-making within the Convention quickly became dominated by its thirteen-member Praesidium, a inner circle steering group, two of whose members were Commissioners under Prodi: Michel Barnier and Antonio Vitorino. Most of its other members were committed pro-Europeans who could be counted as 'natural allies' of the Commission and backers of the EU institution that most purely 'represented the European interest' (Norman 2003: 161).

At the end of the Convention—as well as the subsequent intergovernmental conference (IGC)—it was (again) possible to come to very different conclusions about how well the Commission had fared. Both Vitorino and Barnier contributed significantly to the Convention. In particular, Barnier surprised many with his successful chairing of a working group on defence, perhaps because he assumed the classic role of honest broker, with the Commission having 'no realistic aspirations to get involved in defence policy' (Norman 2003: 116). The Commission's basic legislative and watchdog roles were preserved in the Constitutional Treaty, which even extended its powers (particularly over justice and home affairs policies). A late political compromise in the IGC meant that the college would comprise one Commissioner per member state until at least 2014. But a leaner, more cohesive Commission (equalling two-thirds of the number of states or, say, eighteen in an EU of twenty-seven) was in prospect eventually on the basis of equal rotation between member states. Finally, a proposal backed by the Commission was accepted to make the Union's new Minister of Foreign Affairs a Vice-President in the College (as well as chair of the Foreign Affairs Council), with responsibility for all of the Commission's external activities.

A less generous interpretation was that the Convention revealed the Prodi Commission at its worst. Divisions sprouted within the college about what the Commission's strategy should be. Little or no attempt was made to ensure that Commission staff put to work on the Convention—numbering considerably more than the Convention's own secretariat—worked together (Norman 2003: 267). Most damagingly, the Commission produced two very different contributions to the Convention at a crucial stage in late 2002: one an official communication and the other a maximalist, full draft Treaty prepared in secret

continues

Exhibit 5.2 continued

by Prodi's own hand-picked operatives and code-named 'Penelope'. In presenting the Commission's official paper, Prodi downplayed Penelope as a 'feasibility study, a technical working tool' for which his college had 'no political responsibility' (Norman 2003: 167).

Still, Prodi instructed (the visibly infuriated) Barnier and Vitorino to push for language on several Treaty articles that conformed with Penelope. In the end, when consensus emerged within the Convention in June 2003 on the resolution of outstanding issues, the Commission was almost entirely marginalized. Norman's (2003: 267) verdict was that it 'marked an unhappy end to an unhappy Convention for the Commission President'.

The leading candidate to replace Prodi in 2004, Belgium's Prime Minister Guy Verhostadt, received powerful Franco–German backing, but was opposed intractably by the UK, thus reawakening divisions over the previous year's invasion of Iraq. Eventually, the Portuguese Prime Minister, José Manuel Barroso, emerged as a consensus candidate to lead a new, expanded college, with each member state in an EU of twenty-five appointing one member. Barroso's allocation of powerful economic portfolios to liberals (see Table 5.2) and previous support for the Iraq war were both controversial. Barroso, as Santer before him, also found himself on the sharp end of muscle-flexing by the EP, which threatened to vote to reject his Commission after the initial Italian nominee, Rocco Buttiglione, outraged MEPs by airing his conservative views on gay people and women (see Exhibit 5.3 below). By most accounts, Barroso handled the affair badly, before finally securing the EP's approval of a redesigned college. Hopes that Barroso could restore the Commission's position sank, and fell further when the Constitutional Treaty was rejected by French and Dutch voters in May 2005 referenda. Meanwhile, political rows blazed over the EU's budget and economic policy direction. The early Barroso years showed that the Commission's position serves as a barometer of European integration but also that its ability to influence the process is determined by broad political and economic forces over which it has little or no control.

The structure of the College

Basic norms established over fifty years govern appointments to the college and the relationship between its three basic elements: the President, the College itself, and Commissioners' *cabinets*.

The President

A biographer of Roy Jenkins starkly concluded that:

> The Presidency of the ... Commission is an impossible job. Indeed it can hardly be called a job at all—the President has a number of conflicting responsibilities, but no power. By no stretch of the imagination does it resemble the Prime Ministership of Europe (Campbell 1983: 181).

Table 5.2 The Barroso Commission

Commissioner (nationality)	Portfolio(s)	Relevant previous post(s)	Party affiliation in home country (EP party group*)
José Manuel Barrosso (Portugal)	President	Prime Minister	Social Democratic Party (EPP)
Margot Wallström (Sweden)	Vice-President, Institutional Relations and Communications Strategy	Social Affairs Minister; EU Environment Commissioner	Social Democratic Party (PES)
Günter Verheugen (Germany)	Vice-President, Enterprise and Industry	Minister for Europe; EU Enlargement Commissioner	Social Democratic Party (PES)
Jacques Barrot (France)	Vice-President, Transport	Labour and Social Affairs Minister	Union for a Popular Movement (EPP)
Siim Kallas (Estonia)	Vice-President, Administrative Affairs, Audit, and Anti-Fraud	Estonian Prime Minister	Estonian Reform Party (ELDR)
Franco Frattini (Italy)	Vice-President, Justice, Freedom, and Security	Foreign Affairs Minister	Forza Italia (EPP)
Viviane Reding (Luxumbourg)	Information, Society and Media	MEP	Christian Social People's Party (EPP)
Stavros Dimas (Greece)	Environment	Industry, Energy, and Technology Minister	New Democracy (EPP)
Joaquín Almunia (Spain)	Economic and Monetary Affairs	Employment and Social Security Minister	Socialist Workers' Party (PES)
Danuta Hübner (Poland)	Regional Policy	European Affairs Minister	None
Joe Borg (Malta)	Fisheries and Maritime Affairs	Foreign Affairs Minister	Nationalist Party (EPP)
Dalia Grybauskaite (Lithuania)	Financial Programming and Budget	Finance Minister	None
Janez Potocnik (Slovenia)	Science and Research	European Affairs Minister	None
Ján Figel (Slovakia)	Education, Training, Culture, and Multilinguilism	Research Scientist, Chief Negotiator on EU accession	Christian Democratic Movement (EPP)
Markos Kyprianou (Cyprus)	Health and Consumer Protection	Finance Minister	Democratic Party (EPP)

continues

Table 5.2 continued

Commissioner (nationality)	Portfolio(s)	Relevant previous post(s)	Party affiliation in home country (EP party group*)
Olli Rehn (Finland)	Enlargement	MEP; Adviser to Finnish Prime Minister	Centre Party (ELDR)
Louis Michel (Belgium)	Development and Humanitarian Aid	Deputy Prime Minister and Foreign Affairs Minister	Reformist Movement (ELDR)
László Kovács (Hungary)	Taxation and Customs Union	Foreign Affairs Minister	Socialist Party (PES)
Neelie Kroes (Netherlands)	Competition	Transport, Public Works and Communications Minister	People's Party for Freedom and Democracy (ELDR)
Mariann Fischer Boel (Denmark)	Agriculture and Rural Development	Agriculture Minister	Liberal Party (ELDR)
Benita Ferrero-Waldner (Austria)	External Relations and European Neighbourhood Policy	Foreign Affairs Minister	People's Party (EPP)
Charlie McCreevy (Ireland)	Internal Market and Services	Finance Minister	Fianna Fáil (UEN)
Vladimír Spidla (Czech Republic)	Employment, Social Affairs and Equal Opportunities	Prime Minister	Czech Social Democratic Party (PES)
Peter Mandelson (UK)	Trade	Trade and Industry Minister	Labour (PES)
Andris Piebalgs (Latvia)	Energy	Finance Minister	Latvian Way (ELDR)

Note: * Here we show the affiliation of national parties to party groups within the EP to give a sense of the political balance—especially between Commissioners with ties to centre-right (EPP), socialist (PES) or liberal (ELDR) parties—within the College. See also Chapter 15.

This claim initially seemed to be challenged by the appointment of Prodi, a former Prime Minister of a large member state. Yet, less than a year after his appointment, Prodi was forced to deny rumours that he was considering leaving the Commission to fight a forthcoming Italian domestic election. The only other Italian to have been Commission President, the barely remembered Franco Maria Malfatti, had done precisely that and left Brussels early in the 1970s. Had the Commission gone back to the future?

In a sense, the legacy of Delors continued to haunt Brussels, both in terms of the political aversion of many member governments to a powerful Commission *and* the reality of a Commission that was irreversibly powerful. The internal market was, if by no means complete, at least a political fact. The Commission was responsible for policing it, representing the EU in international trade diplomacy, and suggesting steps towards its full realization. The enormously powerful market forces unleashed by open commerce in the world's largest single capitalist market were often able to overwhelm public power unless it was wielded collectively, with the Commission usually in the lead (see Pollack 1997; Peterson and Bomberg 1999: 67). The freeing of the internal market truly did transform the Commission's institutional position.

Moreover, the EU was increasingly powerful as a player in international politics (see Hill and Smith 2005b). Over time, the Council Secretariat became a formidable institutional rival and clear superior to the Commission on most questions of foreign policy. Still, the Commission packed a punch as purveyors of the EU's programmes for development aid and humanitarian assistance and, particularly, through its lead role in international economic diplomacy. After becoming Commissioner for Ex- ternal Trade under Barroso, Peter Mandelson could plausibly be considered more powerful than perhaps twenty or so Prime Ministers of the EU's smaller states.

Finally, the Commission remained an honest broker between many diverse and competing interests in a system that relied fundamentally on consensus. Arguably, the Commission stood to be empowered in an expanded EU of twenty-five or more member states, around three-quarters of which were small states (with 16 million or fewer citizens), since the Commission had always been the traditional defender of the 'smalls'. Pointedly, Barroso vowed to defend the newest EU countries—all small states besides Poland—from protectionist pressures from long-time member states, some of whom Barroso claimed had 'not yet changed their chip to an enlarged Europe'.[8]

The days when Barroso's job could 'hardly be called a job at all' may be gone, but no Commission President ever makes his own luck. How much any President can accomplish is determined by a variety of factors over which they have little or no control. Even Delors was successful only because of three propitious contextual variables: national receptivity to European solutions, international changes (espe- cially German unification), and a favourable business cycle from 1985 to 1990 (Ross 1995: 234–7). These factors helped Delors exert 'pull' within the European Council, in which the Commission President is the only member who does not head a state or government. Crucially, Delors (and perhaps Jenkins, at least on EMS) was viewed as a political equal in the European Council. There is no evidence that either Santer or Prodi—former Prime Ministers themselves—ever were.

Regardless, the Commission has become more *presidential* over time. Successive Treaty revisions have given the Commission President—considered only 'first among equals' during Delors' time—a progressively stronger grip over the college. Prodi tried to focus on broad political themes, giving himself no specific policy portfolio (unlike Santer, who retained overall responsibility for EMU and external policy) while also seeking to expand his own influence by inserting many of his 'own people' into key positions of authority within the Commission's services. The collective identity of the college seemed a secondary consideration, with Prodi declaring 'I want each Commissioner to be a star, a big star, in his or her own policy area'.[9]

Yet, few argued that it was also more effective or cohesive. Prodi's political mis- judgements were frequent and his communication skills poor. His inability to form coalitions with (especially large state) European leaders led to charges that he had failed to reverse 'the weakness of a Commission that ha[d] not fully recovered from the trauma of the Santer resignation' (de Schoutheete and Wallace 2002: 17).

For his part, Barroso insisted that his would be a dynamic, reform-minded Commission subject to a strong Presidential lead. Promising that his college would be more policy focused and team oriented, Barroso argued that any effort to restore the position of the Commission had to respect the premise that 'the basic legitimacy of our union is the member states'.[10] Yet, even after recovering from the Buttiglione affair (see Exhibit 5.3), Barroso came under attack from the political Left, particularly in the European Parliament where he was accused of pursuing a 'neo-conservative agenda' and privileging a 'liberal Atlantic' clique within the Commission.[11] Barroso's

---

Exhibit 5.3 The Rocco Buttiglione affair

Views on José Manuel Barroso's prospects fluctuated wildly in the first days after his nomination. Barroso was no one's first choice for the job. Immediately after he was chosen, he was lobbied hard by France and Germany to designate their nominees as 'super-Commissioners', provoking fears of another weak Commission President.

Barroso's surprise, early announcement of the distribution of jobs in his college, and his wry comment that he needed twenty-four 'super-Commissioners', temporarily silenced his critics. After first offering the powerful justice and home affairs (JHA) portfolio to the French nominee, Jacques Barrot (who was firm in wanting an economic job), Barroso designated the Italian nominee, Rocco Buttiglione, as JHA Commissioner. An arch-Catholic and close confidante of the Pope, Buttiglione aired ultra-conservative views on homosexuality (calling it a 'sin') and women (who 'belonged in the home') at his EP confirmation hearing, leading the Parliament's civil liberties committee to vote to recommend his rejection. Barroso tried to appease MEPs by delegating Buttiglione's responsibilities for civil liberties to a committee of other Commissioners. Yet, opinion within the EP did not measurably shift. Barroso then made things worse, stating that he was 'absolutely convinced' that his Commission would be approved since only 'extremist' MEPs could possibly vote against it.[12] Ultimately, he had no choice but to withdraw his team from consideration by the EP in order to avoid a humiliating rejection.

Barroso's political instincts seemed to return in subsequent weeks. He was helped by Buttiglione's decision to stand down, as well as Latvia's withdrawal of its original nominee, Ingrida Udre, who was dogged by allegations of corruption. Fresh nominations by both states—particularly Italy's choice of its Foreign Minister, Franco Frattini, to replace Buttiglione—allowed Barroso to propose a new-look college, which was overwhelmingly approved by the EP. Afterwards, Barroso could claim that 'we have come out of this experience with strengthened institutions',[13] including a stronger Commission and, of course, an emboldened EP.

For their part, religious organizations were outraged, with one insisting that the affair showed 'how little trust there is at the heart of the EU'.[14] Supporters of the Parliament accused Barroso of going too far to try to appease European leaders, particularly Italy's Prime Minister, Silvio Berlusconi. A more mundane, but inevitable conclusion was that as long as each state in an EU of twenty-five or more nominates one Commissioner, any nominee for President will find themselves trying to build a team from a large group that includes many (a majority in Barroso's case) they have never met before. In Barroso's own words, 'it is like a blind date'.[15]

defence of small and new EU states provoked the French President, Jacques Chirac, to respond to rising Euroscepticism in France (in advance of the failed 2005 referendum on the Constitutional Treaty) by repeatedly attacking the Commission. One analyst accused Barroso of being an 'intergovernmentalist at heart' and predicted that his Commission would continue on a steady path of decline (Munchau 2005: 17).

The College

The appointment of the College is often a fraught and highly politicized exercise (see Peterson and Bomberg 1999: 40–1). The compositions of the Jenkins and Prodi Commissions were shaped in important ways by the nominees for President himself. Still, provisions in the Amsterdam Treaty[16] that lent weight to Prodi's own preferences in 1999 still 'did not prevent governments from having the upper hand over "their" nomination(s)' (Nugent 2001: 83). Barroso did not appear to influence many choices about who was nominated to his Commission until he was forced to ask for fresh nominees following the Buttiglione affair (see Exhibit 5.3).

The institutional design of the EU is intended to create collective, inter-institutional responsibility for what the Union does. It has given rise to a gradual strengthening of the EP's right to vet the choice of member governments' nominees to the College. The Santer, Prodi, and Barroso Commissions (after the reconfiguration of the latter) all were ultimately confirmed by large margins (of around 300 votes). Yet, if provisions in the Constitutional Treaty were ever implemented, the formal powers of the EP would be reinforced: it would officially elect the Presidential nominee and member states would be legally obliged to take account of the results of the most recent EP election in choosing a nominee for President. Even these changes would pose no threat—in advance of any move to a smaller Commission—to the basic principle that 'each national government is free to select a national Commissioner' (Devuyst 2005: 53).

Collective responsibility is not only built into the EU's institutional system generally. It is also a cardinal principle *within* the College. All members must publicly support all decisions and actions of the Commission. The principle is often difficult to uphold. In contrast to cabinet governments, the college is never united by shared party political, national, or ideological affinities. In fact, no one has ever really explained what is meant to hold it together besides a commitment to 'Europe' (see Coombes 1970).

Formally, the College decides by simple majority votes. In a college of twenty-five, as many as twelve Commissioners could vote against a motion but then have to support it publicly. Our knowledge about how often the College votes is primitive, and frequent voting cannot necessarily be equated with more division in the college. However, when the College votes it is usually an admission that the majority view must be forced on at least a few Commissioners. By most accounts,[17] voting was more frequent in the Santer Commission than in Delors', perhaps because the latter was more clearly dominated by its President. In the Prodi Commission, insiders noted 'a culture of avoiding votes' in a College whose members were 'very focused on their own responsibilities and relatively unconcerned with some larger "big vision"'.

The single most important factor in determining the cohesiveness of the College remains the strength of Presidential leadership. The Prodi Commission was the first in which, according to the Amsterdam Treaty, the college worked 'under the political direction of the President'. Nevertheless, one of its members denied ever having a single substantive discussion with Prodi on any issue related to his own (economic) portfolio, adding: 'Prodi got out of the way, but we needed a sort of control tower. We only avoided a lot of plane crashes at the last minute, and some we did not avoid' (quoted in Peterson 2005*b*).

Barroso appeared to think that his College needed more of a collective identity and more teamwork on actual policy. He thus announced the formation of five 'clusters' of Commissioners in key areas: the Lisbon agenda, external relations (both chaired by Barroso himself), communications, equal opportunities, and competitiveness. Yet, in an early indication of how such devices do not guarantee a cohesive College, Barroso's Commissioner for the internal market, Charlie McCreevy, publicly attacked the Commissioner for Enterprise, Günter Verheugen, dismissing the latter's doubts about the proposed services directive as a case of 'some Commissioners . . . who like to speak out of both sides of their mouth . . . from one day to the next'.[18]

Collective responsibility has become more difficult to enforce as the College has become, over time, a more politically weighty group of individuals. The Santer Commission reinforced the trend towards 'increasing politicisation of the college' (MacMullen 2000: 41), with its inclusion of six former prime ministers, foreign ministers, or finance ministers. Prodi's College contained more policy specialists, with a majority coming to the Commission after being national ministers for agriculture, finance, European affairs, and so on. The Barroso Commission pushed back in the direction of high-powered generalists, with its three former prime ministers, five former foreign ministers, and three former finance ministers. Notably, nearly all who had held such high-level posts hailed from small states, and the early verdict on Barroso's College was that it lacked 'big stars', as Pascal Lamy, Chris Patten, and Antonio Vitorino had been considered to be in their policy areas under Prodi. Nevertheless, even Barroso's line-up seemed to defy any notion that the College consists of mostly grey, apolitical technocrats (see Peterson 1999; 2002).

The *cabinets*

One of the Commission's most vexed problems has always been the proper role of *cabinets*. In principle, *cabinets* are meant to act as a bridge between the college and the services, and thus between the political and apolitical. Most national civil services contain some analogue in the form of party political, temporary appointees to civil services. Yet, members of *cabinets* in the Commission have tended to be particularly vilified as agents of their member state, as opposed to the Commission as an institution. In the past, *cabinets* were usually (not always) packed with officials—often quite young—who shared their Commissioner's nationality, leaving aside a few non-nationals. Many were hand-picked by governments in national capitals. Tensions between the *cabinets* and services were rife, especially during the Delors years. One abiding complaint about *cabinets* was that they intervened aggressively in personnel decisions, acting as lobbyists for national capitals in securing senior posts in the services.

Prodi himself was widely accused of violating the spirit of new meritocratic rules on appointments by placing his own hand-picked operatives in powerful posts. Still,

Prodi instituted major changes at the level of *cabinets*, which were reduced in size to six officials from as many as nine previously (Prodi's own *cabinet* numbered nine). Each Commissioner was required to appoint a head (*chef*) or deputy head (*adjoint*) who hailed from a member state other than their own. Leading by example, Prodi chose as his own *chef* an Irishman, David O'Sullivan (later to become Secretary-General).

Under Prodi, a significant number of new faces appeared in the *cabinets*, with only about one-third having previous *cabinet* experience.[19] The Commission trumpeted the fact that all *cabinets* had officials of at least three different nationalities, and that almost 40 per cent were women (a big increase on past totals). *Cabinets*, along with their Commissioners, were moved out of a central office in Brussels by Prodi and into the same buildings as the services for which their Commissioner was responsible, thus making Commissioners more like national ministers.

Barroso brought Commissioners and *cabinets* back together when the Commission's Berlaymont headquarters were reopened in 2004 after being refurbished and cleared of asbestos. The move was widely expected after complaints that separating Commissioners' office made it harder for them to strike deals and build coalitions. However, Barroso stuck with Prodi's rules on *cabinet* appointments, and the influx of (ten) Commissioners from post-accession states made for an unusually large influx of fresh faces at this level. How much the traditional role of *cabinets* changed in the process was open to question, with one EU ambassador observing that 'the *cabinets* still channel impulses from national capitals, and they probably always will'.

The Commission's powers

The main source of the Commission's power has always been its monopoly right to propose legislation. The Commission also has significant independent powers within the CAP and on external trade and (especially) competition policy. In the latter case, the college often acts as judge and prosecuting attorney—and sometimes jury—on cases of state aids to industry, mergers, and anti-competitive practices by firms. The Commission has considerable powers to set the agenda for policies that 'flank' the internal market, such as cohesion or research policies.

Two important sources of Commission influence—as opposed to power—are its prerogative to deliver opinions on any EU matter, and its obligation to publish an annual report on the activities of the EU. Both give the Commission scope to influence policy debates or steer the EU in specified directions. Generally, however, the Commission must earn its respect by the quality of its analysis, and particularly its judgement of what will play in national capitals and with relevant policy stakeholders (including industry and non-governmental lobbies). For example, the Barroso Commission was challenged in its first months in office by a revolt by some member states over the services directive it inherited from its predecessor, forcing a highly unusual redrafting of its proposal.

Over time, the Commission has become increasingly accountable to the EP. Besides its powers to confirm the College (and its President) and to sack the Commission, the

EP retains the informal right to scrutinize the activities of the Commission, with individual Commissioners expected to appear regularly before its policy-specialized committees. The emergence of the co-decision procedure (see Chapter 6) as the default legislative procedure has had the effect of upgrading the institutional position of the EP at the expense of the Commission. When the EP and Council cannot agree, the Commission risks being marginalized unless it is sensitive to the positions of both of the other institutions, and acknowledges their dominance of the procedure. More generally, the Parliament has 'gained a greater ability not only to hold the Commission more accountable, but also to get the Commission to do things it would not otherwise do' (Stacey 2003: 951).

Historically, the European Court of Justice has usually ruled in the Commission's favour when it has been asked to settle competence disputes. Several underpinnings of the 1992 project became doctrine as the result of individual ECJ decisions, which the Commission then used in the design of new policies (see Armstrong and Bulmer 1999). However, a landmark case in early 1994 saw the Court rule against the Commission in a dispute with the Council over competence on new external trade issues such as services and intellectual property. The Commission also suffered a series of painful court defeats on its competition policy judgements under Prodi, leading to a sweeping overhaul of the EU's regime for state aids to industry under Barroso.

The Commission's most important power may be its right of initiative, but increasingly the Commission's most important role is that of a *manager* of policies set by other institutions. The twenty-first century has found the Commission sharing responsibility for more EU policies, often acting as a broker and facilitator within organizational networks linking the member states and other EU institutions. To cite a prominent example, the launch of the Lisbon agenda of economic reform in 2000 granted few significant new competences to the Commission. However, it allowed just enough room for the Commission to catalyse new initiatives to convince Barroso (five years later) that a revamped Lisbon strategy focused on 'jobs and growth' should be his Commission's top priority. It was also indicative that the Barroso Commission welcomed the proposals of a UK-convened 'Better Regulation Task Force' (2004) to create an informal body composed of officials from the Commission, EP, and Council which could fast-track moves to simplify legislation or adjust it to suit changing circumstances without formally changing it. More than ever, the Commission's work was concerned with advocacy and persuasion within horizontal policy networks, rather than hierarchical compulsion or coercion.

The College in context

The mass resignation of the Santer Commission was clearly a defining event in the life of the institution. Afterwards, one former Commissioner lamented the Prodi Commission's 'astonishing weakness'. A senior official in the services claimed, 'no one is defending the Commission in any major national capital. The Commission as a whole is losing heart'. After its first year, Peter Mandelson claimed that the Barroso college was finding its feet but had found its position eroded by a 'pincer movement':

a loss of leadership to the Council and loss of the internal Commission agenda to the services, which had become more autonomous in the void created by the demise of the Santer Commission.[20]

If the Commission was really so weak, intergovernmentalist accounts of EU politics—which tend to make three arguments about the Commission—could be marshalled to explain why. First, it makes little difference who is Commission President. Second, the Commission is only powerful when and where national preferences converge. Third, the Commission is empowered only to the extent that member government want to ensure the 'credibility of their commitments' to each other (Moravcsik 1998: 492). There is little dispute, among scholars as well as practitioners, that the Commission has traditionally had little influence over most 'history-making' decisions about the broad sweep of European integration.

In contrast, institutionalist theory—now firmly established as 'the leading theoretical approach in EU studies' (Cowles and Curtis 2004: 305)—paints a portrait of a Commission that is often powerful in day-to-day policy debates (see Pierson 1996). According to this view, policy decisions in complex systems such as the EU are difficult to reverse, and policy often becomes locked into existing paths and 'path dependent'. Thus, even as the Stability and Growth Pact, the economic rulebook governing EMU, was rewritten in 2005 amid frustration over the Commission's reprimands of governments running profligate budget deficits, the Commission lost none of its existing mandate or authority over EMU.

Some variants of institutionalism combine insights from rational choice and principal–agent theories (see Pollack 2003). They hold that the principal authorities in EU politics—the member government themselves—make rational choices to delegate tasks to the EU's institutions, which then become their agents in specific policy areas. This body of theory sheds light on the tendency for the EU to make policy by means other than the traditional 'Community method' of legislating (see Devuyst 1999), according to which only the Commission can propose. One of the least flattering features of the Prodi Commission was its frequent insistence that the Community method was the only legitimate path to making EU policy (see Peterson 2005a), even in areas such as the common foreign and security policy where its use was politically unthinkable. There was little dispute that some new policy modes, particularly the so-called 'open method of coordination' (OMC), relying on bench-marking, league tabling, and designating the Commission as a scrutinizer of national policies rather than a proposer of EU policies, produced few tangible, early results (see Borràs and Jacobsson 2004; Dehousse 2004). Yet, EU principals (national governments) were clearly moving towards new kinds of delegation, with the Commission cast as a different kind of agent. By 2005, Verheugen was launching a drive to reduce regulatory burdens on industry and promised to use voluntary codes and other 'soft' forms of regulation in preference to actual legislation.[21]

Increased affinity for new policy modes is also reflected in the creation of a variety of new regulatory agencies, some of which have assumed some of the traditional roles of the Commission (see Chapter 10). EU governments increasingly seem to want new kinds of agents—not just the Commission—to whom they can delegate cooperative policy tasks. Usually, however, the Commission retains the job of identifying and seeking to solve coordination problems within policy networks of (*inter alia*) private actors, consumer and environmental groups, and national and European agencies.

Advocates of multi-level governance as an approach to understanding the EU have long contended that the Commission enjoys a privileged place at the 'hub of numerous highly specialized policy networks of technical experts', even retaining 'virtually a free hand in creating new networks' (Marks *et al.* 1996: 355, 359). Metcalfe (2000: 838) argues that 'the Commission will have to be reinvented as a network organization adept at designing the frameworks of governance and developing the management capacities needed to make them work effectively'. There is little doubt that, insofar as the Commission provides direction to the EU of the future, it will largely do so as a coordinator of networks that seek to make national policies converge (see Héritier 1999; Kohler-Koch and Eising 1999; Peterson 2005*b*), as opposed to replacing them with EU policies.

The College after enlargement[22]

Barroso's College reflected a new political reality in an EU of twenty-five. That is, even if all Commissioners are formally equal, the idea that no Commissioner is more powerful than another is now a practical fiction. If Commissioners from large member states tend to be more successful or powerful, it may be less because of blatant political activism by their national capitals than because they operate in wider networks of contacts (Joana and Smith 2002). Commissioners from small states can 'punch above the weight' of their home country if their performance earns them the respect of their peers and EU member governments. Still, no one pretends that Commissioners from, say, Germany and Malta start out as equals.

To their credit, member governments in the 2004 accession states mostly appointed top members of their political classes to the college. Of the first thirteen appointed by new EU states, six were former prime, foreign, or finance ministers, and several others had been European affairs ministers or national ambassadors to the EU. Thus, most had in-depth knowledge of how Brussels worked from their involvement in negotiating their own state's accession.

Early signals from Barroso's Commission suggested that the President's reformist agenda would be backed by Commissioners whose states had undergone radical, and often painful, reforms to enter the EU. Moreover, Barroso's pledge to defend 'new' EU countries seemed part of a strategy to challenge the *status quo* on key EU issues. For example, (Lithuanian) Budget Commissioner Dalia Grybauskaite raised eyebrows with her assessment that inherited proposals on the structural funds, which targeted more than half of regional funding for the pre-2004 EU-15, were 'difficult to defend'.[23]

The institutional effects of the 2004 enlargement on the Commission, as well as the rest of the EU, will only be revealed years after the event. Yet, there were reasons to think that enlargement might be digested more easily by the Commission than other EU institutions, whose numbers were swelled by a relatively larger influx of new and inexperienced members.[24] At the level of the College, and possibly even more so within the services, enlargement at least held out the prospect of revitalizing and renewing the Commission with a new breed of reform-minded Europeans.

Conclusion

Any analysis of the Commission must consider the normative question of what kind of organization the College should be. A policy entrepreneur? An honest broker? A manager of decisions taken by others? Or an 'engine of integration'?

Increasingly, the Commission seems to have outgrown the last of these roles. It might be argued that there is no other institution that has the independence to identify new directions that European integration needs to take. Moreover, there is historical evidence suggesting that the Commission's declining fortunes can be reversed: after all, it appeared entirely moribund after Hallstein and before Delors.

The Commission spent much of the Prodi era focused on its own institutional position. With its basic role mostly preserved, it can be argued that the Commission now needs to focus on *policy*, as opposed to grand designs. Yet, it has become increasingly difficult, especially in an EU of twenty-five, to design single, EU level policy solutions. As a top former Commission official suggested in 2005, 'most of Europe's worst problem are now micro-level problems. They need to be solved at that level'.

In this context, the EU's added value is mostly as a laboratory for policy learning and transfer. Logically, the new EU will have to adopt new policy modes, and particularly more, and more intensive, exchange and cooperation within networks of national or even sub-national agencies (see W. Wallace 2005). The Union's institutions—including the Commission—will need to embrace more collective types of leadership and advocacy of new policy ideas. Regardless of its eventual fate, the Constitutional Treaty (in Art. 18) gave a clear political signal that the EU's institutions must 'practice full mutual cooperation' if the Union is to thrive.

In an enlarged EU, the Commission may be even better placed than in the past to act as a truly honest broker. It may rarely exercise control over new cooperative networks or reclaim its old function as an 'engine of integration'. But it will logically remain at the centre of many EU policy networks. In any event, it will often find itself in a unique position to steer debates in ways that serve collective European interests, as difficult as they may be to identify clearly in the new EU.

Notes

1 The College remained a men-only club for a shockingly long time. The first women Commissioners were Christiane Scrivener (France) and Vasso Papandreou (Greece), who were appointed to the Delors Commission in 1989.

2 The Luxembourg Compromise was accompanied by a range of new restrictions on the Commission, including a bar on making proposals public before the Council could consider them and the requirement that the Commission could only receive the credentials of non-EEC ambassadors to the Community alongside the Council.

3 It is not clear that Jenkins ever wished to serve another term. His 1979 Dimbleby

Lecture (half-way through his term as Commission President) foreshadowed his ambition to form a new British political grouping—eventually, the Social Democratic Party—of which he became co-leader three years later. By 1980, even Belgium—which originally favoured his reappointment—decided that the 'gap between [Thatcherite] Britain and the rest of the Community was so great that the time had not arrived when any Englishman could be President of the Commission indefinitely' (Jenkins 1989: 601). The Commission's term in office was later extended to five years by the Maastricht Treaty so as to align its tenure with that of the EP.

4 Santer was literally no one's first choice but was chosen after the nominations of Ruud Lubbers (Prime Minister of the Netherlands), Leon Brittan (Commissioner under Delors), and Jean-Luc Dehaene (Prime Minister of Belgium) were all rejected, with the UK under John Major prominently vetoing Dehaene.

5 Santer was not alone in making this claim. The respected Belgian Commissioner for Competition Policy, Karel van Miert, attacked the Experts' report as 'unjust and incorrect' (Santer and van Miert both quoted in *Financial Times*, 17 March 1999). For his part, Brittan (2000: 11) insisted that the Experts had added 'unnecessary and crude journalistic icing . . . to what was a perfectly well-baked and freestanding cake'.

6 Unattributed quote in *Financial Times*, 17 March 1999.

7 This quote (and all others not referenced as otherwise in this chapter) is taken from interviews conducted as part of the research for this chapter in November/December 2000, March 2001, November 2003, June 2004, and January–April 2005. The interviewees included two Commissioners, two former Commissioners, one national ambassador, a former Secretary-General, *cabinet* officials (eight in

the Prodi Commission, including three *chefs* and two *deputy chefs*), and a diverse range of senior officials in the services.

8 Quoted in *Financial Times*, 15 March 2005, p. 8.

9 Quoted in *Financial Times*, 19 July 1999, p. 9.

10 Quoted in *Financial Times*, 7 February 2005, p. 17.

11 The President of the EP Socialist group, Poul Nyrup Rasmussen, and veteran French MEP, Jean-Louis Bourlanges, quoted (respectively) in *Financial Times*, 2 March 2005, p. 6 and *EurActiv.com*, 3 September 2003 (available on *http://www.euractiv.com*).

12 Quoted in *Financial Times*, 22 October 2004, p. 1.

13 Quoted in BBC News, 'MEPs approve revamped Commission', available on *www.newsvote.bbc.co.uk* (accessed 19 November 2004).

14 See commentary by the European Evangelical Alliance (available on *http://www.europeanea.org/TheButtiglioneAffair.htm*); see also Catholic Educator's Resource Centre, 'The New Europe: Catholics no longer need apply' (available at: *http://www.catholiceducation.org/articles/persecution/pch0071.html* (both accessed 25 March 2005)).

15 Quoted in *Financial Times*, 19 December 2004, p. 8.

16 The Amsterdam Treaty promised that members of the College would be chosen 'in common accord' with the nominee for President—not just 'in consultation' with them as in the past.

17 One former Commissioner interviewed for this chapter insisted that there were 'far more votes under Delors and tight votes'. Another indicated that 'voting wasn't very frequent' in the Delors Commission. Previous interviewees with experience of successive Commissions estimated that there were

more votes taken under Santer than Delors (see Peterson 1999: 62).

18 Quoted in *Financial Times*, 4 March 2005, p. 6.

19 As is generally the case in the Commission, personnel records on *cabinet* members are incomplete, thus making precise comparisons impossible. However, using data presented in Hill and Knowlton (2000), a total of 34 (out of all 123 *cabinet* officials) had previous experience working in *cabinets*, or 28 per cent of the total, compared to 74 with no previous *cabinet* experience, or 60 per cent of the total. The data showed no previous information on the former positions held by 15 *cabinet* officials.

20 Peter Mandelson, 'The Idea of Europe: Can We Make it Live Again?', UACES Future of Europe Lecture, Crowne Plaza Hotel, Brussels, 20 July 2005 (available on *http://www.uaces.org*).

21 Quoted in *Financial Times*, 17 March 2005, p. 3.

22 This section and the one that follows both draw heavily on Peterson 2005a.

23 Quoted in *Financial Times*, 24 February 2005, p. 10.

24 By mid-2005, more than 1,000 officials had been recruited to the Commission from the ten accession states, but a number of recruitment targets had been missed. At the same time, pre-enlargement fears that accession state administrations would haemorrhage their top staff to the Commission appeared to be unfounded.

Further reading

The most useful and comprehensive of recent works on the Commission are Spence (2006) and Dimitrakopoulos (2004). Nugent (2001) is still very good on the history of the Commission and Delors (2004) offers an insider's view. Coombes (1970), Ross (1995), and Metcalfe (2000) rank as classics that are always worth revisiting. A typically downbeat assessment of the recent and present position of the Commission is Tsakatika (2005), while Peterson (2005) offers a (very preliminary) view of the likely impact of enlargement on the Commission.

Coombes, D. (1970), *Power and Bureaucracy in the European Community* (London: Croon Helm).

Delors, J. (2004), *Mémoires* (Paris: Plon).

Dimitrakopoulos, D. G. (2004) (ed.), *The Changing European Commission* (Manchester and New York: Manchester University Press).

Metcalfe, L. (2000), 'Reforming the Commission: Will Organisational Efficiency Produce Effective Governance?', *Journal of Common Market Studies*, 38(5): 817–41.

Nugent, N. (2001), *The European Commission* (Basingstoke and New York: Palgrave).

Peterson, J. (2005), *The 'enlarged' European Commission* (Paris: Notre Europe), available on *http://www.notre-europe.asso.fr*.

Ross, G. (1995), *Jacques Delors and European Integration* (New York and London: Polity Press).

Spence, D. (2006) (ed.), *The European Commission* (London: John Harper).

Tsakatika, M. (2005), 'The European Commission between continuity and change', *Journal of Common Market Studies*, 43/1: 193–220.

Web links

The Commission's own website (*http://europa.eu.int*) is a treasure trove which handles something like two million 'hits' per month. The sites of the *European Voice* (*http://www.european-voice.com*) and European Policy Centre (*http://www.theepc.be*) offer insiders' insights from Brussels. It is often useful to see how the Commission's delegations in EU member states (for example, *www.cec.org.uk*) and non-EU member states (see *www.eurunion.org*) present the Commission's line in capitals beyond Brussels.

Chapter 6

The European Parliament

Michael Shackleton

Contents

Summary

The European Parliament (EP) is the European Union's only directly elected institution. For much of its history it has been relatively weak but since the first direct elections in 1979 its powers and status have grown with remarkable speed. It has acquired the right to decide the contents of most EU legislation jointly with the Council and has come to play a major role in the appointment of the Commission and its President, thereby significantly altering the structure of relations between the institutions. The crisis over the Constitutional Treaty has called into question whether the EP's powers will continue to expand. Nevertheless, the issue of the 'democratic deficit' in the EU cannot be addressed without an understanding of how the Parliament has evolved, how it is structured, what influence it exercises and what kind of body it is becoming within an enlarged Union of twenty-seven or more states.

Introduction

On 27 October 2004, EU Commission President, José Manuel Barroso came to the European Parliament in Strasbourg to say that he needed more time before asking for a vote of approval for his new Commission. He knew that following the hearings of the individual Commissioners held earlier that month, he was unlikely to gain the support of the Parliament for the appointment (or 'investiture') of his college as required by the Treaties. Within a matter of days he had reshuffled its composition, paving the way for the Parliament to give its approval by a large majority on 18 November (see Chapter 5, p. 93).

It was a dramatic moment, underlining the conversion of the European Parliament from an arena of discussion to a place where important decisions about the overall direction of the European Union are taken. The change had not come overnight. It was the result of developments stretching back over the whole history of the Parliament but especially during the 1990s when empowering the EP was widely seen as a natural step in the creation of a true 'political union'. The uncertainty in 2005 surrounding the fate of the EU's Constitutional Treaty, which proposed to add to the EP's powers, called into the question the future direction of the Parliament.

This chapter confronts three issues. First, how and why has the Parliament been able to acquire additional powers? Second, what difference has the inclusion of such a directly elected institution made to the evolution of the EU? Third, what kind of institution is the EP becoming and how far can it resolve the so-called 'democratic deficit'? In relation to the first issue, it has proved easier to agree a gradual extension of the institution's role than to say no to the claims of a representative institution with democratic credentials based on direct elections. On the second, the EP has changed the direction of many EU policies. It has also opened up a debate about whether the EU meets the standards of representative democracy. As for the third question, successive decisions taken to develop the Parliament have above all strengthened its role as a legislator. This strengthened role reinforces its position in relation to the other institutions in Brussels, notably the Council of Ministers, but cannot by itself resolve the broader issue of the legitimacy of the EU. The debate about the democratic nature of that system depends on the kind of political structure European governments and citizens want the Union to become and whether they want the same things, an issue that has moved to the centre of EU politics.

Historical evolution

The story of the Parliament has been told as a transition from 'fig-leaf to co-legislature' (Corbett et al. 2005: 1). This change is reflected symbolically in the Parliament's physical surroundings. It has moved from renting premises in Strasbourg that it shared with the Parliamentary Assembly of the Council of Europe to becoming the effective owner of two substantial building complexes in Brussels and Strasbourg,

Table 6.1 Main treaty changes affecting the European Parliament

	Election of MEPs	Legislative and budgetary role	Appointment and scrutiny of executive
ECSC Treaty (1950)	Choice between direct elections or national parliaments to select members		Right to dismiss High Authority
Rome Treaty (1957)	Specific provision for direct elections (implemented in 1979)	Right to be consulted and to give its opinion to the Council	
Budgetary treaties (1970 and 1975)		Right to reject budget, modify level of expenditure and approve/disapprove accounts ('discharge')	
Single European Act (1985)		'Cooperation procedure' providing right to a second reading of legislation and 'assent procedure' to approve enlargement and some international agreements	
Maastricht Treaty (1992)		'Co-decision procedure' with conciliation to apply to 15 legal bases, Right to invite Commission to present a legislative proposal	Right to approve Commission as a whole + Committees of Inquiry, Appointment of Ombudsman and ECB President to report to EP committee
Amsterdam Treaty (1997)		Simplification and extension of co-decision to 32 legal bases	Right to approve Commission President
Nice Treaty (2000)		Extension of co-decision to 37 legal bases	
Constitutional Treaty (2004)		Extension of co-decision to 90 legal bases and to be called 'ordinary legislative procedure' (Art. III-396), Possibility to revoke delegated legislation (Art. I-36)	Commission President to be elected by EP on basis of proposal of European Council that takes into account the elections to the European Parliament (Art. I-27)

both of them with parliamentary chambers (known as 'hemicycles' because of their shape) equipped to seat 750 members. At the same time, the formal powers of the EP have undergone much more significant growth than those of any other institution. Table 6.1 indicates the main Treaty changes affecting the Parliament between 1951 when the original six signed the ECSC Treaty and 2004 when the twenty-five states of the European Union signed the Constitutional Treaty.

When the ECSC was established, a parliamentary body was far from the centre of discussion (Smith 1999: 27–44). The crucial institution was the High Authority, given supranational powers in the management of coal and steel. The creation of a parliamentary institution, called the Common Assembly, was something of an after-thought, perceived as the least imperfect way to address the issue of accountability. The Assembly's only significant power was that of supervising the Authority, with the right to dismiss the entire body by a two-thirds majority of the votes cast, rep-resenting an absolute majority of its members. However, the future evolution of the institution towards something more influential was reflected in the provisions gov-erning its election. Member states could choose whether to have direct elections to the Assembly or to allow its national parliament to select Members. Such a potential direct link to the electorate distinguished the institution from the outset from other international parliamentary bodies, such as the Council of Europe's Parliamentary Assembly.

The Rome Treaty saw significant change in the powers of the Assembly. Specific provision was made for direct elections: it was no longer a matter for each member state to decide. No timetable was laid down, but the commitment to abolish the sys-tem of nominated Members was made legally binding. The Assembly was also given advisory as well as supervisory powers and thus was given its first glimpse of legislat-ive power. These two changes did not have an immediate effect. It took over twenty years for direct elections to be organized and Parliament's formal legislative powers were not altered for nearly thirty years. Nevertheless, a trajectory for further devel-opment in Parliament's powers was laid down.

Subsequent changes in Parliament's role were closely linked with other modific-ations to the EU's structure. Treaty revisions introduced in 1970 and 1975 gave the Parliament budgetary powers, including the right to reject the budget (a right it was to exercise in 1979 and 1984), to amend it within certain fixed limits, and to approve (or not) the annual accounts. The essential source of these changes was the decision to alter the basis for financing the European Community. It was agreed to move away from a system of national contributions linked to each country's gross national product (GNP) to a system of 'own resources', whereby the revenue available for fin-ancing European policies legally belonged to the Community. Under these circum-stances, there was a strong body of opinion among governments, notably the Dutch, that national parliaments could no longer exercise effective control over Community finance and that the task should be passed on to the European Parliament. Already at this stage, the idea of the EP enjoying the kind of rights at EU level traditionally exercised at national level by parliamentarians was proving difficult to resist, with sceptics faced with the task of suggesting a convincing alternative.

However, the Parliament was still composed of national parliamentarians, work-ing there on a part-time basis. The attempt to give life to the provisions of the Rome Treaty on direct elections confronted the institution with a vicious circle, well described in the Vedel report on the enlargement of Parliament's powers:

> [I]f one cannot imagine a Parliament with real powers which does not draw its mandate from direct universal suffrage, it is even more difficult to imagine the election through dir-ect universal suffrage of a Parliament without extended powers. In this way, two equally desirable objectives are making each other's implementation impossible (Vedel 1972: 59).

This dilemma persisted until the election of Valéry Giscard d'Estaing as President of France and Helmut Schmidt as West German Chancellor within five days of each other in May 1974. The subsequent Paris Summit agreed to hold direct European elections after 1978, thereby effectively resolving the dilemma posed by Vedel.

Direct elections paved the way for an extension of the Parliament's legislative powers. A critical moment was the 1980 Isoglucose judgment of the European Court of Justice. This judgment annulled a piece of Community legislation adopted by Council on the grounds that Parliament had not yet given its opinion. The Court made it clear that Council could not adopt Community legislation before receiving Parliament's opinion. Moreover, the Court made a link between the democratic character of the Community and the Parliament's right to be consulted, which the Court described as:

> the means which allow the Parliament to play an actual part in the legislative process of the Community. Such a power represents an essential factor in the institutional balance intended by the Treaty. Although limited, it reflects at Community level *the fundamental democratic principle* (emphasis added) that the peoples should take part in the exercise of power through the intermediary of a representative assembly.

The right to be more than simply consulted came with the Single European Act (SEA) which provided the Treaty base for the establishment of a single European market by 1992. To accelerate the process, member states created a new procedure, with more majority voting, under which Parliament was entitled to two readings of proposed legislation, rather than one. Moreover, providing the Commission was persuaded to back Parliament's amendments, the Council could only overrule the EP by unanimity.

The precise form of Parliament's involvement in the legislative procedure was not pre-ordained. The Vedel Report had argued against the idea that the Parliament be given the right to amend legislation and instead suggested giving it the right to say yes or no to legislation presented to it by the Council. In fact, such a power of 'assent' was granted to the Parliament in the SEA for non-legislative issues. Though restricted to the accession of new member states and the conclusion of certain agreements with non-EU countries, the Parliament was called to give its assent to international agreements thirty times within the first two years of the SEA being ratified. It subsequently was asked to vote on new accessions in 1995, 2003, and 2005.

The Maastricht Treaty ushered in a new and transformational procedure, now generally known as co-decision (though the term is not found in the treaties). It provides for joint decision-taking and direct negotiations between Parliament and Council as well as the possibility for the Parliament to reject draft legislation if such negotiations fail. Supporters of stronger EP powers argued, successfully, that with more majority voting in Council, the position of national parliaments was weakened. A greater role for the EP would improve the democratic legitimacy of EU legislation, by ensuring it had the support of European citizens as well as governments.

Maastricht also gave the EP the right to approve (or not) the Commission before it took office, extended its formal powers of control by providing for the establishment of committees of inquiry, empowered it to appoint a European Ombudsman and made formal provision for the Parliament to invite the Commission to present a legislative proposal, thereby giving it a limited form of legislative initiative. Member states thereby proved receptive to the argument that the broader agenda set for the EU at Maastricht should be matched by a reinforced role for the Parliament.

The process of parliamentarization was still only partial. The role of the Parliament in the second and third pillars (CFSP and JHA) was limited to consultation. The first pillar's provisions for EMU offered a variable role to the Parliament: no co-decision but only 'cooperation' on four articles, alongside a consultative role in the appointment of the board of the ECB. At the same time, the Treaty required the ECB President to report four times a year to the competent Parliament committee (see Chapter 9).

The ongoing process of Treaty revision was used by the Parliament to continue pressing for an expansion of its role and it did so with considerable success. Under the Amsterdam Treaty, co-decision was extended from fifteen to thirty-two Treaty legal bases and simplified to make it possible to reach agreements more quickly. This development can be partly explained by the Parliament proving more 'responsible' than some in EU national capitals had imagined or predicted it would be, readily accepting the obligations imposed by the Treaty. At the same time, the direct negotiations provided for under co-decision proved remarkably successful in facilitating agreement. As a result, more reticent member states, such as the United Kingdom and Denmark, became less nervous about extending Parliament's prerogatives and accepting the arguments of those, such as Germany, who argued that its powers needed to be expanded to increase the democratic legitimacy of the Union.

Amsterdam also legitimized existing practice by giving Parliament the formal right to approve the European Council's nominee as Commission President. Thus by 1999 the Parliament possessed a set of rights to influence the nomination of the Commission which complemented the power of dismissal that originated in the ECSC Treaty, nearly fifty years earlier.

The negotiations over the Nice Treaty were dominated by the dispute over the relative weight of member states in the Council and Commission in an enlarged Union, with a related but less central argument about the number of seats each member state should have in the Parliament. However, there was agreement to extend co-decision (slightly) to thirty-seven Treaty legal bases, with the possibility of limited further extension thereafter by unanimous Council decision. This extension, agreed in November 2004, applies to parts of the JHA pillar that had been explicitly excluded from the scope of co-decision under Maastricht.

In the meantime, the position of the Parliament was subject to major debate and revision in the course of the European Convention (see Chapter 2) and the subsequent IGC that agreed the Constitutional Treaty in June 2004. The most significant change for the Parliament was the effective acceptance of the link between qualified-majority voting in the Council and the application of co-decision. The procedure was extended to ninety legal bases, including the common agricultural and fisheries policies, the common commercial policy and JHA. The centrality of this way of making EU laws was recognized by calling it the 'ordinary legislative procedure'.

Hence the crisis over the ratification of the Constitutional Treaty represented a major brake on the Parliament's ambitions as a legislator. Further widening of co-decision cannot take place without a revision of the Treaties. On the other hand, the proposal in the Constitutional Treaty that the Commission President be elected by the Parliament on the basis of a European Council proposal, 'taking into account the elections to the European Parliament and after having held the appropriate consultations' does not require Treaty revision. It would not give the Parliament the right to elect the Commission President on its own but would mean that the suitability of a candidate could be judged in the light of the political composition of the Parliament after direct elections. Such a link was effectively established in 2004 when the largest group in the Parliament argued successfully that the new President should come from a party represented in its ranks, thereby establishing a precedent that may prove as significant as the formal provisions of the Treaty. Nevertheless, the crisis over the Constitutional Treaty has halted the regular expansion of the Parliament's powers and reopened the question of how the democratic credentials of the EU can be reinforced.

Aggregating interests

It is one thing to be granted significant powers; it is another to use them effectively. More than any other EU institution, the Parliament faces difficulties in aggregating interests in an extraordinarily heterogeneous environment. Before the first direct EP elections there were 198 MEPs, from nine states; by 2004 the number of members had more than tripled to 732, from twenty-five states, with the prospect of two more member states joining by 2007–08.

How can such a large, heterogeneous institution take effective decisions? The European Parliament does not contain a government, and cannot rely on those parliamentarians who belong to the party or parties of a government to ensure that a particular political programme is enacted. What it does have are established leadership structures designed to manage the centrifugal forces at work within it. It elects a President every two-and-a-half years whose task it is to chair the plenary (with the help of fourteen Vice-Presidents), to represent the institution *vis-à-vis* other institutions and the outside world, and to oversee the Parliament's internal functioning. The President also chairs two leadership bodies, the Conference of Presidents and the Bureau. The former, composed of the chairs of all the political groups, agrees, *inter alia*, the draft agenda of plenary sessions, settles conflicts of competence between committees and determines whether or not to send delegations outside the EU. The latter, composed of the Parliament's fourteen Vice-Presidents, deals with internal financial, organizational and administrative matters.

The Parliament's leadership structures ensure that it functions properly but do not guarantee that the institution can use its powers effectively in influencing policy. In fact the EP is very successful in overcoming the clash between efficiency and diversity. It succeeded, for example, in negotiating agreements with Council on more than eighty, often controversial, conciliation procedures under co-decision between 1999 and 2004. Only relatively rarely does it fail to adopt a position for lack of any clear majority, as, for example, on the Iraq war, when divisions present across European society were reflected in the EP itself.

Table 6.2 Composition of the EP in a Union with 27 member states

A	B	C	D	E	F
Germany	82,038	17.1	99	99	829,000
United Kingdom	59,247	12.3	78	72	823,000
France	58,966	12.3	78	72	819,000
Italy	57,612	12.0	78	72	800,000
Spain	39,394	8.2	54	50	788,000
Poland	38,667	8.0	54	50	773,000
Romania	22,489	4.7	—	33	681,000
Netherlands	15,760	3.3	27	25	630,000
Greece	10,533	2.2	24	22	479,000
Czech Republic	10,290	2.1	24	22	468,000
Belgium	10,213	2.1	24	22	464,000
Hungary	10,092	2.1	24	22	459,000
Portugal	9,980	2.1	24	22	454,000
Sweden	8,854	1.8	19	18	492,000
Bulgaria	8,230	1.7	—	17	484,000
Austria	8,082	1.7	18	17	475,000
Slovakia	5,393	1.1	14	13	415,000
Denmark	5,313	1.1	14	13	409,000
Finland	5,160	1.1	14	13	397,000
Ireland	3,744	0.8	13	12	312,000
Lithuania	3,701	0.8	13	12	308,000
Latvia	2,439	0.5	9	8	305,000
Slovenia	1,978	0.4	7	7	283,000
Estonia	1,446	0.3	6	6	241,000
Cyprus	752	0.2	6	6	125,000
Luxembourg	429	0.1	6	6	72,000
Malta	379	0.1	5	5	76,000
Total EU 27	481,181	100.00	732	736	657,000

Note: A: Member states.
B: Population (thousands).
C: Population of each member state as a percentage of total EU population.
D: Seats per member state at present (2006).
E: Seats per member state under Nice Treaty (from 2009).
F: Number of inhabitants represented by each MEP in each member state under the Treaty of Nice provisions.

Political groups

The key agents in the aggregation of interests are the EP's political groups (see also Chapter 15). Since 1952, Members have sat not in national groups but in groups created to reflect shared political affiliation. This structure serves to counteract the logic of the Council where political differences are constructed on national lines. It is also a structure that has proved remarkably stable with members from new member states normally being assimilated into existing groups rather than forming completely new ones. In 2005 there were seven political groups, only one more than in 1979 before direct elections.

Within the group structure there is a mix of competition and cooperation. On the one hand, there is evidence of high levels of group cohesion, with members eager to find agreement with their colleagues in the same group. Hix (2002) has drawn attention to the substantial increase in left–right competition in the EP. He has shown that party allegiance is much more important than nationality in determining how members vote and that members vote the party line more often than, for example, legislators in the United States. This pattern has continued in the Parliament after the 2004 elections. The addition of members from ten new member states has not served to undermine significantly the coherence of groups, despite occasional calls for MEPs from one country to act together to defend the national interest. For example, the Hungarian Prime Minister, Peter Medgyessy, proposed unsuccessfully that there be a single list of MEPs from Hungary at the 2004 European elections to act together in the Parliament. In practice, being a member of a group encourages all to follow the group line in most circumstances.

The obligations imposed by the treaties also create strong incentives for groups to find agreement across party lines. To reject or adopt amendments to the Council's draft budget or to its common position at second reading under the co-decision procedure, to give assent, to approve the accession of new member states, or to adopt a motion of censure on the Commission all require an absolute majority in favour (at present 367) for the Parliament's voice to be heard. No group has anything approaching such a majority: the largest group, EPP–ED, is still at least 100 votes short, even with all its members voting. Thus a strong bargaining culture between the groups has evolved. For some, this development is to be regretted. As two former MEPs have commented, 'political argument is usually displaced by detailed horse-trading to secure the widest possible cross-party support for a given position or set of amendments' (Clegg and van Hulten, 2003: 14). Alternatively, this practice can be seen as an effective way of aggregating interests and perhaps the only way of ensuring the Parliament significant influence in the policy process.

The committee system

Most of the detailed work of the EP is conducted within twenty policy-specialized committees, whose political composition broadly reflects that of Parliament as a whole. These committees enjoy a high level of autonomy under the Parliament's rules. All legislative proposals are referred directly, without debate, from the plenary to one of the committees, which then organizes the examination of a proposal before

it returns to the plenary for a vote. Only one committee can be responsible for a proposal and only its amendments can be considered in plenary; other committees can
table amendments in the responsible committee but do not get a second chance in
plenary. The responsible committee appoints a *rapporteur* who follows a legislative
proposal from its inception to the conclusion of the procedure. On the basis of the
work of the *rapporteur* the committee comes to adopt a position that will normally
prevail in the plenary, unless the members of the committee are unable to overcome
their own differences and the vote on a proposal is very close.

The committees provide an effective mechanism for finding agreement across
political groups but they also embody two other important features that differentiate
the Parliament from the Council. First, all committee meetings are, and since 1999
must be, held in public. The Parliament has traditionally offered a contrast between
its own way of operating and the often less transparent mechanisms of the Council. The result can be very full meeting rooms with all those who wish to influence
the shape of proposals—lobbyists, national governments or officials from the Council Secretariat—free to observe the evolution of debate. Second, the detailed work in
the committees provides an opportunity for those interests that fail to win the argument in the Council or the Commission to have a second chance. The fact that the
Parliament does not mirror the majorities in the Council, with opposition parties often making up the largest number of MEPs from a member state, means that such
efforts to influence policy may have a reasonable chance of succeeding. In both respects, the Parliament offers a distinctive model for reaching political agreement at
EU level.

The 2004 enlargement has undoubtedly challenged this model. The introduction
of ten new languages has posed extraordinarily difficult logistical problems for an
institution committed more than any other to multilingualism. The shortage of suit-
ably qualified translators and interpreters—particularly for smaller new languages
such as Maltese—has obliged committees to share scarce resources and obliged some
members to work some of the time in a foreign language. The difficulty has been mitigated by the high linguistic competence of many members from new member states.
Still there is growing uncertainty about the practical limits of the existing system in
the face of future enlargements.

Exercising influence

To look at what the Parliament is doing on a day-to-day basis is to be confronted with
a bewildering array of reports, debates, and questions. To identify the importance
of the Parliament's role, it is useful to distinguish between history-making, policy-
making and policy-implementing decisions (following with slight variation, Peterson
and Bomberg 1999). Using this distinction one can establish that the Parliament is
more likely to have an effect on outcomes at the level of policy-making than in
history-making and policy-implementing decisions.

History-making decisions

Most of the major decisions in the European Union are taken at the level of the European Council (see Chapter 3). In this framework the Parliament is an outsider: it is not present in European Council meetings except for the relatively brief appearance of its President at the start of the proceedings. It does not have the formal right to say yes or no to the outcome of an IGC, ultimately determined by the European Council. Despite repeated calls to be given such a right of assent, including during the European Convention, ratification of the results of an IGC is a purely national affair, determined by parliamentary vote and/or referendum.

Two powers of decision given to the Parliament after the European Council has taken its decision can be described as history-making ones. As we have seen, the Parliament has the right since Amsterdam to approve the candidate proposed by the European Council as President of the Commission. It also has to give its assent to the accession of new member states. The possibility of the Parliament not approving a Commission President cannot be ignored. In 1994 Jacques Santer was approved by a majority of only twenty-two, despite very heavy lobbying by national governments. After the decision at Nice that the President of the Commission be chosen in the European Council by qualified majority, the opportunity for the Parliament to influence the choice has grown. As suggested earlier, the largest group in the Parliament is likely to press for a candidate from its ranks to be chosen.

Regarding the accession of new member states, the right of assent grows in importance as the number of potential applicants continues to increase. It is a right that is perhaps most empowering during accession negotiations when the Parliament can influence individual issues and try to shape the overall debate. Already in December 2004 Parliament's vote in favour of opening negotiations with Turkey 'without undue delay' (407 votes in favour, 262 against, and 29 abstentions) gave a sense of the balance of political opinion across Europe and paved the way for the formal decisions of the European Council later the same week. Hence the Parliament can influence some history-making decisions but its role is undoubtedly more restricted than it is on policy-making decisions.

Policy-making decisions

The Maastricht agreement on the co-decision procedure established the principle of the Parliament as a joint legislator with the Council in a limited number of areas. As we have seen, the Constitutional Treaty provides the opportunity for the renamed 'ordinary legislative procedure' to apply in future to all areas of policy, with the exception of proposals involving taxation or the revenue sources of the Union.

The overall shape of the procedure and the possibilities it offers are presented in Figure 6.1. Two central features should be underlined:

- first, the EP and the Council have two readings of legislation. If the Council cannot accept the amendments presented by the Parliament at its second reading, the two institutions have to meet in a conciliation committee whose job it is to find an agreement by a process of negotiation. Neither can tell the other one what to do at this stage;

Figure 6.1 The co-decision procedure

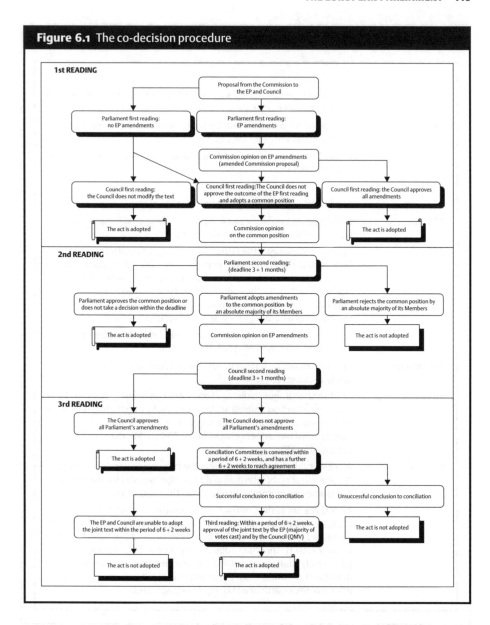

- second, not only are the negotiations subject to time pressure—they have to be concluded in a maximum of eight weeks—but failure to agree in conciliation brings the procedure to an end. Such a prospect necessarily concentrates the minds of the negotiators.

The behaviour of the two institutions under co-decision is illustrated in Exhibit 6.1, a chronology of the directive on railway liberalization. It shows how additional institutional arrangements have been developed to make the procedure work better, notably tripartite meetings, known as trialogues, which bring together representatives

Exhibit 6.1 Railway liberalization package under conciliation — a chronology

2003

23 October — At second reading EP adopts 73 amendments to the four proposals of the Second Railway Package

19 November — EP delegation to Conciliation Committee is constituted and appoints six negotiators to meet the Council

22 December — Council adopts its second reading announcing it is unable to approve all EP amendments

2004

13 January — At a first trialogue the negotiators meet the chair of Coreper I

15 January — EP delegation establishes an initial negotiating position and notes agreement on one of the four directives

27 January — At a second trialogue the EP negotiators meet the Irish Transport Minister and the Commissioner responsible. They draw particular attention to the composition of the board of the European Railways Agency; the date for the liberalisation of national and international rail freight services and of international passenger services; and the setting-up of a European railway safety system

After three hours of discussion at the first Conciliation Committee, agreement is reached on 44 of 73 amendments.

18 February — At a third trialogue further progress is made regarding new national safety measures.

10 March — At a fourth trialogue Parliament proposes compromise texts for 13 of the 21 outstanding amendments. Later, the EP negotiators present to their delegation a compromise suggesting liberalization of international passenger services from 2010 (rather than 2008 as proposed by EP)

16 March — At a fifth trialogue Council accepts the compromise texts relating to the liberalization of international passenger services from 2010 and offers a new compromise in relation to the composition of the board

After three hours the Conciliation Committee reaches agreement on the last outstanding questions: international freight services are to be liberalized from 1 January 2006 and national freight services from 1 January 2007 (rather than 2006 as proposed by EP); EP accepts (reluctantly) that the board should have one member from each member state subject to a Commission commitment to a general reform of the boards of all EU regulatory agencies.

of the Council (in particular, the Presidency), the Commission, and EP. Nowhere are such meetings referred to in the Treaties but they have become a regular feature of all conciliations. Many fewer people attend than at the full conciliation committee where there can be over 100 people in the room. There are usually no more than thirty, with speakers normally restricted to three members of the Parliament delegation, the Deputy Permanent Representative of the member state holding the Council Presidency (most matters in conciliation fall under the responsibility of

Coreper I—see Chapter 14) and a Director or Director-General of the Commission. The major negotiations on the railway package took place in trialogues, with the various compromises first being aired in these meetings. More generally, this example shows that a real negotiation took place with both sides giving ground in the interests of moving towards an overall agreement.

The railway liberalization example is not atypical. In conciliation a high percentage of Parliamentary amendments at second reading are usually either accepted as they stand or in a compromise form more or less favourable to the Parliament (European Parliament, 2004: 13). The procedure has created a new environment where the Council takes the views of the Parliament seriously and is open to modifying its initial position.

The close relationship between Council and Parliament extends beyond the conciliation procedure itself. After Amsterdam, the two institutions increased their cooperation on legislative dossiers to such an extent that it was possible to find agreements at first reading in almost 30 per cent of cases and at second reading in almost half of the 403 proposals dealt with under co-decision between 1999 and 2004. This level of cooperation was only possible because both institutions recognized the need and usefulness of negotiating earlier in the legislative process as a way of avoiding the heavy burden of conciliation. A more specialized form of cooperation has also emerged in the period after the adoption of legislation, with both institutions obliged to join forces to defend the results of co-decisions if they are challenged in the Court of Justice.[1]

This reinforced level of cooperation between Parliament and Council has had two important consequences. First, it has enhanced the institutional status of the Parliament. In particular, co-decision reduces the role of the Commission as the privileged interlocutor of the Council. The Commission no longer can withdraw its proposal once conciliation has begun and is restricted to the often vital but nevertheless circumscribed task of seeking to reconcile the positions of the other two institutions. Second, the Parliament starts to be seen as sharing responsibility in changing the shape of laws that affect all European citizens. Slowly, it is becoming clearer that legislation is not simply a product of agreement within the Council. Parliament can and does alter policy outcomes in significant ways.

Policy-implementing decisions

The implementation of Community policies involves thousands of individual decisions in any one year. No parliamentary body can hope to follow all these decisions in detail. However, the EP has consistently pressed for scrutiny rights equivalent to those of the Council over the implementing bodies, known as comitology committees, that are chaired by the Commission and bring together representatives of all the member states. The EP has consistently argued that it should be informed about the work of these committees and should have the opportunity to block draft decisions with which it disagrees.

This argument became more intense after co-decision was introduced. With the Council able to block draft comitology decisions and take an implementing decision itself, the legislative parity of the two branches in policy making clearly did not

extend to policy implementation. The Council claimed that its role in policy implementation related to its executive functions and that it therefore was in a different
position from the EP. Nevertheless, it was willing to discuss the issue and in 1999 a
new comitology decision was adopted. As a result the Parliament received more information and was given the right to request re-examination of measures adopted
under co-decision if the committee was suspected of acting beyond its powers or *ultra
vires* (Corbett *et al.* 2005: 290).

The debate about comitology may seem arcane but it raises essential questions
about the openness and accountability of the EU system. The decisions are not simply
technical: in the early 1990s, for example, the level of controls needed to stop the
spread of BSE was decided in a comitology committee, the Veterinary Committee.
All such decisions are taken very far from the public gaze, remaining in the hands of
the Commission and national experts. Advocating a more powerful role for the Parliament was designed therefore to improve the transparency of the system. Member
state governments effectively accepted such criticisms and agreed in the Constitutional Treaty to give Parliament effective parity with the Council in the comitology
structure. However, such a reinforced role remains in the future. For the time being,
Parliament exercises considerably less influence over policy-implementing decisions
than it does over policy-making.

The Parliament and the democratic deficit

The crisis provoked by the 'No' votes in the referenda in France and the Netherlands
in May and June 2005 was particularly keenly felt in the Parliament. The Parliament
had championed the Convention as an original and better way of preparing an IGC. It
had achieved equal status with the Council for virtually all EU legislation. And it had
voted by a very large majority in favour of the results of the IGC. For the first time in
its history its acquisition of broader powers was blocked.

Critical outsiders suggested that there was a wider lesson to be learnt. *The Economist*
suggested that the referenda results 'cruelly exposed the fantasy that the EP is the
answer to the disconnect between political elites and ordinary citizens'. It contrasted
unfavourably the turnout in France and the Netherlands for the referenda (70 and 63
per cent respectively) with the much lower figures in the 2004 European elections
(see Table 6.3 below).[2]

The disappointment felt in much of the Parliament and the undisguised glee of
some of its critics reflected very different perspectives on the nature of the European
Union and the possibilities for closing the 'democratic deficit'. At least three such
perspectives can be identified, each offering a different remedy for the democratic
failings of the EU. Yet all share the idea that the structure of the institutions is not a
technical question but one with political values at its core. In this sense the French
and Dutch referendum results brought into the open a debate that had remained half-
hidden.

A first perspective is often referred to as the 'no demos' thesis. It suggests that
democracy is a chimera outside the national context because the peoples of Europe

are not bound together in the same way as national communities with common histories and cultures (Siedentop 2000). If there is no European *demos*, there can be no democracy at European level. From this point of view, the European Parliament can only be an expensive irrelevance.

The most militant advocates of this point of view do not look for a solution within the structures of the Union: they would rather return to the kind of non-binding international cooperation found in the Council of Europe. Milder versions of the thesis accept the existence of the EU institutions but would look to reinforcing significantly the role of national parliaments. There were strong voices, for example, before and during the Convention in favour of this approach. Joschka Fischer, then German Foreign Minister, and Tony Blair both argued in 2000 that the European Parliament should have two chambers, one made up of directly elected members and the other of members of national parliaments.

For the moment these arguments have not prevailed. The Constitutional Treaty did reinforce the role of national parliaments in checking for respect of the principle of subsidiarity, but without creating a second parliamentary chamber at European level. There continues to be great reticence against creating such a new institution that would be likely to face the same kind of organizational and political weaknesses that confronted the European Parliament before direct elections as well as making the European structure still more difficult to understand.

A second perspective suggests that the EU system needs to be less consensual and more politicised to become democratic. On this view the 'EU will only be democratic if European elections are fought by cohesive Euro-parties which present rival agendas for EU policy action, the winning parties form the executive and the parties act cohesively to ensure that their office-holders implement their electoral programme' (Hix 1998: 20).

Such a vision of the future corresponds to the classic parliamentary model found in all EU member states. It can be seen as a natural development from the existing structure of Parliament's powers. However, it is hard to believe that the EU will ever reproduce the national model (Shackleton 2005). For example, the right of censure over the Commission is 'more similar to the power of the US Congress to impeach the American President than to the power of a parliamentary majority to withdraw the support of the government' (Hix 1998: 25–6). Thus when the Commission resigned in 1999 in anticipation of a vote of censure, it did so not because of differences over policy direction, but rather as a result of charges of incompetence and maladministration. To censure a Commission on a question of policy seems an unlikely prospect given the absolute majority required, a much higher figure than can be achieved by any one party in the Parliament.

Similar obstacles stand in the way of applying party logic to the appointment of the Commission President. It has been suggested that a direct link could be created between European citizens and the Parliament, if each European political family nominated a candidate for President of the European Commission in advance of the EP elections (Clegg and van Hulten 2003: 26). Such an apparently attractive arrangement faces major obstacles. It is hard to see national political party structures being willing to accept such nominations, which would weaken their control of the electoral process. Moreover, there would be a marked tension between candidates nominated by European political parties and those nominated by the European Council.

In the event of a dispute between the two bodies, it is not clear that the Parliament would be victorious. In 1994, as already pointed out, when many in the Parliament were unhappy with the nomination of Jacques Santer as Commission President, pressure exercised by national governments succeeded in ensuring that the choice of the European Council prevailed.

Moreover, there is the broader issue of the relationship between Parliament and Commission. As Magnette (2001: 308) has pointed out, 'the Commission is not subordinate to a parliamentary majority that can *sanction* it, but rather scrutinized by MEPs who can only try to *influence* it. The pyramidal and hierarchic structure of the parliamentary state is replaced, here, by horizontal relations of mutual control' (Magnette 2001: 308). Parliament itself has always wanted to uphold the role of the Commission as a separate institution. It has, for example, consistently supported the Commission's right of legislative initiative and not sought to acquire such a right for itself.

Last but not least, the Commission is not an executive in the same sense as a national government is. Executive roles in the EU are split, a tendency accentuated in the Constitutional Treaty, envisaging the formal creation of a post of President of the European Council to be filled every two-and-a-half years. Whatever that person's mandate and relationship with the Commission President might be (assuming the post is ever created), it is difficult to imagine the creation of traditional mechanisms of parliamentary control and accountability applying to him or her. Parliament can only ever hope to have very partial control over the executive at European level.

A third, different narrative sees the democratic credentials of the Union being grounded not by means of a parliamentary majority but rather through the development of a representative system engaged in the search for compromise among competing interests. Such a system would be embodied in a fully bicameral legislature, with the Council representing the member states and the Parliament, the European electorate.

In practice, most EU governments have been persuaded that such a system can be gradually developed at European level as an embodiment of the democratic principle that government should derive its legitimacy from the people (Costa and Magnette, 2003). The Isoglucose judgment referred to earlier provided the underpinnings for the subsequent development of legislative co-decision. The procedure has already changed the behaviour of both Parliament and Council, converting the Parliament into a 'bargaining' body, engaged with Council in the slow process of creating a new legislative culture (Shackleton 2003). If the legislative provisions of the Constitutional Treaty do eventually come into force, the result would be a Parliament that looks much more like a legislature than a chamber for debate, thus prompting comparison with the US Congress (particularly the House of Representatives) and offering a clear contrast with its national counterparts in Europe.

One argument in support of such arrangements would be that it would reinforce the delicate balance between a remarkably wide variety of interests, with all able to identify with one or other part of a divided system of government. The introduction of a logic of partisanship, based on the decisions of a political majority within a parliamentary government, would severely test such a balance. Those who argue that there is no *demos* at European level are right to point to a limited sense of belonging in the EU. Without such a sense of belonging it is very hard to envisage a political system at European level deriving its legitimacy from majority decisions adopted on

Table 6.3 Turn-out in European Parliament elections

	1979	1981	1984	1987	1989	1994	1995	1996	1999	2004
EU	63.0	—	61.0	—	58.5	56.8	—	—	49.4	45.7
Belgium	91.6	—	92.2	—	90.7	90.7	—	—	90.0	90.8
Luxembourg	88.9	—	87.0	—	87.4	88.5	—	—	85.8	89.0
Malta	—	—	—	—	—	—	—	—	—	82.4
Italy	85.5	—	83.9	—	81.5	74.8	—	—	70.8	73.1
Cyprus	—	—	—	—	—	—	—	—	—	71.2
Greece	—	78.6	77.2	—	79.9	71.2	—	—	70.2	63.4
Ireland	63.6	—	47.6	—	68.3	44.0	—	—	50.5	58.8
Lithuania	—	—	—	—	—	—	—	—	—	48.4
Denmark	47.1	—	52.3	—	46.1	52.9	—	—	50.4	47.9
Spain	—	—	—	68.9	54.8	59.1	—	—	64.4	45.1
Germany	65.7	—	56.8	—	62.4	60.0	—	—	45.2	43.0
Austria	—	—	—	—	—	—	—	67.7	49.0	42.4
France	60.7	—	56.7	—	48.7	52.7	—	—	47.0	42.8
Latvia	—	—	—	—	—	—	—	—	—	41.3
Finland	—	—	—	—	—	—	—	60.3	30.1	39.4
Netherlands	57.8	—	50.5	—	47.2	35.7	—	—	29.9	39.3
UK	31.6	—	32.6	—	36.2	36.4	—	—	24.0	38.8
Portugal	—	—	—	72.2	51.1	35.5	—	—	40.4	38.6
Hungary	—	—	—	—	—	—	—	—	—	38.5
Sweden	—	—	—	—	—	—	41.6	—	38.3	37.8
Czech Republic	—	—	—	—	—	—	—	—	—	28.3
Slovenia	—	—	—	—	—	—	—	—	—	28.3
Estonia	—	—	—	—	—	—	—	—	—	26.8
Poland	—	—	—	—	—	—	—	—	—	20.9
Slovakia	—	—	—	—	—	—	—	—	—	17.0

the basis of the programme of one political family. EU institutions reflect a general resistance to the centralisation of power, a resistance reflected in the kind of role that the Parliament plays. The EP cannot initiate legislation and it cannot decide the contents of legislation alone: power and influence are spread across the institutions.

What then of turnouts in European elections? It is one of the ironies of recent years that the steady growth in the powers of the institution has been matched by a steady decrease in the level of participation in European elections. In the 2004 direct elections, as Table 6.3 shows, the average level of turnout fell for the sixth time running, with increases in seven countries more than outweighed by very big drops in turnout in one country (Spain) and particularly poor turnout in most of the new member states, with Slovakia marking the lowest figure (17 per cent) for any country at any time since the introduction of direct elections.

And yet should this tendency be any surprise given the second order nature of the event? Even with all the powers foreseen in the Constitutional Treaty, the legislature at EU level would continue to operate within a much narrower sphere than the United States Congress. Most of the political issues that affect European citizens directly, such as health care, education or taxation, continue to be discussed and decided at national level. MEPs are unlikely ever to have the kind of powers enjoyed by members of Congress in influencing the location of government investment in their constituencies. More generally, the collective character of decisions in the EU makes it difficult for voters to identify whom to reward or punish for particular policy outcomes when they participate in European elections.

At the same time, the tough arguments over the Constitutional Treaty and the growing debate about the future membership of the Union underline the fact that there is no longer what can be described as a 'permissive consensus'. National executives are not free to act as if the European dimension was an intergovernmental affair, a matter for political elites, beyond the reach of democratic debate. And no such debate can avoid a choice between the three perspectives presented here, each with their different visions of the kind of European Parliament that is both possible and desirable.

Conclusions

This chapter has pointed to four general insights into the workings of the Parliament. First, it has shown the power of the democratic idea as driving change in the Parliament's powers. Governments have found it extremely difficult (until now at least) to resist an increase in the role of the EP, as they could not easily formulate an alternative for addressing the democratic deficit. Such ideas have to be integrated into an explanation of institutional change: the separate interests of the participants are not sufficient to do the job.

Second, it has suggested that the shape of the institutions is 'path dependent', and heavily influenced by earlier decisions. Direct elections can be traced back to the provisions of the ECSC Treaty in the early 1950s. Similarly, the establishment of co-decision in the Maastricht Treaty established a trajectory for the Parliament to become one branch of a bicameral legislature.

Third, this chapter has contested the notion that major decisions in the EU are taken exclusively by governments. The Parliament has been able to use its legislative powers to alter the shape of outcomes sought by the Council and has started to exercise influence over the choice of the Commission President, as well as the shape of the Commission. Such developments are difficult to reconcile with a purely inter-governmentalist perspective.

Finally, we have stressed the importance of consensus mechanisms, within the Parliament as well as between it and the other institutions. The result is the spreading of responsibility to ensure that support for policy change is broad amongst a very diverse set of competing interests. Democracy in the EU seems unlikely to develop on the basis of the same kind of majoritarian processes as exist at national level.

Notes

1 Of the dozen or so cases brought so far, the two institutions have only lost one: in October 2000 the Court struck down the directive on the advertising and sponsorship of tobacco that the German government — outvoted in the Council — had challenged (see Chapter 7).

2 *Economist* (2005).

Further reading

There is a growing range of books and articles on the European Parliament. Corbett, Jacobs, and Shackleton (2005) is now in its sixth edition and provides a detailed account of the internal workings of the institution. Judge and Earnshaw (2003) place the role of the Parliament in a wider perspective considering its formal and informal influence as well as its effectiveness as a representative body. Corbett (1998) offers a more historical account of how the institution consciously set out to develop its powers during the 1980s and 1990s, and it can be compared with the Vedel Report (1972) which looked forward to an unknown future for the institution. Rittberger (2005) offers an in-depth analysis of the reasons why governments have been willing to delegate powers to the institution. Kreppel (2002) looks at the increasing legislative role of the institution through the development of the party group structures.

Corbett, R. (1998), *The European Parliament's Role in Closer Integration* (Basingstoke: Palgrave).

Corbett, R., Jacobs, F., and Shackleton, M. (2005), *The European Parliament*, 6th edn., (London: John Harper).

Judge, D., and Earnshaw, D. (2003), *The European Parliament* (London: Palgrave Macmillan)

Kreppel, A. (2002), *The European Parliament and Supranational Party System* (Cambridge: Cambridge University Press)

Rittberger, B. (2005), *Building Europe's Parliament: Democratic Representation beyond the*

Nation State (Oxford: Oxford University Press).

Vedel, G. (1972), *Report of the Working Party examining the problem of the Enlargement of* *the Powers of the European Parliament ('Vedel Report')* (Brussels: Bulletin of the European Communities, Supplement 4/72).

Web links

The Parliament website *(http://europarl.eu.int)* provides up-to-date material on the workings of the institution. It is divided into five sections, looking at what is happening in the Parliament at the moment, what the Parliament is and how it is structured, what the Parliament produces (reports, amendments, minutes, records of debates etc.), who the members of the Parliament are, and an on-line video link to parliamentary debates. In each section there are three levels of information, the first geared to the general reader, the second intended for the specialist and the third providing archive material.

Chapter 7

The European Court of Justice

Tom Kennedy[1]

Contents

Summary

In a quiet and generally low-profile way, the European Court of Justice has made an essential contribution to European integration. It has made clear that the European Community legal order does not simply establish rules between states but confers rights upon their citizens, and operates within the legal and economic systems of the states. It has identified the treaties as constituting a 'constitutional charter of a Community based upon the rule of law' and has defined the extent of and limits to the powers of the other institutions. It has ensured that the aims of the treaties have become a legal reality and not merely rhetorical declarations. This is particularly the case for the four economic freedoms of the single market—the free movement of goods, persons, services and capital—and the application of the rules of fair competition.

The Court of Justice and the rule of law

The inclusion of an independent judicial authority in the European Community's institutional structure was an integral part of the design of the organization from its inception as the European Coal and Steel Community in 1951. The intent was not only to enforce a separation of powers between the EU institutions and between them and its member states, but also to bind together the economies of the nation-states of Europe, with the hope of ensuring lasting peace. The disastrous consequences of the comprehensive violation of the principle of the rule of law during and prior to the Second World War were fresh in the minds of the drafters of the Treaty of Paris.

All six of the original member states belonged to a legal and constitutional tradition in which administrative authority, such as that which would be exercised over the coal and steel industries by the proposed High Authority, was subject to judicial review. In his famous declaration of 9 May 1950 Robert Schuman himself said that 'appropriate measures will ensure that there are means of appeal which may be necessary against the decisions of the High Authority'. Following the 1955 Messina Conference a report to the foreign ministers of the six member states also emphasized the necessity of legal control as being one of the principles upon which the new European Economic Community should be based.

Today, the Court's task is far wider than that of simply ensuring administrative compliance with the rules of the treaties. It is at the heart of an autonomous legal system whose purpose is to ensure that the obligations undertaken by the member states are fulfilled, and that the institutions exercise their respective powers without encroaching on those of the others or those of the member states. The Court also ensures that the rights of individuals and undertakings (firms and other economic and social actors) are respected, and that the treaties and the laws made under their authority are applied uniformly. What most distinguishes the European Communities from all previous models of international cooperation is its system of law, and its obligatory system of enforcement of treaty obligations.

It also distinguishes the European Communities from the European Union. The Maastricht Treaty effectively excluded the Court from exercising its jurisdiction in relation to the EU's second and third pillars. Thus, the full title of the institution is still the 'Court of Justice of the European Communities', and the remainder of this chapter refers to 'Community law'.

The judicial architecture

This expression is widely used to describe the Community judicial system. It includes the courts themselves and the relationships between them, their membership and their internal organization. The Court of Justice is one of the institutions named in Article 7 of the EC Treaty as being responsible for carrying out the tasks of the Community. Confusingly, one of the three courts of which the institution is now

---

Exhibit 7.1 Other European courts

The European Court of Justice in Luxembourg is frequently confused with the **European Court of Human Rights**, based in Strasbourg, or with the **International Court of Justice** in The Hague. The former was established by the Council of Europe to ensure observance of the European Convention on Human Rights and Fundamental Freedoms, while the latter is one of the principal organs of the United Nations and deals with disputes on questions of international law that are submitted to it by the States concerned. The ECJ should also be distinguished from the **European Court of Auditors** (see Chapter 11), whose headquarters are next door in Luxembourg, but which is not a judicial body.

---

constituted is also called the Court of Justice, the others being the Court of First Instance (CFI) and the European Union Civil Service Tribunal (CST). If the Constitutional Treaty were ratified, the institution would become known as the Court of Justice of the European Union. It would include the Court of Justice, the General Court (presently the CFI) and specialised courts such as the CST. The description that follows presents the institution as it appears since the entry into force of the Treaty of Nice and the accession of ten new member states in 2004. The term 'Court of Justice' will be used to refer to the institution as a whole, while 'ECJ' will refer to the higher instance and 'CFI' to the lower.

The courts

From 1957 until 1989 (when the CFI was created) the ECJ was a single-tier judiciary with no possibility of appeal against its decisions. In that respect it was similar to the International Court of Justice (see Exhibit 7.1) but differed from national supreme courts, which generally sit at the pinnacle of a hierarchical structure of lower appellate courts and courts of first instance. Partly to compensate for the existence of only one round of judicial review and the lack of an appeals system, the ECJ includes Advocates-General as well as judges, who provide an additional level of judicial review but have no power to resolve a case (see Exhibit 7.2 below).

The Court of Justice expanded as the EU enlarged. Thus, following the accession of Spain and Portugal, it was composed of thirteen judges and six Advocates-General. However by the mid-1980s it was apparent that the 'one-stop shop' model was insufficient given the needs of an enlarging Community. It was not simply a question of dealing with the management issues arising from the dramatic growth in the ECJ's workload, a tendency that has continued since; as Table 7.1 indicates. Of even greater concern was the increasing length of time necessary to settle cases and in particular, to respond to questions referred by national courts for preliminary rulings. In 1975 a preliminary ruling was given within six months on average, but by 1988 the time taken had risen to 17.5 months. The worry was not only about the delays themselves but the risk of discouraging national courts from referring appropriate cases, hence putting at risk the unity of Community law.

As a result, the Court requested that the member states amend the founding treaties by enabling the Council to attach to the Court of Justice a new court. It would have jurisdiction to decide, at first instance, certain categories of case brought by natural

Table 7.1 Workload of the ECJ and CFI

Year	Member states	Court of Justice — Cases lodged — Direct actions and appeals — Staff cases	Court of Justice — Cases lodged — Direct actions and appeals — Total[iii]	Court of Justice — Cases lodged — Preliminary rulings	Court of Justice — Total	Court of Justice — Judgments[i]	Court of Justice — Cases pending as at 31.12	Court of First Instance — Cases lodged — Direct actions	Court of First Instance — Cases lodged — Staff cases	Court of First Instance — Cases completed	Court of First Instance — Cases pending as at 31.12
1970	EUR 6	35	47	32	79	64	n/a				
1973	EUR 9	100	131	61	192	80	n/a				
1975		26	62	69	131	78	n/a				
1980		116	180	99	279	132	328		The Court of First Instance was established in 1989		
1981	EUR 10	94	214	108	322	128	441				
1985		65	294	139	433	211	574				
1986	EUR 12	57	238	91	329	174	592				
1990		—[iii]	237	141	378	193	583	59	43	82	145
1995	EUR 15	–	157	251	408	172	508	253	79	265	616
2000		–	278	224	502	273	873	398	111	343	786
2001		–	266	237	503	244	943	345	110	340	792
2002		–	254	216	470	269	907	411	112	331	872
2003		–	346	210	556	308	974	466	124	339	999
2004	EUR 25	–	278	249	527	375	840	536	146	361	1174
2005		–	246	221	467	362	740	469	151	610[iv]	1033

(*Source:* Annual Reports of the European Court of Justice.)

Note: [i] This figure does not show the total number of cases completed.
[ii] Including staff cases until 1998.
[iii] After the establishment of the Court of First Instance in 1989, 153 pending cases, including all staff cases, were transferred to it. In 1993 a further 451 cases were transferred, followed by 14 in 1994 and 22 in 2004.
[iv] In 2005 117 staff cases were transferred from the CFI to the CST.

or legal persons (such as private individuals or corporations, as opposed to national courts). The CFI was thus established in October 1989.

More than a decade later, the Treaty of Nice acknowledged the continuing pressure of work on the Court, with the number of cases pending continuing to rise. It further extended the Communities' judicial architecture by enabling the Council to establish 'specialised judicial panels' to deal with specific types of cases.[2] Thus at the time of writing the necessary measures had been adopted to establish the European Union Civil Service Tribunal (CST). It would deal with litigation arising out of disputes between the institutions in their capacity as employers and their respective staff members. It opened its doors for business in December 2005.

The members

The ECJ and the CFI have always been composed of a number of judges equal to that of the number of member states, or one more than that when there was an even number. This has enabled each member state to nominate one judge. For its part the CFI must be composed of 'at least' one judge per member state, presumably to facilitate future expansion to enable it to cope with an increasing case-load. Both courts are therefore currently composed of twenty-five judges in an EU-25, with the ECJ assisted by eight Advocates-General (see Exhibit 7.2). The Statute of the Court now provides that where a case raises no new point of law, the ECJ may determine it without a submission from the Advocate General.

The 'one judge per member state' rule has obvious practical advantages. Among the judges of the Court as a whole, there will be at least one with knowledge of the language and legal system of any member state. Such inclusiveness helps give legitimacy to the Court and encourages member states, their respective judiciaries and their citizens to have confidence in it.

Exhibit 7.2 The Advocates-General

While the role of the judges is generally easily understood (they decide cases), that of the Advocates-General is less easy to grasp. Although there are analogous legal figures in some national judicial systems, the role is better regarded as being a *sui generis* feature of the Community legal order.

According to the Treaty the ECJ is 'assisted by eight Advocates General'. That assistance is provided in the form of a legal opinion (or, to use the wording of the Treaty, 'reasoned submissions') in which the Advocate-General assigned to the particular case which the ECJ is called upon to decide, independently and impartially, examines the legal issues arising and makes a recommendation as to the resolution of the case.

They do not have any right to initiate proceedings, nor are their opinions binding upon either the ECJ or the parties. Nonetheless, their opinions do carry great weight and, usually form the basis of the ECJ's final decision. They are published in the official reports alongside the judgment.

In cases where the ECJ does not follow the Advocate-General's recommendation, the opinion may be regarded as being similar to a judge's dissenting opinion. The opinion may also contain consideration of points which the ECJ finds it unnecessary to decide (*obiter dicta*) but which may well be revisited in future cases.

However, maintaining the link between the number of member states and the number of judges has disadvantages. In particular, significant expansion in the size of the Court, such as that which followed the 2004 enlargement, could change it from a collegiate decision-making body into a deliberative assembly. Furthermore, an increasing number of cases are being dealt with by sub-divisions of the Court (Chambers), thereby potentially endangering the consistency of the case law.

The judges and Advocates-General of the ECJ are, in accordance with Article 223 of the Treaty, 'chosen from persons whose independence is beyond doubt and who possess the qualifications required for appointment to the highest judicial offices in their respective countries or who are jurisconsults of recognised competence'. That broadly stated qualification has resulted in the appointment of members from a wide range of professional backgrounds, including senior judges from the courts in the member states, legal academics (particularly, but by no means exclusively, as Advocates-General), legally qualified politicians and diplomats.

Members of the CFI and the CST must also be chosen from persons whose independence is beyond doubt. However, there is a declining scale in the qualifications required for membership of the lower courts in that members of the CFI must 'possess the ability required for appointment to *high* judicial office' (emphasis added). Those of the CST must 'possess the ability required for appointment to judicial office'.

Members of the ECJ and CFI are appointed 'by common accord of the Governments of the member states'. In principle (but not in practice), each member state thus has a veto over any candidate proposed by another. The appointments, unlike those of the members of the Commission or of the Court of Auditors, are not made by decision of another institution (the Council). Nor are there any provisions for consultation of or approval by the European Parliament. The Parliament has frequently requested that it at least be consulted over judicial appointments on the basis that the involvement of an elected body would give more legitimacy to the institution. However, neither the member states nor the Court of Justice has welcomed the idea. There is the fear of an unacceptable degree of politicization of the process comparable with that witnessed in nominations to the Supreme Court in the United States.

The mandates of members of all the courts are for six years, longer than the mandates of the European Parliament or Commission or any EU member government. The mandates may be renewed and renewal has been the norm with several members of the ECJ serving three mandates and some even four. The result has been considerable stability in the composition of the Court as well as consistency in the development of its case law.

Internal organization and procedure

For practical reasons, the full Court does not sit on every case. Both the ECJ and the CFI have the option of sitting in divisions, known as chambers, of three, five, or seven judges each, to expedite their work. In addition, the ECJ may sit as a Grand Chamber of thirteen judges presided over by the President of the Court where it considers that a case is sufficiently important for the development of EC law or where a member state or an institution so requests. In exceptional cases it sits as a full Court, including the Advocates-General—an impressive thirty-three members. These include cases where it is asked for an opinion on an international agreement (that the

Community wishes to enter into) or where it is considering the dismissal of a member of the Commission, the Court of Auditors or the Ombudsman. However, regardless of the formation adopted, the resulting judgment has the status of a judgment of the Court as a whole.

The procedure before all three courts is based principally on the Statute of the Court, which is annexed to the Treaty. Two general points may be made about the Courts' procedure. First, for reasons of speed and to cope with a multilingual legal system, the proceedings are predominantly conducted in writing. The oral part of the procedure (the hearing) may even be dispensed with altogether. Even in very complex cases, it rarely lasts longer than a few hours.

Second, the Courts operate under particular constraints on the use of languages. To enable the courts of the member states to use the preliminary ruling mechanism (discussed below), they must be able to submit questions and receive answers in their own respective languages. Likewise member states and private parties involved in direct actions must be free to use the language in which they feel most comfortable. To make the Court's case law, like legislative texts, accessible to the citizens whose lives may be affected by it, as well as to the national administrations and lawyers who must apply it, judgments must be translated into all of the official languages. Over thirteen thousand pages of case law were published in each of the then eleven languages in 2003 alone.

To ease the burden of these requirements, the Court has adopted two strategies. First, each case is dealt with in its own language, known as 'the language of the case'. In preliminary rulings the language of the referring court is used. In direct actions the language is selected by the applicant (unless the applicant is an institution in which case the defendant chooses the language). Second, to facilitate its work the Court has adopted French as its internal language for deliberation and drafting.[3]

Pressures arising from linguistic requirements continue to have an important impact on the operation of the Court. Following the 2004 enlargement, which brought with it nine new languages, the Court's staff and budget were substantially increased. In December 2004 the Court counted just under 1,600 staff, an increase of some 500 compared with the previous year. The translation department now accounts for nearly 50 per cent of the total staff of the institution. In a sign that the 2004 enlargement had real institutional costs, the budget of the Court rose from €151 million in 2003 to €235 million in 2004.

The roles of the Court

In key respects, the Court resembles a national supreme court. It acts as a constitutional court, defining the balance between the powers exercised by the member states and those exercised by the Community institutions. It rules upon the extent of and limits to the powers of the institutions themselves, and maintains the system of balances between them. It also acts as a supreme administrative court, reviewing the legality of acts of the other institutions. Since the establishment of the CFI, the ECJ has also had the role of a traditional appellate court. The ECJ even has some penal jurisdiction inasmuch as it may impose financial penalties upon member states and confirm or alter those imposed upon undertakings or firms that the Commission has found to have infringed competition rules.

Despite the broad scope of its tasks, the Court does not have *carte blanche* to intervene as it sees fit. Its actions must take specific forms that are defined in the treaties. These fall into three principal categories: ensuring *observance* by the member states of their obligations under the Treaties; reviewing the *legality* of the acts of the Community institutions and guaranteeing the *uniform application* of European Community law in the member states. The Courts have no power of initiative, nor may they decline jurisdiction in any case lodged that falls within their field of competence. In this sense, the Court of Justice is a reactive institution, not a pro-active one.

Forms of action

The Courts hear cases that fall broadly into two categories: direct actions and references for a preliminary ruling. The former are cases in which one party (the applicant) asks the court for a remedy to right the wrong it claims has been done by the other party. References for a preliminary ruling, on the other hand, arrive at the ECJ not by action of the parties but by a decision of a national court before which the case is pending. This procedure is the primary feature of the Community legal order, accounting for some 40 per cent of the cases brought before the ECJ and resulting in the greatest number of judgments.

Preliminary rulings

Day-to-day responsibility for the application of European Community rules lies with the authorities of the member states. Thus the same customs rules are applied by Italian customs officers in Genoa as by their Dutch counterparts in Rotterdam, by the British in Glasgow, or by the Estonians in Tallinn. Agricultural subsidies are paid to farmers by the agricultural intervention boards in each member state. The common rules on value added tax are applied by the competent authorities in each State. Given the volume and complexity of Community legislation (some 90,000 pages of legislation had to be translated into nine new languages for the purposes of the 2004 enlargement) and the fact that certain forms of legislation (directives) require the member states to transpose European law into national law, it is hardly surprising that legal disputes arise.

In the event of a dispute, it is up to the judicial authorities of the member states to ensure the correct application of Community law. The national courts are therefore courts of general jurisdiction of the Community legal order. They are required both to apply the rules of Community law within the scope of their respective competences and to ensure the protection of the rights which Community law confers upon citizens.

National courts are not free, however, to interpret Community law in accordance with their own legal traditions and methods. If they could, uniformity of interpretation would very soon be lost. The treaties give the ECJ exclusive competence to give definitive and binding rulings on points of interpretation of Community law (Art. 234

TEC). To that end they created a vital channel of communication between the national judiciaries and the ECJ in the form of the preliminary ruling procedure.

This procedure *enables*, and in some cases *requires*, national courts to suspend their proceedings when a question of the interpretation of Community law or of the validity of an act of one of the institutions arises. The issues at stake are then referred to the ECJ, which considers them in the light of observations submitted by the parties to the national proceedings, by member states and by the Community institutions. The Commission, for its part, always submits observations in preliminary ruling cases. The resulting judgment is then referred back to the national court that submitted the question(s). It then applies the answers of the Court of Justice to the case which it must decide.

The word 'preliminary' does not diminish the authority of the judgment of the ECJ. It is preliminary in the sense that it is delivered *before* the final disposal of a case by a national court. Moreover, it is not an appeal procedure: the ECJ does not review the judgment of the national court, nor is it in any hierarchical position in relation to the referring court. The procedure has the character of a judge-to-judge consultation, even if the national judge is bound by the interpretation given by the ECJ.

More generally, the role of national courts in the construction of the EC legal system is one of the most remarkable illustrations of how the EU embeds the national in the supranational, and *vice versa* (see Laffan *et al.* 2000). Anne-Marie Slaughter (2004: 84) speaks of a 'community of courts' in which 'each court is a check on the other, but not a decisive one; the courts assert their respective claims through a dialogue of incremental decisions signaling opposition or cooperation'. To be clear, Community law *is* superior to national law in the areas where it applies. But among national EU courts the German Constitutional Court has been particularly insistent on its co-equal status with the ECJ, even asserting (in the 1993 *Brunner* case) that it retained the right to establish a threshold of constitutional guarantees and that the ECJ could adjudicate their application on a case-by-case basis (Slaughter 2004: 84).

The relationship between the ECJ and national courts remains more cooperative than competitive. The most conspicuous finding of a now large body of scholarship on the relationship between national courts and the ECJ is that many national courts have used the relationship to enhance their own authority and independence, and not just *vis-à-vis* other courts in their member state but also in relation to their national executives and legislatures (see Garrett *et al.* 1998; Stone Sweet 2000; Alter 2001). By its very design, the preliminary rulings procedure gives body to the principle of subsidiarity. The parties to the dispute bring their case before the court in their own member state having appropriate jurisdiction, they instruct their own lawyers, and the case is conducted (including the part before the ECJ) in their own language. It is the national court that finally decides the case. Any appeal lies, not to the ECJ, but to the appropriate national appeal court. The costs in the case are for the national court to decide and the proceedings before the ECJ are free of charge to the parties.

The ECJ has expounded the key legal principles of Community law through its preliminary ruling judgments. These include its primacy over national law and the direct effect of certain treaty provisions (see Exhibit 7.3 below) as well as the liability of member states to pay compensation for loss caused by their non-implementation of Community law. However, perhaps its greatest impact is in making Community law a reality for citizens within the member states. A selection of cases (their names in brackets) illustrates the point:

- a Belgian footballer confronted by restrictive rules on the transfer of players between clubs in different member states successfully relied on the principles of free movement of workers between member states (Bosman);
- a British tourist mugged in the Paris Metro successfully claimed compensation from the French criminal injuries compensation fund as a cross-border recipient of services (Cowan);
- a Belgian airline stewardess was the first of hundreds of employees across the EU to claim effective application of the principles of equal pay for equal work and equal treatment for men and women in the workplace enshrined in the Treaty and in other Community legislation (Defrenne);
- a French travel agent who had secured the financial guarantees needed to trade from an Italian bank rather than a French one successfully relied on the Treaty rules on free movement of capital (Ambry);
- a German pensioner claimed that rules requiring him to reveal his identity when applying for butter being distributed cheaply under a Community scheme infringed his fundamental rights (Stauder).

The willingness of national courts to use the preliminary ruling procedure is demonstrated by the sheer number of cases (over 200 a year; see Table 7.1 above). At times it has risked overwhelming the capacity of the ECJ to deal with them. Perhaps more importantly, though, the acceptance and faithful application of the resulting judgments by national courts has served to anchor Community law within national legal orders. In fact, it could be argued that the strength of the Community legal system lies primarily at the national level since, as Weiler (1999: 28) notes, 'a state, in our Western democracies, cannot disobey its own courts'.

Infringement proceedings

'Infringement' is the term for the main procedure whereby member states can be obliged to fulfill their obligations under the Treaties (Art. 226 TEC). From 1952 to 2004, just under 2,500 infringement cases were brought before the ECJ. Of 155 such cases decided in 2004, an infringement was declared in 144 cases and the action was dismissed in eleven. The cases may be brought either by the Commission, exercising one of its most important prerogatives, or by another member state. The latter are extremely rare (only five cases since 1952) since an aggrieved member state must report an alleged infringement by another state to the Commission before lodging proceedings. The Commission will usually initiate any action that may be required.

In this context the Commission's role is akin to that of a public prosecutor. It investigates complaints of infringements. Where necessary, it initiates proceedings against the state or states concerned. After exercising this power sparingly in the early years, the number of cases has increased steadily: the annual average after 2000 reached 178, with a peak of 214 in 2003. A large proportion of the cases concern purely technical infringements such as the failure to implement directives within the time-limit laid down. Many such cases go undefended, or defended only in a formal manner. Others, however, may involve major national interests such as the German rules on the importation of beer from other member states or the Danish failure to follow public procurement rules correctly for the construction of the bridge over the Storebælt.

The cases finally brought before the ECJ represent only the tip of an iceberg of infringement proceedings started by the Commission. The proceedings begin when the Commission becomes aware of a potential infringement either through its own monitoring procedures or from complaints by member states, corporations, or private individuals. If it considers that there are grounds to suspect that a member state is failing to fulfill its Treaty obligations, it must first give the member state the opportunity to submit its observations. A satisfactory response will result in the proceedings being closed with no further action except monitoring to ensure any promised action has actually been taken. If, however, the response is unsatisfactory or, as is often the case, the member state fails to respond at all, the Commission may move to the next stage, which is the issuing of a 'reasoned opinion'. This is a formal document setting out precisely the obligations concerned and the Commission's reasons for considering the state to be in breach of them, as well as a time limit within which the member state must end the infringement. Again, a satisfactory response will result in the procedure being closed at this stage. Only about one in ten infringement proceedings ultimately is brought before the ECJ.

The Commission's case takes the form of an application to the Court for a declaration that by acting or failing to act in the manner specified, the State concerned has failed to fulfil its obligations under the Treaty. The case proceeds like any other direct action with an exchange of written pleadings and, where required, a hearing and an Advocate-General's opinion. Other member states and institutions may intervene in the case on one side or the other. If the ECJ finds, as it does in the majority of cases which reach this stage, that the member state has indeed failed to fulfil its obligations it makes a declaration accordingly. The question then arises: what effect does such a finding have?

The procedure is effective on several levels. First, all member states accept the principle of the rule of law and the moral authority of court judgments. Member states do not like to see headlines in their national press to the effect that they have infringed the law. Compliance with the judgments of the ECJ is therefore generally assured. Nonetheless, the procedure also has teeth. Article 228 TEC places the member state under a Treaty obligation to comply with the ECJ's judgment. If it fails to do so within a reasonable time, the Commission may open a new procedure, this time for failure to comply with the Court's judgment. The Commission's reasoned opinion will then require the member state to comply with the Court's judgment within a specified time. Since the Maastricht Treaty, when the Commission brings a second action in such cases it has had to specify the amount of a lump sum or a penalty payment to be paid by the state concerned. However, such a penalty payment can only begin to run from the date of the Court's second judgment, by which time the infringement may have lasted for several years.

In the first case in which the procedure was fully applied, the Commission proposed a penalty payment of €24,600 per day for Greece's failure to comply with a judgment on the implementation of a directive on waste disposal. The directive should have been implemented by Greece at the time of its accession in January 1981.

The first judgment was delivered in April 1992. Eight years later, in July 2000, the Court imposed a penalty of €20,000 per day, which ran until the Commission certified that the infringement had been brought to an end some six months later. In a second case, where the first judgment was given in 1991, the Court decided some fourteen years later in July 2005 to impose a fine on France of €20 million, with a periodic penalty payment of €57,761,250 for each six-month period elapsing until the member state complied.

Annulment proceedings

Annulment proceedings are the main vehicle for ensuring that the Community institutions act lawfully and within the scope of their respective powers. Following an application by a member state or another institution (and in certain limited circumstances, individuals), the Court may declare void an act of any institution on one of four grounds: that the institution had no power to adopt the act (lack of competence), that it infringed an essential procedural requirement, that it infringed the Treaty or any rule of law relating to its application, or that the powers of the institution were misused. These powers of the Court extend to any act of an institution that is intended to have legal consequences, whatever its designation.

Member states, the Council, the Commission and (since the Treaty of Nice) the European Parliament are privileged applicants in that they do not have to demonstrate a specific interest in the outcome of the case in order to bring proceedings. The Court of Auditors and the European Central Bank, in addition to relying on one of the four grounds mentioned above, must show that they are acting in order to protect their prerogatives. Individuals or corporations must be either the addressee of the act concerned (in other words, specifically designated in it), in which case the right to challenge it is automatic, or they must be able to show that they are 'directly and individually concerned' by the disputed act.

The latter test has been interpreted restrictively by the ECJ. Its strictness has been widely criticized as effectively depriving individuals or companies of a remedy in cases where they are adversely affected by a change in Community legislation. However, the ECJ has remained unmoved by such complaints (see most recently, *Unión de Pequeños Agricultores* 2002).

Special procedures

A range of special procedures completes any overview of the tasks of the Court. First, in its only consultative capacity, the Court may be asked by the Parliament, the Council, the Commission, or a member state to give an opinion on whether an international agreement which the Community envisages entering into is compatible with the existing Treaty (Art. 300(6) TEC). In the event of a negative opinion, the agreement may only enter into force if the Treaty itself is amended.

Second, the Community is required to make good any damage caused by its institutions or by its servants in the performance of their duties 'in accordance with the general principles of law common to the laws of the member states' (Art. 288 TEC). The Court of Justice has jurisdiction in these disputes, which now generally come before the CFI.

Third, members of the European Commission, the Court of Auditors, or the Ombudsman may be deprived of office, or of their pension benefits, by decision of the ECJ if they no longer fulfil the conditions required for the performance of their duties or if they are guilty of serious misconduct.

Last but not least, staff cases are legal disputes between individual staff members of the EU institutions and those institutions in their capacity as employers. Such cases represent judicial supervision of the internal management of the institutions, and thus are an important constitutional guarantee of the independence of staff members and consequently of the institutions themselves. Moreover, the ECJ and CFI have developed many important principles of administrative law in their judgments in staff cases. Their sheer number (see Table 7.1 above) has been the main driving force for significant developments of the Community's judicial architecture with the creation of the CFI in 1989 and the CST in 2005.

The impact of the Court

The Court has had a decisive impact upon the EU, both in institutional terms and in terms of enabling the Union to achieve closer integration. By no means has the Court's impact been uncontroversial (see Coppel and O'Neill 1992; Weiler 1999; 2003). But no one argues that it has not been powerful in shaping the institutional development of the European Union.

Jurisprudential impact

In the fifty years from its first judgment in 1954, the ECJ delivered 6,465 judgments. Its decisions have not only settled disputes between parties or responded to questions submitted by national courts. In the process, they also have resolved ambiguities in the Treaties, shown how general rules can apply to specific circumstances, and elucidated the general legal principles upon which Community law is based. The establishment of two principles, in particular, direct effect and the primacy of Community Law, has been vital in shaping the constitutional architecture of the Union (see Exhibit 7.3). These two principles enabled the four economic freedoms to be assured via the actions of individuals seeking to enforce their own rights under Community law. This method was particularly important during the early phases of establishment of the common market, when the exercise of the freedoms otherwise depended upon a lengthy legislative process of harmonization of national legislation which could be held hostage to the protection of national sectoral interests.

To illustrate the point, in the Treaty's section on free movement of goods (Art. 28 and 29 TEC), quantitative restrictions on imports and exports and all measures having equivalent effect are prohibited between member states. In the 1974 *Dassonville* case, the ECJ was called upon to define what was meant by the Treaty phrase 'measures having equivalent effect'. It responded with the broad definition that these were 'all trading rules enacted by member states which are capable of hindering, directly or indirectly, actually or potentially, intra-Community trade'. Five years later in *Cassis*

Exhibit 7.3 *Van Gend en Loos* and *Costa v. ENEL*

These two cases, decided in the early 1960s, are the cornerstones of the Community legal order, setting out the principles of the *direct effect* of provisions of Community Law within the legal systems of the member states and of the *primacy of Community Law* over conflicting provisions of national law. The two principles have been accepted by all member states as part of the *acquis communautaire*. The principle of primacy is included explicitly in the Constitutional Treaty (Art. I-6).

Van Gend en Loos is a Dutch haulage company, which was importing a consignment of a chemical product into the Netherlands. Confronted by an increase in the duty applicable to the product, the company objected that the change to the Dutch rules infringed the Treaty. The Dutch authorities responded that the rules in the Treaty did not create rights on which individuals or companies could rely.

The Dutch court referred the case to the ECJ which said:

> The Community constitutes a new legal order of international law for the benefit of which the States have limited their sovereign rights, albeit within limited fields, and the subjects of which comprise not only member states but also their nationals. Independently of the legislation of member states, Community Law therefore not only imposes obligations on individuals but is also intended to confer upon them rights which become part of their legal heritage (*direct effect*).

In *Costa v. ENEL*, in the context of a challenge to the legality of an electricity bill issued by the newly nationalized Italian state electricity authority, the Court first echoed those words:

> By creating a Community of unlimited duration, having its own institutions, its own personality, its own legal capacity and capacity of representation on an international plane and, more particularly, real powers stemming from a limitation of sovereignty or a transfer of powers from the States of the Community, the member states have limited their sovereign rights, albeit within limited fields, and have thus created a body of law which binds both their nationals and themselves.

It then continued:

> The law stemming from the Treaty, an independent source of law, cannot because of its very nature be overridden by rules of national law, however framed, without being deprived of its character as community law and without the legal basis of the Community itself being called in question.' (*primacy*).

---

de Dijon, the ECJ ruled that where a product was lawfully marketed in one member state it must be allowed to be traded freely in all of the others unless restrictions could be justified by imperative requirements, such as the protection of public security, public or animal health, the environment and others (now listed in Art. 30 TEC).

Distribution of powers

The assignment of competences between, on one hand, the areas reserved to the member states and those for which the Community has competence and, on the other, the distribution of powers among the institutions, are determined by the member states. It is they who remain ultimate masters of the treaties. However, these issues are governed by the treaties and the Court has the responsibility of ensuring

---

Exhibit 7.4 The European Parliament in the Court of Justice

Through a number of constitutionally important cases before the ECJ, the Parliament has both asserted and extended its supervisory powers over the other political institutions.

First, in 1980, in the *Isoglucose* case, the ECJ recognized that a requirement to consult the EP 'reflected at community level the fundamental democratic principle that the peoples should take part in the exercise of power through the intermediary of a representative assembly'.

In *Les Verts* (1986), the Court held that acts of the European Parliament which were capable of producing legal effects upon third parties should be open to judicial review.

In 1988, in the *Comitology* case, the ECJ did not accept the Parliament's argument that it should also have the right to bring actions. However, in the so-called *Chernobyl* (1990) case, the Court felt able to allow the Parliament to bring actions for annulment where that was necessary in order to protect the Parliament's prerogatives.

Although both of those changes represented bold interpretations, they were accepted by the member states and incorporated into the texts of the treaties, by the Treaty of Maastricht.

In the Nice Treaty the Parliament was granted the same unlimited rights of challenging the acts of other institutions as the Council and the Commission.

---

their correct interpretation and application. Some illustrations will serve to show how the Court approaches this delicate and often controversial task.

As Exhibit 7.4 shows, the Court has through its judgments played a central part in defining the parameters for the expansion of the European Parliament's role since direct elections. It has developed legal arguments that have served both to restrict the Parliament's actions and to provide the basis for subsequent treaty change by the member states that have reinforced Parliament's powers.

The Court has also been asked to intervene when a member state objected to what Parliament and Council together had agreed. In the *Tobacco Advertising* case, under the co-decision procedure, the EP and Council adopted a directive prohibiting all forms of tobacco advertising. The directive was purported to be based upon considerations of the implementation of the internal market and therefore gave as its legal basis Article 95 of the Treaty, which provides for qualified majority voting in the Council. Germany, which had been outvoted in the Council, successfully challenged the legality of the directive, arguing that in fact its main objective was the protection of public health, a field where unanimity is the rule. This case illustrates that although the member states determine the distribution of powers, it is the Court which, in the last resort, will enforce them, even in the face of objections by the political institutions.

The point is further illustrated by a 1971 case (*ERTA*), which arose after the Council had laid down guidelines for the member states to follow in negotiating revisions to the European Road Transport Agreement. The Commission challenged the guidelines on the basis that they infringed its prerogative of negotiating external agreements on behalf of the Community. Although the Court found against the Commission on the merits of the case, it did affirm the Commission's competence in the area. According to the Court, where the Community implements a common internal policy, the member states are precluded from entering into any commitment in their external relations which might affect the common policy.

The Commission has frequently attacked the legality of Council acts, even when based upon a Commission proposal and when it basically agrees with their contents, when the Council has changed the proposed legal basis of the act concerned. The Court, recognizing that the choice of legal basis governs the legislative procedure (consultation or co-decision), and that the majority required by a given procedure (unanimity or qualified majority) may affect the terms of the measure once adopted, has held that the legal basis must be chosen on the basis of objective criteria, stated in the preamble of the act, and subject to judicial review. It is not a matter for the discretion of the legislative institutions.

A more recent example of the Court's approach in politically sensitive cases is provided by the *Stability Pact* case in 2004. Article 104 TEC provides for an excessive deficit procedure (EDP) to encourage and, if necessary, to compel member states to reduce their budget deficits if they exceed certain limits. In 2003 France and Germany were identified as having budget deficits above the permitted level. The Council, on a recommendation from the Commission, set deadlines for each country to take steps to correct the deficit. Those deadlines expired without either country taking effective measures. The Commission then recommended that the Council give formal notice to the two sides to take the necessary steps. Instead, Council adopted measures by which they held the EDP to be in abeyance and made recommendations to the two states to correct their deficits. The Commission responded by inviting the Court to annul these conclusions.

The ECJ, for its part, made a distinction between those parts of the excessive deficit procedure that depended upon economic and political assessments by the member states and those that were based upon enforceable legal commitments. Relying in part on the 1971 *ERTA* case, it held that economic policy coordination remained the responsibility of the member states in the Council (Ecofin) but that the Commission's role of putting forward recommendations limited the scope for action by the Council at later stages in the EDP. It also pointed out that the Council could not depart from the rules which it had set for itself in the Stability and Growth Pact.

In summary, the Court has been a major player in the evolution of European integration through its major case-law decisions. It has been obliged to adjudicate between the institutions and thus has had a powerful impact on the constitutional shape of the EU. The Court has established major principles that form the basic underpinnings of the European project. It is difficult to imagine today's EU without these principles and the Court as their proponent.

Assessing the Court's role

Given that it has been asked to judge so many politically and legally sensitive questions, it is hardly surprising that the Court has attracted controversy from both political actors and academics. Of the former, one the most dramatic instances occurred in 1975 when Valéry Giscard d'Estaing, then President of France, apparently told other European leaders at the Dublin European summit that something had to be done to stop the Court from issuing its 'illegal decisions.' In the legal academy, every major judgment of the Court is now dissected and scrutinized, and debate about its role is vigorous (see Burley and Mattli 1993; Alter and Meuner-Aitsahalia 1994; Weiler 1999; Alter 2001). Some have argued that the Court's 'uncontrolled judicial activism' was running out of control and posed dangers for the stable development of the Community, on the grounds that the Court had used 'guidelines which are essentially political in nature and hence not judicially applicable. This is the root of judicial activism which may be an usurpation of power' (Rasmussen 1986: 62)

One response has been to argue that any Court with constitutional responsibilities has had active recourse to higher principles of law when faced with otherwise intractable problems (see Cappelletti 1987). One former judge of the Court responded to the charge of 'judicial activism' by considering the very nature of a judiciary. He suggested the charge:

> takes no account of the context of every judicial decision, the purpose of which is ... to settle a dispute between opposing points of view. 'Activism' means something fundamentally different depending upon whether one puts oneself in the position of the strong or the weak; of public authority or of the individual; of the general interest or of particular advantage; of the polluter or of the environment; of a managed economy or of the free market .... What is described by one as activism is seen by another as a necessary safeguard' (Pescatore 1994).

Defence of the Court's prerogatives and role by insiders, however robust, has not ended the argument. Ongoing controversy about the Court is hardly surprising given the expanding role of the Union. What is uncontroversial is that the Court is firmly rooted in the larger system of EU institutions. Crucially, it also is a nodal point in a network of European national courts more than it is a command post at the top of a hierarchy. Perhaps above all, the politics of Community law are a lively and prominent feature of almost any debate about where European integration has been and where it is now going. Joseph Weiler (1999), a leading scholar and often a sharp critic of the Court of Justice, has argued that while legal (or 'constitutional') changes brought about by the Court have been crucial, their importance is a consequence of their interaction with the Community political process.

Conclusion

The often technical legal language in which the European Court of Justice seems shrouded cannot conceal the importance of its work for the themes of this book. First, the Court illustrates the depth of the interdependence that binds together the EU institutions, as well as its member states. No institution or member state is exempt from scrutiny by the Court. Member states are constantly being reminded through the legal process of the obligations that they have assumed under the treaties.

Second, we can see how the national level of governance becomes embedded in the supranational, and *vice versa*. National courts work with the Court in Luxembourg to ensure compliance with the Treaty, with each side dependent on the other for the system to work. EU law enters into national law through the procedures described in this chapter, in particular the system of preliminary rulings.

Third, the Court is an essentially reactive institution that responds to requests for rulings and cannot initiate action on its own. Still, the Court has played a central role in giving direction to the European Union. The establishment of the principle of direct effect was not pre-ordained but once established, served to transform the Community Treaty into a set of directly effective provisions enforceable by interested individuals. Similarly, the Court's support for the primacy of Community law was crucial in enabling the legal order that exists today to emerge. The process has certainly not been short of critics, but no party has at any time indicated its refusal to accept the decisions of the Court as authoritative.

The ratification of the Constitutional Treaty, if it ever happens, would oblige the Court to enter new legal terrain, where it would be likely to court much more controversy. For the first time, the Court would have jurisdiction over all of the areas covered by the Treaty on European Union as well as the task of interpreting some of the innovative rights created by the European Charter of Fundamental Rights. Even without the Constitutional Treaty, the Court faces major challenges associated with enlargement and the incorporation of new legal cultures. It will need to work hard to ensure that it retains the coherence it has displayed up to now with the inevitable increase in workload and strong pressures operating against coherence between the judgments of the different chambers. The future is as uncertain for the Court as it is for the other EU institutions.

Notes

1 Head of the Legal Service, European Court of Auditors, and formerly Head of the Press and Information Division of the European Court of Justice. The views expressed are those of the author alone and are not necessarily shared by either of the institutions or their members.

2 Judicial panels would become 'specialised courts' under the provisions of the Constitutional Treaty.

3 However, when presenting their opinions, the Advocates-General use their own respective languages.

Further reading

One of the most readable and comprehensive texts on the ECJ is Craig and De Búrca (2003). Arnull (2006) provides a comprehensive overview of the material law as it results from the Court's judgments. One of the most perspicacious commentators on the Court is Weiler (1999) who has written extensively on the Court's relationship with the broader development of the Union, including its attempts to agree and ratify a Constitutional Treaty (Weiler

et al. 2003). For discussions of the relationship between the Court and national courts, see Slaughter et al. (1998), Stone Sweet (2000) and Alter (2001). Slaughter (2004) offers a stimulating view of the ECJ's role in an emerging global 'community of courts'.

Alter, K. J. (2001), *Establishing the Supremacy of European Law* (Oxford and New York: Oxford University Press).

Arnull, A. (2006), *The European Union and its Court of Justice* 2nd edn (Oxford: Oxford University Press).

Craig, P., and De Búrca, G. (2003), *EU Law: Text, Cases and Material*, (Oxford: Oxford University Press).

Slaughter, A.-M. (2004), *A New World Order* (Princeton, NJ: Princeton University Press).

Slaughter, A.-M., Stone Sweet, A., and Weiler, J. H. H. (1998) (eds.), *The European Court and National Courts—Doctrine and*

Jurisprudence: Legal Change in its Social Context (Oxford: Hart Publishing).

Stone Sweet, A. (2000), *Governing with Judges* (Oxford and New York: Oxford University Press).

Weiler, J. H. H. (1999), *The Constitution of Europe* (Cambridge: Cambridge University Press).

Weiler, J. H. H., Begg, I., and Peterson, J. (2003) (eds.), *Integration in an Expanding European Union* (Oxford and Malden, MA: Blackwell).

Web links

The Court's website, *www.curia.eu.int*, provides access to all cases brought before the Court of Justice since 1953 and the Court of First Instance since 1989, with access to the full text of all ECJ and CFI judgments delivered since mid-1997 as well as most of the opinions of the Advocates-General. The Annual Report of the Court of Justice and the Annual Report of the Commission to the European Parliament on the implementation of European community law are available on the websites of the respective institutions. Both are goldmines of detailed information and statistics.

Part II

Managing the Union

Chapter 8
The Commission's Services

Liesbet Hooghe and Neill Nugent

Contents

Summary

The Commission has always been considered the 'engine of Europe.' However, an increasingly sceptical public, the managerial challenge of Eastern enlargement, and allegations of mismanagement have forced the Commission to rethink its role. In 2000, the Commission embarked on an overhaul of its services. We ask how the reform programme has affected the organization, functions, and people of the Commission services. We conclude that the reforms have probably not weakened its capacity or will to play a supranational role, though we note distinct changes in appetite: the Commission's leadership has become more managerial, and more wary of bold new initiatives.

Introduction

Commentaries on the European Commission tend to focus more on the College, the political arm of the Commission (see Chapter 5), than on the services, the Commission's permanent bureaucracy. This is not surprising; commentaries on national political systems also tend to pay more attention to political executives than to bureaucracies. But in the case of the Commission it is unwise to over-focus on the College, for the Commission services are not a normal bureaucracy. They exercise a central role—sometimes in a leading and sometimes in a supporting capacity—in virtually everything the Commission does. Few Commission initiatives are launched, few Commission proposals are made, and few Commission decisions are taken without being extensively examined and approved by the services.

The Commission was initially designed by the founding fathers to be the 'engine of Europe,' and it has generally lived up to this role. But over the past decade European integration has changed dramatically. Three exogenous shocks—a politicized climate, the resignation in 1999 of the Santer College, and the 2004 'big bang' enlargement—have forced the Commission to rethink its role. This rethinking provided the context for a reform programme, launched in 2000 by Commissioner Neil Kinnock, which reshaped the organization and the culture of the Commission services.

This chapter examines how the reform programme has affected the Commission's role as the engine of Europe. Has the institution been weakened, as some anticipated? How have the reforms affected the organization and functions of the services, and how have they influenced the people who work within them?

Origins and evolution

The Commission's services have their origins in the High Authority of the European Coal and Steel Community (ECSC). Jean Monnet, the High Authority's first President, wanted the High Authority to be small and informal. Shortly after becoming President, Monnet remarked to a fellow member of the High Authority, 'If one day there are more than two hundred of us, we shall have failed' (Monnet 1987: 405).

Monnet's hopes were quickly dashed. After its foundation in 1952, the High Authority rapidly acquired more staff, a more formal organization, and more bureaucratic procedures than Monnet had envisioned. When, in 1957–58, the Commissions of the European Economic Community (EEC) and the European Atomic Energy Community (Euratom) were established, their administrations were built on the High Authority model. With the mergers of the High Authority and the two Commissions in 1967, the single Commission that we know came into existence. Over the intervening years, the Commission's services have expanded their tasks enormously as the Union has come to touch on many aspects of European citizens' lives. Yet core features of the services have remained durable:

- The services have always been relatively impartial—that is, neutral in their policy stances, save perhaps for a certain pro-integration bias—and independent—that is, autonomous from national and sectoral interference. This impartiality has facilitated close working relationships with a host of governmental and non-governmental organizations. More than most national or international administrations, the work of the Commission is intimately interwoven with that of national, regional, and local administrations.

- The administrative structure, organized around Directorates-General (DGs) and services, has remained essentially unchanged, though the number of units has varied. The number of DGs and services increased from fifteen DGs and services in 1958 to forty-five by the late 1990s. Recent Commission Presidents have reduced that number to counter organizational fragmentation, and when José Manuel Barroso took office as Commission President in late 2004 there were 37 DGs and services.

- The services have always been small in size compared with national administrations. There are good reasons for this. National governments have been reluctant to increase the EU's administrative budget in step with the expansion in its tasks. Also, the Commission rarely implements EU policies and does not undertake much routine administration—two common bureaucratic activities that require large numbers of civil servants. In 1959 there were just over 1,000 full-time staff in the EEC Commission; in 1970 there were close to 5,300 in the merged Commission; by 1990 the number had increased to 16,000; by 2005 there were just over 24,000 full-time officials.

- Recruitment has been primarily meritocratic. Officials are recruited through competitive procedures, although this has not always been applied strictly at the most senior levels. National governments have often insisted on a broadly proportional representation of their nationals in the top layers of the bureaucracy. Commissioners sometimes violate the rules of competitive recruitment to reward *cabinet* members with a permanent appointment.

- The services have consistently been involved in political as well as administrative activities, with the relative importance of the political being greater than in national administrations. Preparing EU legislation, managing funds, or conducting trade negotiations—tasks undertaken mainly by the services—have significant political ramifications. Monnet intended the Commission to set the agenda for Europe, and the services have generally lived up to his expectations.

What kind of bureaucracy does this make the Commission—or 'the House', in the language of Commission officials? The foundations of most core features can be traced back to three diverse bureaucratic models.

The Monnet model

Jean Monnet had a strong hand in shaping the early years of the Commission services. His vision was to recreate at European level a sort of Planning Commission, based on the *Commissariat du Plan* he had headed after the Second World War in France. The *Commissariat* was composed of a small high-level team of civil servants and experts outside the normal bureaucratic hierarchy, whose main job was to produce five-year national economic plans. In the same vein, Monnet wanted the High Authority to be made up of a small, organizationally flexible and adaptable, multi-national nucleus of individuals. It was to be their role to develop ideas, to stimulate and persuade others, but to leave implementation to national administrations. As François Duchêne put it in his much-admired biography of Monnet, there was 'a comic incompatibility of humour between Monnet and routine administration' (Duchêne 1994; 240). Monnet did not want a permanent core of civil servants.

This Monnet spirit is still palpable. By and large, Commission officials focus on designing policies and rely on national or regional administrations to implement most EU legislation. They are an exceptionally diverse and multinational collection of people. And though Commission officials now have career tenure, the Commission is more inclined than national administrations to attract experts from outside.

National bureaucratic models

Monnet was never able to wholly mould the High Authority according to his vision. From the start, the nature and range of its responsibilities and the watchfulness of member states on its functioning meant that it came to have much in common with national bureaucracies. That is to say, from an early stage the services were strongly shaped by Weberian-type principles and modes of operation. As such, hierarchy, formality, and impartiality became key organizational principles.

Particular national bureaucratic traditions and preferences have also fed into the shaping of the services. The strongest national signature remains French, which though weaker now than in the early years of European integration is still apparent in the Commission's organizational structure and terminology. For example, the terms for senior positions are borrowed from the French model: *directeur-général, directeur-général-adjoint, directeur, conseiller*, and *chef de cabinet*.

International organization models

The Commission also echoes features of an international bureaucracy. Indeed, the League of Nations secretariat and the United Nations secretariat were models for the High Authority. The influence of international organization bureaucratic models is evident in the special work conditions of Commission officials, such as their relatively high pay and secure status. Generous terms of employment should help officials resist outside pressures. In return, Commission officials (as well as Commissioners) have to pledge neither to seek nor receive instructions from their home state. Like international civil servants, Commission officials also benefit from tax privileges and from limited immunity against prosecution.

The international legacy is also evident in persistent conundrums the Commission faces: how to wed meritocracy with national representation; how to guarantee officials' impartiality while recognizing their national allegiances; and how to provide political entrepreneurship in the absence of electoral accountability?

The Commission has always been an amalgam of diverse traditions, but these are now partially under revision. The unstated purpose is to make the Commission services look more like just any other professional administration. However, as we observe the Commission during an age of reform, the threads of continuity appear as strong as those of change.

Powers, structure, and functioning

What is the role of the services in the Commission as a whole? What are their powers and functions, and how are the services organized? As we will see, the basic structural features have remained relatively untouched by the Kinnock reforms launched in 2000. The thrust of the reform pertains to how the services organize their work—both in-house and in relation to member states, third parties and the public—as well as to how they recruit and promote personnel, which we turn to in the next section.

The College and the services

If political and administrative tasks could be disentangled, the College would be responsible for politics and the services for administration. In the wake of the Santer College's resignation, Romano Prodi sought to make the distinction between political and administrative tasks clearer by 'reducing the grey areas which currently tend to blur demarcation lines of autonomy and responsibility between those performing more political tasks and those more involved with administration' (Prodi 1999).

In practice, the role of the services is not easily separated from that of Commissioners and their *cabinets*. There are a number of reasons for this. To begin with, what is 'a political decision,' and what is 'routine' or 'administration?' So, for example, deciding whether a new product is subject to an existing EU law on product standards may appear to be an administrative matter. However, the decision may be contested by important economic or social interests. Second, Commissioners usually rely on the services for information, advice, and the preparation of documentation. The services are the main repository of accumulated wisdom in the Commission. While Commissioners and *cabinets* come and go, the services hold the fort. Third, Commission officials are often the hub of policy networks involving key EU actors, and therefore inevitably influence political choices. And fourthly, and arguably most importantly, Commissioners have to contend with a strong tradition of policy entrepreneurship among Commission officials. Monnet's intent to create a team of creative thinkers still echoes powerfully. This is reinforced by the fact that officials often have career reasons to defend their right to make policy.

Powers and functions

The role of the European Commission is described in the Treaty Establishing the European Community. The Commission has a constitutional obligation to set the legislative agenda in the European Union (Art. 211). It has exclusive formal competence to initiate and draft EU legislation. The Council of Ministers and the European Parliament may request the Commission to draft an initiative, but the Commission can, and sometimes does, refuse. The Treaty also instructs the Commission to serve the European interest. And it requires the Commission to be independent from any national government (Art. 213.2).

Most powers and functions of the Commission apply to the services as well as to the College, and they combine to put the former in a position that is unparalleled among the administrations of international and national civil services. It is true that ultimate political responsibility for Commission actions lies with the College, but in practice the services have considerable leeway in acting on behalf of the Commission. Commissioners and their *cabinets* usually just do not have the time, information, or political will to monitor their civil servants or fully control their actions.

The Commission's powers and functions can be grouped under six headings: policy initiator, legislative facilitator, executive roles, legal guardian, mediator and broker, and external representative and negotiator.

- **Policy initiator**: The single-most important power of the Commission is its exclusive Treaty right to draft legislative proposals, save for a few exceptions in justice and home affairs and in external relations. This guarantees the Commission pole position in initiating policies, whether this concerns broadly based policy initiatives or proposals to develop/revise narrow 'technical' policies.

  Many different actors in addition to the Commission may attempt to initiate EU policy. The European Council and the Council of Ministers regularly request policy papers from the Commission. The European Parliament can prod the Commission to start initiatives. Member states, especially when they occupy the Council presidency, table policy documents and proposals at Council meetings. Interest groups make policy submissions to relevant DGs. However, to be turned into legislation, such proposals must be picked up by the Commission. No other body can draft legislation or direct how the Commission should respond to requests to bring forward legislative drafts.

- **Legislative facilitator**: The Commission also acts as a key legislative facilitator. It is the only institution present throughout the legislative process—at meetings in the Council of Ministers, in the Parliament, and at inter-institutional meetings. This continuing presence gives it knowledge not only of what the legislators in the Council and the European Parliament ideally want, but also what they are prepared to accept.

  The Commission's legislative role varies depending on the decision-making procedure. Outside the co-decision procedure its role is pivotal. At any stage, it can withdraw its proposal, thereby aborting the legislative process. The Commission's legislative role is more constrained for matters decided by co-decision, for once the Council and the European Parliament convene in a conciliation meeting the Commission loses the right to withdraw its proposal. At that point, it is merely charged with taking 'all the necessary initiatives with a view to reconciling the positions of the European Parliament and the Council' (Art. 251 TEU). This means that it remains an important actor, but not such a pivotal one.

- **Executive role**: In a few policy areas, the Commission has direct implementation responsibilities. By far the most important of these is competition, where it has to decide, for instance, whether state aids and certain types of takeovers or mergers are permissible under EU law. In most policy areas, however, the Commission relies on national or regional governments, or external agencies, to do the work. About 80 per cent of the EU budget is implemented by third parties. The Commission's role is to organize implementation, including by developing rules that tell national governments and agencies how to implement EU legislation. In some areas, such as cohesion policy, it has the authority to withhold funds; in others, it must rely on its powers of persuasion.

Such implementation frameworks—for example rules prescribing how to test technical product standards, or how to set prices for agricultural products—must normally be channelled through a so-called comitology committee, of which there are approximately 300. Here member state representatives, sometimes complemented by scientific experts or interest group representatives, watch closely how the Commission monitors the implementation of EU policies by third parties. Comitology is the living embodiment of how different institutions and different levels of governments have become intertwined. Unilateral action by one institution has become virtually impossible.

- **Legal guardian**: The Commission—along with the European Court of Justice (ECJ)—is also charged with ensuring that EU law is applied rigorously and uniformly throughout the member states. The Commission is heavily dependent on 'whistle blowing' to be made aware of possible breaches of EU law. Its limited resources mean that only a relatively small number of likely breaches can be pursued all the way to Court. The usual approach is to resolve the matter informally. But from time to time, the Commission organizes dawn raids on suspected firms, which, if found guilty, may end up paying hefty fines. Since the 1993 Maastricht Treaty, the Commission can also take member states to court. The first fine imposed on a member state was in July 2000 when the ECJ ordered the Greek government to pay €20,000 for each day of continued non-compliance with a 1992 Court judgment concerning the disposal of toxic and dangerous waste.

- **Mediator and broker**: EU decision-making involves a multiplicity of actors eager to influence EU policy making. Within this multilevel system there is a strong need for mediation and brokerage, for which the Commission is particularly well placed. The Commission tends to have the best overall understanding of the positions of decision making actors—a knowledge that stems from its contacts across the EU and its extensive involvement in EU policy processes. It is also more likely to be perceived as impartial, in contrast to, say the Council presidency, parliamentary factions, or interest group representatives.

- **External representative and negotiator**: The Commission is a principal international actor. It negotiates trade matters on behalf of the EU; it takes the lead during enlargement negotiations; and it shares responsibilities with member states in foreign policy, development policy, and the external dimensions of such policies as transport, environment, and competition. The Commission's influence depends on the character of the policy. It is greatest in policy areas that: fall under the first (EC) pillar, notably trade; have been subject to extensive transfer of competence, such as enlargement; do not normally raise too much political sensitivity, such as development; require impartial leadership, such as competition; and need technical expertise, such as agriculture.

Structure

The Commission services are organized into Directorates-General (DGs) and general and internal services. DGs are normally concerned with policy sectors, such as trade, environment or competition. Other services usually handle horizontal tasks. Examples of other services are the Secretariat General, the Legal Service, and the Publications Office.

The Commission's most senior official is the Secretary-General. There have only been five Secretaries General in the history of the Commission: the Frenchman Emile Noël (1958–87), the British David Williamson (1987–97), the Dutchman Carlo Trojan (1997–2000), the Irishman David O'Sullivan (2000–5), and since November 2005, the first female Secretary General, the Irishwoman Catherine Day. The Secretary-General is the captain on the ship. She and her service ensure that all parts of the Commission coordinate activities, act in accordance with formal procedures, and liaise properly with other institutions—notably the Council of Ministers and the EP—and outside bodies. Under Emile Noël and to a lesser extent David Williamson the Secretary-General was also a formidable policy shaper. Several important new policy ideas—including cohesion policy, justice and home affairs policy, asylum policy, and foreign policy—were nursed in the Secretariat-General. But Trojan and O'Sullivan interpreted their role in more strictly managerial terms, and many expect Day to continue in this tradition.

Each Directorate-General or service is headed by a Director-General, who may be assisted by one or more deputies. Directors-General give instructions to Directors, who head a directorate. An average-sized DG has between three and five directorates, each of which is composed of between three and seven units—the lowest organizational level in the Commission. A typical unit contains between twelve and fourteen officials, of whom, aside from the unit head, four to six work on policy development, two to three are assisting clerks and three to five are mainly involved in secretarial and other administrative work. These people are often supplemented by one or two contractual positions, such as officials from national civil services on secondment to the Commission.

Reforming the Commission

In the 1990s the Commission's services came under intense pressures to reform. This was largely a consequence of three external shocks to the system.

The first shock was the demise of the 'permissive consensus' on European integration. The Danish 'no' and the very narrow French 'yes' in referendum votes on the Maastricht Treaty heralded a new era—a time in which European integration has become more politically contentious. Governments have found it increasingly difficult to control debate on key issues of European integration: should national sovereignty be diluted; should further market integration be implemented; should the EU be expanded? More people, from political parties to ordinary citizens, have wished to have their say. Just in case this had not quite dawned on the political elites, the 'no' votes in the 2005 referenda on the Constitutional Treaty in France and the Netherlands reinforced the message. Politicization has weakened the Commission's claim to be the primary agenda-setter for Europe. In a polity that struggles to be democratic, decisions by unelected Commission officials have questionable legitimacy. There has therefore been increased pressure on the Commission to justify what it is doing, and to be more deferential to elected politicians.

Second, from the mid-1990s the EU moved towards the most challenging enlargement in its history, to include a swathe of former communist states. With the 2004 enlargement, the EU is facing a policy environment where problems are more diverse across the Union, resources scarcer, decisions more contentious, and implementation more haphazard. No institution has been left unaffected by enlargement, but the impact on the Commission services has been particularly great. For over a decade now, the Commission has invested extensive personnel resources in the accession process and it will continue to do so for some time to come. It has also been overhauling its own organization to make space for new nationals. In all likelihood, enlargement will result in the Commission finding it a taller order to produce effective and efficient policy.

Finally, the EU struggled through a major institutional crisis in 1999 provoked by alleged faulty practices in the Commission services. In March 1999, the Santer College resigned in the face of allegations of nepotism, fraud and mismanagement of funds. The immediate cause was the publication of a report by a Committee of Independent Experts (1999a), which had been established at the European Parliament's insistence, to investigate accusations of mismanagement in the Commission. Most media attention went initially to those parts of the Committee's report that detailed acts of favouritism by some Commissioners, but the real message of the report was that there were numerous performance problems in the Commission services. A second Experts' Report, published in September 1999, exposed in great detail shortcomings in financial management (Committee of Independent Experts 1999b). This provided the immediate context for a comprehensive reorganization of the services.

The reform programme

Aims

Against the backdrop of politicization, enlargement, and the 1999 resignation crisis, a concerted effort has been made to reshape the Commission into a more professional bureaucracy. The incoming Prodi College had no option but to make internal Commission reform a top priority. Accordingly, a Commissioner—Neil Kinnock, former leader of the British Labour Party—was appointed with a specific brief to draft a reform programme. A White Paper on reform was subsequently adopted by the College in May 2000, and largely implemented during the Prodi Commission.

In the introduction to the White Paper, the Commission stated that:

> We want the Commission to have a public administration that excels so that it can continue to fulfill its tasks under the Treaties with maximum effectiveness. The citizens of the Union deserve no less, the staff of the Commission want to provide no less. To

fulfill that objective, we must keep the best of the past and combine it with new systems designed to face the challenges of the future. The world around us is changing fast. The Commission itself, therefore, needs to be independent, accountable, efficient and transparent, and guided by the highest standards of responsibility.

Source: Commission, 2000, Part I: 3

These ringing tones have been given effect by aiming to make the Commission more professional, more efficient, and more focused on core tasks.

Content

Exhibit 8.1 outlines the main goals and measures of the reform programme. The Commission's basic organizational structure has not changed much, but some operational principles have been affected.

One set of measures is aimed at making the Commission more 'service-oriented' and more accountable to its principals—the European Parliament, member states, interest groups, and Europe's citizens. Among other things, the Commission has ensured faster payment of invoices, vastly increased electronic access to documents, and adopted guidelines for consultation with civil society.

Perhaps the single most important change is the introduction of a system of centralized strategic policy planning, which is designed to constrain the services' penchant for initiating new policies. The system tries to achieve a sensitive balancing act. On the one hand, the Commission's responsibility to conceptualize policy is reinforced so as to 'fulfil its institutional role as the motor of European integration' (Commission 2000: 5). On the other hand, the Commission is induced to do less by confining officials' creativity to designated priority areas—so-called 'core tasks.' What is meant by 'core tasks' is left vague, though some observers have interpreted it to mean retrenchment to managing the single market. The first moves of the Barroso Commission seem consistent with such an interpretation. This retrenchment is reinforced by rules that make it easier for the Commission to externalize 'non-core tasks' to national administrations, EU agencies, and private contractors, of which more below.

At first sight, this new system seems at odds with the Monnet tradition of policy activism and political entrepreneurship. But the implications of the new rules are ambivalent. To the extent that the services' energies are refocused on 'core functions such as policy conception, political initiation and enforcing Community law' and 'away from managing programmes and projects and directly controlling the latter' (Commission 2000: 5), the services may end up doing *less* hands-on routine administration and *more* policy initiation—and that would be close to Monnet's heart.

There have also been major changes in personnel policy. Meritocracy is now given clear preference over nationality in recruitment and promotion, and that should make it more difficult for national governments to interfere with Commission personnel policy. The Kinnock reforms also encourage mobility throughout the services and make management training mandatory.

Finally, the Commission has rewritten its financial management rules. It has decentralized financial responsibility to units and even to individual officials, separated financial control and auditing, simplified accounting procedures, and

Exhibit 8.1 The Commission's internal reform programme

Principles and goals	Most important measures
Service-oriented Commission culture Five core principles: ■ Independence from national and sectoral interests. ■ Clear division of responsibility. ■ Accountability. ■ Efficiency. ■ Transparency.	■ New codes of conduct for Commissioners and for relations between Commissioners and departments. ■ Faster payment of invoices: no more than 60 days after receipt. ■ Agreement to streamline relations with European Parliament. ■ Whistleblowers' charter. ■ Improved public access to documents. ■ Guidelines for consultation of civil society groups; public listing of interest groups in committees or working groups. ■ E-Commission: electronic accessibility of documents and contacts.
Priority setting, allocation and efficient use of resources ■ Strategic planning. ■ Externalization of non-core tasks.	Introduction of New Public Management ■ Activity-based management (ABM): new system that organizes what Commission does in substantive rather than budgetary categories. ■ Annual policy strategy (APS) combined with annual management programme (AMP): Commission sets policy priorities and allocates resources in APS, which provides basis for departments' AMP. Updated every three months. ■ Detailed, regularly updated job descriptions for each official. ■ New rules for externalization of non-core tasks: devolution to executive EU agencies, decentralization to national administrations, and contractual outsourcing to private parties.
Meritocratic human resources ■ Merit above nationality. ■ Managerial training. ■ Mobility and flexibility.	■ Staff reform: two-track career structure, re-organization of non-permanent staff, changes in pay and pension provisions. ■ Training: fourfold increase of budget, management skills criterion for promotion. ■ New statute for seconded national officials. ■ Senior management: open competition, merit and experience, no national quotas, compulsory mobility. ■ Transitional rules for enlargement candidates.

continues

Exhibit 8.1 continued

Principles and goals	Most important measures
Financial management ■ Decentralization ■ Faster and simpler procedures	■ Separation of financial control and internal auditing; creation of two centralized services — one to help DGs manage their finances, the other to conduct internal auditing. ■ Financial accountability decentralized into DGs, if feasible down to official who decides a particular action. ■ Closer cooperation with national administrations. ■ Strengthening of OLAF, the anti-fraud office.

Source: Commission website: *http://europa.eu.int/comm/reform/index_en.htm* (and links); Kassim (2004).

reorganized and intensified cooperation with national administrations, which are often the culprits of mismanaging EU funds.

The thrust of the reforms reflects the new public management (NPM) philosophy, which applies principles and practices from the private sector such as competition, cost effectiveness, outsourcing, and customer satisfaction to public service. Therefore many reforms look very much like what has been happening in national bureaucracies such as in Britain, Scandinavia and Spain (Levy 2003; Suleiman 2003). So the Commission still seeks to emulate best practices from Europe's national administrations, though the models are no longer so much Franco–German as Anglo–Scandinavian.

Externalizing Commission work

A particularly contentious aspect of the reform programme concerns the externalization of financial, administrative and support tasks to agencies outside the Commission. Externalization is not a new phenomenon; many subsidy programmes in agricultural or regional policy have been managed by contractors, who organize (but do not decide on) project selection and administer funds. The main purpose of externalization is to allow Commission staff to concentrate on policy making, and to save money. However, the Commission is walking a fine line between economizing on the one hand and ensuring accountability on the other. This was the flashpoint in the 1999 crisis when the Commission was accused of having encouraged mismanagement in outsourced offices because it did not have proper supervision in place.

The reform package distinguishes between three kinds of externalization: devolution to executive EU agencies, decentralization to national administrations, and outsourcing through contracts with private parties. For each category, rules of engagement and oversight have been standardized and tightened. The basic principle is that the Commission remains responsible for making policy, but external agents take on implementation. By streamlining the rules, Kinnock paved the way for a substantial increase in externalization, even over and beyond substantive policy programmes and into administration. For example, in January 2003, the DG for Personnel spun off part of its tasks to three offices, one for the payment of all Commission staff, and the other two for managing Commission buildings and infrastructure in Brussels and Luxembourg. The Commission justified the decision by pointing out that externalizing these tasks should shave 18 per cent off operational costs.

Streamlining personnel policy

Contrary to popular myth, the Commission services are small in size. In 2005, the Commission's core of full-time employees consisted of about 7,400 policy-making officials—the so-called *fonctionnaires* who make policy, negotiate with other EU institutions and outside bodies, and represent the European Union abroad. Prior to the reforms, these officials were known as 'A-category officials' in what was a four category personnel career structure. Now they are described as 'Administrators'—a misnomer if there ever was one—in what is a two-track system. There are also about 600 to 700 temporary appointments at *fonctionnaire* level. Members of Commission *cabinets* fall into this category, as do individuals attracted to meet temporary staff shortages or to provide short-term expertise (for example, to evaluate Commission-funded research programmes).

Fonctionnaires are assisted by administrative assistants, clerks and translators, of which there are about 10,600 in total. Before the personnel reforms, these people populated B and C grades; they are now called 'Assistants', and constitute the second track of the new two-track system. There are also some 3,700 researchers, mostly employed in the Ispra/Varese facilities of the Commission in northern Italy on fixed-term contracts. And there are a further 2,500 posts in various EU agencies and offices, such as the fraud-prevention office OLAF, the Translation Centre, the Publications Office, and the Plant Variety Office. A solid 70 per cent of Commission staff reside in Brussels; the other 30 per cent work in Luxembourg (such as for the Statistical Office), in Italy, in one of numerous (see Table 10.1) EU agencies across the European Union, or in the 120 Commission delegations in third countries.

One goal of the reform programme is to scale down non-*fonctionnaire* numbers by reducing temporary staff, and by off-loading non-core tasks to national administrations or to contract staff. Conversely, two important categories outside the core are set to grow: seconded national officials, and contract agents. *Seconded national officials* are usually sent from national or regional civil services to work in the Commission for up to four years (until the Kinnock reform, up to three years). Exceptionally they may be detached from the private sector or from non-profit organizations. New rules make it easier for DGs to attract national officials, though the number is not to rise above 30 per cent of a DG's permanent policy-making staff. Secondment allows the Commission to attract specialist expertise from national administrations or from the private sector. It also gives national, regional or local civil servants the opportunity to gain experience with EU programmes. That is particularly important for new member states. Precise numbers on seconded officials are not easy to come by, but according to the European Ombudsman, there were about 900 seconded national officials in the Commission in 2004.

The second category to expand consists of *contract agents*. Most of these agents work in the outsourced agencies, some are temporarily employed as in-house 'consultants', 'experts', or 'advisers' (previously called auxiliary staff), whilst others are locals working in the various Commission offices and delegations in and outside the EU. Before the reforms began to take effect, the Commission employed about 1,250 con-tract agents.

Seconded national officials and contract agents are cheaper for the Commission than permanent staff. Seconded national officials are almost 'freebies': they receive their salary from their national employer, and only a top-up for daily living expenses from the Commission. Contract staff usually are paid 10 to 15 per cent less than com-parable Commission staff.

The Commission also hosts about 1,200 trainees per year—known as *stagiaires*. These are usually graduate students, who spend up to five months in the Commis-sion gaining work experience. Competition for these jobs is cut-throat, especially for popular DGs such as external relations or press and communication. To be appoin-ted, it can help to know someone in the services who can make a recommendation from the long list of candidates. *Stagiaires* perform supportive tasks, which can range from photocopying, to researching background information, to assisting discussions in Commission committees.

Recruitment and training

The reform programme leaves existing recruitment policy basically intact, but up-grades training. Nearly all new officials in policy-making positions are recruited by written and oral examination—the *concours*. Competition is intense, and usually there are, for each vacancy, well over a hundred qualified candidates—that is, people with a good academic qualification and high proficiency in at least one language in addition to their mother tongue. Candidates who pass the *concours* are placed on a re-serve list from which they may be cherry-picked by an interested DG. Nationality is in principle not a criterion, but overrepresented nationalities, such as Belgians and Italians, find it difficult to jump from the reserve list to a permanent job.

A minority of middle- and higher-level officials are recruited directly. The rules for recruitment from outside have been tightened, and as a result there are fewer external appointments: between 2000 and 2002 the figure was about 20 per cent among the most senior level (Directors-General) and about 8 per cent among Direct-ors, which is down from about 50 per cent in the mid-1990s. All vacancies need to be posted publicly and require a competitive process.

There are good reasons for maintaining flexibility at senior levels. For one thing, recent member states would otherwise have to wait a very long time before they would have nationals in the senior ranks. Lateral appointments also make it possible to attract scientific or managerial talent to take on specialist jobs.

The biggest change in personnel policy is the virtual elimination of nationality as a criterion for the Commission's top management. National quotas used to be quite strict at the most senior level, and this included informal country flags for some key positions. For example, Germans were usually in strategic positions in the Competition DG, French officials were prominent in the Agriculture DG, Itali-ans in economic and monetary affairs posts, and British in external affairs posi-tions. However, rules now explicitly state that merit and experience should prevail over nationality: 'The nationality of the outgoing post holder is not a factor in the appointment of the new occupant' (Commission 2002*a*). The only nod to nationality is that 'each nationality should have at least one post as Director General, Deputy Director General or equivalent.' In its first senior appointments the Prodi and Barroso Commissions demonstrated that the practice of national quotas and informal country flags had indeed ended.

The new personnel policy also places a much greater emphasis on mobility. All officials have a non-binding benchmark of staying between two to five years in the same post. Mobility is compulsory for sensitive posts, such as those awarding contracts, determining rights and obligations, and awarding grants, and for top managers. As a rule, senior officials normally do not stay in a post for longer than seven years, and they may even be asked to move after five years. Mobility within five years is compulsory for Directors General.

When new members join the EU, special derogations are made from the rule that 'no posts shall be reserved for nationals of any specific member state' (Art. 27 of the new Staff Regulations 2005) to facilitate recruitment from those countries. For the ten countries that acceded in 2004, some 3,400 permanent new posts have been budgeted for by the Commission, plus some 1,000 contract staff, which the Commission seeks to fill by 2010. These posts are distributed across all levels in the Commission, and are allocated to each of the new members according to population size, weighting of votes in the Council and seats in the EP. The most detailed provisions are at the senior level, with forty-one positions at Director level and ten positions at the level of Director-General or equivalent to be distributed among the ten countries. The objective is that at least one national from each member state holds a Director-General, Deputy Director-General, Head of Department or similar function. So the effects of enlargement on Commission personnel will be phased in over a seven-year period. Except for the most senior posts, recruitment is based on competitive exams.

The budget for training tripled between 2000 and 2004. Much attention is given to enhancing managerial skills, with candidates for senior posts now needing to demonstrate solid management experience. The development of financial reporting and accounting skills has also been prioritized.

The 2004 enlargement has presented an unusually tough linguistic challenge, with the number of official EU languages jumping from eleven to twenty. This is deeply affecting the Council and the European Parliament, which are legally bound to conduct much of their work in all official languages. The Commission's working environment is simpler in that it conducts its internal business in English, French or German. This means that all Commission officials—be they from Latvia, Slovakia, or Cyprus—are required to master at least one, and preferably two or all three, of these working languages. However, all official documents and many Commission working documents—and this number has increased dramatically under the EU's new rules on transparent governance—have to be available in all official languages. To meet this challenge, the Commission has been actively involved in recruiting and training translators and interpreters, but has found it difficult to keep up with rising demand. This has led to processing delays, and to officials being encouraged to produce shorter documents whenever possible. Europe's multilingual pluralism does not come cheap: linguistic training and recruitment have absorbed more than a third of the additional administrative expenditure connected with enlargement. However, the Commission is confident it can deliver language convertibility at a cost of just over €2 per citizen per year. This economy notwithstanding, it comes as no surprise that the EU has been at the forefront of language computerization!

A decade of turmoil

The Treaty creates clear expectations for Commission officials. It obliges them to put the Union interest first, to set the agenda for the Union, and to promote the Union interest independently from national pressures. The Commission's internal staff regulations reinforce these prescriptions by instructing that 'an official shall carry out his duties and conduct himself *solely with the interests of the Communities in mind*; he shall neither seek nor take instructions from any government, authority, organization or person outside his institution. ... *He shall carry out the duties assigned to him objectively, impartially and in keeping with his duty of loyalty to the Communities*'.[1]

These norms have roots in the pioneering days. The Commission's autonomy, pro-European bias, and its exclusive power of initiative were crucial to Monnet's supranational conception of the Commission as the engine of Europe, and he persuaded member states to enshrine them in the Treaty. In the early 1960s, Emile Noël, the Commission's first Secretary-General, institutionalized them in Commission staff rules and practices. No other national or international organization, with the partial exception of the ECJ, represents so patently the notion that supranational interest is irreducible to national interests. These norms have been reinforced by the Kinnock reforms. Thus the 2000 Commission White Paper on reforming the Commission states that, 'the original and essential source of the success of European integration is that the EU's executive body, the Commission, is supranational and independent from national, sectoral or other influences. This is at the heart of its ability to advance the interests of the European Union' (Commission 2000: 7).

How widespread is support for these norms in the Commission? A solid half century later, do Commission officials still subscribe to Monnet's core philosophy? Are they—as Monnet wished them to be—true Europeans with a continental loyalty that transcends national loyalties? And has the most challenging decade in the Commission's existence weakened the core norms, or have Commission officials weathered the storm? We bring to bear evidence from two surveys of senior Commission officials—one collected in 1996, before the external shocks, and the other in 2002, after the shocks. The surveys were conducted with Directors-General, Deputy Directors-General, Directors, and Principal Advisers: that is to say, the people who hold the reins of the Commission administration (Hooghe 2002; 2005).

The public image of Commission officials usually takes on one of two caricatures, neither of them particularly flattering. The favourite is to portray Commission officials as Euro-centralizers, keen on maximizing power in Brussels and in their own hands. The other caricature is to suspect Commission officials of currying favours for their nationals while short-changing other nationalities. The two caricatures are difficult to combine logically, though it is not uncommon for the popular press to accuse the Commission of both sins in the same breath.

The Commission and theory

The caricatures reflect contrasting expectations generated by the two classical theories of European integration. Neofunctionalist theory emphasizes that supranational organizations set the pace of European integration. These organizations identify functional needs for regional cooperation, translate these needs into supranational policy, and mobilize support among transnational interest groups to persuade national governments to shift authority. As supranational organizations gain power, so more interests are drawn to them, and this in turn strengthens their resolve to shift authority to the European level (Haas 1958; Lindberg and Scheingold 1970; Stone Sweet and Sandholtz 1998). The Commission is the most powerful supranational organization, and it is expected to identify with Europe first and foremost.

This view is contested by liberal intergovernmentalism. The thrust of this theory is that European integration, and the Commission in particular, is an instrument for national governments to maximize national economic benefits of international cooperation while minimizing the loss of national sovereignty (Hoffmann 1966; Moravcsik 1998). So national governments—not supranational actors—call the shots. Liberal intergovernmentalists conceive of the Commission as a servant of national interests, not an independent actor. They expect Commission officials to reflect the interests of their country. Commission officials should not differ substantially in their views or identities from national actors.

More recently, theorists have emphasized that the EU is a multilevel polity where shared authority is a vital feature of decision-making; in few policy areas can one institution, national or European, take authoritative decisions unilaterally (Hooghe and Marks 2001; Pollack 2000; Sbragia 1993; Scharpf 1994). Multilevel governance plugs top Commission officials into diverse institutional contexts, where they interact with national governments, political parties, public opinion, and other EU institutions, as well as cope with the internal demands of the Commission. Multilevel governance scholars, then, expect the attitudes of Commission officials to vary depending on the relative importance of these multiple influences on their lives.

If Commission officials were to project Monnet's supranational legacy, they would favour increasing the authority of the Commission to enhance its role, advocate a policy-initiating role for the Commission to maximize its agenda-setting powers, and champion autonomy from national interests to minimize interference. In the 1996 and 2002 surveys, senior Commission officials were asked where they stood on these matters, and Table 8.1 reports what they said.

An absolute majority of senior officials subscribe to all of the supranationalist norms bar one. This would appear to give support to neofunctionalist expectations and to undermine intergovernmentalist theory. However, except for the broad norm that the Commission should speak for the European interest, there is no consensus amongst the officials. Sizeable minorities reject the supranationalist stance. There is, then, considerable disagreement within the Commission about its proper role—a variation that is consistent with multilevel governance.

Note the upward trend in supranational support from 1996 to 2002. Contrary to what many pundits claim, politicization, enlargement, and the Commission crisis

Table 8.1 Senior Commission officials and supranationalist support		
Supranationalist norms	**1996**	**2002**
Political authority for Commission		
Member states should not be the central pillars of the EU	65.0	83.7
Commission should be the government of the European Union	51.0	60.2
Agenda-setting by Commission		
Commission needs a vision for European integration/Commission should speak for European public interest	94.3	93.5
Commission should not give up sole right of initiative to European Parliament	62.1	83.7
Administration, management should not be a Commission priority	42.9	36.6
Autonomy from national interests in Commission		
Qualifications should prevail over national quotas/posts should not be distributed according to national quotas	74.7	62.4

Note: All figures indicate the percentage supporting a statement. N = 105 in 1996; N = 93 in 2002. For details on the surveys, see: *http://www.unc.edu/~hooghe*.

have (thus far) not weakened supranationalism. There is significantly *more* support for the idea that member states should not run the European Union (from 65 per cent in 1996 to 84 per cent in 2002), that the Commission should become the embryonic European government (from 51 to 60 per cent), and that the Commission's sole right of initiative should be defended (from 62 to 84 per cent). On basic issues of EU governance, supranationalism has gained ground in the Commission.

Most Commission officials explain this deepening supranationalism in pragmatic terms. They argue that Commission leadership tends to produce better outcomes than member state guidance. Time and again during interviews, officials contrasted the relatively smooth handling of enlargement, where the Commission took the lead, with well-documented examples of inefficient or botched member state guidance, such as the failure to manage the break-up of Yugoslavia, the failed attempt to negotiate external trade in services, and deadlocks in immigration and asylum policy. Furthermore, many top officials warn that enlargement will grind EU decision making to a halt unless the Commission gains more power and can preserve its right of initiative. Monnet could not have formulated it better. Significantly, this support is consistent with one of the key objectives of the reform programme—to concentrate Commission personnel resources on the Union's 'core tasks directly linked to the two main Commission remits, i.e. *right of initiative and guardian of the Treaties*' (Commission 2002b, our emphasis).

Two areas buck the trend of rising supranational support, and both are directly related to the Kinnock reforms. The first concerns the reform programme's objective to strengthen Commission attention to administrative management. Monnet saw a basic contradiction between the need to provide political leadership and the urge to engage in administration. He downplayed the Commission's administrative and managerial tasks—a choice not always appreciated by his colleagues. But the

Commission's senior officials are more with Kinnock than with Monnet. As Table 8.1 shows, even in 1996—before the resignation crisis broke—a majority of senior Commission officials wanted management and administration to be a priority. By 2002, support for this view had grown, with only 37 per cent of officials agreeing with the statement that administrative management should *not* be a priority. Thus by 2002, fewer shared Monnet's view that attention to management saps policy initiative, with more having come to share Kinnock's views that an effective Commission needs to get its books in order first.

The second area where supranational support has weakened relates to personnel policy. Monnet emphasized the need for officials to be independent from national interests. The reform programme reinvigorates this principle by asserting that merit, not nationality, should determine promotion and recruitment, especially at the highest ranks. In Table 8.1, support among senior officials for this principle is considerable, but it softened from 75 per cent in 1996 to 62 per cent in 2002.

Interviews reveal that many top officials take a more nuanced view than either Monnet or Kinnock on national representation in the Commission. Geographical variation among senior Commission officials ensures a range of views in policy making and bestows greater legitimacy on EU policy. Many believe that a policy blind to the realities of a diverse multilevel polity could do more harm than good. Senior officials' instincts about how to balance national sensitivities and impartiality have been honed by experiences over the last decade. A Commission that appears to speak in a foreign tongue is vulnerable to Eurosceptic rhetoric, and a Commission perceived to be the handmaiden of particular national interests loses credibility. That is why officials make a sharp distinction between communicating with compatriots and making policy for compatriots. While the former finds broad approval, the latter meets wide-spread condemnation. When asked in 2002, only 12 per cent believed that Commission autonomy would be better served if officials avoided contact with compatriots, but eighty per cent agreed that national policy dossiers should not be handled by officials of the same nationality.

So Monnet's vision is alive and well in the Commission. His views seem to have remarkable resilience. But some of his principles have received a blow. While there appears to be firm supranational support on the basic choice between an intergovernmental or supranational/federal European Union and wide approval of the Commission's right of initiative, fewer officials now support Monnet's singular focus on creative policy entrepreneurship. Most senior officials—like Kinnock—believe that creativity and managerial savvy-ness must go hand in hand.

Do Commission officials identify with Europe?

Monnet thought of his team as the 'first Europeans' in a Europe where destructive nationalisms give way to a common European identity. As supranational institutions deepened integration, they would help convert national into European allegiances. To what extent do the people in the Commission identify with Europe, and how does this affect their national identities?

Table 8.2 compares feelings of national and European identity among senior officials with those of 'ordinary' European citizens in 2002. It reveals stark differences. While 42.4 per cent of citizens describe their identity as exclusively

Table 8.2 Identity perceptions—top Commission officials versus EU citizens

'In the near future, do you see yourself as . . . '	Top Commission officials	Public
National only	0.0%	42.4%
National and European	38.7%	45.3%
European and National	43.0%	5.8%
European only	2.2%	3.4%
Don't know/refuse	16.1%	3.1%

Note: Commission (N = 93 in 2002); public opinion.
Source: Eurobarometer 54.1, 2001.

national, not a single top Commission official does. Conversely, only 9.2 per cent of citizens give European identity priority over national identity, while 45.2 per cent of top Commission officials do. Thus the people who work in the Commission have decidedly stronger European loyalties than Europe's citizens. But top Commission officials do not abandon national identities for a European identity. Rather, they embrace inclusive, multiple identities. Only 2.2 per cent describe themselves as exclusively European, while 81.7 per cent feel both European and national. Commission officials do not perceive a conflict between being national and being European. Some even object strenuously to the idea that one or the other could be more important: 16 per cent of officials refused to answer the survey question because it compelled them to rank-order national and European identity!

The notion that national and European identities are compatible is deeply engrained among senior Commission officials, and this notion is also growing amongst citizens. Analysing perceptions of identities over more than a decade, Citrin and Sides find that 'while the nation retains primacy in most people's minds, the growing sense of Europeanness implies that more people are integrating a sense of belonging to two overlapping polities' (2004: 170). For both Commission officials and citizens, multiple identities are consistent with life and work in a multilevel polity.

Conclusion

After an eventful decade—shaped by the triple shocks of politicization, enlargement, and the resignation of the Santer Commission—the Commission services have been reformed. The reforms have put the organization on a more professional footing, most particularly by upgrading on-the-job training, focusing more on managerial skills, scrapping national quotas and country flags, and decentralizing accountability. However, contrary to what pundits had thought, there are few signs that these changes have weakened the Commission's traditional role of being the engine of Europe. A central purpose of the reforms has been to free the 7,000 to

8,000 Commission administrators from routine administration and implementation so that they can focus on initiating policy—in the spirit of Jean Monnet's original ideas.

The many changes in staff policy and work practices seem to re-affirm, not weaken, the special role of the Commission in the EU architecture. And thus organizational change paves the way for institutional continuity. Surveys of the Commission's senior officials before and after the reform corroborate this conclusion. Support for supranationalism—understood here as a preference for a privileged role for the Commission in setting Europe's agenda—has grown among the Commission's senior management.

Does this suggest that more policy may flow from the services? This is unlikely since a major goal of the reform programme has been to constrain the Commission's penchant for policy entrepreneurship. Measures such as the introduction of the Commission's Annual Policy Strategy and its associated Annual Management Programme are designed to achieve this, by compelling Commission officials to pursue initiatives within the guidelines set by the College. Combined with the increasing 'completion' of the internal market and a market-liberal turn in the College and among top Commission officials, these measures may well keep the Commission services' entrepreneurship on a short leash.

Notes

1 Art. 11 Commission Staff Regulations 2005 (emphasis added).

Further reading

The academic literature on the Commission has grown considerably in recent years. However, most remains generally unconcerned with the distinction between the College and the services within the Commission, and focuses on the roles and influence of the Commission as a whole. The references provided here concentrate on sources that include extensive discussions and analyses of the services.

Committee of Independent Experts (1999a), *First Report on Allegations Regarding Fraud, Mismanagement and Nepotism in the European Commission* (Brussels: European Parliament, 15 March).

Committee of Independent Experts (1999b), *Second Report on Reform of the Commission: Analysis of Current Practice and Proposals for Tackling Mismanagement, Irregularities and Fraud*, (2 vols.) (Brussels: European Parliament, 10 September).

Dimitrakopoulos, D. G. (2004) (ed.), *The Changing European Commission* (Manchester and New York: Manchester University Press).

Hooghe, L. (2002), *The European Commission and The Integration of Europe: Images of Governance* (Cambridge: Cambridge University Press).

Hooghe, L. (2005), 'Many Roads Lead To International Norms, But Few Via International Socialization. A Case Study of the European Commission', *International Organization*, 59(4): 861–98.

Nugent, N. (2001), *The European Commission* (Basingstoke and New York: Palgrave).

Websites

The Commission's website is at *http://www.europa.eu.int/comm/index_en.htm*. Specialised websites include:

- Commission (2004) *Reforming the Commission: Reform of Europe's Public Services*: *http://europa.eu.int/comm/reform/index_en.htm.*
- Commission (2005) *Staff Regulations of Officials of the European Communities. Conditions of Employment of Others Servants of the European Communities*: *http://europa.eu.int/comm/dgs/personnel_administration/statut/tocen100.pdf.*

Chapter 9

Managing the Euro

The European Central Bank

Kathleen R. McNamara

Contents

Summary

This chapter evaluates the economic and political reasons for the creation of the European Central Bank (ECB), and describes its structure with particular reference to the balance between the centralization of power within the ECB and ongoing involvement by national policy-makers in related economic policy realms. The policy areas surveyed include monetary policy, economic policy coordination, and exchange rate policy. In all these areas, challenges arise from the movement of monetary policy to the supranational level while other economic policies are maintained at the national level, particularly in the context of an enlarging EU. The chapter concludes with a discussion of democratic accountability and legitimacy, and argues that the ECB's unique degree of institutional independence makes these issues of enduring importance.

Introduction

On 1 June 1998, the European Central Bank (ECB) began operation. Housed in a gleaming glass and steel office tower in Frankfurt, Germany, the ECB seems a rather prosaic institution, charged with managing Europe's new currency, the euro, making monetary policy for the participating countries, and directing and coordinating the national central banks who together with the ECB make up the European System of Central Banks. On closer reading, however, the ECB is not simply a grey, apolitical organization filled with technocratic central bankers, but rather a unique supranational entity with the potential for deep transformation in the nature of European politics. The ECB's decisions profoundly affect not only the economies of the EU but may also be transforming its politics as critical decisions, formally jealously guarded by states, are transferred to the European level. The ECB is quietly revolutionary, and this EU institution, soon to be moved to a cutting-edge, architecturally soaring building on the Main River, more than merits our attention. This chapter will review the theory and history of the ECB and its euro, and assess the structure and functioning of the ECB and its linkages to other policy areas in the EU. It also speculates about the pressures that are likely to promote change in the ECB's management of the euro in the next few decades. The chapter begins, however, with a brief discussion of where the ECB fits within the broader set of European banking institutions.

The ECB and the 'other' European banks

The European Central Bank is responsible for formulating and executing monetary policy with the goal of providing a stable economic environment across the EU. While the ECB's interest rate decisions profoundly shape the economy, the ECB is prohibited from investing money or lending out funds. But two other Euro-banks, established before the ECB, do play an important role in direct financing and in granting loans. Their work has stimulated growth and development in regions facing economic hardship, both inside the EU and in neighbouring areas, and is now providing capital for research and development in emerging sectors of the economy. These institutions are the European Investment Bank (EIB), which was founded by the Treaty of Rome, and the European Bank for Reconstruction and Development (EBRD), founded in 1991 as a multilateral institution outside the EU (see Exhibit 9.1).

While these European-oriented banks continue to grow in importance, it is the European Central Bank that is the central site of monetary governance and whose deepening authority represents a key transformative innovation within the institutional landscape of the EU.

Exhibit 9.1 The 'other' European banks

The European Investment Bank

The European Investment Bank (EIB) was created in 1958 by the Treaty of Rome, and is owned by the twenty-five states that make up the European Union. It is the world's largest bank of its kind, with loans totalling €43.2 billion in 2004 (€39.7 to EU members, and €3.5 billion to non-member states). The EIB has traditionally financed capital investment in the EU, often lending support to large infrastructure projects and helping to bind together the single market. The EIB's bond issues enjoy the highest credit rating, so it is able efficiently to raise funds and then lend at low rates.

In June 1998, the responsibilities of the EIB expanded to include the Amsterdam Special Action Program, focusing on health and education projects, and the targeting of entrepreneurial firms. The idea is to promote job creation and capital investment throughout the EU, and the EIB has been surprisingly nimble in adjusting to its new tasks. Responding to decisions taken at the Lisbon Summit, the EIB has been working with the European Investment Fund (EIF), a previously low-profile subsidiary that now acts as an aggressive venture capital enterprise in partnership with private investment managers in areas such as biotechnology. Finally, the EIB can be a useful tool of statecraft, as in 1999 when its Balkan Task Force was set up to provide expertise and loans to address the infrastructure needs in post-war south-eastern Europe.

The European Bank for Reconstruction and Development

The European Bank for Reconstruction and Development (EBRD) was established in 1991 at the suggestion of François Mitterrand, then President of France, as a multilateral organization autonomous from the EU with shareholders from around the globe, including the US. The purpose of the EBRD is to promote economic restructuring and liberalization in the economies of the former communist European states. The EBRD struggled to gain credibility in 1993, after it was discovered that the institution had spent more money on its headquarters than on loans to Central and Eastern Europe. Reformed, the EBRD now plays a significant role in the redevelopment and reorienting of the former Soviet states towards market capitalism and democracy.

The origins of the ECB

Economic and political rationales

The ECB is the institutional expression of a process of monetary integration that began early on in the history of the European Union but underwent a multitude of setbacks before becoming a reality. Why have the European states had such a longstanding interest in creating a common currency, despite what seem high odds against success? There are two sets of reasons, economic and political, which are often offered for the development of a single currency and central bank. The following brief review of both the theoretical reasoning and the historical evidence on the

European case suggests that it is not economics, however, but rather politics that explains the creation of the ECB.

The economic benefits from a single currency and monetary institution seem straightforward: the more trade and investment activity there is across an area, the more desirable a single currency should be. A single currency is assumed to ease economic interactions by eliminating the transaction costs of doing business in many different monies, as well as eliminating the risks to business associated with fluctuating currencies (Frieden 1991). The Commission's report *One Market, One Money* stated emphatically that 'Indeed, only a single currency allows the full potential benefits of a single market to be achieved.' (Emerson *et al.* 1992: 20).

However, the evidence is not conclusive as to whether exchange rate uncertainty and currency transaction costs actually do hinder trade flows. Many of the world's closest trading partners, such as the US and Canada, have not shared a single currency, yet have seen their trade and investment flows increase dramatically. In addition, the economic costs of giving up a national currency might be substantially higher than the benefits. Moving monetary policy authority to the ECB means that monetary policy and the exchange rate cannot be tailored to fit national conditions but must be collectively decided for the whole of the union, whether twelve or twenty-five states. Such a collective monetary policy is most appropriate under a series of conditions: when regional trade levels are high, when labour is very mobile, when economic shocks, such as an oil crisis, affect the different geographic parts of currency union in similar ways, and when there are compensating fiscal transfers across the monetary union to make up for uneven economic development.[1] Under such conditions, the costs of giving up a national, independent exchange rate and monetary policy will be minimized, as economic adjustment can occur without reliance soley on the exchange rate or monetary policy but rather on actions such as workers moving from depressed areas to areas where jobs are plentiful.

Given these economic guidelines, what may be puzzling to observers is that the European Union does not seem to meet these criteria. Fortunately, this does not mean, however, that EMU will not succeed. In fact, the great majority of existing national currencies and sovereign central banks also do not match up to these ideal economic conditions even within their own national borders. For example, the economic region bounded by the United States does not qualify as a likely candidate for a single currency and central bank, yet few have questioned the viability of a single US dollar. In the American case, as with the majority of states, *politics*, not economic logic, seems to be the overwhelming factor shaping the geography of money and the success of unified currency standards. The EU is no exception.

What is the political logic, then, that has compelled the creation of the euro and the ECB? There were several key political motivations for monetary union. For some countries, most importantly France, one key benefit was to replace the existing exchange-rate arrangement, centred on the German mark, with a formal European level institution where each national central bank governor would have a seat at the table of monetary decision-making. More generally, the political benefits of a supranational monetary institution lay in its potential to serve as an engine of political integration. Currencies have a powerful symbolic value to their users (Cohen 1998; Helleiner 1998), and leaders have promoted the consolidation of monetary authority in the euro as a way to bind the EU states and encourage political unity. Some leaders, again, particularly in France, have long championed the potential for the single European currency to present a more unified face to the international system and enable Europe to play a larger role in the management of the global economy. Given the size of the single market, the euro, if attractive to investors, has the capacity to rival the dollar as a key international currency. All these elements therefore link currency to the political goals of European integration and projection of power abroad.

Finally, the political rationale for a single currency and central bank was also rooted in the perception that a European central bank would produce more effective policy than the national banks could on their own.[2] A new, politically independent central bank might be able to project a more credible image about its policy capabilities to investors, resulting in a more stable currency than those found among states, such as Italy, with historically high levels of inflation and political instability. All of these motivations played a role in the push for EMU.

Politics in practice: the long road to EMU

While motivations were strong for a common central bank, the road to the euro was not smooth and until the moment EMU began it was by no means certain that a common currency and European central bank would ever be a reality. Political conflict all along the way, and economic concerns about how to reduce the costs of EMU, were also very much on the minds of policy-makers through its long history, as will be outlined below.

Although the original Treaty of Rome did not contain any explicit call for a single currency or central bank, by the 1960s European leaders had begun to discuss the possibility of a monetary union. This early interest was prompted in part by the instability of the international Bretton Woods system, which was no longer effective in smoothing out exchange rate fluctuations among the world's major economies. Dissatisfaction with continued monetary instability and the desire to forge a cohesive European response prompted the political leaders of the six member state governments, at the Hague Summit of December 1969, to call for a plan to create a European monetary union. The first and only stage of this plan to be implemented was the short-lived currency 'Snake,' a fixed exchange rate regime created in 1972. Movement towards monetary union was hampered by the oil crisis, economic instability and inflation, and perhaps most importantly, by a political divergence of views across Europe on what would constitute an appropriate policy (McNamara 1998). At this point, it looked as though a common European monetary institution would never become a reality.

Creating the ECB

By the second half of the 1980s, European leaders, led by the French in partnership with the Germans, began to consider reviving the monetary union project. The success of the single market programme in moving towards the dismantling of barriers to trade and commerce seemed to forge a logical link with movement towards a single currency. The success of the single European market also created a sense of excitement and support for bold steps to further Europe's integration. At the June 1988 European Council in Hanover, EU Heads of State and Government charged the

Commission President, Jacques Delors — a key protagonist in the revival of the single currency project — with developing a plan for Economic and Monetary Union. The committee formed to address this goal delivered its Delors Report to the European leaders at a summit in Madrid in 1989. The report's conclusions formed the basis for the subsequent Treaty on European Union, signed in Maastricht in December 1991.

The Maastricht Treaty called for EMU to be achieved in three stages, beginning with a period of financial market integration and economic convergence. The next stage, begun in January 1994, was to be devoted to the transition to EMU. In this stage, a new body, the European Monetary Institute (EMI) was created to assist in the coordination of national monetary policies and to encourage a convergence in economic fundamentals. The EMI was the precursor to and laid the procedural groundwork for the final stage, comprising the creation of the ECB and the single currency. The national central banks were to continue to exist as members of the European System of Central Banks (ESCB), carrying out the policies of the ECB, somewhat like the US regional Federal Reserve Banks.

The starting date of the final stage of EMU remained subject to a political decision by Europe's leaders. The Maastricht Treaty's 'convergence criteria' were meant to guide that decision, a necessary concession to those states, most importantly Germany, that feared EMU would be inflationary if the participating economies were not adequately prepared. The criteria called for member states to achieve low and convergent inflation rates, a budget deficit of 3 per cent of GDP or less, public debt levels of 60 per cent or less, and a stable exchange rate. The rules of Maastricht left substantial room, however, to allow the heads of state to make their own judgments about entry into EMU.

In the end, the decision to begin EMU on 1 January 1999 was effectively made by a special European Council meeting in Brussels in May 1998. While most EU states had made strenuous efforts to meet the convergence criteria by the time of the launch of Stage III, not all conditions were met for all eleven countries slated to participate in the euro. The political desire to continue moving towards a common monetary authority carried the day, and shortly after, the European Central Bank replaced the EMI at the end of 1998 and began business preparing for the start of EMU.

The structure of the ECB

The overarching institutional framework for EMU is the European System of Central Banks (ESCB), made up of the national central banks of the participating countries with the ECB itself at the centre. Although the formulation of monetary policy is highly centralized within the ECB, the execution and operation of monetary policy is more broadly decentralized within the ESCB. The basic tasks of the ECB and the ESCB are the formulation and implementation of monetary policy, most prominently through the setting of interest rates; the execution of exchange market operations; the holding and management of official reserves; and the promotion of the smooth operation of payment systems.

The ECB's formal structure was established in the Maastricht Treaty, and it is this structure that has been followed in practice. The ECB is made up of three separate, but closely linked and somewhat overlapping decision making bodies (see Fig. 9.1). The first body, and arguably the most important, is the Executive Board of the ECB. The Executive Board consists of the ECB's President, Vice-President, and four other board members. The Executive Board is responsible for the day-to-day management of monetary policy, implementing decisions made by the second body, the Governing Council, and issuing the necessary instructions to the national banks. Strictly speaking, the primary responsibility of this Executive Board is to carry out monetary policy, but, as will be discussed, it is also heavily involved in the formulation of policy itself.

The six members of the Executive Board are appointed by consensual agreement among the Heads of State or Government of the EU member states, on a recommendation from the Council and after consulting the European Parliament and the Council. The terms of office for the Executive Board members are eight years, and non-renewable. None of these individuals is allowed to hold any other position while on the Executive Board, and all are to be appointed 'from among persons of recognized standing and professional experience in monetary or banking matters'.[3]

The first Executive Board of the ECB was indeed consensually chosen from the ranks of highly respected economists and policy-makers long associated with the EMU project. Although the Board's appointments were largely uncontroversial, the decision over who would serve as the first President provoked a political tussle

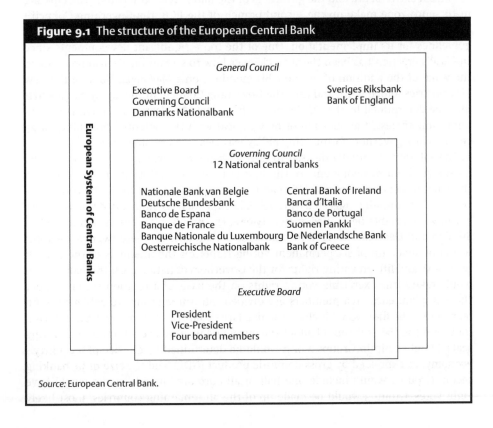

Figure 9.1 The structure of the European Central Bank

European System of Central Banks

General Council

Executive Board
Governing Council
Danmarks Nationalbank

Sveriges Riksbank
Bank of England

Governing Council
12 National central banks

Nationale Bank van Belgie
Deutsche Bundesbank
Banco de Espana
Banque de France
Banque Nationale du Luxembourg
Oesterreichische Nationalbank

Central Bank of Ireland
Banca d'Italia
Banco de Portugal
Suomen Pankki
De Nederlandsche Bank
Bank of Greece

Executive Board

President
Vice-President
Four board members

Source: European Central Bank.

among the member states. A compromise was reached which put the former Dutch central bank Governor, Wim Duisenberg, at the helm, but purportedly only for four years with the French candidate, Jean Claude Trichet, Governor of the *Banque de France*, his presumed successor. After some suspense about whether he would in fact step down early, Duisenberg finally announced his retirement plans in 2002. Another round of intrigue about who would take over ensued, with Trichet finally getting the nod and assuming the Presidency on 1 November 2003. Given the strongly convergent views across the majority of central bankers in Europe that price stability was the primary goal of monetary policy, the policy positions of the two did not differ substantially, but different national styles and prestige played a role in the dissension over the appointment. The President's public role may be more important than any internal policy posture. The relative ability of the President to project a unified, strong position on matters such as the foreign exchange value of the euro and the health of the European economy is often viewed as a crucial part of the job. Indeed, Duisenberg was subject to considerable criticism during the early part of his tenure by financial market participants, who argued that the ECB did not send clear enough signals about the state of the economy, how the economy was being evaluated, and what might constitute appropriate interest rate changes. Trichet's reputation as a more deft policymaker and communicator has largely been borne out in approbation in the financial press and in the continued strength of the euro so far under his tenure.

The Executive Board and the governors of the national central banks participating in the euro zone make up the second branch of the ECB, the Governing Council.[4] The Governing Council is responsible for formulating monetary policy and adopting guidelines for its implementation. One of the more significant developments since the ECB's creation has been the struggle over how to streamline decision-making in the wake of the addition of ten new EU members on 1 May 2004. None of the new EU countries joined EMU, and thus the Governing Council, immediately as they first must be determined by the EU Council to have met the Maastricht convergence criteria. Nonetheless, the question of how to deal with the potential possibility of 25 central bank governors formulating policy was clearly a pressing issue.

The solution eventually devised to deal with the ever-widening EU is one of the most significant developments of the first years of the ECB as an institution, even though it has not yet gone into effect and remains poorly understood. The voting procedures were initially suggested by the ECB itself, which recommended that the number of voting rights be capped at twenty-one, the number it would reach if the UK, Sweden and Denmark decided to join before enlargement. These twenty-one votes would be made up of six permanent voting rights for the members of the Executive Board, and fifteen voting rights for the Governors of national central banks, who would take turns exercising voting rights on the basis of a rotation system. Under the ECB plan, euro area members are divided into three groups to achieve the fifteen votes. The first would include the five large countries (Germany, France, Spain, Italy, and the UK, if it should adopt the euro) and would have a total of four voting seats. Membership in Groups 2 or 3 would be determined by the size of a country's economy, as expressed by gross domestic product (GDP), and the size of its banking sector. Group 2 would include one half of all euro area members and would have eight votes. Group 3 would be made up of the all remaining countries, most likely including most of the newest EU members who have smaller GDPs and banking sectors, and would share three votes. The division into three groups, and the rotation of voting rights within each group, has created a complex and opaque voting system for the ECB. Unhappiness over this initiative was evidenced in the (non-binding) vote against it in the European Parliament, whose members called the new system complicated and unfair, proposing instead a simple majority system. Specific complaints include the point that using the size of the banking sector as a key determinant gives Luxembourg more voting time than other much larger members, while Group 1 seems to unduly privilege the current, core EMU states from having their votes diluted.

Despite these criticisms, the EU leaders decided to follow the ECB's recommendations and adopted the new voting system in March 2003, The decision, contained in an amendment to Article 10.2 of the Statute of the European System of Central Banks and of the European Central Bank, is still subject to ratification by EU member states before it can go into effect.

The question of voting is important less because of the specifics of the decision but because it highlights a broader critique of the mechanisms of euro zone governance in the ECB. The voting system seems to privilege nationality over the needs of the euro zone as an economic area, unsurprising perhaps as the EU is ultimately a political body. However, some observers, such as economist Francesco Giavazzi, have also argued that the 21 vote level is far too high. He has noted that the current Council's size tends to produce a status quo bias: interest rates are sometimes kept unchanged simply because it proves difficult to gather consensus in favour of a change. What he calls 'best practice' in central banking indicates that interest rate decisions are better made by an independent committee within the bank. In the US case, a strong personality, former Federal Reserve Chairman Alan Greenspan, often shaped interest rate decisions in decisive ways. In the ECB case, the increase in votes of non-executive board members tips the balance away, again, from the President and his or her board members, potentially slowing down decision-making.

In practice, it does appear that currently the Executive Board takes a large measure of agenda setting power and shapes the decisions made in the Governing Council. At the twice-monthly meetings of the Governing Council, the Executive Board presents information to the national central bank governors on the state of the 'Eurozone' economy, provides projections on future developments, and then recommends a specific course of action. Given the large size of the Governing Council and the uniquely European wide perspective of the Executive Board, the latter's lead role is understandable. The proposed increase in votes on the side of the ECB governors may decrease this role, but on the other hand, if the Executive Board provides persuasive leadership, they may serve as an anchor for the enlarged ECB. At present, it also seems that decisions in the Governing Council are more likely to be taken by consensus, not formal votes, which means that the agenda setting powers of the Executive Board may be more important than their minority voting position might indicate. However, such consensus politics become harder and harder the more, and more disparate, members enter into the Euro.

The third and least powerful branch of the ECB is the General Council, comprised of the president, vice-president, and governors of all the EU national central banks, including those not participating in the euro. The remaining four members of the

ECB's Executive Board can participate in the meetings of the General Council, but have no voting rights. It is the right of the General Council to be notified before the Governing Council implements most legal acts, so that its members can study and submit observations. However, the General Council's role in practice is very limited, and those members not participating in the Eurosystem are effectively shut out of policy-making.

It should be noted that not all of the action in EMU lies with the ECB—the national central banks and their Governors continue to be quite important to the operation of the ECB, as they collect and analyse data crucial to the modelling of the eurozone for monetary policy, as well as providing the banking supervision for their econom-ies. The national central banks also are politically important in providing a direct link to the European publics, as they have long-standing relationships with govern-ing bodies in their countries and are an accepted and legitimate part of their national political landscape.

One of the most notable features of the institutional structure of the ECB is that its statute makes it the most politically independent central bank in the world, even surpassing historically independent entities like the German Bundesbank or the US Federal Reserve. The Maastricht Treaty states that the ECB cannot seek or take in-structions from any EU or national entity or any other body. Its independence is argu-ably more secure than that of any national bank because a modification of its statute would require an amendment to the Treaty, which can only occur with unanimous agreement among the member states. The ECB is linked, but only minimally, to the political bodies of the EU in the following ways.[5] The President of the EU's Coun-cil of Ministers may participate in the deliberations of the Governing Council of the ECB and may submit motions for consideration, but cannot vote. A representative of the European Commission may also attend meetings of the Governing Council, but may not vote or present motions. The ECB President will also be invited to at-tend meetings of the Council of Ministers when it is discussing matters of relevance to the ESCB. In addition, the ECB must fulfill a number of reporting commitments to European bodies and the public.[6] It must issue retrospective annual reports on its activities, and present this report to the Council and the European Parliament, which may hold a general debate on it. The Maastricht Treaty states that the ECB's Presid-ent 'may' be required to appear before (but not take direction from) committees of the European Parliament, and indeed the EP took the initiative in its resolution of 18 June 1996 to request that the President of the ECB appear every three months to discuss developments in EMU. This degree of independence raises many important is-sues about the desirability and functionality of such a highly delegated institutional structure, issues which will be taken up in the last section of this chapter.

The organizational culture overlaying the ECB's formal institutional structure is still in formation. However, the ECB does seem to have certain distinct qualities that set it apart from the other institutions of the EU. First, the ECB is not subject to the same administrative rules and regulations as the rest of the EU institutions but rather has created its own rules regarding the hiring, promotion, and firing of personnel.[7] The ECB is still a relatively small organization compared to most national central banks, and staff members pride themselves on being flexible, sensitive to the need for adjustments and change. In interviews, they claim to see themselves as much closer to a private-sector firm in organizational culture than what they view as the overly bureaucratized Brussels institutions. In addition, the ECB is not set up on the French-influenced EU Commission *cabinet* system, a fact those working in the ECB see as also quite important in making the dynamics inside the central bank more like a private corporation than the other EU institutions. Neither do they view themselves as just an extension of national-level central banks. While the formal structure of the ECB mimics the German Bundesbank in many ways, there is a conscious effort on the part of some of the highest-level staff to pioneer a truly new institutional culture and identity. The ECB's location in Frankfurt has made it easier to attract staff from Northern Europe, while making it a less attractive post for other EU nationals, skewing the culture of the ECB towards the formidable Bundesbank model. However, asked to draw an analogy between the EU and national banking institutions, some within the ECB approvingly cite the Bank of England, which is viewed as somewhat more 'competitive' and 'market oriented' in its monetary policies, instruments and organizational rules than the other national central banks. It is not inconsequential that English is the *de facto* working language of the ECB as it is in international banking circles, in contrast to the Commission where French is still important. This combination of design and aspiration seems to set the ECB somewhat apart from the national central banks and the other EU institutions, although it remains to be seen to what degree this culture will become more bureaucratized as the ECB ages.

The powers of the ECB: centralization versus national control

The creation of the ECB has had myriad effects on policy-making, moving some policy processes to the European level while leaving other related policy areas in the hands of national governments. These transformations have the potential to ignite serious tensions between centralization and national control in governance and economic policy-making within the EU. The following sections evaluate the likely organization and character of EU policy-making in the key areas of monetary policy, economic policy (particularly fiscal policy), and exchange rate policy.

Monetary policy

Despite the novelty of the ECB's formal institutional framework, there is significant overall continuity in the substance of European monetary policy-making. In the past two decades, there has been an increasing consensus in Europe on the importance of price stability and central bank independence (McNamara 1998). This consensus has been an important underlying contributor to exchange rate stability in advance of EMU. The Maastricht Treaty codifies this consensus, stating that the 'primary objective' of the European Central Bank is 'the maintenance of price stability' (Art. 105 TEC). The ECB must also 'support the general economic policies in the Community' but 'without prejudice to the objective of price stability'. Price stability is not defined by the Treaty in quantitative terms, but is usually agreed by European central bankers to mean an inflation rate close to but under 2 per cent, a position clarified in a May 2003 ECB internal review of monetary policy strategy.

Underlying the emphasis on price stability is the belief that monetary policy cannot have any long-lasting influence, through monetary expansion, on real economic variables such as output growth and employment. European officials have viewed such expansion of the money supply through lower interest rates as dangerous, because they may produce permanently higher and more variable rates of inflation that will have negative effects on the real economy. Then ECB President Wim Duisenberg has stated that 'the monetary authorities can support job creation and the attainment of higher living standards by fostering a stable macroeconomic environment in which business decisions can be made' (Duisenberg 1998b). In this view, low inflation can enable growth and employment only indirectly, by providing a stable economic environment. This monetary policy consensus has not been entirely uncontested. Observers have argued that a strict emphasis on price stability by the ECB may have a deflationary effect, slowing growth within Europe and its trading partners (Eichengreen 1996; Cameron 1998).

To achieve the goal of price stability, the Executive Board early on developed a two-track operational approach. The first strategy is monetary targeting, in which the amount of money flowing through the European economy is measured, and the central bank adjusts its policies to achieve a set money supply goal. The second strategy is inflation targeting, the identification and publication of an inflation target that is used by the bank to guide policy. Both these strategies have their critics and adherents. When these strategies are used together, some critics claim there is a danger that the objectives of policy may be too opaque for observers to determine what they are and if they are being met.

Other critiques of the ECB's monetary policy have been more comprehensive. Some observers have argued that the existing decision-making structure of the ECB is cumbersome, and has produced a more static monetary policy than conditions warrant. A more nimble ECB would be better able to pull the EU out of its economic stagnation, in this view. In addition, enlargement makes monetary policy even more challenging. One important reality of the Eurozone (and many national currency settings) is that as it does not comprise an optimal currency area, the ECB's 'one size fits all' monetary policy will have real costs for participating states whose economies are outliers to the rest. For example, a slow-growth Germany would benefit from lower interest rates than the ECB has set, while a sizzling Irish economy with concurrent inflationary pressures would probably warrant higher rates than those set by the ECB. The size of the euro zone, should it eventually grow from the current twelve members to the full twenty-five, will increase the potential for such divergence in economic conditions. Granted, the GDP weight of the new entrants is relatively low, as the nominal GDP of the euro area in 2003 was €7,254 billion and that of the ten new member states was €436 billion (thus around 6 per cent of the euro area's GDP). However, the ten new EU members have a total population of 74 million people (approximately 25 per cent of the euro area's), as opposed to the current euro area's population of 309 million people. Fortunately, there is in place a well-functioning process of consultation between the national central banks and the ECB, which may help with coordination in the wake of any euro enlargements. Meeting in Frankfurt in series of Eurosystem committees, representatives of the national central banks and the ECB engage in preparing decisions of the Governing Council, which provide an important link between domestic expertise and Eurozone policymaking. Nonetheless, ECB officials will be challenged to provide a monetary policy that can meet the needs of the entire population of the euro zone should it increase to include all of the new member states.

In addition, a remaining issue for the ECB in the monetary realm is the question of financial regulation. Although the formulation of monetary policy is located solely within the ECB, much of the execution and operation of monetary policy continues through the national central banks. The ECB is responsible for the promotion of the 'smooth operation of the payment system', which refers to the workings of TARGET, the intra-European large payments clearinghouse system, for which the ECB could be a lender of last resort in the event of a crisis. But two tasks traditionally vital to national central banks have not been transferred to the supranational level in Europe, namely ultimate responsibility for stability of the European financial system, and the issuance of system wide debt instruments. Even some years into the full operation of EMU, uncertainty remains over how intra-EU disputes and systemic crises will be contained and resolved due to the lack of clear legal direction in the treaty. Although some have advocated it, the ECB does not yet have broader supervisory capacity over the ever more closely integrated EU financial markets. One thing that is clear, however, is that the Maastricht Treaty features a 'no bail-out' clause prohibiting the ECB from rescuing member states who find themselves in financial dire straits. Also, the ECB is barred from creating an EU-level financial instrument, such as a European treasury bill, to finance EU expenditures. Instead, the national governments have individually issued their own bonds denominated in euros, and there is a highly competitive market in such bonds across the EU. These elements of traditional national monetary capacity are absent at the EU level, thus making the ECB's tasks in certain ways more difficult.

Economic policy coordination

The question of economic governance and coordination in EMU involves an ongoing set of issues that officials do not appear to be close to resolving, despite repeated calls in a variety of expert reports on the topic. In the Treaty itself, there is little statutorily to increase the degree of coordination in areas such as fiscal policy. In practice, what coordination there has been is centred in Ecofin, the EU Council of Ministers for Economic and Financial Affairs, which will continue to be a key locus for general discussions of issues like taxation and national budgeting. National governments are still responsible for the individual development and execution of their economic policies, although they are expected to take account of their EU neighbours and work to coordinate their policies where appropriate.

Indeed, concerns have been raised about whether this policy apparatus will enable member states effectively to coordinate fiscal and monetary policies, and the possible implications of coordination problems for the management of the external value of the Euro. Two political initiatives have addressed this concern by moving beyond the general guidelines for policy coordination established in the Maastricht Treaty. The first important post-Maastricht policy innovation was the Stability and Growth Pact (SGP), which builds on language in the Treaty regarding 'excessive government deficits' (Art. 104 TEC). The Treaty language specifies that a government whose budget deficit exceeds 3 per cent of GDP or whose public debt exceeds 60 per cent of GDP may be required to correct its situation, and may be subject to sanctions and penalties if it fails to do so.

Prompted by the German Finance Minister, Theo Waigel, Heads of State and Government came to agreement in Dublin in December 1996 on procedures for increased policy surveillance, the specific penalties to be imposed when countries have excessive deficits, and the automatic imposition of those penalties. In practice, however, over the first years of EMU, the SGP has not proven to be a resilient tool for fiscal coordination, but rather has disintegrated into squabbles over its execution and application. Most obviously, as of this writing, four countries have been found to be in violation of the SGP, and the Pact has been 'suspended' for a time *vis à vis* these truants, while the rules have also been loosened.

In 2003, France received an 'early warning' and was instructed to get its financial house in order, while Portugal, Italy, and Germany all went from initial 'early warnings' to being judged as having 'excessive deficits'. However, EU finance ministers rejected the Commission's recommendations to sanction these countries and voted instead to give them room to make adjustments without fines. This decision was viewed by many as suspending the Pact, and angered some member states who believed that the two largest actors in the Eurozone were being given *carte blanche* to flout the rules their partner states were struggling to meet. The Commission subsequently decided to refer the matter to the European Court of Justice to decide if the SGP Treaty was being upheld. In August 2004, the ECJ, while condemning the EU's finance ministers for suspending the Pact's recommendations on deficits, upheld the rights of the national governments to ignore these recommendations and the disciplinary procedures attached to them (see p. 140 cf.).

The controversy about truants from the Pact is only part of the problem: more damaging to its future are the serious questions raised about its appropriateness in meeting the needs of economic governance in Europe. The precise numerical targets of the SGP do not have a solid foundation in economic theory but rather appear to be the product of political bargaining. In addition, many view the budget targets as overly restrictive and likely to inhibit recovery at exactly those moments that European states may need to stimulate their economies by spending public funds. Indeed, most of the EU states have been plagued by economic underperformance, making the flouting of the rules less than surprising. In lieu of strict rules, it might be more appropriate to pursue more aggressively coordination among EU economic and finance ministers so that policies can be more appropriately tailored to the needs of the moment. Some long-time official participants in the EMU project have stated privately that some form of fiscal federalism—that is, a more federal European structure with centralized redistributive policies of taxing, borrowing, and spending—is a certainty in the long run, although this remains a publically taboo idea.

Concerns such as these have prompted the second important political initiative affecting the character and organization of economic policy-making in EMU, the establishment of a new informal group, now called the Eurogroup, which had its inaugural meeting on 5 June 1998 in Luxembourg (the draft European Constitution was slated to formally embed it in the legal structure of the EU). The Eurogroup is a subset of the Ecofin, made up of the ministers of the euro states and acting as a forum for coordination within the euro zone, with some states such as France advocating a strong role for this body. Although this ambition has been strongly criticized as a threat to the independence of the ECB, it should not be dismissed. It is instructive to recall that even the very independent Bundesbank is embedded in a framework of political institutions and long participated in an ongoing dialogue with its 'social partners', that is, business and labour (McNamara and Jones 1996; Hall and Franzese 1998). Germany initially argued, however, that the Eurogroup should serve merely as an informal body to promote information exchange, and that the SGP would provide direction on the appropriate fiscal policies. Britain has been even more resistant to a major role for the Eurogroup, fearing that it will be shut out if the Eurogroup gains real institutional power. Nonetheless, the Eurogroup's formal inclusion as an EU institution in the drafting of the European Constitution indicated a certain realism about the inadequacies of the Stability and Growth Pact, and a need for more pro-active coordination of fiscal policy.

Exchange rate policy

While the structure of monetary policy decision-making within the ECB is relatively clear, the Treaty on European Union was less clear in the area of exchange rate policy making for the Euro. Operational responsibility for exchange rate values, through the conduct of foreign exchange operations (interventions and the daily management of exchange reserves), is the sole responsibility of the ECB. The Treaty is less clear, however, about the locus of responsibility for the formulation or creation of exchange rate policy. Article 109 TEC treats three aspects of exchange rate policy, as well as two broader questions of economic governance.

According to the Treaty, the decision to enter into a formal exchange rate agreement with non-EU countries is the responsibility of Ecofin, and any such agreement would be binding on the ECB. In the absence of such an agreement, the Council, acting on a proposal from the Commission and after consultation with the ECB, may adopt (by a qualified majority vote) 'general orientations' for exchange rate policy towards non-EU currencies, but only insofar as they do not interfere with the ECB's primary goal of price stability.

As the resurrection of a formal system such as the post-war Bretton Woods international exchange rate regime is unlikely in the foreseeable future, the vague language regarding 'general orientations' is more likely to govern the informal cooperation that has characterized the international monetary system since the early 1970s. One result is an opening for increasing the Commission's institutional power. The policy discussion about the locus of competence for exchange rate policy is, in any event, ongoing.

The European Council attempted to resolve some of the ambiguities at its meeting in Luxembourg in December 1997. It adopted a resolution designed to clarify Article 109 TEC, stating that the Ecofin may 'in exceptional circumstances, for example in the case of a clear misalignment, formulate general orientations for exchange-rate policy in relations to non-EC currencies'. At Luxembourg, the heads of state also agreed that the Ecofin Council 'should decide on the position of the Community at international level as regards issues of particular relevance to economic and monetary union'. It interpreted the Council's jurisdiction broadly by including 'bilateral relations between the EU and individual third countries and to proceedings in international organizations or informal international groupings'.

Then ECB President Wim Duisenberg stated the consistent view of the ECB, however, when he argued that an exchange-rate objective is not an appropriate monetary policy strategy for the ECB, 'given that for an area as potentially as large as the Euro area, such an approach might be inconsistent with the internal goal of price stability. The external value of the euro will thus mainly be an outcome of the ECB's monetary policy'. Formal arrangements with non-EU countries are unlikely, he went on to say, although the ESCB will of course have the technical capacity to 'intervene in order to counteract excessive or erratic fluctuations of the Euro against the major non-EU countries' (Duisenberg 1998a). In contrast, the European Commission and some member states, notably France, have argued that the Treaty does leave the door open for a more activist policy on the part of Ecofin and the Commission. One likely motivation for such a stance is the desire to manage the value of the euro to increase the competitiveness of EU products in world markets.

The initial experience of the euro in exchange-rate markets has been marked by dramatic swings in its value, making the issue of who has authority over the exchange-rate management of real world importance. The euro began on 1 January 1999 valued at $1.18, but by its first birthday was trading at around 1 euro to 1 US dollar. In its second year, the euro declined to the value of only 87 cents per euro. However, this decline began to reverse and by its fifth birthday in January 2005, it was the dollar's turn to be traded at historic lows against the euro, as those paying in dollars had to hand over $1.34 for the EU's currency. There is disagreement on the implications, economically and politically, of this decline. A good argument can be made that the euro simply began at too high a value, hurting European exporters, and that a certain decline was desirable. However, the very low levels of the early years of the ECB were frustrating for those who championed the euro as a way to develop a strong, stable counterpart to rival the dollar internationally. Yet the very strong euro that emerged in 2004 caused concern on the part of commercial interests in Europe whose exports now were much more costly, and thus less attractive, to American consumers. The ECB has sent somewhat mixed signals at times about the desired level of the euro, and a variety of actors have criticized the ECB for not presenting a more coherent front. There has been an effort at currency intervention coordinated with American officials, but exchange rate management is not high on the agenda of either the ECB or the US government. Fluctuations of the euro *vis-à-vis* the currencies of EU countries not participating in EMU and those of other states in Europe may be of perhaps greater ultimate concern given the high level of economic and political interaction within Europe.

The uncertainly regarding the legal division of responsibility for exchange-rate policy-making between Ecofin and the ECB is troublesome but not unusual, however, when considered in light of national policy arrangements. Henning (1997: 32) notes that 'In most countries, the relationship between the central bank and finance ministry is treated in legislation only vaguely, if at all'. Historically, the finance ministries have played an active role in exchange-rate management and policy-making throughout the EU. The ECB's view that exchange-rate policy will simply be subordinate to the internal objective of price stability, although enshrined in the Treaty, has already been proved not to be the case in practice. Its doctrine will probably evolve as the ECB matures as an institution. The larger issue raised by exchange-rate policy, however, is one of the relationship of monetary policy to other economic and social goals. Developing the institutional capacity to integrate monetary policy capacity into a broader set of political institutions, at both the EU and national levels, is a challenge that may remain unsolved for some time to come.

Democratic accountability and legitimacy issues

The ECB has successfully overcome a series of difficult technical tasks in its first years, from developing new European-wide measurements of the economy to the changeover to euro coins and paper currency. However, important political tasks remain for the ECB. The main political question confronting Europe's central bankers is how the ECB can maintain independence while at the same time being viewed as legitimate and accountable to the European public. Democratic accountability is not only an ideal that one might be philosophically committed to, but rather should be seen as the key to the success of this new EU institution by safeguarding the policy effectiveness of the ECB. The searing public defeat of the European Constitutional Treaty in France and the Netherlands in the spring of 2005 has only raised the stakes for the legitimation of the ECB and the euro in many European citizens' eyes.

The ECB is a unique supranational organization with powers far beyond what we could have imagined sovereign states would delegate to such an institution. But, as argued above, the ECB is also notable for being the most independent central bank in the world. Its statute begins by prohibiting the ECB from seeking or taking any directions from 'Community institutions or bodies, from any government of a Member State or from any other body'. Its personnel rules, the fact that it requires a Treaty revision to change its mandate, and the barring of financing of national deficits all contribute to the ECB's independence. But this legal independence is only half the story.

The nature of European Union politics adds to the ECB's independence in more subtle ways because the ECB is not embedded within a larger network of governing institutions. The formal institutions of the EU that might provide accountability, such as the European Parliament, are institutionally weak. The informal political institutions that might provide a legitimating foundation are also tenuous, in that the political loyalties of citizens and sense of connection to the EU level are also limited across the nation states. Any institution needs political friends to help it survive in the advent of difficulties. While a degree of independence is merited, it can be a problem if it means that there is little in the way of substantial dialogue across various groups and only weak legitimating foundations for policy delegation.

Regardless of its eventual fate, the deliberation process around the Constitutional Convention provided the potential for a discussion of the broader economic policy context in which the ECB operates. But aside from the formal recognition of the Eurogroup, there was little evaluation of the delicate balance that must be struck between independence and accountability, and between the supranational nature of the ECB and the continuing national-level economic institutions. In practice, improving accountability may rest on expanded communication and transparency, achieved in part by strengthening the institutional linkages with a broad range of interlocutors throughout the EU. The President of the ECB is regularly called before the European Parliament, and although having no formal obligation to appear, Trichet (like Duisenberg before him) has proven willing to go beyond the confines of the Treaty in interactions with the EP. However, not enough attention is paid by the average citizen in Europe to the central bank president's testimony. Unlike former US Federal Reserve President Alan Greenspan's visits to the US Congress, which were avidly watched on television by millions, Jean-Claude Trichet's forays in front of the EP receive less attention from the broader public than they do from financial market participants.

Unfortunately, the parliamentarians themselves are limited in their resources and capacity to provide comprehensive oversight of the ECB. The ECB Executive Board members often give the impression that communication, for them, is a one way street, instead of acknowledging that communication can flow both ways, *from* political leaders and their publics about the values and goals of economic policy *to* the ECB. To overcome this *lacuna*, the role of the Eurogroup in providing a broader context for formulating economic policy could be critical. As the national ministers do more directly represent their publics, developing the linkages between the Eurogroup and the ECB would seem to be an important way forward, without jeopardizing the ECB's independence. More communication with the social partners, particularly EU trades unions, might also strengthen, not erode, the position of the ECB. The most effective national central banks have long had quite close relationships with business, labour and social groups that help determine the success of their monetary policies; developing those relationships at the European level will also be a crucial determinant of the ECB's success.

The issue of transparency is contentious, but cannot be separated from the issues of democracy and communication. In a widely read article, Willem Buiter (1999) criticized the ECB for not being sufficiently open, transparent and accountable and argued that its strategies and objectives need clarifying. To correct this, Buiter argued that the ECB should publish its voting records, minutes, and its inflation forecasts. ECB Executive Board member Otmar Issing (1999) responded that confidentiality is essential for the central bank to fulfill its public mandate of good governance over the euro area by ensuring unbiased voting and discussion among the board members. If the minutes of General Council meetings are published, Issing (1999: 513) asserts, council members might be inhibited from stating their true opinions, instead worrying how their views will come across to the public in the minutes of the meeting. However, others have argued that the ECB's lack of transparency may result in a lack of credibility, and ultimately, a lack of public support for its policies (Lohmann 1998; Berman and McNamara 1999).

The central bankers inside the ECB are not immune from these debates. Indeed, one key cleavage that has emerged in the first years of the ECB is the ongoing internal discussion over how to ensure that the ECB is indeed politically legitimate. Some, such as Issing, believe that performance and policy outputs determine legitimacy, and that independence may improve the chances of price stability, thus allowing the ECB to fulfil its primary mandate. In this view, the performance of the ECB will itself take care of accountability. There are others, however, who believe active communication with the public is crucial, that accountability is a political process, not based solely on economic outcomes. Some in the Governing Council see the national central bank governors as playing a crucial role as channels of 'representation', or communication to their publics, as they are familiar, mostly well regarded, and literally speak the right language. The debates in the Governing Council over the instruments of monetary policy—whether to use monetary targeting or inflation targeting—are in the view of some more about accountability than technical merit. Some Governors view inflation targeting as more transparent than a monetary target, and want to be sure to include it for that reason. As most central banks use a pragmatic mix of the two policies, it seems likely that different perceptions about the transparency and communicability of each policy may indeed have been a large factor in the intensity of the early debates on this issue. Outside the ECB, transparency remains a concern of financial market actors, who continue to be somewhat dissatisfied with the amount of information volunteered by the ECB about its policies, in publications, press conferences, and appearances before the EP.

In all, it is important to stress that monetary policy, like any other act of governance, requires political constituencies to evaluate and support its actions. If the ECB is able to develop in a context of increasing linkages with both national and other EU level institutions and social groups, without jeopardizing its independence, it will be to the benefit of the economies and the people of Europe.

Conclusion

By the year 2010, the ECB is scheduled to move into a dramatic new building being built on the banks of the River Main. The twisting glass towers and innovative design suit the unique and surprising institution that is the ECB. Despite the many odds against monetary union, EMU has been successfully launched with the ECB at its helm, presiding over a huge political economy and managing a new global currency. This chapter has outlined the reasons, theoretical and historical, behind the ECB's creation. The challenges it still faces in achieving more effective monetary policy, in embedding itself in a more extensive framework of EU economic governance, and in increasing political accountability and legitimacy while not compromising its independence, are formidable, particularly in light of the unease of European publics after the rejection of the European Constitutional Treaty. The enlargement of the EU to twenty-five in 2004 has only raised the stakes for the successful resolution of these questions. How all of the levers of economic policy can be juggled between the national capitals, Brussels, and Frankfurt remains to be seen. More proposals will no doubt be forthcoming for increased fiscal policy coordination and perhaps simultaneously a dialogue within the European Parliament and elsewhere on the need for more genuine communication with the citizens of Europe. Managing the euro will continue to be a challenging task. The ECB now joins other critically important EU institutions such as the Commission and the European Court of Justice in formulating policy for Europe. Like them, it also must confront the issue of democratic legitimacy while maintaining its policy effectiveness.

Notes

1 This analysis rests on the Optimum Currency Area (OCA) theory developed by Mundell (1961), McKinnon (1963), and Kenen (1969).

2 More generally, Oatley (1997) provides a deft account of the variety of distributional and coalitional rationales across the different EU states that contributed to monetary integration.

3 Treaty on European Union, Protocol on the Statute of the European System of Central Banks and of the European Central Bank, Chapter 3, Art. 11. The

terms of the original founding board members varied in length initially; now, they are all eight years.

4 The ECB and the twelve national central banks of the euro area also are referred to as the Eurosystem.

5 As per Art. 113 TEC.

6 Art. 113(3) TEC.

7 However, it is still subject to judicial review on the part of the European Court of Justice in relation to its compliance with EU law.

Further reading

For an overview of the history and the rationales behind EMU, see Sandholtz (1993), Dyson and Featherstone (1999), McNamara (1998), and Moravcsik (1998). The emerging literature on the ECB includes Lohmann (1999), McNamara (2001), and de Haan *et al.* (2004). See Galí *et al.* (2004) and earlier volumes of the series *Monitoring the European Central Bank* for excellent economic policy analyses of the ECB.

De Haan, J., Amtenbrink, F., and Waller, S. (2004), 'The Transparency and Credibility of the European Central Bank', *Journal of Common Market Studies*, 42/4: 775–94.

Dyson, K., and Featherstone, K. (1999), *The Road to Maastricht* (Oxford: Oxford University Press).

Galí, J., Gerlach, S., Rotemberg, J., Uhlig, H., and Woodford, M. (2004), 'The Monetary Policy Strategy of the ECB Reconsidered', *Monitoring the European Central Bank* 5, (London: Centre for Economic Policy Research).

Lohmann, S. (1999), 'The Dark Side of European Monetary Union', in E. Meade (ed.), *The European Central Bank: How Decentralized? How Accountable? Lessons from the Bundesbank and the Federal Reserve System* (Washington, DC: American Institute for Contemporary Germany Studies).

McNamara, K. (1998), *The Currency of Ideas: Monetary Politics in the European Union* (Ithaca, NY: Cornell University Press).

McNamara, K. (2001), 'Where Do Rules Come From? The Creation of the European Central Bank', in A. Stone Sweet, N. Fligstein, and W. Sandholtz (eds.), *The Institutionalization of Europe* (Oxford and New York: Oxford University Press).

Moravcsik, A. (1998), *The Choice for Europe: Social Purpose and State Power from Messina to Maastricht* (Ithaca, NY: Cornell University Press).

Sandholtz, W. (1993), 'Choosing Union: Monetary Politics and Maastricht,' *International Organization* 46/1: 1–39.

Web links

Key official websites include the website of the ECB (*www.ecb.int*); the EU's official euro website (*www.europa.eu.int/euro/html/entry.html*); the website for the European Commission's Directorate on Economic and Financial Affairs (*www.europa.eu.int/comm/economy_finance/*); and that for the European Parliament's Committee on Economic and Monetary Affairs (*http://www.europarl.eu.int/committees/econ_home.htm*). The websites of the *Financial Times* (*www.ft.com*) and *The Economist* (*www.theeconomist.com*) are the two definitive English-language news sources for developments in the euro zone and the ECB. The Centre for European Policy Research (*www.cepr.org*) funds research on a wide range of economic issues, including monetary policy and the ECB, and posts summaries of research publications on its website.

Chapter 10

Managing Europeanization

The European Agencies

Giandomenico Majone

Contents

Summary

This chapter analyses the rise of European regulatory agencies. The rate of agency creation in recent years, at both national and European levels, suggests the existence of functional needs that are not satisfied by centralized policy-making institutions. What has been achieved so far in the EU, however, is more in the nature of stop-gap measures than stable solutions. Most European regulatory agencies cannot take final and binding actions. Hence, they cannot be held accountable in case of regulatory failure. The underlying problem is the difficulty of institutional innovation within the rigid framework of the classic Community method. To provide adequate answers to the diverse regulatory needs and preferences of a greatly enlarged Union it will be necessary to enlarge this framework by delegating rule-making powers to independent regulatory networks.

Introduction

'Agency' is not a technical term but rather an omnibus label to describe a variety of organizations which perform functions of a governmental nature, and which generally exist outside of the normal departmental framework of government. The United States Administrative Procedure Act (APA) of 1946 probably provides the most comprehensive definition of the term. According to this important law—the product of almost a decade of efforts to systematize the decision-making procedures of all federal agencies, whose number had grown rapidly during the New Deal—an agency is a part of government that is generally independent in the exercise of its functions, and that by law has authority to take final and binding actions affecting the rights and obligations of individuals. Most of the agencies that have proliferated in the member states of the EU in recent years—such as Regulatory Offices in Britain, *Autorités Administratives Indépendantes* in France, *Regulierungsbehörde* in Germany, and *Autorità Indipendenti* in Italy—are agencies in the sense of the APA.

At European level, the first agencies were created in the 1970s, but these were operational or promotional, rather than regulatory, bodies. The 1990s produced a second wave of agencies, now dealing with regulatory issues, including the environment (EEA) and the medicines (EMEA) agencies discussed below. A third wave of agency creation started at the beginning of this decade with the creation of the Food Safety Authority, the Maritime Safety and the Aviation Safety Agencies, the European Network and Information Security Agency, and the European Railway Agency. In addition, the Commission has put forward proposals for the creation of additional regulatory bodies: a Community Fisheries Control Agency and a European Chemicals Agency. Most European agencies of the second and third generation advise the Commission on the technical or scientific aspects of regulatory problems, but have not been given the authority to take final and binding regulatory decisions. Hence, they are not 'agencies' in the sense of the APA, and lacking final authority, they cannot be held accountable for the outcomes of regulatory measures. On the other hand, the European Commission, which usually takes the final decisions, is a collegial body—it can be removed from office through a vote of no confidence by the European Parliament, but only in its entirety. The EP is understandably reluctant to dismiss the entire college in order to sanction a single Commissioner. To complicate matters further, the Commission has been given a large number of separate tasks—executive and regulatory—making it extremely costly to remove it in response to even intense dissatisfaction with how it carries out one particular task. The result is a very unsatisfactory accountability framework.

Why agencies?

The current popularity of the agency model at the national and European levels should not obscure the fact that there are alternative ways of making and implementing regulatory policies. In parliamentary systems, for example, assignment of rule-making functions to government departments is the normal mode of delegation. In the case of economic and social regulation, however, it is today generally admitted that direct ministerial oversight seldom represents a satisfactory solution (Baldwin and McCrudden 1987). The case in favour of delegation to agencies includes such reasons as: the need for expertise and the independence from government which is demanded by at least some applications of expertise; the need of constant fine-tuning of the rules to adapt them to scientific and technical progress; and the opportunity for consultations through public hearings, which is considerably greater for agencies than for departments. Regulatory powers may also be delegated to courts. In the United States, for example, courts are the final decision-makers in competition (antitrust) cases. In parliamentary systems, however, there are serious constitutional and practical obstacles to the delegation of regulatory powers to courts.

Self-regulatory organizations (SROs) are a third alternative to agencies. Self-regulation—delegation of regulatory responsibilities to private bodies—plays a significant role in highly technical areas such as industrial standardization, and wherever product or service quality is an important consideration. An SRO can normally command a greater degree of expertise and detailed knowledge of practices within the relevant area than a public agency. A second advantage is that the rules issued by a private body are less formalized than those of public regulatory regimes. This informality reduces the cost of rule-making, and facilitates quick adaptation of the rules to new technical knowledge and changing conditions. A problem of self-regulation is the risk of capture of the SROs by the regulated interests. Capture is a problem also for agencies, but with self-regulation, regulatory capture is there from the outset since the members of the SROs come from the same groups or organizations they regulate. Monitoring is another potential problem since the willingness of an SRO to publicize and punish wrong-doers is likely to be less than that of a public regulator. One possible solution to these problems is a two-tiered system where a public agency acts chiefly as a regulator of regulators, with the SROs handling day-to-day rule-making and enforcement. A large market like the United States, for example, is remarkable for the high decentralization of its standardization system. There are literally hundreds of SROs involved in the development of technical standards. At the same time, the US regulatory system is characterized by the presence of powerful independent agencies to monitor the activities of the private bodies, and to fill any gaps in the system. In the EU, by contrast, political and legal constraints (such as the 'Meroni Doctrine' discussed in a later section) create serious obstacles to the emergence both of a variety of SROs—matching the expanding size of the European market, and the increasingly diverse preferences of producers and consumers—and of fully fledged regulatory agencies capable of monitoring the activities of the SROs (Majone 2005).

Delegation and policy credibility

We have not yet mentioned what is arguably the most important reason for delegating regulatory powers to independent agencies, namely to enhance the credibility of long-term policy commitments. *Political uncertainty* and *time inconsistency* are the main causes of the credibility problem. Political uncertainty is a direct consequence of the democratic process. One of the defining characteristics of democracy is that it is a form of government *pro tempore* (Linz 1998). The requirement of elections at regular intervals implies that the policies of the current majority can be subverted by a new majority with different and perhaps opposing interests. Hence the uncertainty about future policies.

The other threat to policy credibility—time inconsistency—occurs when a government's optimal long-run policy differs from its preferred short-run policy, so that the government in the short run has an incentive to renege on its long-term commitments. In the absence of some binding commitment, the government will use its discretion to pursue what appears now to be a better policy. However, if people anticipate such a policy change they will behave in ways which prevent policy makers achieving their original objective. For example, a policy of low inflation may be optimal over the long run, but at any time there can be short-run political gains from surprise inflation. If the policy-makers have the possibility of revising the original policy to achieve such short-term gains, economic actors will recognize this and change their behaviour accordingly.

An effective way of enhancing the credibility of long-term policy objectives is to delegate the implementation of those objectives to politically independent institutions. An independent central banker, for example, has no incentive to pursue time-inconsistent monetary policies for short-run political gains. Similarly, the point of insulating regulators from the political process is to increase the credibility of a government's regulatory commitments. The delegation of regulatory powers to some agency distinct from the government itself is best understood as a means whereby governments can commit themselves to regulatory strategies that would not be credible in the absence of such delegation (Gatsios and Seabright 1989). Similarly, the commitment of the member states to the integration of the national markets was thought to lack credibility without the delegation of significant regulatory powers to the independent European Commission. However, the progressive politicization of this institution, in particular its increasing dependence on the support of the European Parliament, poses again the issue of credibility, now at European level: a less independent, more 'parliamentary' Commission faces problems of credible commitment that are analogous to those of the national governments. This is a strong argument in favour of independent European regulatory agencies.

Legal and political obstacles to delegation

As already mentioned, European agencies do not have the powers granted to American regulatory bodies, and even lack the more limited competence enjoyed by the regulatory authorities of the member states. Thus, the Regulation setting up the European Environment Agency (EEA), does not include regulatory functions in the agency's mandate.[1] The task of the agency is mainly to provide information that may be useful in framing and implementing environmental policy. Even the European Medicines Agency (EMEA), which comes closest to being a fully fledged regulatory body, does not take decisions concerning the safety and efficacy of new medical drugs, but submits opinions concerning the approval of such products to the European Commission.[2] Similarly, the European Food Safety Authority (EFSA) is only allowed to assess risk, not to manage it.[3] Only the Commission can make final determinations concerning the safety of the food we eat.

There are several reasons why the European agencies are not granted broader powers. A significant factor is the traditional emphasis on an essentially legislative approach to market integration. The Community adopts a directive which is subsequently transposed by the member states into their own legal order, and implemented by the national administrations. Hence the delegation of full regulatory powers to autonomous European bodies was always resented by the member states as too intrusive. The separation of rule-making and enforcement is also convenient for the Commission, which is more interested in the rewarding task of developing new rules rather than in the thankless and politically costly task of seeing that the existing ones are implemented by the national authorities.

The politically motivated opposition to fully fledged regulatory agencies at European level finds some justification in a narrow reading of Article 7 of the EC Treaty, which lists the institutions—European Parliament, Council, Commission, Court of Justice, and Court of Auditors—which may carry out Community tasks. This has been interpreted as a general prohibition of the establishment of additional policy-making bodies, so that nothing short of treaty revision would allow for the creation of truly independent agencies. As early as 1958, the European Court of Justice with its 'Meroni Doctrine'[4] ruled that the Commission could delegate certain of its executive functions to bodies not named in the Treaty, but only subject to strict constraints. In particular, such bodies must not be given any discretionary powers, and the Commission must retain oversight over the delegated competence, and is responsible for the manner in which it is performed. This reasoning is reflected in the current status of the European agencies, most of which engage only in the preparation of regulatory decisions. However, it can be shown that the model of delegation underlying the Meroni Doctrine is totally out of step with the development of social scientific knowledge about means of controlling agency discretion without excessively intruding upon the delegated authority implicit in the enabling statute (Majone 2005). This doctrine is also out of step with the institutional developments shown in Table 10.1; lip service notwithstanding, the doctrine has *de facto* been repealed.

Table 10.1 European regulatory agencies

	Start of activities	Mission	Location	Official website
European Environment Agency (EEA)	1994	To collect and disseminate timely and reliable information on the state and trends of the environment at European level; to cooperate with relevant scientific bodies and international organizations	Copenhagen	http://www.eea.eu.int/
Office for Harmonization in the Internal Market (Trade Marks and Designs) (OHIM)	1994	To contribute to harmonization in the domain of intellectual property, and, in particular, the domain of trade marks	Alicante	http://oami.eu.int/
Community Plant Variety Office (CPVO)	1995	To implement the regime of Community plant variety rights, a specific form of industrial property rights relative to new plant varieties	Angers	http://www.cpvo.eu.int/
European Agency for Safety and Health at Work (EU-OSHA)	1995	To provide the Community bodies, the member states and stake holders with all relevant technical, scientific, and economic information; to create a network linking up national information networks and facilitate the provision of information in the field of safety and health at work	Bilbao	http://agency.osha.eu.int/
European Medicines Agency (EMEA)	1995	To protect and promote public and animal health through the evaluation and supervision of medical products for human and veterinary use	London	http://www.emea.eu.int/
European Food Safety Authority (EFSA)	2002	To provide independent scientific advice on all matters with a direct or indirect impact on food safety; to carry out assessments of risks to the food chain; to give scientific advice on genetically modified non-food products and feed	Parma	http://www.efsa.eu.int/

continues

Table 10.1 continued

	Start of activities	Mission	Location	Official website
European Aviation Safety Agency (EASA)	2003	To assist the Community in establishing and maintaining a high level of civil aviation safety and environmental protection in Europe; to promote cost efficiency in the regulatory and certification processes; to promote world-wide Community views regarding civil aviation safety standards	Cologne	*http://www.easa.eu.int/*
European Maritime Safety Agency (EMSA)	2003	To provide technical and scientific advice to the Commission in the field of maritime safety and prevention of pollution by ships; to contribute to the process of evaluating the effectiveness of Community legislation	Lisbon	*http://www.emsa.eu.int/*
European Network and Information Security Agency (ENISA)	2004	To assist the Community in ensuring particularly high levels of network and information security; to assist the Commission, the member states and the business community in meeting the requirements of network and information security, including those of present and future Community legislation	Heraklion	*http://www.enisa.eu.int/*
European Railway Agency (official acronym not yet available)	2006 (expected)	To provide the member states and the Commission with technical assistance in the fields of railway safety and interoperability, in particular by carrying out continuous monitoring of safety performance, and producing a public report every two years	Lille/ Valenciennes	*http://europa.eu.int/ comm/transport/rail/ era/index_en.htm*

Source: Official home page of the Agencies: *http://europa.eu.int/agencies/index_en.htm.*

The growing role of agencies

An expanding body of specialized academic literature (see Further reading) is only one of several indicators of the growing importance of European agencies. Thus, unlike previous treaties, the new Constitutional Treaty explicitly mentions agencies in three articles of Title VI of the First Part, dealing with 'The Democratic Life of the Union'. In these articles, agencies are raised to the same level as European institutions and other bodies, at least as far as their duties and responsibilities vis-à-vis European citizens are concerned. According to Article I-48, the European Ombudsman is supposed to investigate and report on complaints about maladministration 'within the Union Institutions, bodies or agencies'. The following article states that any citizen of the Union, as well as natural or legal persons domiciled in one of the member states 'shall have a right of access to documents of the Union Institutions, bodies and agencies . . .'. Again, Article I-50 announces that a European law will lay down the rules relating to the protection of individuals 'with regard to the processing of personal data by the Union's Institutions, bodies and agencies . . .'. Agencies are also mentioned in Part III of the same Treaty.[5] Such references may be less than what some observers had expected—namely an explicit treaty basis for the creation of independent agencies—but they are an important acknowledgment of the growing significance of agencies in EU governance.

Their significance has been recognized also by the Commission in recent official publications. Thus, the White Paper on European Governance contains a section on 'Better application of EU rules through regulatory agencies'. The advantage of agencies, we read, 'is often their ability to draw on highly technical, sectoral know-how, the increased visibility they give to the sectors concerned . . . and the cost savings that they offer to business. For the Commission, the creation of agencies is also a useful way of ensuring it focuses resources on core tasks' (Commission 2001: 42). The White Paper announced a new document setting out the criteria for the creation of new regulatory agencies, and the framework within which they should operate. The promised document is the Communication on the Framework for European Regulatory Agencies of 11 December 2002. The Communication makes several proposals that, if implemented, would introduce some interesting innovations. One such proposal is that the legal basis for establishing an agency be the same as that authorizing the corresponding policy, rather than the general Article 308 EC. The logic of the proposal is clear—the agency is simply an instrument of policy implementation—and in fact it has already been followed in the creation of the EFSA and of the two agencies dealing with aviation and maritime safety.

More controversial is the proposal concerning the management boards of the agencies. At present, these boards—whose task it is to define the agencies' general operating guidelines and work programmes, approve their budgets, and appoint their executive directors—are composed of one or two representatives of each member state and a Commission representative. In some cases, they also include members appointed by the European Parliament or by the social partners. The Commission argues that such arrangements are administratively too cumbersome, especially in the enlarged Union, and too dominated by the member states. It proposes smaller boards where national and supranational interests should be more evenly represen-ted. Concretely, the boards should consist of six representatives appointed by the Commission, six by the Council, and three, with no voting rights, representing the interested parties. It seems highly unlikely, however, that the member states will ac-cept the idea of smaller boards, with rotating national representatives and an equal number of Commission representatives (but see discussion of the EFSA below).

A third proposal has a better chance of being accepted. While in the past the Com-mission always pleaded in favour of including in the boards representatives of the European Parliament, now it argues that appointments by the EP are 'inappropri-ate in view of the regulatory agencies' work and the fact that the Parliament must be free to exercise external political supervision over their activities, without feel-ing tied by the membership of the administrative board' (Commission 2002c: 9). The point is well taken, since most agencies depend, at least for part of their revenue, on subsidies from the EU budget. As the EP shares control of the Union budget with the Council, the presence of members of Parliament in the management boards could create situations of conflict of interest.

The Communication contains several other innovative proposals, but on the central issue of the delegation of regulatory powers the official position has hardly changed: agencies may not be empowered to make rules, i.e., quasi-legislative mea-sures of general applicability. At most, agencies may be allowed to adopt individual decisions in clearly specified areas of Community legislation, 'where a single pub-lic interest predominates and where they do not have to arbitrate on conflicting public interests, exercise powers of political judgment or make complex economic assessments' (Commission 2002c: 11). The Office for Harmonization in the Internal Market, the Community Plant Variety Office, and the European Aviation Safety have been deemed to satisfy these conditions and hence allowed to adopt legally bind-ing decisions in the adjudication of particular applications. In these three cases, it is claimed, the task is simply to verify that individual applications satisfy certain con-ditions precisely defined by the relevant regulations. However, the EMEA and the EFSA seem to satisfy the same conditions: EMEA is exclusively concerned with the safety and efficacy of new medical drugs; EFSA, with the safety of the food we eat. Yet, these agencies have been denied real decision-making powers: the Commission takes the final decisions, subject to the usual comitology oversight. The only relev-ant difference between the two groups of agencies seems to be the greater economic and political significance of EMEA and EFSA, and the consequent reluctance of the Commission to surrender control over these agencies and the corresponding regu-lated activities. The Commission's refusal to delegate regulatory powers entails seri-ous costs in terms of the credibility and accountability of European regulators. Before discussing such costs, however, it may be helpful to review the origin, structure, and powers of three representative agencies.

The politics of institutional choice: the birth of the European Environment Agency

Political actors and interest groups are well aware that institutional choices have significant consequences for the context and direction of policy, so that issues of institutional design are caught up in politics as much as issues of policy (Moe 1990). The inevitable political compromise offers a chance for the opponents of a policy to have a say in the design of the implementing agency and thus, as Moe shows, to impose structures that make effective performance difficult to achieve. This simple model of institutional choice helps us to understand the origin, powers, and position within the EU policy process of the European Environment Agency.

Member states, European institutions, and environmentalist groups all voiced support for the proposal of a European environmental agency made by Commission President Delors in January 1989. However, this general agreement concealed deep divisions concerning specific structural choices, especially those concerning the regulatory powers and effective independence of the new agency. The European Parliament favoured a body with regulatory 'teeth'. In varying degrees all member states opposed the idea that the agency could monitor the implementation of European environmental legislation by national regulators, preferring to restrict its task to the collection of environmental information, and to networking with national, European, and international research institutions. The position of the Commission was ambivalent. On the one hand, executives of the Directorate General for the Environment were concerned about the criticism of industry and of some member states that the Commission's environmental proposals were not grounded in 'good science'. They were even more concerned by the poor implementation of environmental directives. Hence, the idea that the EEA could become a sort of inspectorate of national environmental inspectorates had a number of influential supporters within the Commission. On the other hand, this institution was reluctant to surrender regulatory powers to an agency operating at arm's length. In its proposal of 21 June 1989, the Commission outlined four functions for the new body: a) to coordinate the enactment of EC and national environmental policies; b) to evaluate the results of environmental measures; c) to provide modelling and forecasting techniques; and, d) to harmonize the processing of environmental data. Because of the expected opposition by the member states, no inspection tasks were contemplated.

This proposal was quite distant from the EP's 'ideal point'. The fact that Beate Weber, the *rapporteur* of the Parliament's Environmental Committee, travelled to Washington, DC to gain first-hand knowledge of the US Environmental Protection Agency suggests the model of regulatory agency that European parliamentarians had in mind. The Environmental Committee maintained that the EEA should be given power to police environmental abuses, to supervise national enforcement of EC environmental regulations, and to carry out environmental impact assessments on certain projects funded by the EC both inside the Community and in third countries. Also the composition of the management board became a point of contention. According to the EP, environmentalist groups should be represented in the board, along with representatives from the member states, the Commission, and the EP itself, and the board should be allowed to take decisions by majority vote.

Comparing the preferences of the main political actors—member states, Commission, EP—with the provisions of the Regulation setting up the agency, one sees that the member states clearly won the contest over the structure and powers of the agency. The decisive influence of the national governments is revealed by the composition of the management board which consists of: one representative of each member state and of the three EFTA countries—Iceland, Liechtenstein and Norway—which have joined the agency as full members; two Commission representatives; and two scientific personalities designated by the European Parliament. As already mentioned, the main task assigned to the agency is to provide the EU and the member states with environmental information and, in particular, 'to provide the Commission with the information that it needs to be able to carry out successfully its tasks of identifying, preparing, and evaluating measures and legislation in the field of environment' (Art. 2 of the Regulation). The wording is sufficiently vague, however, to make it unclear whether the agency would be allowed to directly influence policy formulation, for example by evaluating alternative proposals for regulatory measures. So far, the EEA has not been allowed to carry out research that is directly policy relevant. In fact, the agency has not been given any significant role in the EU regulatory process. Political compromise has produced an institutional design characterized by uncertain competences, unresolved conflicts, and failure to deal with the serious implementation problems of EU environmental policy.

From committees to agency: the development of the EMEA

Our next example provides valuable insights into how the present comitology system may evolve into a structure where committees become the operational arm of European agencies, and link up with national authorities to form transnational regulatory networks. The first attempt by the EC to regulate the testing and marketing of pharmaceutical products was a directive introduced in 1965 with the dual objective of protecting human health and of eliminating obstacles to intra-Community trade. This directive only established the principle that no medical drug should be placed on the market without prior authorization, and defined the essential criteria of safety and efficacy for drug approval.

The second phase of regulatory developments began in 1975, with another directive setting up the 'multi-state drug application procedure' and establishing the Committee for Proprietary Medicinal Products (CPMP). This Committee composed of national experts has played, and continues to play, a key role in the EU approach to the regulation of pharmaceuticals. Under the multistate procedure, a firm that had received a marketing authorization from the regulatory agency of a member state could ask for the recognition of that approval by at least five other member states. The agencies of these countries had to approve or raise objections within 120 days. In case of objections the CPMP had to be notified, and would express its non-binding opinion within 60 days. The procedure did not work well: the national agencies did not appear to be bound either by the decisions of other regulatory bodies or by the opinion of the CPMP. Subsequent simplifications failed to streamline the approval process, as national regulators continued to raise objections against each other almost routinely. Hence, firms generally chose to continue to seek authorization from each national agency separately.

A different approval process was introduced in 1987 for biotechnology and other high-technology products. This new 'concertation procedure' required that the application for the authorization be filed both with the national authorities and with the CPMP. The country where the authorization had been filed acted as *rapporteur*, but unlike the old multistate procedure, no decision on the application was to be made by any member state before the CPMP had expressed its opinion. The final decision remained with the member states, however. The evaluation of the application, led by the *rapporteur* country, was carried out at the same time in all the member states—hence the name 'concertation procedure'. The new process was an advance with respect to the old practice, but was nevertheless problematic for firms because, as with the previous procedure, there was a tendency for delays in the notification of decisions following the CPMP opinion. Waiting for all countries to notify their decisions following the Committee's opinion could result in serious delays in a firm's ability to start marketing a new drug.

On 1 January 1995, the problematic multistate and concertation procedures were replaced by three new approaches and a new agency (see Table 10.2). The multistate procedure was replaced by a decentralized procedure, which continues and reinforces the principle of mutual recognition introduced in 1975. Meanwhile, the concertation procedure was replaced by the centralized procedure set out in the same Regulation which also established the European Medicines Agency (see Exhibit 10.1).[6]

Under the centralized procedure, applications are made directly to the agency, leading to the granting of a European marketing authorization. Use of this procedure is compulsory for products derived from biotechnology and optional for other innovative medicinal products. EMEA is also called on to arbitrate disputes arising under the decentralized (mutual recognition) procedure. Opinions adopted by the EMEA in either the centralized procedure or following arbitration lead to binding decisions formally adopted by the Commission.

The technical work of the agency is carried out by the Committee for Medicinal Products for Human Use (CHMP, the successor of the old CPMP), by the Committee for Veterinary Medicines (CVMP), and by two smaller and newer bodies: the Committee for Orphan Medicinal Products (COMP), established in 2001 and charged with reviewing designation applications from persons or companies who intend to develop medicines for rare diseases ('orphan drugs'); and the Committee on Herbal Medicinal Products (HMPC), established in 2004 to provide scientific opinions on traditional herbal medicines. A network of some 3,500 European experts underpins the scientific work of EMEA and its committees and working groups.

The CHMP (and similar rules apply to the CVMP) is composed of two members nominated by each member state for a three-year renewable term. These members in fact represent the national regulatory authorities. Although Commission representatives are entitled to attend the meetings of the Committee, the Commission is no longer represented, no doubt to emphasize the independence of the CHMP.

Table 10.2 An overview of the European authorization system

Human and animal health

The European system for the authorization of medicines for human and veterinary use has been in place since 1995. It is designed to promote both public health and the free circulation of pharmaceuticals. Access to the European market is facilitated for new and better medicines — benefiting users and European pharmaceutical research.

EMEA: a network agency

The European system is based on cooperation between the national competent authorities of the member states and the EMEA. The EMEA acts as the focal point of the system, coordinating the scientific resources made available by member state national authorities, including a network of some 3,500 European experts.

The EMEA is designed to coordinate the scientific resources of the member states, acting as an interface between the national competent authorities rather than as a highly centralized organization.

The European procedures

The European system offers two routes for authorization of medical products:

Centralized procedure: Applications are made directly to the EMEA, leading to the granting of a European marketing authorization. Use of this procedure is compulsory for products derived from biotechnology, and optional for other innovative medicinal products.

Decentralized procedure: Applicable to the majority of conventional medicinal products. Applications are made to the member states selected by the applicant and the procedure operates by mutual recognition of national marketing authorizations. Where this is not possible, the EMEA is called on to arbitrate.

Opinions adopted by the EMEA scientific committees in either the centralized procedure or following arbitrations lead to binding decisions adopted by the European Commission.

Purely national authorizations remain available for medicinal products to be marketed in one member state.

Exhibit 10.1 The European Medicines Agency (EMEA) mission statement

To contribute to the protection and promotion of human and animal health by:

- mobilizing scientific resources from throughout the European Union to provide high-quality evaluation and supervision of medicines for human and veterinary use;
- developing efficient and transparent procedures to allow timely access by users to innovative medicines through a single European marketing authorization;
- controlling the safety of medicines for humans and animals, in particular through a pharmacovigilance network;
- providing useful and clear information to users and health professionals;
- cooperating closely with international partners, thus reinforcing the EU contribution to global harmonization.

In fact, the Committee has become more important, as well as more independent, since the establishment of the EMEA. In the new situation, Committee members have greater incentives to establish the agency's, and their own, international reputation than to defend national positions. Using Alvin Gouldner's (1957–58) terminology, we may say that the agency creates a favourable environment for the transform-ation of national regulators from 'locals'—professionals who have primarily a na-tional orientation—to 'cosmopolitans,' who are likely to adopt an international reference-group orientation. It does this by providing a stable institutional focus at the European level, a forum where different risk philosophies are compared and mu-tually adjusted, and by establishing strong links to national and to extra-European regulatory bodies.

The uncertain pursuit of regulatory credibility: the European Food Safety Authority

The food sector is an area where EC regulation dates back to the earliest days of the Community. Traditionally, policy on food safety was developed by the Commission assisted by a large number of comitology and expert committees. Several regulatory failures—of which the BSE epidemic attracted the greatest public attention—revealed the inadequacy of the traditional approach. The BSE (Bovine Spongiform Encephalopathy, or 'mad cow' disease) tragedy exposed serious shortcomings in the overall coordination of European policies on agriculture, the internal market, and human health. On 18 July 1996, the European Parliament set up a temporary Committee of Inquiry into BSE. The Committee concluded that both the Council and the Commission had neglected their duties, and that the UK gov-ernment had exerted pressures on the Commission's veterinary services in order to avoid Community inspections and prevent publicization of the extent of the epi-demic. The Commission was criticized for having given priority to the management of the beef market rather than to the risks to human health posed by BSE, and for having downplayed the problem despite concerns raised by a number of experts. The Committee of Inquiry also noted that there had been severe problems with the work-ings of the Commission's Scientific Advisory Committee.

Responding to these and other criticisms, on 30 April 1997 the Commission issued a Green Paper on the general principles of food law in the EU. This was followed, on 12 January 2000, by a White Paper on Food Safety, proposing the creation of an independent European Food Authority (EFA, later renamed European Food Safety Au-thority) in the context of a reform of the entire food safety system, 'from farm to table'. The EFA was to take on responsibilities relating to the risk assessment and risk communication parts of the regulatory system envisaged by the Commission. How-ever, risk management, comprising legislation and control, was not to be transferred to the agency. The EFA was to be guided by the best science; independent of indus-trial and political interests; open to public scrutiny; scientifically authoritative, and closely linked to national scientific bodies. The reform proposals contained in the

---

Exhibit 10.2 The European Food Safety Authority (EFSA) mission statement

- To provide independent scientific advice on all matters with a direct or indirect impact on food safety.
- To carry out assessments of risks to the food chain, and scientific assessments of any matter relating to the safety of the food supply.
- To give scientific advice on genetically modified non-food products and feed, and on nutrition, in relation to Community legislation.
- To provide scientific opinions which will serve as the scientific basis for the drafting and adoption of Community measures.
- To cooperate with the Commission and the member states in order to promote effective coherence between risk assessment, risk management, and risk communication.

White Paper on Food Safety formed the basis of the already mentioned Regulation 178/2002, which lays down the general principles and requirements of food law, establishes the European Food Safety Authority, and sets out the EFSA's mission (see Exhibit 10.2).

The organizational design of the EFSA is broadly similar to that of the EMEA: a Management Board, an Executive Director, a Scientific Committee, and a number of Scientific Expert Panels and their working groups. There are, however, some important differences which are best understood in light of the credibility crisis of EU food safety regulation following the BSE crisis. The EFSA is the only case where the member states have been willing to accept something less than full representation in the Management Board. The EFSA Board comprises fourteen members appointed by the Council—in consultation with the European Parliament, from a list drawn up by the Commission—plus an additional representative of the Commission. Four members must have a background in organizations representing consumer and other interests in the food chain, and no member is an official government representative. Instead, the principle of one representative per country has been retained in the composition of the Advisory Forum, which assists the Executive Director and advises on scientific matters, priorities, and work programmes. From May 2004, this body comprises twenty-five members (including the ten representatives of the new member states) who come from national bodies that play a role similar to that of the EFSA.

In spite of these innovative features, it seems unlikely that the present arrangements will succeed in resolving the credibility problem, or in ensuring an acceptable level of public accountability. The tension between the desire to enhance regulatory credibility by appealing to independent scientific expertise, and the refusal to delegate regulatory powers to the EFSA, has been temporarily resolved by the doubtful expedient of an organizational separation of risk assessment (the function assigned to the Authority), and risk management, which remains the responsibility of the Commission. Similar organizational separations of regulatory functions have been tried in the United States and other countries, usually with disappointing results. The separation of risk assessment and risk management is problematic because while the two functions are conceptually distinct—one dealing with scientific issues, the other with economic, legal, and political issues—they are closely intertwined in practice. The setting of rational regulatory priorities, for example, entails economic, political, and scientific judgements that cannot be easily separated. Again, the determinations of the risk analysts can effectively preempt the decisions of the risk managers. Thus, it is often impossible to determine with certainty whether a dose-response function—measuring the probability of an organism's response to different levels of toxicity—follows a linear or a non-linear model, yet the scientists' choice of one or the other model is crucially important to the determination of an acceptable level of risk (Majone 2003). If risk assessment and risk management are not separable in practice, then it follows that both efficiency and accountability are best served when the head of an expert agency, rather than a collegial body of political executives or bureaucratic generalists, such as the Commission, is personally responsible for the outcomes of the regulatory process. The refusal to set up a regulatory agency fully responsible for food safety entails a serious accountability deficit, without solving the credibility problem.

Independence and accountability

As we saw at the beginning of this chapter, policy credibility is arguably the main reason for delegating regulatory powers to an independent agency. Such powers, entrusted to a non-elected body, must be balanced by a sophisticated system of accountability that goes well beyond the controls needed to discipline the limited discretion of the ministerial bureaucracy. The basic problem is always how 'to control and validate the exercise of essentially legislative powers by administrative agencies that do not enjoy the formal legitimacy of one-person, one-vote election' (Stewart 1975: 1688). The solution requires a framework where independence and accountability are complementary and mutually supportive, rather than antithetical; values. Such a framework will largely consist of procedural and other indirect means of inducing the desired agency behaviour. An outstanding example is provided by the already mentioned US Administrative Procedure Act. The Act prescribes an agency's obligation to make public information about its organization, procedures and substantive requirements, and to provide advance notice of proposed rulemaking. Interested persons must be given opportunity to participate in the regulatory process through public hearings. General conditions for judicial review of agency decisions are also defined. These, together with other procedural requirements introduced by later statutes, provide an effective accountability framework, without interfering with the legitimate exercise of agency independence. As a result, although American regulatory agencies are independent from direct political control, they are hardly free from strict requirements of public accountability (Freedman 1978).

In contrast, the present European agencies are in many ways beyond the scope of public scrutiny, without any generalized administrative rules or standards laid down which they must observe, and the process by which they reach their conclusions are subject to limited external monitoring or review. This lack of clear mechanisms of accountability is highly problematic within a polity like the EU whose legitimacy is often contested. The above-mentioned requirements of the new Constitutional Treaty are helpful as far as they go, but they are not specifically tailored to the tasks of regulatory agencies. It is also important to keep in mind that agency independence is a necessary, but certainly not a sufficient, condition of accountability—an agency may use its autonomy to favour particular interests, including its own. Hence, when the Commission contends that agencies like EMEA or EFSA are independent, it chooses to highlight only one aspect of the general problem. As long as such agencies have no authority to take final and binding actions, but must share responsibility with the Commission and a variety of comitology committees, accountability by results is reduced to vanishing point. Regulatory failures such as the BSE disaster are always possible, and in such cases citizens want to know whom to blame. This legitimate demand cannot be satisfied under the present institutional arrangements.

The network model

It is clearly impossible to transpose to the EU the American model of federal agencies operating independently from the regulatory authorities of the states. Regardless of what one thinks of the alleged legal obstacles to the adoption of such a model, it is certain that the member states would reject it. However, their attitude could be different towards a system where the national regulators are the components of an EU-wide network, coordinated by an independent European body. A heuristically useful model is provided by the European System of Central Banks (ESCB), which is composed of the European Central Bank and of the national banks of the member states (see Chapter 9). The ECB is completely independent from the European institutions as well as from the member states, while the national banks must be independent from their respective governments as a condition of membership in the monetary union. Although regulators could not, and probably should not, be as independent as central bankers, the broad relevance of the ESCB model is increasingly recognized.

In fact, the European agencies have not been designed to operate in isolation, or to replace national regulators, but are expected to operate in networks including national, and possibly international, agencies. To qualify as fully fledged regulatory networks, however, the European agencies and their national counterparts need autonomous decision-maker powers, and a firmer legal basis for their independence. In addition to the independence of its decision centres—the agencies—an effective transnational regulatory network must satisfy several other conditions: a high level of professionalism; a common regulatory philosophy; intense information exchange; and mutual trust. Although these conditions may not be satisfied from the beginning, the very existence of the network provides an environment favourable to the development of the requisite qualities. An agency that sees itself as a member of a group of organizations pursuing similar objectives and facing analogous

problems, rather than as part of a large bureaucracy pursuing a variety of objectives, is more motivated to defend its professional standards and policy commitments
against external influences, and to cooperate with the other members of the network. This is because the agency executives have an incentive to maintain their
reputation in the eyes of their international colleagues—as we saw in the case of
the EMEA. Unprofessional, self-seeking, or politically motivated behaviour would
compromise their international reputation and make cooperation more difficult to
achieve in the future. Thus, a network facilitates the development of behavioural
standards and working practices that create shared expectations and enhance the effectiveness of the social mechanisms of trust and reputation.

A well-designed network is also characterized by a mode of coordination, known
as 'coordination by mutual adjustment', that relies primarily on information exchange and adaptive behaviour, rather than on a central coordinator. As Michael
Polanyi has shown, a set of autonomous decision centres can coordinate their actions by each centre adjusting to the results achieved by all other centres in the
set. A 'polycentric task' is the problem of coordinating a network of such autonomous decision centres. The proper method of managing a polycentric task, according to Polanyi, is not by collecting all the data at a central coordinating authority.
Rather, the desired result is achieved by each individual centre reacting to the whole
range of signals that reach it from the other parts of the network. Each centre evaluates the joint significance of the signals, and thus guided all centres collectively
produce a solution to the polycentric task, or achieve, at any rate, a measure of success in this direction (Polanyi 1951: 170–6). In a regulatory network, the solution of
the polycentric task—the adoption of rules tailored to the specific needs of the various national and subnational communities, while avoiding negative policy external-
ities for the other jurisdictions—is greatly facilitated by the properties mentioned
above: a shared regulatory philosophy, common professional standards, and intense
information exchange. It should also be noted that the notion of coordination by
mutual adjustment is closely related to some of the 'new governance' approaches,
such as the Open Method of Coordination, recently adopted as alternatives to the
classical Community method (Majone 2005: 59–60).

Conclusions

As shown by many chapters in this volume, the rate of institutional innovation in
the EU, after fifty years of integration, is still remarkable. Also, the present chapter
has revealed a certain amount of change. What is particularly striking in the case of
regulatory agencies, however, is the gap between the quantitative and the qualitative dimension of change. While the number of European agencies created since the
early 1990s matches the scale of parallel developments in many member states, the
majority of these new European bodies lack the powers normally granted to their
national counterparts. The reason for this discrepancy must be sought in the politics of inter-institutional relations in the EU, and ultimately in the logic of the Community method.

As the French constitutional scholar Jean-Paul Jacqué noted some years ago, the organizing principle of the Community is not the separation of powers but the representation of (national and supranational) interests. Each European institution is the bearer of a particular interest that it strives to protect and promote, and the nature of the prevailing interest determines the structure of decision-making. Thus, when the framers of the Rome Treaty deemed that national interests should have precedence in an area of particular interest to national sovereignty, such as fiscal harmonization, they required a unanimous vote in the Council. Where, on the other hand, it appeared that national interests had to be reconciled with the supranational interest, it was decided that the Council should legislate by qualified majority. Again, where it was thought that the supranational interest should prevail, the Commission was given an autonomous power of decision. In the domain of application of the Community method, the balance between the institutions representing these different interests has constitutional significance. It follows that in this domain, which includes most areas of regulation, it is impossible to achieve more than incremental adjustments. For radical change to take place it would be necessary that an institution renounces to exercise its powers to the full possible extent, but this goes against the principle of institutional balance (Jacqué 1991).

Under the Community method, moreover, only the Commission can propose specific reforms; hence, no departures from current practice that would in any way reduce its own powers may be expected. But without far-reaching reforms the credibility and legitimacy deficits of EU regulation can only deepen. This is especially true in a Union of twenty-five and more member states. From the regulatory viewpoint, a greatly enlarged EU implies, above all, a much greater diversity of national needs, preferences, and resources, and a corresponding increase in the costs imposed by uniform rules. It is highly doubtful that this diversity can be managed with the traditional instruments of central coordination, such as harmonization. A more flexible mode of agency coordination, based on information exchange and mutual adjustment, will be needed. Regulatory networks are the institutional realization of this approach.

Notes

1 Council Regulation 1210/90 of 7 May 1990.

2 Council Regulation 2309/93 of 22 July 1993.

3 Regulation 178/2002 of the European Parliament and the Council of 28 January 2002.

4 Stated in *Meroni* v. *High Authority*, Case 9/56, [1957–58] ECR 133.

5 Arts. III 398–9 of the Constitutional Treaty.

6 See Regulation 2309/93.

Further reading

Recent examples of the burgeoning literature on regulatory agencies in Europe are the volumes edited by Zwart and Verhey (2003), and by Gerardin *et al.* (2005). Freedman (1978) considers only US institutions but still provides the most extensive discussion of the legitimacy problems of regulatory agencies, and many of his arguments are general enough to be applicable to the European context. Recent developments in risk regulation, with special emphasis on food safety, are discussed in Majone (2003). Regulatory reform at European and national levels is the topic of the volume edited by Jordana and Levy-Faur (2004), while the Community method and its implications for institutional reform are analyzed by Majone (2005).

Freedman, O. (1978), *Crisis and Legitimacy* (Cambridge: Cambridge University Press).

Gerardin, D., Munoz, R., and Petit, N. (2005) (eds.), *Regulation through Agencies: A New Paradigm of European Governance* (Cheltenham: Edward Elgar).

Jordana, J., and Levy-Faur, D. (2004) (eds.), *The Politics of Regulation* (Cheltenham: Edward Elgar).

Majone, G. (2003) (ed.), *Risk Regulation in the European Union: Between Enlargement and Internationalization* (Florence: European University Institute).

Majone, G. (2005), *Dilemmas of European Integration — The Ambiguities and Pitfalls of Integration by Stealth* (Oxford: Oxford University Press).

Zwart, T., and Verhey, L. (2003) (eds.), *Agencies in European and Comparative Law* (Antwerp: Intersentia).

Web links

The website *http://europa.eu.int* is the place to start any search for basic information on the institutions and bodies of the EU. For the different European agencies, see specifically *http://europa.eu.int/agencies/index_en.htm*

Chapter 11

Financial Control

The Court of Auditors and OLAF

Brigid Laffan

Contents

Summary

This chapter analyses the evolution of two of the Union's institutions designed to protect the financial interests of the Union: the Court of Auditors, a full EU institution since the Treaty on European Union (1993) and OLAF, the EU's Anti-Fraud Office. The chapter examines the origins of the institutions, how their internal structures have evolved, their powers and their place in the institutional landscape of the Union. Their growing importance arises from the expansion of the EU budget, evidence of mismanagement and fraud against the financial resources of the Union, the emergence of an accountability culture in the EU, and enlargement. Notwithstanding institution-building and a tightening of the regulatory environment, allegations of financial mismanagement continue unabated in the press.

Introduction

The focus in this chapter is on the EU's institutions that were created to protect the interests of Europe's taxpayers in relation to the Union's public finances. Those institutions are the European Court of Auditors (ECA) and OLAF (*Office européen de lutte antifraude*), known in English as the European Anti-Fraud Office. The two bodies are very different. The Court of Auditors is a public audit institution akin to the national audit offices of the northern member states, notably the UK, the Netherlands, and the Nordic states. OLAF is not an EU institution; rather it is a specialist body with a remit in combating fraud.[1] The Court of Auditors, based in Luxembourg, is already more than 25 years old, dating back to 1977. In contrast, OLAF is a much newer body, only created in June 1999. The European Parliament, exercising its role of fostering political accountability, played an important part in the establishment of both institutions. The member states were persuaded that an independent audit body was warranted given the emergence of an EU budget with supranational characteristics. The creation of the Court represented polity-building at the EU level. The fight against fraud assumed greater salience as the size and reach of the EU budget expanded. Peterson (1997) highlights the challenge facing the EU arising from the co-existence of pooled sovereignty and divided accountability. The two bodies are part of an attempt to re-configure systems of accountability in Europe to take account of pooled sovereignty.

Financial management, and in fact management more generally, tends to be marginalized in scholarly discussions of the European Union (Bauer 2002). We should not forget, however, that it was a pronounced failure of management that led to the first resignation of an entire Commission in the history of the Union. The political crisis that culminated in March 1999 with the departure of the Santer Commission had its origins in deep-rooted and perennial problems of financial management in the European Union (MacMullen 1999). Moreover, a continuing stream of sensational newspaper headlines highlighting the smuggling of animals, cigarettes, or liquor act to undermine public confidence in the effectiveness of EU institutions and its policy regimes. Whistleblowers working in European institutions have featured prominently in public disclosures about financial management in the Union. One of the most prominent of these, Paul van Buitenen, was elected to the European Parliament in June 2004.

Following the 1999 crisis, the next Commission under Romano Prodi was given a strong mandate by the European Council to make financial management more robust in the Commission. The Prodi Commission embarked on a series of structural and managerial reforms, known as the Kinnock reforms, with Vice-President Neil Kinnock given the lead role in the Commission reform programme. Although committed to reform, the Prodi Commission was not immune to problems of financial management. The Eurostat investigations, discussed below, put considerable pressure on Prodi. Commissioner Siim Kallas, former Estonian Prime Minister, took over the onerous responsibility for administration, audit, and anti-fraud in the Barroso Commission.

Effective management of the EU budget poses a considerable challenge to the EU and the member states. The budget amounting, to some €106.3 billion in 2005, is largely managed by the member states, with only some 12 per cent managed directly by the Commission and an additional 6 per cent spent on the administrative costs of running the institutions. The effective management and control of the budget is not just, or even primarily, a task for the EU's institutions but can occur only if member states have the capacity and willingness to protect the financial interests of the Union.

That said, the work of OLAF has highlighted numerous cases of irregularity within the European institutions such as mismanagement of contracts, misleading declarations of expenses, and collusion between a Commission official and a contractor (OLAF 2004: 33–4). Combating fraud, corruption and waste—much of it transnational—is a formidable task. The Court of Auditors and OLAF operate in a challenging environment given the complexity and reach of the EU budget. The future of OLAF has become bound up with discussion of a European Public Prosecutor, an office designed also to protect the financial interests of the Union. The Commission produced a Green Paper on a European Public Prosecutor in 2000 and the Constitutional Treaty made provision for the creation of such an office if unanimously agreed in Council. The idea of a European Public Prosecutor remains highly contested in the Union.

The origins of the institutions

The Court and OLAF evolved from pre-existing bodies with responsibility for financial control and fighting fraud. The Court of Auditors replaced two audit bodies, the European Communities Audit Office and the Auditor of the European Coal and Steel Community (ECSC). OLAF evolved from the Commission's internal anti-fraud unit known as UCLAF (*Unité de coordination pour la lutte antifraude*), established in 1988 by the Delors Commission. Both were created as a response to the perceived weakness of their precursors as well as broader changes in the EU as a whole. The provision for a Court of Auditors in the 1975 Budget Treaty was directly related to the transition from national contributions to a system based on 'own resources', an independent revenue base. In addition, the granting of the power of the purse to the European Parliament was seen to require a related shift in the locus of financial auditing. The political argument in favour of a Court of Auditors was made in 1973 by the President of the EP's Budgetary Committee, Heinrich Aigner, who argued that a more supranational EU budget necessitated an independent EU audit body. His case was reinforced by a series of well-publicized frauds against the EU budget and the limited and patchy nature of the financial investigation undertaken by the Audit Board and the ECSC Auditor (Wallace 1980: 101–2; Strasser 1992).

The establishment of OLAF in 1999 can be traced back to 1988 when the Delors Commission felt compelled to create UCLAF in response, notably, to repeated requests from the European Parliament to the Commission to enhance its fight against fraud. For many years, it was a largely symbolic response to the problem of fraud, rather than a serious anti-fraud unit. With an initial staff of ten in addition to temporary agents from the member states, UCLAF could do little more than co-ordinate the anti-fraud units in the big spending DGs—Agriculture, Customs Union and Structural Funds. The need to go beyond a symbolic response was heightened by repeated reports of fraud against the EU budget in the media, reports from the UK's House of Lords, the Court of Auditors reports and in UCLAF's own annual reports (Laffan 1997a).

In 1993, Commissioner Peter Schmidhuber was given direct responsibility for combating fraud and a new director, Per Brix Knudsen, was appointed to UCLAF. The European Parliament insisted in that same year that all anti-fraud divisions in the Commission should be integrated into UCLAF rather than dispersed throughout the organization. After 1994, consolidation took place alongside an increase in the number of staff in UCLAF (sixty permanent staff and sixty-two contract staff by 1997), with the effect that all those with responsibility for combating fraud in the Commission were finally within one chain of command.

The decision in 1998 to create OLAF was taken as the relationship between the Commission and the European Parliament worsened on the whole question of the Commission's management capacity. The prospect of a new body failed to ward off attacks on the Commission in the EP and from the Committee of Independent Experts it established in January 1999 (see Exhibit 5.1). After the Santer Commission resigned in March 1999, the Prodi Commission immediately identified OLAF as a central plank in its response to the criticisms of the Commission's ability to combat fraud (Pujas 2003: 778–97). The Committee of Independent Experts was critical of UCLAF, finding that 'its intervention sometimes slows the procedures down, without improving the end result' (Committee of Independent Experts 1999).

The remit of OLAF may appear more functional than that of the European Court of Auditors, with the emphasis on protecting the financial interests of the Union and combating fraud. However, like the Court of Auditors—whose web page slogan is 'Helping the European Union achieve better value for your money'—OLAF claims a normative purpose, suggesting that it is the engine of a 'Europe of legality' against international crime (OLAF 2000).

Structure of the institutions

European Court of Auditors

The Court of Auditors consists of twenty-five members, one per member state, the members' cabinets (two staff per member, a chef and an attaché) and about 786 staff, who form the operating core of the organization. Just under half are professional auditors. The members elect a President for a three-year renewable term The Council appoints the members of the Court for a six-year renewable term after consultation with the European Parliament. The Parliament's Budgetary Control Committee holds formal investiture proceedings on appointments to the Court, which have led on two occasions to a candidate being replaced. In 1989, when the Parliament issued an opinion objecting to two nominees from a total of six, one of the two member states concerned agreed to nominate another candidate (Strasser 1992: 271). In 2004, the Cypriot Government withdrew its candidate following a negative vote in Parliament. The investiture proceedings established a right of parliamentary involvement that was later followed in relation to the appointment of the Commission. According to the Treaty, the members of the Court must be from the national external audit bodies or have 'special qualifications' for the office (Art. 247 TEC). The stipulation that those 'who are especially qualified' may serve means that the Court of Auditors consists mainly of a mixture of professional senior auditors, finance officials and former politicians. Unlike the European Central Bank, its members do not constitute a cohesive professional college.

The President of the Court is essentially *primus inter pares*: his/her authority rests on the fact that fellow members of the Court elect him or her. The President oversees the operation of the Court and is the public face of the institution, presenting the COA's Annual Report to the European Parliament and to the Ecofin Council and representing the Court *vis à vis* national audit offices. The role of the President has been enhanced by the growing importance of financial control in the Union. Since its inception, the Court has had nine Presidents (see Table 11.1).

Hubert Weber was elected President in January 2005. Mr Weber, who joined the Court of Auditors in 1995 as Austria's first member, has considerable auditing experience at both national and EU levels. He faces the challenge of moulding the post-enlargement Court into a cohesive body.

One of the most outspoken Presidents of the Court was André Middelhoek, who served until 1995. As a member of the Court from the outset, Middelhoek was very committed to the idea that the Court should be an EU institution, formally and legally (as it was so designated by the Maastricht Treaty), and was also determined to heighten the profile of the Court and to give greater salience to the issue of financial management. Middelhoek went on to play a major role in the 1999 Commission resignation crisis when he chaired the Committee of Independent Experts in a particularly muscular fashion.

Regardless of the personality of its President, the Court is a collegiate body characterized by a vertical hierarchy between the auditing staff and the college of

Table 11.1   Presidents of the European Court of Auditors

Sir Norman Price	(UK)	1977
Michael Murphy	(IRL)	1977–81
Pierre Lelong	(F)	1981–84
Marcel Mart	(Lux)	1984–90
Aldo Angioi	(I)	1990–92
André Middelhoek	(NL)	1992–95
Bernhard Friedmann	(G)	1996–98
Jan O. Karlsson	(S)	1999–2004
Hubert Weber	(A)	2005–

Source: Court of Auditors,
http://www.eca.eu.int/index_en.htm

Figure 11.1 Distribution of responsibilities in the Court of Auditors (2005)

Presidency
Coordination and follow-up of the activities of the Court, Legal Service, Institutional external relations and public relations

Audit Group I (6 Members)
Agricultural policies

Audit Group II (6 Members)
Structural and internal policies

Audit Group III (5 Members)
External actions

Audit Group IV (5 Members)
Own resources, banking activities, administrative expenditures, community institutions

CEAD Group (6 Members)
Coordination, evaluation, assurance, development responsible for ADAR sector (audit and training) and DAS (statement of assurance)

Source: Court of Auditors, *http://www.eca.eu.int/index_en.htm*

---

members, and a horizontal division between the sectoral auditing areas. From the outset, the Court had organizational autonomy and was solely responsible for the organization of its work and rules of procedure. The court is divided into eight units—four sectoral audit groups, two horizontal groups responsible for Coordination, Evaluation, Assurance, and Development (CEAD Group), and an Administrative Committee, and the offices of the Presidency and the General Secretariat. The audit staff are organized into divisions reporting to a group of auditors (see Figure 11.1).

The Court as a College meets approximately every two weeks and is attended only by the members and the Secretary-General. Decisions are taken, as in the Court of Justice, by a simple majority vote. Since the middle of 2004, the Court has instituted an 'A' and 'B' point procedure. Items that are categorized as 'A' are adopted without discussion by the Court if the responsible audit group so recommends. Discussion of 'A' points only takes place if several members object and request a full discussion in the Court. This development enhances the role of the audit groups which have become the primary arena for debate and decision. This may represent the development of chambers in practice, if not formally, in the Court.

The structure of the Court has developed on the basis of one member per state, thus giving it an increasingly top-heavy structure over time. The size of the Court has grown from nine to twenty-five as the number of member states expanded. The Treaty of Nice made explicit provision for 'one national from each member state'.[2] Following the accession of ten new states in May 2004, the Court gained ten additional members and their supporting cabinets. A second change that resulted from Nice was the provision that the Council shall adopt the 'list' of candidates put forward by the member states. Prior to this, the Council took a separate decision on each nominee. It is too early to tell if this will make it more difficult for the EP to attempt to block individuals. Given the disparate backgrounds of the members of the Court ensuring that the College works effectively and to the highest professional standards required in an auditing institution is a genuine challenge.

OLAF

OLAF's structure grew out of UCLAF, the office that it replaced in 1999. The key difference between UCLAF and OLAF is that the latter was given a special independent status in the regulations that led to its establishment. It remains, however, a part of the Commission under the responsibility of the Commissioner in charge of the budget. Its independence is clear in its investigative powers and OLAF's Director-General (Franz-Hermann Brüner at the time of writing) is independently responsible for its investigations. (S)he is appointed by the Commission for a five-year period, renewable once following a favourable opinion from the Supervisory Committee of OLAF, the Council, and the EP. The Director-General of OLAF may neither seek nor take instructions from any government or EU institution, including the Commission, and may uphold its prerogatives before the European Court of Justice. The management of the Office is under the guidance of a Supervisory Committee of five persons who have no links to EU institutions and are specialists in its area of work. After its creation, OLAF underwent a process of rapid expansion and had a staff complement of 340 staff by 2004. OLAF is organized in three directorates. Directorate A has responsibility for Policy, Legislation, and Legal Affairs, Directorate B manages Investigations and Operations and Directorate C is a support Directorate with responsibility for Intelligence, Operational Strategy, and Information Services. The Directorate for Investigations has two pools of investigators that are multidisciplinary in character and consist of former members of national police forces, anti-fraud units, customs services, and lawyers, instead of the sectoral teams that characterized UCLAF.

The relationship between the Commission and OLAF is ambiguous. On the one hand, OLAF has independent powers of investigation but on the other it works closely with the Commission concerning its responsibility for advising on anti-fraud measures. Yet in the conduct of its work it has to investigate Commission officials on occasion. This hybrid nature of OLAF was raised as a serious issue in a 2004 Report by the UK House of Lords (House of Lords 2004).

Powers of the institutions

European Court of Auditors

Notwithstanding its title, the Court of Auditors does not have any judicial functions. It deals exclusively with financial auditing, even though its remit has been expanded in the Treaty on European Union (TEU), the Treaty of Amsterdam and the Nice Treaty. Article 248 TEC specifies that the Court is required to 'examine whether all revenue has been received and all expenditure incurred in a lawful and regular manner and whether the financial management has been sound'. In other words, the

Court, like other public audit institutions, was given responsibility for three core facets of financial auditing: notably legality, regularity, and sound financial management. The Financial Regulation, in Article 27, defines sound financial management as economy, efficiency and effectiveness. The stipulation that it audit 'all' revenue and expenditure meant that its remit included the budgets of the European institutions, the European Development Fund, the Union's borrowing and lending activity and all satellite bodies established by the Union. Its task is a vast one given that the EU's financial instruments are deployed in the member states and in third countries throughout the world. The Commission estimates that in any one budgetary year, it engages in 400,000 budgetary transactions (Laffan 1997b).

The tasks of the Court were expanded by the Maastricht Treaty in 1993 when it was given responsibility for providing the Council and the European Parliament with what is known as a Statement of Assurance (SOA) concerning the reliability of the accounts and the legality and regularity of the underlying transactions. The SOA was a requirement that the Court use its audit powers in a systematic manner to certify the reliability and regularity of the accounts and the transactions underlying the accounts. Each year the Court in its Statement of Assurance has qualified its assurance concerning the legality, regularity, and reliability of the accounts. The Treaty of Amsterdam in 1997 made a number of minor changes to the mandate and working methods of the Court, by making provision for the publication of the Statement of Assurance in the EU's *Official Journal*. The Nice Treaty mandated the Court to supplement the Statement of Assurance with specific assessments of 'each major area of Community activity' and also paved the way for the eventual establishment of internal chambers in the Court. Formal chambers have not materialized as yet.

The Court has developed a number of non-treaty based practices. The President of the Court may issue what is known as a Presidential letter to any of the institutions to raise important issues arising from an audit. The Presidential letter excerpted here (see Exhibit 11.1) provides a chilling account of challenges of financial management in the European Union and of the politicized nature of the Commission when faced with high-level national intervention

---

Exhibit 11.1 The Fléchard case[3]

This letter was sent to the Commission by the President of the Court of Auditors, Jan Karlsson. It provides a detailed twelve-page analysis of a case of fraud against the EC budget and the manner in which the Commission handled it. It draws particular attention to the role of OLAF.

Facts of the case

A French company, Fléchard, won a tender to supply butter to the Soviet Union. The company bought 58,645 tonnes of butter including 6,750 tonnes of Irish intervention butter from the Department of Agriculture in Dublin. The Irish butter was exported in December 1991 by the French company with the declared destination of the Soviet Union but it was diverted to the Polish market. A joint investigation carried out by the Irish Department of Agriculture and DG Agriculture of the Commission concluded that the 'transaction had been orchestrated as a fraud from the outset'.

continues

Exhibit 11.1 continued

Involvement of the Court and OLAF

The Court received two anonymous letters of complaint concerning the Commission's management of the case in 1998–9 and a further letter was received by the Parliament's Budgetary Control Committee. The Court informed UCLAF which immediately began an investigation.

Findings concerning the case

Regulation 863/91 provided that a security would be forfeited if a product did not reach its destination. In this case the security, lodged by Fléchard, amounted to €17.6 million. In March 1992, DG Agriculture of the Commission requested that the Irish authorities demand the full payment of €17.6 million. But between May 1992 and September 1993, the French authorities intervened on behalf of the French company on four occasions to try to reduce the amount of the forfeit that would have to be paid by Fléchard. During 1993, there was considerable attention given to the case in the Commission with the involvement of the Legal Service, Financial Control, the President of the Commission's Cabinet and DG Agriculture. The Commission eventually agreed to a settlement of €3 million, or less than 20 per cent of the total of €17.6 million. (The settlement was a source of difficulty for Pascal Lamy, who had served as Delors' *chef du cabinet* during the Fléchard affair, when he was vetted by the EP after being nominated for the Prodi Commission.)

Conclusions of the Court

The Court was clearly uneasy about the Commission's management of this case. It felt that the terms of the settlement had no legal basis, that Fléchard had acted in bad faith from the outset, that the administrative arrangements in DG Agriculture were breaking down, and that the Commission needed to strengthen its arrangements for high risk subsidized exports.

Output of the Court

The Court is a prolific producer of reports. The core of its work is to undertake audits and to publish the results of such audits in the form of reports. Between 1989 and 1995, it produced ninety-six reports including five annual reports (Laffan 1997*a*: 197). The tempo has increased since then (see Table 11.2 for a summary update). The Court's work programme and auditing cycle enters the policy process in the form of the Court's Annual Report, published in the autumn of each year for the preceding year, the Statement of Assurance which has been drafted since 1994, a myriad of special reports on particular institutions, policy programmes or financial processes, and Opinions when requested by the Council or Observations on the initiative of the Court.

The Annual Report is a very large document, running to some 400 pages each year. The massive tome consists of detailed observations of different spending programmes and the replies of the Commission and other EU institutions on its observations. The length of the report and the level of detail it contains is a deterrent to all but the most eager followers of EU finances. There was an attempt to produce shorter and sharper Annual Reports towards the end of the 1990s and to focus more on special reports dealing with the results of audits on specific sectors. A 2001 report on the COA by the British House of Lords found 'the Special Reports of generally greater

Table 11.2 Reports of the European Court of Auditors (1977–2004)			
Years	1977–86	1987–96	1997–2004
Annual reports	10	10	8
Special reports and studies	47	55	112
Total	57	66	120

Source: Court of Auditors, http://www.eca.eu.int/index_en.htm

Table 11.3 Focus of Court of Auditors' special reports (1999–2003)		
	Number of reports	%
Own resources	3	4
CAP	27	36
Structural measures	12	16
Internal policies	7	9
External action	22	29
Administrative expenditure	3	4
Financial instruments	2	2
Total	76	100

value than the Annual Report, although variations in the quality of the former were recognised' (House of Lords 2001). The growing emphasis on Special Reports can be gleaned from Table 11.3, which outlines the focus of the Special Reports between 1999 and 2003. In the past the majority of the COA's reports involved audits of the Union's internal policies with a particular emphasis on the CAP and structural expenditure. The evidence in Table 11.3 highlights the growing focus on the Union's external expenditure.

From the outset, there has been considerable consistency in the findings of the Court. In 1981, its benchmark study of the financial systems of the European Communities, included the following key findings:

- limited staff resources devoted to financial management;
- serious delays in the clearance of European Agricultural Guidance and Guarantee Fund accounts;
- financial accounts hardly intelligible to users;
- insufficient emphasis placed on the evaluation of results by the Commission;
- problems in the definition of the tasks of the Commission's internal controller;

- no comprehensive strategy for computer software, hardware and operating staff resources.[4]

These criticisms have been repeated regularly in the Annual Report, the Special Reports and since 1994, in the Statement of Assurance. In its report on financial year 2003, the Court asserted that it had 'no reasonable assurance that the supervisory systems and controls of significant areas of the budget are effectively implemented so as to manage the risks concerning legality and regularity of the underlying operations' (Court of Auditors 2004: 6).[5]

The Court's institutional position

In analysing the Court's position in the Union's institutional landscape, it is important to distinguish between its relationship with its auditees, on the one hand, and its place in the Union's system of financial control, on the other. Inevitably, tensions exist between the Court as an audit institution and the other EU institutions that are subject to its audits. Although the work of the Court covers all EU institutions and bodies, the most critical relationship is the one with the Commission as the institution that is responsible for EU expenditure (even if it only directly manages a small part of it). The relationship with the Commission was very difficult for many years as the young Court strove to find its niche in the Union's institutional landscape. One of the first controversial issues with the Commission related to the issue of a 'right of reply' to the Court's observations. In the early years, the Commission never fully reconciled itself to the role of the Court in 'value for money' auditing, and clearly felt that the Court was straying from its audit function into policy or political judgements. Auditing remains a contested area between the Commission and the Court. Gradually, however in the 1980s, the Court and the Commission developed a working relationship as the latter came to accept that the audit body was a permanent feature of the Union.

Relations deteriorated again during Jacques Delors' term as President of the Commission. During the negotiations of the Delors II budgetary package (covering 1993–99), the Commission was furious at a report from the Court to the Council on management problems in the structural funds. Delors complained that the report made it more difficult for him to get the member states to agree to a larger budget.

The Santer Commission made improving relations with the Court one of its main objectives. Santer had considerable contact with the Court during his time as Prime Minister of Luxembourg. The Santer Commission attempted to upgrade its relationship with the Court. It is paradoxical then that the Court contributed to the resignation of the entire Santer Commission in March 1999 when the 1996 discharge procedure became embroiled in a wider debate on management problems in the Commission (see below).

The Court is not the only cog in the wheel of financial management in the Union. Such management is also the responsibility of the financial controllers in all of the EU institutions, OLAF, the national authorities that manage EU finances, and the national audit offices. Given the extent and range of the Union's budgetary activities, the Court needs to work in partnership with national audit offices. Court audits in the member states are carried out in liaison with the national audit authorities, all of which have appointed a liaison official with the Court. In the period since the ratification of the Maastricht Treaty in 1993, the Court has devoted considerable energy to improving its links to the national audit offices, especially given the latter's staffing resources and responsibility for national financial interests. The Treaty of Amsterdam stipulated that 'The Court of Auditors and the national audit bodies of the member states shall co-operate in a spirit of trust while maintaining their independence' (Art. 248 TEC).

The Court's formal relations with the Council and the European Parliament take place within the so-called discharge procedure. Under this procedure the EP has the power to grant or withhold approval for the Commission's implementation of the annual budget. The Council also offers a recommendation but the Parliament takes this decision alone. The Commission is legally bound to take the EP's discharge resolutions into account. The procedure is based on the analysis by the EP's Budgetary Control Committee of the Court's Annual Report, its Statement of Assurance and any special reports published during the budgetary year in question. The EP drafts a discharge report largely based on the work of the Court. Because of the discharge procedure, contact is continuous between the Court and the EP's Budgetary Control Committee. The Parliament refused to grant a discharge in 1984 with respect to the 1982 budget and has delayed the discharge on a number of times since then.

However, in spring 1998 the most politically charged discharge process in the history of the EU began. In March, the EP Budgetary Control Committee recommended that the EP delay giving the Commission a discharge for the 1996 budget following one more critical report from the Court of Auditors. The issue then became entangled with additional allegations of mismanagement involving Commissioner Cresson and later the European Community Humanitarian Office (ECHO). An internal Commission whistleblower—one of an increasing number to come forward in recent years (see Exhibit 11.2)—added to the politically charged atmosphere (see also van Buitenen 2000 and Chapter 5).

Exhibit 11.2 EU whistleblowers

A number of officials working in EU institutions have, over the last decade, made their concerns about financial management in EU institutions public. These whistleblowers have received considerable exposure in the media and hence have had high visibility and nuisance value. The institutions generally responded to the whistleblowers very defensively, although Vice-President Kinnock felt obliged to establish a whistleblowers' charter in 1999. Among the whistleblowers were:

- Paul van Buitenen, who brought his concerns about financial management to an MEP in 1998. He was suspended from his post but his revelations led to the downfall of the Santer Commission in 1999. He first wrote a book on his experiences (2000) and later (in 2004) was elected to the European Parliament.
- Marta Andreasen, who was appointed as chief accountant in the Commission but was suspended in 2002 when she refused to sign off on the Commission's accounts. She was highly critical of the book-keeping standards in the Commission. Following suspension, she was dismissed from her post for breaching staff regulations.

continues

Exhibit 11.2 continued

- Dougal Watt, an official in the European Court of Auditors, who raised serious issues of financial mismanagement concerning one of the members of the Court. On the basis of his allegations, OLAF conducted an investigation that led it to recommend charges of fraud be taken against the former member of the Court.

The Commission survived a motion of censure but only because a special Committee of Independent Experts was appointed to investigate the charges of mismanagement. The ultimate result was the resignation of the entire Santer Commission. In an indirect way the Court's highly technical work of auditing therefore contributed to what was a history-making event in the politics of the Union. Most of its activity, however, is directed towards the less dramatic but still crucial task of improving the financial control procedures of EU institutions and protecting the financial interests of the Union.

OLAF

OLAF exercises the following tasks in the fight against fraud, corruption or any other activity affecting the financial interests of the EU:

- it conducts all the investigations conferred on the Commission by Community legislation and in third countries through agreements;
- it safeguards the Community against behaviour that might lead to administrative or penal proceedings;
- it exercises a coordinating role *vis à vis* the national auditing authorities in the fight against fraud;
- it contributes to the development of methods for combating fraud.

In order to carry out these tasks, OLAF conducts external audits in the member states and where permissible in third countries and has the power to conduct internal investigations in the EU institutions when fraud or corruption is suspected.

OLAF's 2004 Activity Report marked the first five years of this fledgling organization's work. OLAF's Case Management System listed 3,992 cases during this time including 1,423 cases that it inherited from UCLAF. The number of cases in any one year rose from 322 in 1999–2000 to 637 in 2003–04 (OLAF 2004: 17). The balance between external cases and internal cases was 153 to 619. Internal cases were investigations into the activities of EU officials and institutions. External cases involved investigations in the member states, candidate states and in the wider world. Of the external cases, a very high proportion, 73 per cent (2004), related to activities jointly carried out with member state authorities. This underlines the necessity for EU-level bodies to work with national authorities in the fight against fraud (OLAF 2004: 19). OLAF's external cases cover a wide range of EU activity.

The Eurostat case was one of the most controversial cases involving an investigation by OLAF since its establishment. Following the mass resignation of the Santer Commission and the stated commitment to tackling fraud by President Prodi, the emergence of serious problems in Eurostat was most unwelcome. Fraud allegations emerged concerning an irregular bank account set up in Luxemburg during the 1990s, known as the Eurodiff account, which appeared to hold money from the sale of Eurostat publications that should have been channelled into the Commission account. Faced with mounting political pressure from the European Parliament, the Commission and OLAF set up a special OLAF Task Force to deal solely with the investigation into Eurostat. A total of fourteen investigations were pursued; four external cases and ten internal cases some of which are not yet complete. The Task Force found that most of the irregularities had their origins before 1999 (OLAF 2004; House of Lords 2004). The Eurostat investigation was the source of considerable conflict between the Commission and OLAF. The former felt that it should have been informed sooner of the investigation as it was accountable for the Agency and was itself under considerable pressure from the European Parliament. The Commission suspended three senior Eurostat officials and terminated a number of contracts with private companies.

OLAF, like all EU institutions, operates in an institutional environment that is multilevelled, cross-national and very diverse. It has to develop strategies for managing diversity and for dealing with the multiple anti-fraud agencies in Europe. It seeks to work closely with national authorities not as a substitute for national action but as a means of more effectively fighting fraud that is transnational in nature. As much crime and fraud in Europe today has a transnational dimension, OLAF itself is partly a response to transnational pressures. In short, legal Europe is attempting to catch up with criminal Europe.

The institutions in context

Financial control and the larger EU system

The evolution of the Court of Auditors and OLAF in the EU system illustrates how institutions and their external environments interact. These institutions were established at different times, more than twenty years apart, in response to changes in the salience of financial management, control and accountability in the EU system. The establishment of the Court was recognition of the supranational nature of the EU budget and OLAF of the failure of self-regulation within the Commission. Both institutions represented a strengthening of the relatively weak organizations that preceded them. The Court of Auditors had to devote considerable organizational energy to becoming a 'living institution'—to becoming embedded in the EU system. The Court had to evolve a culture of auditing that was suitable to the extended scale and reach of the Union's financial activities. Like all EU institutions, it had to work with diversity—auditing cultures, attitudes to financial management, diversity of professional background, legal arrangements in the member states and multiple languages.

No less important than its internal structures are its relationships with other parts of the EU system. The Court is part of the system of financial audit and control that exists in the EU involving internal financial control, external audit and measures to combat fraud. It is part of the Union's accountability structures in that the Parliament's Budgetary Control Committee relies on reports of the Court for its annual discharge process. The Court has played its part, albeit a secondary one, in the unfolding drama of EP–Commission relations. The Court has gradually established working relationships with all EU institutions and its institutional status gives it the same legal status as the institutions that it audits. Its stronger, formal status in treaty terms matters in the day-to-day politics of auditing in the Union. As the salience of good financial governance has gained prominence in the Union and received the backing of the Council and the European Council, the Court has turned its attention to enhancing its relationship with national auditing authorities.

OLAF, like the Court of Auditors, is part of the Union's accountability structure with a specific remit to combat fraud and crime. Its remit is based on the clear recognition that there is an important transnational dimension to budgetary fraud in the EU. The establishment of OLAF as an independent unit attached to the Commission but with a separate chain of command was a response to the problems the Commission had in conducting internal investigations when there were allegations of fraud by individuals in the Commission's services. Its future is bound up with the possible creation of a European Public Prosecutor. The idea which was floated in 1997 in a Commission funded study entitled *Corpus Juris* carried out by eight academic lawyers was later backed by the Commission in a 2001 Green Paper on the protection of the financial interests of the Union.[6] The proposal re-emerged in the Convention and formed part of the Constitutional Treaty agreed by the member states in June 2004. Article III-175 of the Treaty makes provision for the creation of a European Public Prosecutor (EPP) subject to unanimous agreement in the Council. According to the Constitutional Treaty's provisions, the EPP would be responsible for 'investigating, prosecuting, and bringing to judgement, where appropriate in liaison with Europol, the perpetrators of . . . offences against the Union's financial interest' (Art. III 175). The EPP provisions were controversial and were opposed by a number of countries in the negotiations, notably the UK and Ireland who did not want the Union to encroach on their systems of criminal law. Hence, there is considerable uncertainty concerning the place of OLAF in the emerging financial architecture of the Union. The creation of the EPP, if it is established, will alter OLAF's operating environment in a fundamental manner. One could envisage that OLAF becomes an investigating arm of the EPP or that it is absorbed into a re-organized Europol.

Theories of integration and institutional development

From the outset, scholars of integration paid considerable attention to what they saw as the novel characteristics of the Union's institutional architecture. In fact, institutions were central to neofunctionalist analysis, as well as early volumes on the EU's policy process. Not unexpectedly, the growing volume of literature on the factors driving integration—liberal intergovernmentalism, supranational governance/new institutionalism and social constructivism—all address different dimensions of institutionalization and institutional evolution in the EU.

How well do these theories of European integration explain the establishment and evolution of the European Court of Auditors and OLAF? Both institutions are non-majoritarian institutions with a role as guardians of the EU purse. All political systems have institutions whose *raison d'être* is supervision and control. Social constructivism draws our attention to the importance of ideas and discourse in shaping political action and structures. In the case of the two institutions analysed in this chapter, established concepts of democratic government, and accountability, shaped the institutions from the outset. The fact that external audit was a well-established norm and practice in domestic government would have made it very difficult for any member state to argue against the establishment of the Court of Auditors. By conducting audits and reporting on the findings of such audits the Court of Auditors contributed to the diffusion of democratic practices of governance in the EU. In particular, social constructivism provides a useful lens for analysing the normative dimension of institution-building and related processes of learning and socialization (Checkel 1999: 548). The Court of Auditors, together with other actors in the system, had a responsibility to strengthen the norms of sound financial management, legality and regularity in relation to the EU budget, and did so through its recommendations and opinions concerning the Financial Regulation. In an effort to enhance its effectiveness, the Court of Auditors and more recently OLAF have promoted learning and socialization on issues of financial management and fraud in the EU system.

The literature on institutionalization and supranational governance provides a lens with which to analyse the development of these institutions over time (Stone Sweet and Sandholtz 1998: 16–20; Pierson 1996; Pollack 1998). The processes highlighted in this literature, such as rule-making and institutionalization, are clearly evident in the evolution of the Court of Auditors and OLAF. The member states may have established the Court of Auditors to oversee their agent the Commission in its management of EU monies but over time the Court, because of its audit remit, has had to follow the audit trail into the member states. One of the unintended consequences of the establishment of the Court was the manner in which national financial management came under increasing scrutiny. Treaty revision and changes in the Financial Regulation all contributed to an enhancement of the norm of sound financial management in the EU and to creating a web of rules around the control of EU expenditure. The Court and OLAF are but part of the wider development of an institutionalised control/accountability culture in the Union. Nor has the process been limited to these two institutions. Provisions for the establishment of a European Public Prosecutor underline the tendency for institutional spillover in the system, notwithstanding the controversial nature of this proposal.

Liberal intergovernmentalism is more concerned with why institutional delegation takes place rather than the consequences of such delegation. A liberal-intergovernmental analysis of the development of the Court of Auditors and OLAF would privilege an explanation based on the need for credible commitments. From this perspective, the role of both these institutions is to assure predictable, fair and transparent compliance with the rules. However, the credibility of the commitment is bolstered by both of these institutions not by limiting democratic involvement, a key argument in liberal intergovernmentalism, but by reinforcing democratic control, because both institutions are part of the democratic fabric of the EU polity (Moravcsik 1998). Liberal intergovernmentalism could not easily account for the establishment of the EPP if it is created because it is opposed by a number of powerful players.

The impact of the institutions

Given the perennial problems associated with the management of EU finances in successive reports of the Court of Auditors, the Commission's Annual Reports on *The Fight Against Fraud*, and OLAF's annual reports, it begs the question of just how intractable are the problems associated with financial management in the Union. Establishing effective systems of financial management is a challenge even within states. In the EU, there are additional structural factors, notably the range of auditing institutions, practices, and cultures in the member states and beyond, the geographical range of EU finances and the multilingual environment within which the staff of the Court of Auditors and OLAF work.[7]

The reports of the Court since the end of the 1970s did much to highlight management inadequacies in the first place, and the COA's constant pressure on the Commission led to an acceptance—however tardy—that there were very real problems of financial management in the Union. The Commission responded by strengthening formal systems for overseeing the implementation of the budget, but as Levy (2000: 187) has concluded: 'moving beyond formal change is a general problem that bedevils most aspects of EU programme management'. The Commission continues to struggle to enhance its internal management processes and to strengthen its links to the member states. This effort has borne some fruit but the continuing evidence of weak management and fraud contained in the reports of the independent experts on the Commission in 1999 underlined just how chronic the problems are. The continuation of problems during the Prodi Commission, highlighted by the Eurostat investigation, underlines just how difficult it is to overcome the fragmented accountability structures in the Union and the prevailing culture of financial management.

The Court of Auditors played a particularly important role in EU institutional politics by altering the balance in relations between the EP and the Commission. Its reports provided the Budgetary Control Committee with the raw material to exercise the discharge procedure in a manner that strengthened parliamentary control over the Commission. The resignation of the Santer Commission was the most dramatic event to result from the problems of self-regulation in the Commission. Without the slow drip feed of COA reports, it is unlikely that it would have happened. OLAF has undertaken a large number of investigations in the EU institutions, the member states and in third countries. These investigations have led to criminal investigations in Romania, the extradition of a Lithuanian national from Lithuania to Belgium, a guilty plea by a multinational company in Lesotho, and an investigation into the use of EU monies by the Palestinian Authority (OLAF 2004: 38–40).

Conclusions

The establishment of the Court of Auditors in 1977 was dependent on the changing nature and funding of the EC budget. In turn, once the Court found an institutional identity and established its approach to auditing, it began to highlight the problems of financial management in the Union. Its effectiveness improved with the internal development of an agreed audit culture and growing human resources. For well over ten years, the Court had to fight to ensure that its findings were taken on board in the Commission, the Council and at national level. With the major expansion of the Union's budgetary resources after 1988 and a growing net contributors club, financial management found its way from the margins of the agenda to centre stage. Gradually the rules surrounding financial management were strengthened and the member states were forced to accept a tighter regime of financial control. The Court of Auditors, whose institutional position was strengthened in this period, contributed to but also benefited from the growing salience of financial management in the Union. The establishment of OLAF in 1999 was a response to the problems of fraud against the financial interests of the Union and more specifically to the problems of self-regulation in the Commission. The Court of Auditors and OLAF represent institutional innovation in the EU system. Subsequent provisions for a European Public Prosecutor suggest that the process of institutional innovation continues. Such developments bring the continuing autonomy of national criminal law systems and the need to combat transnational problems sharply into focus.

Notes

1 The author would like to thank David Bostock, member of the European Court of Auditors, for his thorough review of an earlier version of this chapter. The chapter has benefited greatly from his corrections and observations.

2 Art. 247 TEC.

3 Presidential letter from President Jan Karlsson to the Commission President, 11 May 2000.

4 Court of Auditors, C342, 31 December 1981.

5 The Court is attempting to get agreement on a single audit model for the EU as a whole (COA Opinion 2/2004).

6 COM (2001) 175 final.

7 These issues were taken up in a speech delivered by Maire Geoghegan-Quinn, Member of the Court to the Parliament's Budgetary Control Committee, ECA/04/21.

Further reading

Levy (1996) highlights the difficulty posed by diverse national auditing traditions for external auditing in the Union, while the same author's monograph (2000) is the most in-depth analysis available of financial management in the EU. Laffan (1999, 2003) analyses (respectively) the Court of Auditors's relationship with other EU institutions and charts how it became embedded in the Union's institutional system, and the general dynamics of financial accountability in the EU. Pujas (2003) provides insight into the governance of EU anti-fraud activities. House of Lords (2001) offers fascinating material garnered from expert witnesses on the role of the Court of Auditors.

House of Lords (2001), *The European Court of Auditors: The Case for Reform*, 12th Report, 3 April, available on http://www.parliament.the-stationery-office.co.uk/pa/ld200001/ldselect/ldeucom/63/6302.htm

Laffan, B. (1999), 'Becoming a "Living Institution": The Evolution of the European Court of Auditors', *Journal of Common Market Studies*, 37/2: 251–68.

Laffan, B. (2003), 'Auditing and Accountability in the European Union',

Journal of European Public Policy, 10/5: 762–77.

Levy, R. (1996), 'Managing Value for Money Audit in the European Union: The Challenge of Diversity', *Journal of Common Market Studies*, 43/4: 509–29.

Levy, R. (2000), *Implementing European Union Public Policy* (Cheltenham: Edward Elgar).

Pujas, V. (2003), 'The European Anti-Fraud Office (OLAF): a European policy to fight against economic and financial fraud?', *Journal of European Public Policy*, 10/5: 778–97.

Web links

The most important web link is to the *http://europa.eu.int* site which provides access to all of the EU institutions. The ECA is at *http://www.eca.eu.int/index_en.htm*. The link to the Commission provides access to the Budget Directorate and the Financial Control Directorate in addition to OLAF which is found at *europa.eu.int/comm/dgs/anti_fraud/mission*. Europa leads to the Court of Auditors' extensive site which gives access to the annual reports, special reports, and a bibliography on the Court of Auditors. The link to the European Parliament provides access to the work of the Budgetary Control Committee which is central to the annual discharge of the budget.

Part III

Integrating Interests

Chapter 12

Security Interests

Police and Judicial Cooperation

Theodora Kostakopoulou

Contents

Summary

Police and judicial cooperation are no longer an optional extra for European integration. Justice and home affairs (JHA) cooperation has matured to the point where the Constitutional Treaty, regardless of its fate, attempted to complete a transition from intergovernmentalism to the Community method. The trajectory of JHA cooperation has spawned loose intergovernmental cooperation, then problem-solving outside the Community framework, followed by the creation of an 'Area of freedom, security and justice' (AFSJ), and most recently ambitious developments in criminal law and counterterrorism. JHA institutions have evolved through incremental adaptation and *ad hoc* compromises, rather than systematic planning. An eclectic approach that draws on neofunctionalism and neoinstitutionalism, but which also pays attention to time, context and discourse, is needed to understand the dynamics of institutional change.

Introduction

This chapter examines the institutional evolution of Justice and Home Affairs (JHA) policy—extending to issues of internal security, human mobility, and judicial co-operation—and more recently (and optimistically) designated an 'area of freedom, security and justice'.[1] Although incrementalism is a familiar feature of European integration in this area as it is in others, the distinctive features of JHA should not be overlooked. First, policing, criminal law and immigration policy are matters of 'high politics'. They are intimately linked with national sovereignty and state-hood. The perception that closer JHA cooperation comes at the cost of compromising state sovereignty has been a brake on integrationist institutional solutions. Second, law and order have traditionally been the prerogative of national executives in all member states. Politicians and bureaucratic elites have been determined to main-tain this control in the European arena. Accordingly, JHA cooperation has been ex-ecutive driven, secretive and, until the mid-1990s, insulated from close scrutiny by outsiders. Third, threat perceptions (real or imagined), ideological orientations, and political expediency blend and shape choices, with the effect that politics and rhet-oric—about open borders, immigration, and security deficits—subjugate policy. JHA cooperation thus has developed complex, *ad hoc*, and 'crowded' institutional arrange-ments.

However, European integration has been a process of learning by doing and JHA cooperation is no exception. Throughout its thirty-year history (1975–2005), national executives have had to face transnational challenges including terrorism, drugs traf-ficking, international crime, and human mobility. They have been forced to interrog-ate the doctrine of sovereignty, to learn to trust each other, and search for improved institutional arrangements. A distinctive trait of JHA cooperation is institutional rest-lessness: lacking a robust institutional framework or clear objectives, JHA coopera-tion has always been in transition in some form or another.

The discussion below draws on the distinction introduced in Chapter 1 between institutions as organizational actors, as opposed to rules, conventions, norms and formal legalistic means that constrain and facilitate action. Understanding how changes in the latter category of 'institution' affect the adaptation and role of organ-izational actors sheds considerable light on JHA, which by many measures has been the fastest-growing area of EU policy activity in recent years.

Origins

Phase 1: *Ad hoc* intergovernmental cooperation: 1960s–1985

The origins of JHA cooperation date to the 1960s. Following the design of the com-mon agricultural policy (CAP), initiatives were taken to tackle fraud in Community finances, advance civil judicial cooperation and promote mutual assistance among customs authorities. Thereafter political extremism prompted the establishment of the TREVI Group in Rome in 1975. By some accounts, TREVI was named after the Trevi fountain in Rome (near to which its first meeting was held under a Dutch Council Chairman whose name translated as 'fountain'). By others, it is an acronym for 'terrorism, radicalism, extremism, and violence international'. In any case, TREVI became a policy forum for the exchange of national strategies and expertise in counterterrorism. Drawing on the experience of European political cooperation (EPC), it was hoped that regular meetings of interior ministers and senior civil servants would advance police cooperation.

After 1984, TREVI was convened once during each Council Presidency. It spawned cooperation between officials (and sometimes police officers) that extended over time to football hooliganism, serious international organized crime, especially drugs trafficking, and border controls. Eventually, police and customs officers established 'a chain of equivalence' within TREVI between the single market and security deficits. That is, the abolition of internal border controls foreseen for the end of 1992 was seen to require compensation in the form of tightened external border controls and internal surveillance.

Phase 2: Advanced intergovernmental cooperation: 1985–92

By 1985, the prospect of a frontier-free internal market led France, Germany and the Benelux countries to opt for an early experiment in 'reinforced cooperation' outside the EC itself. These six states agreed to abolish border checks across their shared borders to promote the free movement of persons. The 1985 Schengen Agreement was signed in the small village of Schengen in Luxembourg. In an early sign of how political agreements in JHA are often subject to protracted negotiations, Schengen's implementing measures were not agreed until mid-June 1990, after becoming bound up in the unexpected unification of Germany and fears of mass migration from Central and Eastern Europe.[2]

Policy cooperation within Schengen extended to:

- the design of an external frontier policy and the harmonization of visa policies;

- common rules on asylum and migration-related issues;

- the establishment of a central Schengen information system (SIS) in Strasbourg to link the various databases in the member states, thereby allowing law enforcement authorities to exchange personal identification data and descriptions of lost or stolen objects.[3]

Schengen's main institutional body was its Executive Committee, comprising national ministers and secretaries of state. The Committee was assisted by a Central Group of senior civil servants and police officers, which directed and supervised detailed work done by a range of other working groups and committees. Schengen undoubtedly has made it easier and quicker for travellers to cross the internal borders of its member states. Yet, its complexity of institutional structure, coupled with the secretive character of its meetings, gave rise to charges of a serious accountability deficit.[4]

Schengen also demonstrates that the formation of national preferences do not always precede interstate cooperation, as liberal intergovernmentalist theory claims (see Moravcsik 1998). Often, objectives have been formulated and strategies pursued only *after* protracted European discussions within a highly specialized elite drawn from national justice and interior ministries. The embedded beliefs shared by members of this elite matter. To illustrate the point, the link between the abolition of internal frontiers and increased crime and migration has rarely been either called into question or verified by empirical research. Whether border controls make much difference to the overall level of serious international crime is open to doubt: a report of the United Kingdom (UK) House of Commons (1990) Home Affairs Committee urged that an effective anti-terrorist policy depended on police intelligence more than the apprehension of terrorists at borders. Nevertheless, the single market became a pretext for restrictive measures, including new mobile controls internally and the erection of new barriers externally.

One effect of the creation of 'an internal security continuum'—the perception of a security deficit in a Europe without frontiers (Bigo and Leveau 1992)—was to help justice and interior ministries and security agencies maintain their levels of public funding despite the removal of border controls. It also precipitated a proliferation of JHA working groups. Monar (2001) estimates that EU member states created over twenty new intergovernmental bodies between 1986 and 1991, the most prominent of which was the Ad Hoc Working Group on Immigration. Created in 1986, the Group drafted the 1990 Dublin Convention (which came into effect in 1996) to try to prevent 'asylum shopping', or the practice whereby migrants seek asylum in the EU state most likely to grant it. In an attempt to provide some organizational infrastructure and coordination to the work of it and other working groups, the European Council set up a Group of National Coordinators in 1998, consisting of senior civil servants from national interior and justice ministries. This Group compiled the so-called Palma document which outlined the 'compensatory measures' required by the abolition of border controls.

These steps elicited sharp responses from human rights groups, such as Amnesty International, and migrant organizations, such as the Joint Council for the Welfare of Immigrants. Alarms were raised in particular about the concentration of power in the hands of national executives and their civil servants, who were often acting as quasi-legislators. Worse, they often did so with little or no parliamentary oversight or judicial scrutiny (Schermers *et al.* 1993; Bunyan 1991).

Fears of a new 'authoritarian Europe' did not prevent Schengen from becoming the primary laboratory for European JHA cooperation. Its principal advantage for its supporters (equally, in the view of others, its major weakness) was its flexibility. That is, it enabled JHA cooperation outside of, but in parallel with, the framework of the EC. The benefits of enhancing cooperation and fostering a culture of trust were seen to outweigh the accountability and transparency deficits associated with 'pure' intergovernmental cooperation. Moreover, it was argued, a unique institutional design featuring linkages with EC institutions could remedy these deficiencies over time.[5]

Justice and home affairs: the third pillar

Phase 3: Diluted intergovernmentalism: 1993–98

JHA cooperation was truly institutionalized for the first time by the 1992 Maastricht Treaty. The failure of existing procedures and tools to deal effectively with the abolition of internal border controls and cross-border threats outweighed concerns about sovereignty at the IGC that agreed the Treaty. The secrecy that surrounded deliberations in the pre-Maastricht phase, the lack of coordination between various workings groups (often resulting in duplication), and the difficulty of agreeing binding measures and then monitoring them suggested that a new institutional architecture was needed. Formal linkages with the Community process became widely viewed as necessary. Accordingly, nine areas of JHA cooperation became matters of common interest located in a separate intergovernmental pillar (the so-called 'third pillar'; see Exhibit 12.1)

In line with the institutionalized intergovernmentalism used elsewhere, the Council of Ministers took the lead and the predominant decision-making mode was unanimity. A JHA configuration of the Council was created to take over decision-making in this area from the General Affairs Council (of Foreign Ministers), and was assisted by a new Coordinating Committee. The latter prepared JHA Council meetings (three to four a year) together with the Committee of Permanent Representatives (Coreper) and gave opinions to the Council. In reality, however, the so-called K4 Committee (named after Art. K4 of the Treaty on European Union, or TEU), which absorbed the Coordinators' Group, strictly limited the role of Coreper. Generally, the input of diplomats remained unwelcome in a realm dominated by justice and interior ministries. The K4 Committee's substructure formalized the TREVI structure, in particular reproducing its complex system of working and steering groups.

Exhibit 12.1 The Maastricht Treaty's 'third pillar'

The policy areas subject to the Treaty on European Union's new institutions for JHA were:

- asylum policy;
- rules on crossing external borders;
- immigration policy;
- drug addiction;
- international fraud;
- civil judicial cooperation;
- criminal judicial cooperation;
- customs cooperation;
- police cooperation.

Here, we find a clear illustration of the historical institutionalist insight that path dependence often develops from past institutional choices (see Pierson 2004). The emergence of a complex, five-tiered, decision-making structure (JHA Council, Coreper, K4, Steering Groups and Working Groups), instead of the normal three-tiered Council working structure (see Chapter 4), gave rise to coordination problems and undermined effectiveness. For this reason, the Irish Council Presidency introduced reforms in the second half of 1996 and the UK Presidency abolished the Steering Groups altogether in 1998.

Meanwhile, the expansion of formal linkages with the Community process acted to dilute intergovernmentalism. The Maastricht Treaty required that the European Parliament be 'regularly informed' of JHA discussions and 'consulted' by the Presidency of the Council on the 'principal aspects of activities'. For the first time the Commission was formally associated with Justice and Home Affairs policy-making. It shared the right of initiative with the member states in all areas (except judicial cooperation in criminal matters, police and customs cooperation). A JHA policy portfolio was established within the remit of the Social Affairs Commissioner, and a new division in the Secretariat General monitored and supported the third pillar. The Commission began cautiously, but increasingly exercised its shared right of initiative strategically, proposing both legislative instruments and funding programmes. The Commission also used the overlap between the second and third pillars[6] to propose measures concerning the Community's financial interests, a list of (129) countries whose nationals required a visa when crossing the external borders of a member state, and a uniform format for visas. By developing credible policy ideas, the Commission signalled to member states the potential benefits of granting it future agenda setting powers.

The European Court of Justice was given no mandatory jurisdiction in the third pillar. A system of judicial review was optionally provided for in Conventions, one of the main third pillar instruments along with joint positions and joint actions. As the legal effect of joint actions and joint positions was not clarified by the Maastricht Treaty, Conventions remained the main 'hard law' instrument in the third pillar. However, since Conventions had to be agreed unanimously, they tended to be lowest common denominator agreements. Most also required long and slow periods of ratification. For example, the Dublin Convention only entered into force seven years following its agreement (in 1997). Dublin, Rome and Schengen were the only three of eleven Conventions agreed in 1985–92 to be ratified by 1999 (Peers 2000: 16). And quite apart from the relative scarcity and slow ratification of Conventions, the post-Maastricht era found ministers favouring soft law instruments, such as resolutions, recommendations, declarations, and conclusions, thus effectively avoiding the stipulations of formal legal obligations.

Another problem was national opt outs from specific legal obligations, as illustrated by the Convention establishing Europol (see Exhibit 12.1). Britain and Denmark opposed any involvement by the ECJ in Europol, while Germany and the Benelux countries considered it necessary. Despite attempts by the 1995 French Council Presidency to resolve the matter, the dispute became bound up politically with the row over BSE ('mad cow' disease), before a complex compromise on the ECJ's role was found at the Florence summit in June 1996. The result was a Protocol to the Europol Convention, which gave member states wide discretion to opt out of the ECJ's preliminary rulings jurisdiction (see Chapter 7) and modify the procedure at will, thus threatening the uniform application of rules.

An institutional architecture of 'diluted intergovernmentalism' seemed to appease concerns about national sovereignty. Nevertheless, intergovernmental negotiations had to be conducted under the shadow of future Community competence. The *passerelle* (literally, in French, 'footbridge') provision of Maastricht's Article K9 opened the possibility of the transfer of all areas of JHA cooperation (with the exceptions of customs, police and criminal judicial cooperation) into the Community pillar, thereby bridging the first and third pillars. The transfer required unanimous Council

---

Exhibit 12.2 Europol

The institutional origins of the European Police Office—based in The Hague and usually re-ferred to as 'Europol'—can be traced to discussions within TREVI in the late 1980s. Even-tually, they led to the creation of an Ad Hoc Working Group on police cooperation in 1991. Capitalizing on the Maastricht Treaty's reference to 'a Union-wide system for exchanging information' and an attached Declaration on Police Cooperation, the Working Group sug-gested the formation of a European Drugs Unit (EDU) as a point of exchange of criminal in-telligence data among police forces. EDU, the precursor of Europol, was up and running by the mid-1990s, with a remit ranging from illicit trafficking in drugs, radioactive and nuclear substances, vehicles and human beings, to criminal organizations and associated money laundering activities. Europol was then established by a 1995 Convention, although dis-agreements about the role of the European Court (ECJ) and the immunity of its staff delayed its entry into force for another three years.

Europol does not possess executive powers in the same way as US federal enforcement agencies. Rather, it facilitates the exchange of criminal data and intelligence and the co-ordination of criminal investigations. It has a complex institutional structure, comprising a management board (one representative from each member state and the Commission with observer status), which meets about six times annually, a director and several deputy directors. The board makes annual reports on Europol's activities to the Council, which, in turn, submits an annual report to the EP. The ECJ has no jurisdiction to review whether Europol has exceeded its powers or whether national enforcement agencies have stepped beyond their mandates in EU approved operations. The absence of effective parliamentary scrutiny is also a continuing cause for concern.[7]

The Amsterdam Treaty recognised Europol's crucial role in coordinating national law enforcement authorities. The 1999 Tampere European Council proposed the extension of Europol's powers to all money-laundering activity. The same year, Europol was given a new counter-terrorism mandate and competence to act against child pornography. Following the 9/11 terrorist attacks, a team of counter-terrorist specialists was created at Europol and the Council approved cooperation agreements between Europol and the US on the exchange of personal data. The absence of human rights safeguards or clear references to the right of privacy in these agreements was striking. In November 2003, the Council adopted a protocol amending the Europol Convention that extended the powers, research and advisory functions of Europol and allowed designated national authori-ties to have direct contact with Europol. Europol thus illustrates both the transparency and accountability deficits endemic to JHA policy, as well as its institutionalization over time.

approval and ratification in accordance with national constitutional requirements (the 'double lock' procedure). However, the unthinkable had already happened. The inclusion within the third pillar of the *passerelle* clause fuelled supranationalist aspirations and paved the way for the partial communitarization of the third pillar at Amsterdam.

The area of freedom, security and justice

Phase 4: Contained intergovernmentalism: 1999–

The Maastricht Treaty's third pillar illustrated most of the shortcomings of intergovernmental cooperation: frail compromises due to the prevalence of unanimity, a cumbersome decision-making structure, a lack of clear objectives, weak enforcement mechanisms, and an absence of parliamentary and judicial scrutiny. However, three important differences distinguished cooperation in this phase from earlier phases. First, JHA cooperation now had a clear legal basis in the treaties. Second, the member states became locked into an institutionalized dialogue. Third, the Commission and EP enjoyed increased input.[8] Their critique of the intergovernmental method could not be ignored at a moment when the EU was trying hard to appeal to its citizens. The 1996 Intergovernmental Conference represented an opportunity to shift towards 'communitarizing' the third pillar, or subject it to the rules and institutions of the first pillar, a move favoured by the Commission, the 1996 Irish Presidency, the European Parliament and numerous non-governmental and quasi-governmental actors.

The Amsterdam Treaty (in force by May 1999) transferred migration-related issues to the Community pillar. A new Title (IV) was inserted in the EC Treaty regulating external border controls, the rights of third country nationals, migration, asylum, and judicial civil cooperation. Police and judicial cooperation in criminal matters was kept within a reformed third pillar (Title VI TEU), which was extended to action against racism and xenophobia and offences against children. Customs cooperation and the protection of the financial interests of the Community were transferred to other parts of the EC Treaty. The term 'justice and home affairs' was replaced by 'an area of freedom, security and justice' (AFSJ), which became both a designated policy area and a stated objective of the Union.

Although the AFSJ spanned both the first and third pillars, the institutional configurations differed. The Council continued to lead in the third pillar and unanimity remained the rule. Special qualified-majority voting (a specified number of votes in favour cast by at least ten of fifteen member states) was required for the implementation of third pillar decisions, and a majority of two-thirds of the states was needed for the adoption of measures implementing Conventions. Coreper II was to be assisted by 'JHA counsellors', or experts from the national ministries who often met as an informal group. The K4 Committee became the Article 36 Committee and its remit was confined to third-pillar matters. The Committee coordinated

Figure 12.1 The post-Amsterdam working structure of the Council in JHA policy

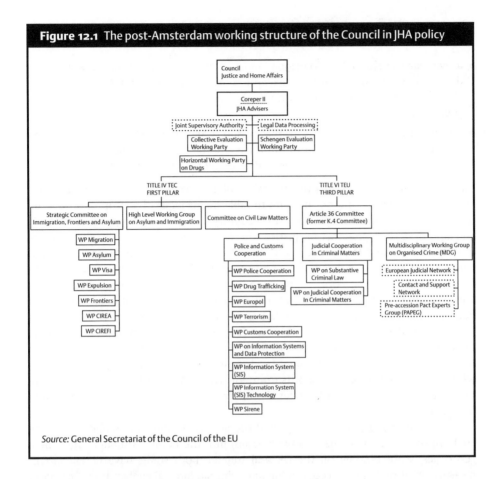

Source: General Secretariat of the Council of the EU

the activity of working groups on police and customs cooperation, criminal judicial cooperation, and organized crime, while also working closely with the Strategic Committee on Immigration, Frontiers and Asylum (established in 1999) and a new Civil Law Committee (see Fig. 12.1).

The Commission gained a shared right of initiative in all areas of the third pillar. The role of the European Parliament was also extended, since it had to be consulted on all measures except common positions.[9] These declarations defined the approach of the EU on a particular matter and were complemented by a range of specific instruments: framework decisions, decisions, and conventions. Framework decisions would be used for the approximation of national laws or administrative provisions, while decisions served any other purpose consistent with the objectives of Title VI (such as countering racism or xenophobia). Both framework decisions and decisions were designated as binding on member states, but without direct effect: that is, they did not create rights for individuals enforceable before national courts. The Amsterdam Treaty also tightened the ratification process for conventions and stipulated that they would enter into force once they had been ratified by at least half of the member states that adopted them. Measures implementing conventions could be adopted by the Council by a two-thirds majority.

The Migration Title, on the other hand, weaved together Community and intergovernmental features by distinguishing two phases:

- a five-year transitional period (1999–2004) during which the Council would take decisions by unanimity (with the exception of visa matters), with the Commission sharing the right of initiative with member states and the EP playing only a consultative role;

- a phase at the end of the transitional period (1 May 2004) when the Commission would have an exclusive right of initiative and the Council could decide by unanimous vote to switch to co-decision and qualified-majority voting.[10]

The requirement of unanimity on migration-related issues hampered progress. However, the Commission did not hesitate to table major legislative proposals (on family reunification, long-term resident third country nationals, and asylum). A dynamic and ambitious Commissioner for Justice and Home Affairs, Antonio Vitorino, was appointed in 1999, and the Justice and Home Affairs Task force was turned into a full Directorate-General. The input of the Court was also enhanced, although with a variety of complicated restrictions. Some member governments clearly remained hesitant to expand the ECJ's role, fearing that it might undermine national control and empower individuals, particularly in the area of data protection.

Institutional arrangements for JHA were further complicated by opt-outs from the migration title on the part of the UK, Ireland and Denmark. The UK and Denmark had long-standing reservations about border controls and sovereignty (respectively), while Ireland wished to maintain its Common Travel Area with the UK. All were allowed to opt in to agreements under the migration title via a series of complicated procedures.

The Amsterdam Treaty also integrated the Schengen Convention and the associated implementing acts (the Schengen *acquis*) into the EC/EU. Although the Schengen *acquis* is not binding on the UK and Ireland, both states have taken part in measures relating to police cooperation and criminal judicial cooperation. Denmark, on the other hand, can decide to opt in to measures adopted by the Council which 'build upon the Schengen *acquis*', but the incorporation of any such decision into national law would create an obligation of international law. Finally, Iceland and Norway—both members of the Nordic passport area with Finland, Sweden, and Denmark (which allow free movement across its members' borders)—were accommodated by two separate agreements outside the institutional framework of the Union. In short, whatever its advantages in terms of enhanced accountability, transparency, and scrutiny, the integration of the Schengen *acquis* considerably increased the complexity of the JHA institutional framework and invited inconsistency in the application of JHA provisions across the EU.

The development of such a complex institutional framework, coupled with considerable variable geometry, suggests that national governments have not behaved as rational and strategic actors in the JHA area, as liberal intergovernmentalist accounts would predict (den Boer and Wallace 2000: 518). Lacking clear objectives, a well thought through strategy or comprehensive forward planning, member governments have often adopted what Wessels (2001: 201) has termed 'parallel strategies', which are difficult to link in a coherent way. Specifically, member states have sought increased efficiency yet wished to retain national autonomy. They have resisted pooling sovereignty but later 'opted in' and adopted specific policies that they played no role in deciding. They have treated the free movement of EU nationals as a right, while regarding the movement of non-EU nationals as a problem.

Federalists might view the partial communitarization of the third pillar as a step closer to supranational statehood. Neofunctionalists would regard it as an incremental spillover effect of the internal market. However, the fact that spillover did not extend to criminal judicial cooperation and policing shows both the continuing salience of politics and the uneven character of institutional change. The Amsterdam Treaty certainly did not displace the intergovernmentalism of the third pillar. Nevertheless, at the very heart of the revised third pillar one finds again the 'communitarization constant': that is, the possibility of transferring third pillar matters to the first pillar by a unanimous vote in the Council (Art. 42 TEU). This provision exerted a serious gravitational pull that, as we shall see, was clearly visible in the Convention on the Future of Europe.

Institutionalization and the European Council

The Amsterdam negotiations prompted the European Council to take a position of leadership on JHA matters. Before the new Treaty entered into force, the 1998 Cardiff European Council called for a plan to determine how best to implement the provisions of the Treaty establishing an area of freedom, security and justice (AFSJ). Within a few months, the Commission (1998: 459) responded with a precise agenda and proposed objectives, while urging that

> freedom loses much of its meaning if it cannot be enjoyed in a secure environment and with the full backing of a system of justice in which all Union citizens and residents can have confidence. These three inseparable concepts [freedom, justice and security] have one common denominator—people—and one cannot be achieved without the other two.

Arguably, the Commission thus embraced the tendency of member states to treat security threats as objective realities, without undertaking the (highly political) processes of articulating and defining security threats. In particular, the 'securitisation of migration' (Huysmans 2000) was felt by applicant states in their accession negotiations. Only a few existing EU member states were willing to grant immediate free movement and residence to applicants' nationals after their accession. The 1998 Vienna European Council revealed the prevalence of the security paradigm by establishing a high level working group on asylum and migration and adopting the Commission's action plan. The latter outlined a basic list of measures designed to implement the AFSJ, ranging from the development of Europol and the incorporation of the Schengen *acquis* on police and customs cooperation to the adoption of a European migration strategy based on reducing migration pressures at the source, combating illegal immigration, and so on.

The 1999 Tampere European Council diluted the restrictive character of these provisions. It agreed that a scoreboard would review progress towards the implementation of a number of new policy orientations and priorities. The Tampere

---

Exhibit 12.3 Eurojust and the European Judicial Network

Eurojust, a central judicial cooperation unit, was formally established in February 2002. Eurojust is endowed with wide, albeit advisory, responsibilities on serious cross-border and organized crime. It provides legal advice and assistance to national investigators and pro-secutors and facilitates the coordination of cross-border investigations and prosecutions among competent national authorities.

Eurojust is headquartered in The Hague (along with Europol) and is the world's first permanent network of national judicial authorities. Comprising a high-level team of 25 national prosecutors, senior magistrates, judges, and other legal experts (one nominated by each member state), it is an independent body endowed with legal personality and fin-anced from the Community budget. Eurojust can act either through its national members or as a college, and its President reports to the Council every year. In 2002 the national members elected Michael Kennedy, the UK member and a former Chief Crown Prosecutor, as its President. Drawing on the team's knowledge of legal systems as well as Europe-wide patterns in serious organized crime, Eurojust can recommend the initiation and/or coordin-ation of investigations and prosecutions by national authorities of serious organized crime.

Eurojust cooperates closely with other EU agencies, such as Europol, OLAF (the EU's anti-fraud office; see Chapter 11), and with liaison magistrates (national judges appointed in other member states in order to function as 'legal adapters' between different legal sys-tems). It has a particularly close working relationship with the European Judicial Network (EJN), created in 1998 to advise and assist judicial authorities in the member states.

Unlike Eurojust, EJN has a decentralized structure involving central national authorities, and is meant to link judicial contact points in the member states and the Commission. The secretariat of the EJN forms part of the Eurojust Secretariat, thereby enhancing the effect-ive interaction of these agencies. By improving contacts among national representatives, establishing directories of information by means of a telecommunications network, and enabling national judges and prosecutors to carry out cross-border investigations and pro-secutions, the European Judicial Network has fostered a tangible increase in judicial cooper-ation.

'milestones' included action to ensure better access to justice, the mutual recognition of judicial decisions and judgements, more rapid extradition, the free movement of evidence, and greater convergence in civil law. European leaders also agreed to address crime prevention and cooperation, establish a European Police Chiefs operational Task Force, create a European Police College, and set up EUROJUST (see Exhibit 12.3). They also set up a Convention, composed of individuals drawn from governments, national parliaments, the EP, and the Commission to draft the EU Charter of Fundamental Rights, which was 'proclaimed' by the Presidents of the Council, the Parliament, and the Commission at the 2000 Nice Summit. By this time, the AFSJ had become a matter of high politics. Two important upshots were accel-eration in both the institutionalization of JHA cooperation and the securitization of migration, moderated slightly over time but never fundamentally questioned.

Single market institutions for JHA

A prime catalyst for JHA cooperation has been the adoption of the single market principle of mutual recognition. Originating in the European Court of Justice's judgment in the *Cassis de Dijon* case (see Chapter 7), mutual recognition refers to the horizontal (at state level) abolition of barriers to free movement across the EU. Relying on a form of negative integration—the presumption that the member states have mutual trust and confidence in each other's regulatory standards (as opposed to 'positively' replacing them with EU standards)—the Tampere European Council endorsed the application of the principle to criminal matters to try to overcome divergence in national laws and judicial systems and to unblock progress. Mutual recognition was thus proclaimed 'the cornerstone' of a 'genuine European area of justice', since decisions taken by judicial authorities in one member state would be recognized and, where necessary, executed by judicial authorities in other member states without political involvement and 'with a minimum of formality'.

In 2000 the Commission presented a Communication on Mutual Recognition which furnished the basis for the adoption of a programme containing 24 measures by the Council later the same year. These included actions to enforce pre-trial or pre-hearing orders, the definition of common minimum standards to facilitate mutual recognition, and the determination of the grounds for refusing recognition. The first measure agreed was the Framework Decision on the European Arrest Warrant, which abolished cumbersome extradition procedures among the member states. It was followed by the adoption of a Framework Decision on Freezing of Assets and Evidence in 2003, as well as later moves on other issues, such as the 'double jeopardy' principle (that is, avoiding more than one trial for a single crime), the adoption of a European evidence warrant, and the mutual recognition of sentences.

The European arrest warrant

In line with the Tampere decision on extradition proceedings, and prompted by the 9/11 attacks, the Commission moved quickly to propose a Framework Decision on a European arrest warrant on 19 September 2001. Political agreement was reached in less than four months. After concerns of the Italian Government under Silvio Berlusconi concerning the inclusion of corruption on the list of offences were appeased, the Framework decision was formally adopted in mid-2002.[11] By 1 January 2004, the deadline for transposition into domestic legislation, only eight states had implemented it.

The European arrest warrant transforms the extradition regime into one of administrative transfer between EU member states. Extradition procedures have traditionally been protracted and complex. States have been reluctant to extradite their own nationals. They have also tended to confine extradition obligations to a select list of crimes and invoke the 'political offence exception', that is, they have refused requests for extradition if the offence is deemed to be political in character. The EU adopted Conventions in 1995 and 1996 that simplified and expedited extradition procedures, abolished the political offence exception, and limited the grounds allowing states to refuse extradition. However, delays in the ratification of both Conventions, which never entered into force, led the heads of state or government at Tampere to commit formally to abolishing existing extradition procedures.

Drawing on the Extradition Conventions and relying on the principle of mutual recognition, the European arrest warrant allows a judicial decision to be issued by a member state to secure the arrest and surrender of a person, accused of an offence carrying at least one year's imprisonment or sentenced to imprisonment of at least four months, by another member state. European arrest warrants may be issued in respect of committed or alleged offences contained in a list of 32 Euro-crimes, which have a much broader scope than counterterrorism. Member states can no longer refuse to surrender their own nationals and their powers of refusal are confined to specific certain grounds (such as that the requested person has already been finally judged by a member state). On this basis the Italian judicial authorities approved the extradition within 35 days of Hussain Osman, a suspect in the failed London bomb attacks of 21 July 2005.

Whatever the advantages of replacing the political dimension of extradition with a judicial process, serious concerns have been expressed about human rights safeguards and democratic accountability. The European arrest warrant was adopted by the Council under an exceptional 'urgent procedure' with minimal parliamentary involvement.[12] The abolition of the dual criminality rule means that a member state must hand over suspects to other jurisdictions, even when the offence is not a crime under their own laws. The European arrest warrant also contains no explicit references to the European Convention on Human Rights or rights to liberty and a fair trial. Critics have argued that the European arrest warrant needs to be accompanied by measures designed to ensure that standards of law enforcement and rights protection for citizens are equally high across the EU. It thus comes as no surprise that Constitutional Courts in Germany and Poland have ruled that national implementing legislation conflicts with constitutional guarantees.

Mutual assistance in criminal matters

Mutual assistance, a well-established institutional norm in international judicial cooperation, is also anchored by mutual recognition. In 2003, the Commission proposed a Framework Decision on the European Evidence Warrant, enabling the free movement of evidence among the judicial authorities of the member states and replacing overlapping international and EU conventions governing the gathering of evidence in cross-border litigation. A Convention on Mutual Assistance in Criminal matters was adopted in 2000, and a Protocol on cooperation in the monitoring of bank accounts in another member state, which forms an integral part of the Convention, was adopted a year later.[13] The Convention and the Protocol, which still awaited ratification by all member states by late 2005, updated and further developed the 1959 Council of Europe Convention. Specifically, they enabled the spontaneous exchange of information (that is, without a prior request) concerning criminal offences and administrative infringements among national judicial authorities without the involvement of central authorities, and limited the grounds for refusal of such assistance.

Mutual assistance under the 2000 EU Convention goes well beyond the scope of the 1959 Convention. It entails the provision of evidence by video conferencing, telephone conferencing, the setting up of joint investigation teams, requests for

---

Exhibit 12.4 The post-9/11 transatlantic agreements on JHA

The events of 9/11 in the US prompted closer cooperation in criminal law between Europe and America. Following protracted (and secretive) negotiations, the Council agreed the text of EU–US Agreements on extradition and mutual legal assistance in mid-2003. The latter extends to many of the same issues as the EU's own, internal agreement on mutual legal assistance in criminal matters, with special emphasis on improved cooperation in investigations into organized crime, terrorism, and financial crime.

The impact of the Extradition Agreement is variable and more limited. The member states have reaffirmed the Union's opposition to capital punishment. Portugal has stated that it will not grant extradition if the offence is punishable with the death penalty. At a minimum, EU member states require that death penalties imposed prior to extradition requests from the US should not be carried out. Finally, the Extradition Agreement provides scope for a refusal to extradite persons whose right to a fair trial, including the right to adjudication before an impartial tribunal, is not guaranteed.

In 2004, the Council (at foreign minister level) adopted a controversial EU-US agreement that obliges European airlines to give access to passenger name record (known as PNR) data to US agencies. Critics alleged that the agreement institutionalized the global surveillance of movement and violated the European Data Protection Directive. It was opposed by the European Parliament, which sought its annulment by the ECJ. Together with other US–EU agreements that came before it, PNR showed how transatlantic cooperation on JHA post-9/11 had mushroomed even as debates raged about how far it should extend.

---

covert investigations, and the interception of telecommunications for the purpose of a criminal investigation. One inevitable effect is to put at risk the rights of suspects and defendants in criminal proceedings, account holders whose financial transactions may be disclosed, and individuals whose telephone calls may be intercepted (see also Exhibit 12.4).

Security interests and terrorism

Significant progress was made in AFSJ matters after Tampere, not least because of the application of the principle of mutual recognition. Meanwhile, new security priorities, accentuated by 9/11, were increasingly seen to require a different approach: put simply, the harmonization of substantive criminal law (that is, 'positive integration'). The most important harmonizing initiative was the Framework Decision on Combating Terrorism, which became the core of the Union's policy on terrorism. At its extraordinary meeting of 21 September 2001, the European Council made the fight against terrorism a 'priority objective' and approved an action plan that included, among other things, the development and implementation of international anti-terrorist legislation, the freezing of terrorists' assets, the strengthening of air security, and co-ordination of the EU's global action. Sixty-eight (new and old) initiatives were listed in a 'road map' whose scope extended beyond counterterrorism and criminal judicial cooperation to cover external border controls and visa policy.

The Framework Decision on Terrorism was formally adopted in mid-2002.[14] It provided a common definition of 'terrorism' (previously defined differently in different member states), defined crimes linked to terrorist acts, and specified the penalties that could be imposed on conviction. Terrorism was defined on the basis of a combination of objective criteria—for example, acts that 'may seriously damage a country or an international organisation'—and subjective criteria, such as the context of the action, the aim of the action ('intimidating a population') and the specific acts being committed. The Framework Decision listed eight types of specific terrorist offence, set out the terms of offences for directing or participating in a structured terrorist group, and specified maximum sentences.[15]

The Framework Decision contains a very broad definition of terrorism. The list of offences is considerably wider than that included in UN Conventions. Its detractors claim that it could result in the criminalization of public protest and certain kinds of industrial action. The Council has sought to appease such concerns by including a reference to 'fundamental rights or freedoms such as the right to strike, freedom of assembly and association or of expression, including the right of everyone to form and join trade unions with others for the protection of his or her interests and the related right to demonstrate'. Despite this reference and member states' human rights obligations (under Art. 6 TEU), critics have argued that the security paradigm that has traditionally characterized JHA cooperation was allowed to trample on civil liberties post-9/11. It is by no means always clear that the EU takes a 'balancing approach' that openly weighs security concerns, perceived risks and fears, and the adequate protection of the rights of individuals.

Such concerns were intensified by the adoption of two common positions on terrorism in 2001, which essentially evaded parliamentary and judicial scrutiny. The first criminalized the wilful provision or collection of funds for terrorist activities and required member states to prevent 'any active or passive support' to terrorists. However, it did not define 'terrorism' and the human rights safeguards mentioned in the Framework Decision were omitted.

The second common position dealt with the freezing of assets and the blocking of transfers of funds to 'international terrorists'. It contained a blacklist of individuals, groups, and organizations, which was adopted without debate and extended by the Council twice in 2002. This list includes, among others, the Irish Republican Army (IRA), Protestant Groups in Northern Ireland, Palestinian groups, the International Sikh Youth Federation, the Kurdistan Workers' Party, and certain Latin American groups. The Council's wide discretion to designate a person or group as 'terrorist(s)', without allowing those concerned to bring about judicial challenges to their listing, reaffirms the Union's 'securitarian' JHA policy.

The train bombings in Madrid (11 March 2004) placed the fight against terrorism at the top of the EU's agenda. An extraordinary JHA Council followed by a European Council within weeks of the bombings led to the appointment of an Anti-terrorism Coordinator (Gijs de Vries), the adoption of a declaration on combating terrorism,[16] and another on solidarity against terrorism. Thus, on one hand, the EU showed considerable agency in response to the threat of international terrorism, and in JHA policy more generally. On the other, critics worried that EU action on counter-terrorism made 'security' a pretext for setting aside the civil liberties norms so painstakingly established over fifty years. Moreover, it was notable that the 2005

Prüm Convention on the 'stepping up of cross-border cooperation, particularly in combatting terrorism' (and other offenses) was agreed intergovernmentally by only seven member states (Austria, Belgium, France, Germany, Luxembourg, the Netherlands and Spain) and not within the framework of the EU treaties.

The Constitutional Treaty

The Laeken Declaration on the Future of Europe (2001), which defined the mandate for the Convention on the Future of Europe, called for a 'deeper and wider debate' about European governance. The final report of the Convention's Working Group on JHA endorsed a number of reforms based on two 'golden rules'. First, the pillar structure should be formally abolished and the legal framework for JHA unified. Second, legislative and operational tasks should be clearly separated from one another. The Working Group also called for a new standing committee within the Council to be formed on internal security to improve operational coordination. Its report further recommended the standardization of co-decision and qualified-majority voting on JHA matters, with few exceptions, and the inclusion of the principle of mutual recognition of judicial and extrajudicial decisions in the Constitutional Treaty.

It is worth pausing to consider how the Constitutional Treaty, regardless of its fate, aimed to restructure the institutional framework for JHA cooperation. It abolished the pillar structure entirely, placing all JHA under a single institutional framework. The unification of law-making meant that the distinctive third pillar instruments would be replaced by European laws (directly applicable regulations) and framework laws (directives), which might have direct effect. Co-decision would be the standard decision rule, with unanimity usually replaced by qualified majority voting in the Council. Most decisions would require the approval of 55 per cent of the member states representing at least 65 per cent of the EU's population.[17] In the case of a member state initiative, QMV would consist of two-thirds of the member states representing at least three-fifths of the population of the Union.

The extension of co-decision to the majority of police and criminal judicial cooperation matters, where the EP previously had only a consultative role, offered a chance to increase accountability and enhance individuals' rights. The empowerment of the EP was complemented by the enhancement of the role of national parliaments. In addition to widening access to documents and the introduction of a formal scrutiny procedure of draft legislation for compliance with the principle of subsidiarity, national parliaments could 'participate in the [new] evaluation mechanisms' foreseen in the Treaty and would be involved in the political monitoring of Europol and the evaluation of Eurojust's activities. The promise of increased transparency and scrutiny, coupled with the constitutionalization of the openness of legislative proceedings in the Council, seemed welcome reforms.

The communitarization of JHA matters also meant that the Commission's exclusive right of initiative would be strengthened on migration-related matters, without prejudice to that of groups of member states in the sensitive areas of police and criminal judicial cooperation. But in order to ensure that member states' initiatives did not reflect purely national policy preferences, the Treaty imposed the threshold of a quarter of the member states for a proposal to be admissible. The European Court of Justice would assume full jurisdiction for all JHA matters (with the exception of the validity and proportionality of policing actions). Meanwhile, the Charter of Fundamental Rights would become legally binding and justiciable. The Treaty also envisaged possible accession by the EU to the European Convention on Human Rights.

Moreover, the Treaty proposed to formalize the institutional role of the European Council, which would 'define the strategic guidelines for legislative and operational planning within the AFSJ'. The election of a European Council President for a period of two-and-a-half years, renewable once, held out the prospect of increased policy continuity and a bridging of legislative and operational programmes. The new Council committee on internal security, replacing the Article 36 committee, seemed likely to improve coordination of operational collaboration, even if the all embracing concept of 'internal security', coupled with the fact that the committee would not be accountable to parliaments, gave rise to concern. The Treaty did not envisage the creation of federal agencies endowed with executive power, thereby alleviating fears about the 'federalization' of JHA. However, the creation of new legal bases concerning the integrated management of external borders, criminal procedure and the establishment of a European Public Prosecutor's Office reflected integrationist pressures.

On criminal judicial cooperation, the Constitutional Treaty confirmed the principle of mutual recognition as the basis for further developments. The Union's competence was also extended to substantive criminal law where the EU would have powers over the definition of offences and sanctions in twelve listed areas of serious and cross-border crime, ranging from terrorism and trafficking in human beings to computer and organized crime. The Council could extend these powers if it agreed unanimously and had the consent of the EP. The powers of Eurojust were extended to the initiation of criminal investigations and proposing the initiation of prosecutions by competent national authorities, particularly those relating to crimes against the EU's own financial interests, and the resolution of conflicts of jurisdiction. The Treaty extended further the remit of Europol, which would have powers to carry out investigations and participate in operational actions undertaken jointly with competent national authorities or jointly with Eurojust.

Finally, the Constitutional Treaty proposed to extend further the Union's JHA *acquis* by establishing a legal basis for a European Public Prosecutor's Office within Eurojust. The European Public Prosecutor (EPP) would investigate and prosecute crimes against the Union's financial interests. However, the EPP's powers could be extended to include serious crime having a cross-border dimension by a unanimous European Council decision after it obtained the consent of the European Parliament. Although certain member states believed that the need for an EPP had not been sufficiently demonstrated, and felt reassured by the retention of a veto over its establishment, the extension of judicial criminal cooperation into the field of law enforcement generated anxieties about the Union's creeping competence.

In short, the Constitutional Treaty proposed radical, even revolutionary changes to the EU's institutional architecture for JHA policy. It would be wrong to claim that all of these changes were supported enthusiastically by all member states. Yet, on JHA as much as any other area of policy, it was plausible to view the Constitutional Treaty

as containing—in the words of the UK Prime Minister, Tony Blair—a 'perfectly sens-
ible set of rules to govern Europe'.[18] How many of its provisions, on JHA as well as
other areas of policy, will eventually be adopted and when remain very open
questions.

Conclusions

Concerns about sovereignty still matter in JHA policy, and they are reflected in the
EU's (still) complex institutional architecture in this area. They are likely to continue
to impact on its future direction and effectiveness, regardless of the fate of the Constitutional Treaty. The retained opt outs of Britain, Ireland and Denmark are illustrat-
ive. We have shown how these concerns have shaped institutional choices since 1975.
Still, the evolution of JHA has been broadly consistent with a neofunctionalist view
of European integration. New institutionalist insights about 'path dependency' and
'lock-ins' also help us understand the process of incremental, but transformative, institutional change.

The general trend has been towards more proactive and better-coordinated JHA cooperation. Mutual recognition has clearly enhanced the array of policy options at the
Union's disposal. Yet, JHA cooperation still faces a number of important challenges. A
reduction in the Community budget for the period between 2007 and 2013 could result in a loss of momentum and impede progress. Differentiated integration also poses
a challenge, particularly in light of the simplification of the enhanced cooperation
procedure proposed by the Constitutional Treaty. Political signals indicating acceptance of a 'concentric circles Europe' in JHA could eventually produce incoherence
and variable patterns of responsibility across the EU.

The recent enlargement of the EU (2004) poses a further challenge. JHA was, for the
first time, part of the *acquis* that new members had to take on board in order to join
the EU. Ensuring its implementation still remains a major test for numerous post-
accession states. The Commission provided €380 million for 2004–06 to reinforce
the new members' administrative capacity to implement the *acquis*. However, the
increased diversity of interests, national legal systems, administrative and law enforcement structures could well slow the pace of JHA policy output.

Finally, we have seen how the framing of security as a supplement of freedom
and justice in the AFSJ has arguably promoted security at the expense of freedom
and justice. Perhaps the greatest challenge for the EU is to break from the security
paradigm that has traditionally characterized JHA cooperation (Huysmans 2000; Kostakopoulou 2000). In important respects, JHA policy needs to be reconceptualized. If
security becomes an overriding policy goal and an enabling condition of 'freedom',
the range of policy options at the Union's disposal will be limited and unbalanced.
No one doubts that the AFSJ is a major political project for the further development
of the Union. It has the potential both to enhance the Union's social legitimacy and
help alleviate security concerns. Yet, a protective Union needs to work hard to ensure
that human rights and civil liberties are respected if its citizens are not to condemn
it as a defective Union.

Notes

1 The focus of this chapter, in line with this volume generally, is on JHA institutions. For a treatment that focuses more on policy content and process, see Lavenex and Wallace (2005).

2 Its entry into force was delayed for another five years due, *inter alia*, to difficulties associated with the Schengen Information System (SIS), a computerized database at the disposal of police and customs officers in the Schengen countries. By then (1995), all EU member states, with the exception of UK and Ireland, had either acceded to or were moving towards full membership (with Denmark, Sweden, and Finland becoming 'observers').

3 SIS went on line on 26 March 1995, and was complemented by SIReNE, a communication system which enables law enforcement agencies to exchange information — within a few minutes — in relation to specific queries.

4 This charge has been made frequently by the non-government organization Statewatch (see *http://www.statewatch.org*). See also the many sources cited in Cain (2000).

5 See European Commission Communication SEC (91) 1855 final.

6 A number of areas of overlap also existed between the first and third pillars which gave rise to jurisdictional conflicts, on (for example) the Community policy on public health and action to combat drug addiction, and fraud affecting the financial interests of the Community and action to combat fraud on an international scale.

7 See the Commission's Communication on Democratic Control of Europol, COM (2002) 95 final.

8 See EP's Resolution A3-01123/92, 7 April 1992, No. C125/81; Commission Communication on the Possibility of Applying K.9 to Asylum Policy, SEC(93) 1687 Final, Brussels, 4 November 1993; Commission Reports to the Reflection Group and the IGC in 1995 and 1996 respectively.

9 These common positions are specific to JHA and different from those of the second pillar relating to the common foreign and security policy (see Chapter 13).

10 The Treaty of Nice inserted a fifth paragraph in Art. 67 EC which allowed for measures relating to civil judicial cooperation and asylum to be adopted using the co-decision procedure, under certain conditions.

11 OJ L 190, 18.7.

12 House of Commons Select Committee on European Scrutiny, 33rd Report, Democracy, Accountability and the role of National Parliaments HC 152 – xxxiii – I, 21 June 2002.

13 See (respectively) OJ C 197 (12 July 2000) and OJ C 326 (21 November 2001).

14 OJ 2002 L 190/1 (arrest warrant) and OJ 2002 L 164/3 (terrorism).

15 The EU has also set in motion a system of peer evaluation of the anti-terrorist laws of the member states; see Council Decision 2002/996/JHA of 28 November 2002 (OJ L 2002 349/1).

16 According to Statewatch, 27 out of 57 proposals contained in the Declaration have little or nothing to do with terrorism. Rather, they concern surveillance and crime in general. See *Statewatch European Monitor*, Vol. 4, no. 5, May 2004, para. 30.

17 Unanimity was preserved for family law, the establishment of minimum rules on specific aspects of criminal procedure, the identification of new areas of serious crime, the adoption of a European law on the establishment of a European Public Prosecutor, operational cooperation between

law enforcement authorities, and cross border actions by police.

18 BBC News, 'Blair calls for "EU Reflection"', 30 May 2005 (*www.bbc.co.uk*).

Further reading

General works on JHA/AFSJ include Barrett (1997), Bieber and Monar (1995), Peers (2000), Walker (2004), and Lavenex and Wallace (2005). The *Journal of Common Market Studies*, the *Journal of European Public Policy* and the *European Journal of Migration and Law* should be regularly consulted for articles and updates on developments. *Agence Europe* and the *Statewatch European Monitor* are good sources of information on JHA matters. There is a surprising lack of theoretical accounts of JHA, with the notable exception of Monar (2001).

Barrett, G. (1997) (ed.), *Justice Cooperation in the European Union* (Dublin: Institute of European Affairs).

Bieber, R., and Monar, J. (1995), *Justice and Home Affairs in the European Union: The Development of the Third Pillar* (Brussels: European Interuniversity Press).

Lavenex, S., and Wallace, W. (2005), 'Justice and Home Affairs', in Wallace, H., Wallace, W., and Pollack, M. (eds.), *Policy-Making in the European Union*, 5th edn. (Oxford and New York: Oxford University Press).

Monar, J. (2001), 'The Dynamics of Justice and Home Affairs: Laboratories, Driving Factors and Costs', *Journal of Common Market Studies* 39/4: 747–64.

Peers, S. (2000), *EU Justice and Home Affairs Law* (Harlow: Longman).

Walker, N. (2004) (ed.), *Europe's Area of Freedom, Security and Justice* (Oxford: Oxford University Press).

Web links

The most useful sites for information on JHA policy are the homepages of the DG Justice and Home Affairs of the Council of the European Union (*http://ue.eu.int/jai/default.asp?lang=en*) and of the Commission's DG Justice and Home Affairs (*http://europa.eu.int/comm/justice_home/index_en.htm*). The EP's Committee on Citizens' Freedoms and Rights, Justice and Home Affairs has its own website: *http://www.europarl.eu.int/committees/libe_home.htm*. Statewatch provides analysis and critical discussion of EU measures on JHA matters (*http://www/statewatch.org*).

Chapter 13

International Interests

The Common Foreign and Security Policy

Michael E. Smith, Brian Crowe, and John Peterson

Contents

Summary

Among all that sets the EU apart, its aspirations in foreign policy rank high. No other international organization claims to have a 'common foreign policy', let alone an emerging defence policy. The common foreign and security policy (CFSP) seeks to combine the political weight of twenty-five EU member states in the pursuit of common goals. But 'European foreign policy' must also integrate a wide range of other policies to be effective. This chapter highlights the CFSP's relative youth (compared to other EU policies), mixed record, and uncertain future. Compared to the rest of what the EU does, foreign policy has resisted pressures for integration. Nonetheless, it has witnessed a significant degree of institutionalization and is an area where the EU's ambitions remain high.

Introduction

The creation and development of what is now the European Union (EU) has not only promoted cooperative relations between its member states. It also has given them an opportunity to speak with a common, sometimes even single, voice in world politics. Potentially, at least, the Union has the power to influence global events in pursuit of European values and interests. By the early twenty-first century, no other international actor had such a diverse foreign policy 'tool kit' (Everts and Keohane 2003: 177). It could even be argued that the EU's power matched or exceeded that of the United States (US) in every area besides the deployment of military force (Moravcsik 2005: 349). Yet, possessing such power is not the same as being able to deploy it effectively.

The EU's capacity for common external action developed earliest and most rapidly in trade policy. From the origins of the European Economic Community (EEC), there was a clear and necessary connection between the creation of a customs union and a common commercial policy towards the rest of the non-EU world (the former is impossible without the latter). Purely functional necessity resulted in the effective delegation by member states of trade policy authority to the EU's institutions, with the European Commission in the lead. Today the EU acts for the member states in international trade negotiations, including within the World Trade Organization, usually managing to negotiate as a single bloc.[1]

However, there is no obvious connection between (what has become) a single market and a common foreign policy. The EU shares representation with member states

---

Exhibit 13.1 Defining 'foreign policy' and 'external relations'

In ordinary English, foreign policy and external relations mean much the same thing. However, they have quite different meanings in Euro-speak. *External relations* is used in Brussels to refer to the foreign affairs responsibilities of the Commission, in practice trade and aid but also external aspects of other EU policies (such as agriculture). Decisions are taken by the Council on the basis of a Commission proposal, increasingly by qualified-majority voting (QMV) and sometimes with a strong role for the European Parliament (EP). In contrast, *foreign policy* refers to policies and actions in those areas that are normally in the remit of national foreign ministries and on which nearly all decisions are taken unanimously. The Commission is only 'fully associated' (that is, it has a lesser position than member states) and the EP has no power (and little influence) over the common foreign and security policy (CFSP). Proposals can be made by anyone, although in practice the Council Presidency takes the lead.

Since the 1992 Maastricht Treaty, the CFSP along with the rest of what the EU does have been the responsibilities of a single set of institutions, or 'single institutional framework'. Thus, decisions on the CFSP and external relations are, in the end, taken by the same people—mainly foreign ministers and heads of government with Commission support—but according to different decision rules. These differences would remain even if the Constitutional Treaty were to be ratified, despite its provisions for assigning responsibility for external relations and foreign policy to a single EU Minister for Foreign Affairs (see Crowe 2005).

in key forums such as the Group of 8, and is entirely absent from others, such as the United Nations (UN) Security Council or International Monetary Fund (IMF). EU member states have vastly different foreign policy capabilities, and vary sharply in their willingness to employ the EU's complex and often time-consuming procedures. One consequence is a stubborn persistence of different views about the EU's ultimate aim in foreign policy: *intergovernmental coordination* of pre-existing national foreign policies (at a minimum) or the *supranational governance* of a single European foreign policy (at a maximum).

When decisions on foreign policy action must be taken, key EU member states (particularly larger ones) often act like 'normal' nation-states. That is, they reject the delegation of foreign and security policy to international bodies except on the basis of unanimity. This intergovernmental approach dominates most other international organizations, such as NATO. At the same time, however, it has become increasingly recognized within European political classes, and still more among national and EU foreign policy officials, that even the largest EU states have limited influence unless they act together with their European partners. All EU member states have accepted this reality for decades, but have drawn different conclusions from it, with most of the smaller ones but also Germany arguing consistently for a more supranational CFSP, notably with decisions by qualified-majority voting (QMV).

Even as it aspires to a *common* foreign policy, the EU has learned from experience that it may never have a *single* foreign policy, in the sense of an EU foreign policy that replaces national policies. The CFSP remains only one element in what is often referred to as 'European foreign policy', or the sum total of all external action by EU member states whether it is pursued via the Union itself, national channels and instruments, or other (non-EU) multilateral organizations (see Ginsberg 2001; White 2001; Carlsnaes *et al.* 2004; Hill and Smith 2005). And when the perceived national interests of member states clash, as over the 2003 Iraq war, there simply is no EU foreign policy, common or otherwise (Hill 2004).

What the CFSP offers is a mechanism for consensus-building and seizing on the 'politics of scale' (Ginsberg 1989), or the basic reality that the EU is far more powerful when it speaks with one voice, as opposed to twenty-five or more. The EU has even developed something approaching a doctrine for its foreign policy, in the shape of the European Security Strategy adopted in 2003 by the European Council (see Exhibit 13.2). More generally, the Union has gone much further in institutionalizing foreign policy cooperation than has any other regional organization.

The origins of CFSP institutions

One of the first laws of politics is that nearly all institutions have effects that their creators did not intend them to have. The founding fathers of what is now the European Union clearly had little or no ambition to create a new and unique foreign policy power. Foreign policy was thus a bit player in the European 'project' of the early 1950s, which began as a mostly economic enterprise although with a strong political purpose: to make war impossible between Germany and France via

> **Exhibit 13.2** The European Security Strategy
>
> Agreed in the aftermath of painful divisions over the US-led invasion of Iraq, the European Security Strategy (ESS; see EU 2003) identifies the key challenges and threats facing the EU. It also identifies the Union's strategic objectives, throwing the EU's weight behind effective multilateralism (especially via the UN), democracy promotion, and respect for human rights and the rule of law. The ESS espouses the need for more active policies across the whole range of 'political, diplomatic, military and civilian, trade and development activities' and an EU strategic culture fostering 'early, rapid, and when necessary, robust intervention'. The *leitmotiv* is multilateralism: promoting good governance, international cooperation and the use of all the policy instruments at the EU's disposal, especially economic instruments but not excluding force. There is little dispute that the ESS was partly, at least, a European response to the controversial 2002 US National Security Strategy, which appeared to embrace the doctrine of 'pre-emption' of threats to American security without prior consultation with European (or any other) allies. There is far more dispute about whether the ESS and its American counterpart signal transatlantic convergence or divergence of strategy in a new and uncertain security environment (see Dannreuther and Peterson 2006).

the integration of their coal and steel industries. The next major step, the creation of a European Defence Community (EDC) in 1952 sought to harness a still occupied and distrusted (West) Germany into a European army to bolster Western Europe's defence against the Soviet threat (see Table 13.1). But the EDC collapsed in 1954, following its rejection by the French National Assembly, leading the founding fathers once again to turn to economic integration to fulfil political objectives.

The supranational governance endemic to the Coal and Steel Community and, later, the EEC, was always unimaginable in the security realm. Defence was left to NATO and the new Western European Union (WEU; see Rees 1998), and their strictly intergovernmental institutions. However, the coming to power of Charles De Gaulle as French President led to a serious effort to 'intergovernmentalize' the EEC by grafting on to it the so-called Fouchet Plan in 1961–62. De Gaulle's clear intent was to turn the EEC into a voluntary union of member states with extensive national veto powers, with action possible only by unanimity in foreign and defence affairs. The Fouchet Plan was rejected by the other EEC five, partly because some (such as the Netherlands) were unhappy that it excluded the United Kingdom, and partly because it was seen as a French move against NATO. In any event, the debate on the Fouchet Plan — with intergovernmental cooperation competing for support with the Community method — set a pattern of tension that survived far into the future.

European political cooperation

Interest in foreign policy coordination did not disappear with the Fouchet Plan. Buoyed by the resignation of De Gaulle and the prospect of the Community's first enlargement, EC Foreign Ministers agreed the 1970 Luxembourg Report and thereby established the European Political Cooperation (EPC) mechanism. EPC had no basis other than a political declaration (legally non-binding) of the Council. Member states agreed to consult and cooperate on issues of foreign policy, but not on defence and

Table 13.1 The expansion of EU foreign policy — a chronology

1952	EDC Treaty signed by six founding states of the EEC
1954	EDC Treaty rejected by French National Assembly
	Brussels Treaty for the WEU signed by six EEC states plus the UK
1958	Treaty of Rome founding the European Community (EC) enters into force
1961–62	Fouchet Plan for purely intergovernmental political cooperation rejected
1970	EPC mechanism created
1971	EPC used to present (for the first time) collective EC positions at the UN
1973	EPC used to develop collective positions toward key allies (such as the US)
1974	First institutionalised regional political dialogues (Euro–Arab)
1975	Helsinki Final Act of the CSCE, in which EPC plays a key role
1977	EPC establishes Code of Conduct for EC firms operating in South Africa
1981	EPC/EC coordinated economic embargo against Argentina during Falklands War
1986	Single European Act agreed, bringing EPC into the EC treaty framework
1989–91	Communist governments fall in Central and Eastern Europe, culminating in German unification (1990) and the collapse of the Soviet Union (1991)
1992	Maastricht Treaty on European Union agreed, with provisions for a CFSP and links to the WEU
1993	Maastricht Treaty (and the CFSP) enters into force
1997	Amsterdam Treaty agreed, creating High Representative for the CFSP
1998	UK and France agree the St Malo Declaration on European defence
1999	Cologne and Helsinki summits (respectively) create European Security and Defence Policy (ESDP) and agree to create Rapid Reaction Force
2003–04	Convention on the Future of Europe agrees Constitutional Treaty
	First ESDP police mission in Bosnia, followed by ESDP military missions (Macedonia, Democratic Republic of Congo, Bosnia)
2005	Constitutional Treaty rejected by French and Dutch voters

only outside the EEC treaty framework. For several years France prevented any discussion of foreign policy in an EC framework. Foreign ministers were even forced on one occasion in 1975 to hold an EPC meeting in the morning in Copenhagen and then fly to Brussels to reconvene in the afternoon for 'separate' EC discussions.

Still, EPC slowly became more institutionalized, with a number of informal rules and substantive policies gradually codified during the 1970s. There was no shortage of opportunities to put EPC to the test: common European positions were sought during this period on the Yom Kippur War in the Middle East, relations with the US, crises in Cyprus and Portugal, the Soviet invasion of Afghanistan, and the Iranian revolution. Actual policy output remained modest for two main reasons. First, all decisions were made by consensus, and just one member state could block or water down any proposal. Second, EPC had no resources, policy tools or staff of its own.[2] Some of its early participants viewed it as little more than a diplomats' dining club.

Over time, however, EPC began to produce substantive policy successes. The 1980 Venice Declaration on the Middle East affirmed the right of Palestinians to self-determination (in defiance of the US) for the first time. The member states, using both the EPC and EC frameworks, played a leading role in the Conference on European Security and Cooperation (CSCE[3]). Despite US scepticism towards what was originally a Soviet initiative, the CSCE produced the Helsinki Final Act in 1975, a political declaration which (among other things) reaffirmed fundamental rights and freedoms, made frontier change permissible only by peaceful means and opened to international discussion the ways countries treated their citizens and cooperated with their neighbours. Later, the CSCE was regarded as an important factor in the political process leading to the end of the Cold War.

From EPC to the CFSP

Despite EPC's successes, the 1970s and 1980s were mostly a time of missed opportunities for European foreign policy. Member states, including France, gradually accepted that a large part of the problem was the separation of EPC from the European Community itself. EPC thus began to develop its own brand of 'soft law', which allowed its participants to refer to and (with the cooperation of the Commission) to draw upon Community instruments such as economic aid and sanctions (such as trade sanctions against Argentina during the 1982 Falklands War). Still, these arrangements remained mostly *ad hoc* and unsatisfactory.

Over time, an increasing number of member states became both less hesitant to use Community instruments and institutions to support EPC objectives, as well as frustrated by problems rooted in the compartmentalization of economic and political affairs. The Commission became gradually more accepted as a necessary partner in EPC in order to align Community policies with EPC-identified policy objectives. Eventually, member states decided that EPC should be given formal status within the Treaties in the Single European Act in 1986.

Even the new-model EPC was exposed as inadequate in the face of major foreign policy challenges such as the fall of the Berlin Wall, ethnic tensions and war in Yugoslavia, and the first war with Iraq. The opportunity was taken in the 1992 Maastricht Treaty to strengthen it by bringing it into the new EU's institutional structure and to give it, for the first time, aspirations in the defence field, all with an ambitious-sounding new name, the common foreign and security policy (CFSP; see Exhibit 13.3). Maastricht integrated the hitherto autonomous EPC secretariat (working under the Council Presidency) into the General Secretariat of the Council. It also established new CFSP policy instruments and marked the first steps towards an EU defence policy (see below). What it did *not* do was to modify the strictly intergovernmental decision-making processes of the old EPC. Thus, little changed in practice.

The structure of the CFSP system

The Maastricht Treaty gave birth to a new 'European Union', putting into a single treaty framework the European Community, CFSP, and the newly emerging area of justice and home affairs (JHA). But it kept these policy areas separate by giving the CFSP and JHA their own distinct decision-making procedures and 'pillars' (pillar II for the CFSP). Maastricht also launched the EU on the road towards a military capability. It provided for a common defence policy and gave the Union the right to call on the Western European Union (WEU), a mutual defence organization founded in 1948 and kept alive for various purposes (most notably the first ever commitment of the UK to

Exhibit 13.3 CFSP policy instruments

In contrast with the purely political decisions taken under EPC, the CFSP initially provided for two types of legally binding decisions: *common positions* to be implemented through coordinated national actions, and *joint actions* to make use of EC instruments, such as aid and sanctions. The record of common positions (on biological and toxic weapons, the creation of an emergency travel document for EU nationals, and so on) and joint actions (for instance, renewal of the Nuclear Non-Proliferation Treaty and action against anti-personnel landmines) revealed no clear distinction in terms of actual activity regardless of which category of instrument was employed.

Common strategies, a third instrument introduced by the Amsterdam Treaty in 1997, were intended to provide greater long-term coherence to the EU's major external policies. The first, for Russia, was agreed in 1999 and others followed for Ukraine and the Mediterranean region. Yet, a 2001 report prepared by Javier Solana, the High Representative for the CFSP (see below), was scathing about how common strategies had added little or no value to existing EU foreign policy activities, and their tendency to consist of lists of vague good intentions for the future. A fourth common strategy, on the Balkans, was identified in 1998 but was never even written. Common strategies thus have become a dead letter.

station forces on the continent) despite the creation of NATO in 1949, to undertake military missions on the EU's behalf.

The new Treaty also ensured a strong measure of continuity between the old EPC and new CFSP. Responsibility for managing the CFSP remained with the rotating Council Presidency, which also remained responsible for its implementation. Decisions could be taken on the proposal of any member state, as well as the Commission, but the Commission's inferior status was formalized by making it only 'fully associated' with the CFSP. While the EU appeared to embrace higher foreign policy ambitions, it dedicated few new resources to this purpose. The CFSP remained stubbornly intergovernmental and a matter for unanimous agreement. As under EPC, the Union continued to look extensively to the policies and instruments of the EC, especially its economic tools, to realize its foreign policy ambitions.

The European Council formally gave the CFSP strategic direction and took the highest profile political decisions (see Chapter 3). Foreign ministers meeting monthly in the General Affairs Council took most policy decisions.[4] On CFSP matters, foreign ministers' agendas were prepared as in EPC by a committee of senior officials, the Political Committee (PoCo), which did the sort of preparatory work that Coreper performed in Brussels for pillar I questions. Composed of Political Directors—very senior diplomats—from national foreign ministries, PoCo normally met once a month on its own, usually in the capital of the Presidency, as well as in the margins of foreign ministers' and European Council meetings. PoCo was serviced by a diverse array of working groups of national EU officials covering geographical regions (such as the Middle East) and functional issues (such as non-proliferation).

The CFSP also inherited the Coreu system, named after the acronym for the French *Correspondant Européen*, from EPC.[5] This encrypted communications network allows for direct communications among foreign ministries of all the member states, the Commission, and the Council Secretariat, and is a critical real-time means of exchanging information and views. The longer the EU system of intensive exchange has operated, the more it has become accepted that major foreign policy problems should be discussed at the EU level before national positions are formed. Thus, a 'co-ordination reflex' has emerged: consultation before action is the norm and unilateral action is shunned. As former British Foreign Secretary Douglas Hurd once noted (1981: 389): 'Perhaps one reason why ... unilateral efforts now usually come to nothing is precisely that they are unilateral.'

The 1997 Treaty of Amsterdam was an opportunity to address some of the defects in the CFSP (see Peterson and Sjursen 1998). The treaty created a new High Representative for the CFSP (HR/CFSP), who would also retain the existing post of Secretary-General of the Council, to 'assist' the Presidency in managing the CFSP. A new Policy Planning and Early Warning Unit was also established within the Council Secretariat, bringing together staff from the Council, Commission, WEU, and member states' diplomatic services. Some spoke of a 'nascent EU foreign ministry'. More sober analysts noted that the new Unit expanded the EU's Brussels-based foreign policy machinery, but kept it under the firm grip of the Council (Allen 1998: 54–5; see also Spence 2002).

In themselves these were not far-reaching changes. What made them important, and what really changed CFSP, was less Amsterdam's provisions than the way they were implemented. Amsterdam came into force (in 1999) when the EU was under pressure after a humiliating performance in the Balkans, where it appeared powerless without US political as well as military leadership to prevent extensive bloodshed, first in Bosnia and then in Kosovo (see Bildt 1998; Holbrooke 1999; Clark 2001). In particular, the exposure of Europe's institutional and military ineffectiveness in Kosovo focused minds on the Union's inability to manage a security crisis without strong American participation.

Thus the Cologne European Council in June 1999 created a new European security and defence policy (ESDP), building on the 1998 Anglo–French St Malo initiative and assimilating into the EU the military arrangements of the WEU.[6] It also appointed Javier Solana as the CFSP High Representative, thus opting for a former Spanish Foreign Minister and NATO Secretary-General instead of a low-profile official as many had been expecting. Six months later, the Helsinki European Council agreed the main features of the EU's defence policy, with substantial knock-on effects for the CFSP (of which ESDP forms a part). The so-called 'headline goal' was agreed, specifying the military capabilities member states would aim to put at the EU's disposal (see below), as were parallel 'civilian and conflict prevention dimensions'.[7]

New politico–military structures had to be grafted onto what was previously a purely civilian organization in order to manage the EU's new military capability. Thus, a Military Committee consisting of senior military officers representing their national chiefs of staff (similar to NATO's arrangements) was set up. It would be serviced by a new Military Staff made up of military personnel seconded from member states located in the Council Secretariat. On the political (CFSP) side, the Political Committee was superseded by a new Political and Security Committee (PSC), consisting of national ambassador level officials stationed, significantly, not in their capitals but in Brussels. The PSC would meet regularly (typically twice a week) and take responsibility, under the chairmanship of the Council Presidency for the day-to-day supervision of the CFSP. Uniquely in the EU's institutional set-up, it was given scope to make actual decisions (as opposed to recommendations) on the political control of military operations if the Council so mandated.

These institutional changes, along with the appointment of Solana as HR/CFSP, resulted in a distinct European foreign policy system. Over time, it became increasingly robust, action-oriented, and Brussels-centred. Still, foreign policy remained an area where the EU clearly failed to 'punch its weight'. Perhaps the CFSP's main weakness was the leadership conflicts inherent in a system where the Presidency changed every six months, the High Representative was increasingly seen as the external face of EU foreign policy but lacked real power, and the Commission was autonomously responsible for many of the instruments needed to make CFSP effective. Thus, CFSP reform emerged as a prominent theme of the 2002–03 Convention on the Future of Europe, and the new Constitutional Treaty that emerged in 2004.

Following its rejection in the 2005 French and Dutch referenda, the Constitutional Treaty looked doomed. Few were more disappointed than those for whom strengthening the EU's foreign policy performance was a priority. Most importantly, the Constitutional Treaty had proposed to abolish the rotating Presidency in external relations and transform the High Representative into an EU Minister for Foreign Affairs (MFA), who would also serve as a Vice-President of the Commission in charge of external relations (see Exhibit 13.4).

The Constitutional Treaty also embraced doctrinal as well as institutional changes. It included a 'solidarity clause' committing the EU to 'mobilise all the instruments at its disposal', including national military resources, in the event of a terrorist attack or natural or man-made disaster in any of its member states. More strikingly, given the strong obligation felt by many member states to NATO, it created for all member states the obligation to aid each other 'by all the means in their power' if any

---

Exhibit 13.4 The EU Minister of Foreign Affairs

The desire to make the EU a more effective global actor was widely shared across the EU after the 2003 Iraq crisis. The 2004 Constitutional Treaty thus contained a number of proposed reforms:

- abolishing the rotating European Council presidency and replacing it with an appointed President to serve up to two two-and-a-half-year terms. The European Council President would be responsible at their level for external representation of the EU on matters concerning the CFSP, without prejudice to the powers of the EU Minister for Foreign Affairs (MFA);
- abolishing the Presidency in the external relations field and giving the chairmanship of the Council in that field to the newly created EU Minister of Foreign Affairs;
- transforming the post of High Representative for the CFSP into the EU Minister of Foreign Affairs (MFA, and appointing Javier Solana to the post in the first instance);
- making the MFA also a Vice-President of the Commission with responsibility for external (economic) relations;
- putting at the EU Minister of Foreign Affairs' disposal a new External Action Service which would consist of the Commission's nearly 130 overseas delegations (and two Council liaison offices in Geneva and New York), officials in Brussels now dealing with CFSP and external relations in the Council Secretariat and Commission, plus diplomats on secondment from member states.

EU member state was the victim of armed aggression, although without prejudice to NATO commitments.

What would *not* change, even if the Constitutional Treaty were somehow ratified, are the basic ground rules of the CFSP, notably decisions by unanimity. Nor would the MFA reduce the importance of national foreign ministers or the Council Presidency, whose agreement would continue to be needed for each and every common policy. However, the MFA would be in a far stronger position than any previous European official to broker agreements, and implement them once agreed. Following the 2005 referenda, it became a matter of considerable debate how many—if any—of its foreign policy reforms would eventually come into force, and how.

The CFSP system in action

One of the abiding features of the EU foreign policy system is its emphasis on consensus. No single official or body enjoys a monopoly over policy initiation, although the Council Presidency traditionally has been expected to provide leadership and manage business. The new Minister of Foreign Affairs (MFA) was meant to take over these functions and provide leadership of a kind the CFSP traditionally has lacked. The basic problems of multiple EU foreign policy representatives plus inconsistent and often weak leadership and implementation were prime motivators of the decision to create this new post.

Other changes proposed in the Constitutional Treaty were of secondary importance, but nonetheless would probably have helped. Double-hatting the MFA as Commissioner (Vice-President) for external relations would have had built-in institutional contradictions but would nonetheless have made for greater coherence between political ends and economic means. This institutional move could arguably not be introduced without treaty amendment. Conversely, the External Action Service could be introduced without a new treaty, relying on Council–Commission agreement. The problem is that it would hardly be a major reform without a powerful boss to report to, even if it usefully gave the HR/CFSP the eyes and ears abroad which member states have and the lack of which has been a severe handicap to Javier Solana.

A more fundamental problem with the CFSP system is that member states are bound by agreed common approaches and have an obligation to consult each other, but retain freedom of action where there is no agreed common policy. Even where an EU agreement exists, member states may still act themselves, so long as they do so in accordance with the agreed position. This practice can be seen for example in the succession of EU foreign ministers who follow each other making the rounds in the Middle East—sometimes to the despair of Council Presidencies (especially from small countries). Put simply, there is no obligation on a member state to conduct its foreign policy 'exclusively' or even primarily through the CFSP, or even to leave CFSP action exclusively to the Presidency (unless it has been agreed otherwise).

The difficulty of reaching common policies and/or the conviction that (especially) larger member states can achieve better results by other means sometimes leads to the creation of small groups outside the EU for the pursuit of European foreign policy objectives. One prominent and traumatic (for the young and fragile CFSP) example was the so-called Contact Group, in which France, Germany, the UK, and (eventually) Italy engaged in multilateral diplomacy after 1994 with the US and Russia on the conflict in the former Yugoslavia, with other EU member states effectively excluded.[8] Another occurred when France, Germany and the UK (the 'EU-3') gave themselves in 2004 the task of convincing Iran on behalf of the EU to agree to international controls on its nuclear development programme. Sensitivities between large and small EU member states remain tender, but with enlargement to twenty-five (and more) there is an increasing if still reluctant recognition that some member states are more equal than others, and that similar groups are necessary if the CFSP is to function. In any event, foreign policy for all EU member states has over time become more 'Europeanised' (Wong 2005): that is, more Brussels-based, frequently linked to EC external economic policies, and an increasingly central part of the EU's personality.

Powers of the institutions

As the rules governing EU foreign policy have expanded over the years, so too have its policy instruments and capabilities. As we have seen, EPC often did little more than issue declarations and coordinate diplomatic activity among EU member states. On some issues, however, such as the Euro–Arab Dialogue and CSCE, the coordination of views and even common actions were quite sustained and intense. In fact, these two efforts in the mid-1970s were early examples of *institutionalized political dialogues*. Such dialogues became useful ways to coordinate all EPC (and later, EC) activities toward an important region or country, such as the Mediterranean or the countries of Central and Eastern Europe. In particular, trade and cooperation agreements were linked to broad political goals, particularly democracy, respect for the rule of law, and human rights (Szymanski and Smith 2005). These arrangements also enabled the EU to promote regional integration in other key areas of the world, such as the Middle East, Latin America, and Asia (see K. E. Smith 2003: 69–96).

Each of the EU's 'positive' economic measures (financial aid or trade agreements) involves a negative component as well: the EU's ability to stop aid or suspend trade negotiations (at a minimum), or impose diplomatic or economic sanctions (at a maximum). During the first twenty years of the EEC's existence, economic sanctions were imposed in only two cases: against Rhodesia (1965) and Greece (1967). Following the creation of EPC in 1970, the EU imposed sanctions against a growing list of countries, including Iran, the Soviet Union, Argentina, Poland, Libya, South Africa, Yugoslavia, and Iraq. Still, then as now, the EU generally favours diplomacy over coercion (Hill and Wallace 1996).

CFSP powers

The Maastricht Treaty was important in giving the EU for the first time the capacity for military action via recourse to the WEU. Elaborate arrangements were thus established between the EU and WEU and between the WEU and NATO (so that the WEU could call on NATO assets). The only case when the Union drew upon the WEU's resources in the 1990s was in assisting in the EU's administration of the Bosnian town of Mostar. On the one occasion when the Union might have asked the WEU to undertake a military operation on its behalf, to defuse a crisis in Albania in 1997, EU foreign ministers were unable to agree, and Italy ended up leading a coalition of the willing.

Over time, the cumbersome, slow-moving and bureaucratic procedures for EU-WEU joint action became a source of frustration. Influenced by events in Kosovo, the European Council decided in June 1999 that the EU should have its own military capability, in consequence of which the WEU's military capability simply fell away. The core tasks of the new ESDP, like the WEU's before it, were the so-called 'Petersberg tasks'[9]: that is, humanitarian and rescue missions, peacekeeping, and crisis management, including (the curiously ambiguous task of) 'peacemaking'. ESDP's military cornerstone was the 'headline goal' agreed by the subsequent European Council in Helsinki in December 1999. The EU decided to equip itself with the capability to deploy a military force—popularly known as the Rapid Reaction Force (RRF)—of up to 60,000 troops by 2003 that could be deployed with two months' notice and sustained for at least a year. As was the case for NATO's own reaction force, the RRF would not be a standing force. Rather, EU member states would earmark their national troops and capabilities for the force during specific operations, thus 'double-' or even 'triple-hatting' them.

Since the RRF's launch, member governments have worked intensively to identify shortfalls in European military capabilities and have taken steps to remedy them, even though the target date of 2003 has slipped to 2010. Meanwhile experience has shown that smaller forces, even more rapidly deployable but for a shorter time, can be useful, as was demonstrated by Operation Artemis in the Democratic Republic of the Congo (see Mace 2003). Paralleling steps in NATO towards smaller and more deployable formations, the EU decided in 2004 to create (eventually) as many as twenty 'battle groups' of up to 1,500 troops. Most will combine European resources at the hard end of their military capabilities in specialized areas such as desert or jungle fighting or dealing with a chemical weapons attack. The aim is to have the battle groups available at near immediate notice for short-term deployments.

On the civilian side, considerable effort has been put into developing the capability to prevent conflicts before they occur or 'win the peace' and help failing or post-conflict states with their civilian infrastructure, particularly law and order. A headline goal for rapid-response police as well as for administrative, judicial and other law enforcement professionals was established in parallel to the military headline goal. The very first ESDP operation was in fact a civilian police mission, which the EU took over from the UN in Bosnia in January 2003. It was followed by relatively small military operations in Macedonia and Congo later that year, but also a more substantial military commitment in Bosnia (taking over from NATO) in 2004.

Often, efforts to give substance to the dramatic 1999 foreign and security policy decisions taken in Cologne and Helsinki have lacked conviction. Member states have failed, predictably, to live up to their more ambitious goals (such as the RRF headline goal). Defence budgets have generally fallen rather than increased. Arguably, the gap between capabilities and expectations that has troubled the EU since the CFSP was first launched has widened, not narrowed (Hill 1993, 1998), though probably due to increased expectations of the EU as much or more than the slow growth of EU capabilities.[10]

There is no denying tangible progress compared to just a few years ago. The EU's military options, while still small scale, are steadily widening. ESDP can be deployed 'where NATO as a whole is not engaged'. Obviously, any EU-led military operation will depend on a handful of countries, in the first place the UK and France, with expeditionary military capabilities to mount and lead them. For anything beyond small-scale operations the EU would have to call on NATO assets, but that is a sign of good sense (avoiding duplication and additional cost) and not weakness. The so-called 'Berlin Plus'[11] arrangements between the EU and NATO are far less cumbersome than the old EU–WEU–NATO procedures.

To the ambitious, the EU's effort remains disappointingly slow and militarily weak. But the EU's ability to contribute to international security by combining the military and civilian dimensions of the ESDP is unique, and certainly beyond what NATO can offer. Eventually, the EU could offer the United Nations a rapidly deployable and effective military capability, thus strengthening multilateralism more generally. Gradually, the EU is buttressing its 'soft power', or ability to attract or persuade in international affairs (see Nye 2004), with hard power to coerce or deter.[12]

The EU's foreign policy record

The sum total of the EU's foreign policy activity—diplomatic, economic, and military—goes far beyond that of any other regional organization. Yet, hard, even brutal questions about whether it results in demonstrable EU influence in world politics cannot be avoided (for contrasting views, see Zielonka 1998 and Ginsberg 2001). The EU's record as a foreign policy actor is decidedly mixed.

After early failures, the EU's chief success—in a still continuing story—has been the Balkans. A large part of this success has come from lessons learnt from the success of using enlargement as, in a sense, a tool of 'foreign policy'. Specifically, the promise of EU membership has been used to promote reform in Central and Eastern Europe, and establish and consolidate democracy, liberalization and the rule of law. Deliberately transposing this success to the Balkans, the EU has offered the prospect of accession as a way of changing behaviour. The attraction of enlargement has induced Balkan political leaders to pay heed (in many cases still only intermittently) to political pressure from the EU. Thus, the EU has shown itself to be more powerful because of what it *is*—a geopolitical magnet—than for anything it actually *does*.

After the 2004 enlargement the Union hoped it could achieve similar results in other neighbouring countries to the EU's east and south, even though many were not prospective candidates for accession (see Dannreuther 2004). The EU offered to form special relationships with such states via a new 'neighbourhood policy' that combined political, economic, trade and other policy instruments. Whether the Union can offer enough to change the behaviour of its non-EU candidate neighbours is open to question. The EU (particularly Javier Solana) played a significant role in the resolution of the Ukrainian election crisis at the end of 2004, but probably less on the basis of the 'neighbourhood' status that the EU was offering Ukraine than because the Ukrainians saw themselves as future EU members. The EU's record further afield, notably in Africa, has its defenders (see Lowe 1996) but generally has been patchy and unimpressive.

Similarly, the ESDP's record during its short lifespan has been patchy. Operation Artemis showed that the EU could respond quickly to a UN appeal in a humanitarian crisis, and save lives in the process (see Mace 2003). But the EU Police Mission to oversee reform of the police in Bosnia was ridiculed as an expensive 'laughing stock'.[13] Beyond the EU's 'neighbourhood', on the wider international stage, the Union's ability to influence events remains very dependent on, not to say subordinate to, the United States. That is, its success is largely determined by the extent to which, and if so how, the US is engaged in areas where they share a foreign policy interest, notably in the Middle East, or on counterterrorism and non-proliferation.

Accountability and lobbying

Two dimensions of accountability—operational and democratic—help us come to grips with the question of who controls the CFSP. Operational accountability for specific CFSP policy actions varies. Where CFSP objectives are implemented through EC decisions, accountability is assured by the usual means for Community policies. However, provisions for monitoring and evaluation of CFSP decisions and implementation are much weaker than they are for other EU policies. This gap is partly a function of the foreign policy process itself and applies equally to national foreign policies. But there are problems that are particular to EU foreign policy.

One is that there are no provisions for punishing defectors from common positions. It is generically more difficult to 'regulate' cooperation in foreign policy as compared to other domains, including trade or monetary policy. Moreover, democratic accountability in the form of parliamentary control is weak. The EP does have the right to be informed and consulted on the main lines of the CFSP, but the Council is under no compulsion to pay attention to the EP's views, and usually—leaving aside budgetary matters—does so to the extent that it is convenient. Democratic control over the CFSP and ESDP effectively is through the accountability of foreign ministers to their own national parliaments. Some informed commentators are very critical of this situation, although there is little evidence that it much bothers the public in most European countries. On the contrary, surveys show that European publics favour EU unity in foreign and defence policy (far more than they support other EU policies, including enlargement and monetary union; see Howorth 2004), but also that ordinary citizens also show little interest in what the EU actually does in this domain. A major challenge for EU foreign policy is to increase public awareness of and active support for its increasingly wide range of activities.

The CFSP also mostly escapes the attention of lobbyists (the application of economic sanctions is a major exception). In fact, the most active lobbyists of EU foreign policy are non-EU governments such as the US, the states of the Middle East, Russia, and other players in the global system. Much of this diplomatic lobbying is directed towards the holder of the Council Presidency, the High Representative, and the Commission, although third countries which understand how the EU works (notably the US) also lobby in European national capitals.

EU foreign policy has always been an elite-driven process. It might be argued that so are national foreign policies. Still, the CFSP's institutional system clearly insulates the national elites conducting it, let alone the Brussels elite in the Council machinery, from ordinary democratic pressures as it produces policies with increasingly powerful effects. It thus illustrates Hill's (2003: xvii) more general maxim that foreign policy has become 'a key site for responsible action, and for democratic accountability in a world where the facts and myths of globalization have obscured the locations of decision-making and confused the debate over democratic participation'.

The institutions in context

One of the CFSP's major problems is that the CFSP does not represent or dominate any specific policy problem. Unlike the EC, which has exclusive competence over a number of policy issues, the CFSP must often compete with other actors and forums, such as functionally related EU policy domains, other international organizations, and even the independent activities of EU member states. In this sense the CFSP must often struggle just to make itself relevant.

The CFSP in the EU system

Foreign policy is effective to the extent that its 'targets' are open to persuasion, influence, or coercion by the foreign policy actor. The EU is no different: its success depends on its ability to supply or withhold certain resources in exchange for compliant behaviour. However, the CFSP by itself has only limited resources and few instruments of its own, even if that is changing, notably via the ESDP. It is therefore most effective when it harnesses resources available as Community instruments. In these cases, Commission involvement is essential, if only because it has the sole right of proposal. Sensitive to its prerogatives, the Commission often bridles at any suggestion that CFSP decisions might be taken that tell it what to do or what the EU member states want of it in EC policy areas.

Under the Constitutional Treaty, the right of proposal in the CFSP would have lain exclusively with the EU Minister of Foreign Affairs and the member states, although the Commission could have made proposals jointly with the MFA who, after all, would be a Vice-President of the Commission. However, the Commission would have remained excluded from decision-making on military matters (it has never been present in the Military Committee). EU member states have gone to considerable effort to maintain their control over ESDP and isolate it and their national defence industries completely from integrative pressures that might push it in the direction of the Community method. However, even without ratification of the Constitutional Treaty, a European Defence Agency was launched in 2004, with Solana chairing its Board of Directors, to begin long overdue work on upgrading and integrating the EU's military capabilities.

As is often the case, what is most interesting is not where the EU is but where it is in relation to where it started. Less than a decade ago the mere mention of an EU military capability was unthinkable. Today, the ESDP is an accepted growth area for common European action. No other regional international organization possesses its own military component, although some (such as the African Union) have nascent military capabilities or have made feeble pledges to cooperate on foreign policy issues. Despite all its problems, the EU can claim to be uniquely successful in this realm.

The CFSP and national policies/ministries

Foreign, security, and defence policies are core prerogatives of nation-states. All EU member states have their own highly institutionalized foreign and defence ministries and policies (see Hocking and Spence 2002). There is little sign that they intend to abandon them. Yet, the EU has become a central, though not exclusive, reference point for national foreign policies, especially for smaller EU states (Manners and Whitman 2000). Since the early 1970s, we have witnessed a gradual contraction of *domaines réservés*, in which former colonial powers regard their own interest and influence as paramount, and a simultaneous expansion of the topics considered appropriate for the CFSP (Belgium's experiences in Congo and Rwanda, where it was helpless acting on its own to prevent humanitarian disasters in its former colonial possessions, no doubt contributed). Virtually no foreign policy topic is considered off-limits for EU action, although discussions do not always lead to common action. The exception is issues before the UN Security Council, of which Iraq was a prime example: the two European permanent members of the Security Council—the UK and France—have insisted that their UN obligations preclude any coordination of their positions with the EU, let alone accountability to the Union for them.

Otherwise, communication between national capitals—which is crucial to consensus-building—is now highly institutionalized. The growth of the CFSP as a policy domain and the intense networking that takes place within it often make it difficult for outsiders to determine where national foreign policy-making ends and the CFSP begins. Some would even argue that purely national foreign policy preferences—entirely unaffected by EU deliberations—no longer exist (see Glarbo 2001).

Theorizing the CFSP

Applying theory to the practice of all of this activity, involving the EU's member states, institutions, non-member actors, and other policy domains (EU and otherwise), is a daunting challenge. Most theories of European integration or EU policy-making provide partial explanations at best since the CFSP contains elements of intergovernmentalism, supranationalism, and transgovernmentalism. Equally for theorists of European integration or international relations (IR) more generally, 'the issue of the meaning of European foreign policy cooperation for the international system, and conversely the impact of international relations on the EU, has been of marginal concern' (Hill and Smith 2005b: 404).

One of the most compelling theoretical accounts of the CFSP is an institutionalist one (see M. E. Smith 2003). Institutional theory explains not only what is expected but also appropriate behaviour by actors in any social setting. Institutions help 'filter' disparate social activities into explainable, purposeful policy outputs. Institutionalism stresses the importance of (mostly) incremental changes in terms of their accumulation: consider the High Representative's (proposed) transformation into the

MFA, or how the EU started with EPC and eventually equipped itself with a defence capability.

Institutionalism offers a kind of moving picture rather than a snapshot of European integration (see Pierson 1996). The differences between these two accounts of the CFSP are crucial. The CFSP began as an intergovernmental discussion forum (EPC), then developed its own complex infrastructure, and finally allowed the involvement of existing EC institutions (namely the Commission). A process of 'learning by doing' led to the embedding of foreign policy in the EU, actively drawing upon Community resources.

Perhaps more than any other single perspective, institutionalism helps explain why EU foreign policy institutions have developed sufficient proficiency to make member states not only unable but *unwilling* to interrupt, reverse, or exit from a process of further institutionalizing foreign, security, and (now) defence policy cooperation (see Hill 2004), even if clear policy successes remain elusive. Even theorists who reject the institutionalist account have to concede that foreign policy cooperation is now sufficiently institutionalized in Europe as to defy the assumption—which still underpins much IR scholarship—that all alliances between states are temporary and expedient. Amongst students of IR, consensus is beginning to emerge—slowly, gradually and somewhat begrudgingly—that 'the EU can no longer be treated as a peculiar side-issue in international relations' (Hill and Smith 2005b: 388).

Conclusion

The history of EU foreign policy is punctuated by critical junctures when the Union ran up against the limitations of its institutions, and elected to reform them. The inadequacies of the CFSP system, exposed first by the Balkans and then by Iraq, combined with the 'big bang' 2004 enlargement, brought another such juncture. Afterwards, it was impossible to imagine an effective CFSP without more 'coalitions of the willing', or which continued to rely on leadership by whoever happened to be foreign minister of the rotating Council Presidency. Stronger leadership was seen as necessary in itself as well as an important means of resolving other problems, notably tensions between small and large member states, and achieving more coherence in the EU's external policies.

There was no shortage of opportunities, and indeed demands, for the EU to speak with a single voice in the years immediately after its 2004 enlargement. Continued tension in the Middle East, the unfinished peace in the Balkans, problems in the Caucasus and other countries close to the EU's borders (Ukraine, Moldova, Belarus, North Africa), threats associated with terrorism and WMD, the rise of China as a global actor, ongoing disputes with North Korea, tensions in transatlantic relations, and the erosion of democracy in the former Soviet Union all put pressure on the EU. There was a widespread feeling that things could not go on in foreign policy as before.

As always, institutional reform was a necessary but far from sufficient condition for an effective CFSP. Member states, especially large ones, will always weigh the virtues of 'multiplying' their own power via common EU action against the difficulties of getting others to agree, resorting instead to working with smaller groups, or even alone. The 2004 enlargement has made consensus-building even more delicate and time-consuming than before. The external relations provisions of the Constitutional Treaty had the potential, at least, to give the CFSP consistent leadership with international name-recognition and authority to pull together the strengths of its member states and the Commission. With the survival of the Constitutional Treaty now unlikely, the EU and its CFSP will have to muddle through as best they can for the foreseeable future on the basis of the existing treaties. It is impossible to introduce reforms without treaty change if they clearly violate the current treaties. Formally abolishing the Presidency in external relations and double-hatting the HR/CFSP as a Commissioner for external relations would evidently fall into that category.

There will be other chances. We should recall that major reforms of the CFSP (the appointment of Javier Solana and the creation of the ESDP) were made in 1999 by a European Council decision, not a treaty change. Changes of this magnitude—including the creation of combined Council/Commission delegations overseas—are still possible and will no doubt be introduced when the dust has settled.

Still, tomorrow's historians may consider the rejection of the Constitutional Treaty in 2005 as marking a critical juncture when the chance of a genuine breakthrough towards making the EU an effective global power was missed. If so, it will not have been just the rejection of the Treaty's new foreign policy arrangements that weakened the EU's voice in the world, but also the host of ancillary issues which surveys showed contributed to the negative votes in France and the Netherlands. These included concerns about enlargement as well as about the dilution of national influence within the enlarged EU. Suddenly the whole concept of enlargement, a key factor in the EU's external influence (at least close to home), was thrown into doubt, not least but not only in relation to Turkey. At a more general level, there may well be a significant impact on the EU's external effectiveness from what has been widely seen as the popular rejection of top-down policies successfully pushed through by political elites.

The Constitutional Treaty would not have solved all of CFSP's institutional problems, let alone problems arising from a lack of political priority being given to arriving at common policies. Having the best institutional arrangements in the world cannot guarantee the right solutions or even solutions at all to intractable problems. Still, under the terms of the Constitutional Treaty, the EU would have likely developed a more 'centred' foreign policy. That process now looks likely to take much longer, certainly years or even decades, with quite a lot of improvisation.

On one hand, EU foreign policy coordination has been institutionalized in important respects. On the other, EU foreign has been stubbornly resistant to pressures for integration in key respects. As institutionalist theory tells us, institutions can shape and sustain political action. Rarely, however, can institutions 'create' such action entirely on their own.

Notes

1 Some important trade policy areas remain matters of shared competence with member states, notably services.

2 In its first years EPC was staffed by the foreign ministry of the holder of the Council Presidency, reflecting its informal and non-institutionalized status.

3 The CSCE was renamed the OSCE when it was made a standing 'Organization' (rather than a 'Conference') in 1995.

4 The CFSP is no different from other EU policies in that only ministers take decisions. 'Decisions' by officials — leaving aside those made by the Political and Security Committee — are formally recommendations to ministers.

5 A Coreu is a mid-level official in each Foreign Ministry responsible for coordination of arrangements and consultations with the Presidency and other colleagues.

6 This bilateral summit held at a French coastal resort produced a joint declaration by Europe's two major military powers endorsing the creation of an ESDP with the means to allow the EU to act autonomously when NATO decided not to be involved in a military action (see Sloan 2003: 172–5).

7 This rather opaque phrase refers to 'civilian' (that is, non-military) policy tools, such as diplomacy or economic sanctions, and command structures (such as EU defence ministers meeting in the Council of Ministers), as well as instruments for preventing conflicts, including the addition of policing or judicial expertise to EU military missions, as was done in the Balkans.

8 Nuttall (2000: 269) notes that the Contact Group 'did after all preserve a façade of EU organizational coherence' through a variety of procedural fixes that linked the participation of EU states to the CFSP as a whole. However, the Contact Group came at a time — during the first year of the CFSP's existence — when the EU's new mechanisms for foreign policy seemed to be failing more generally.

9 This designation arose from the Petersberg hotel outside Bonn at which WEU ministers adopted the tasks in 1992.

10 It is worth mentioning that the EU has proved capable of settling or at least managing open disputes that have flared with the US (about the relationship with NATO) and Turkey (primarily about Cyprus) externally, and between the UK and France internally (about the nature of ESDP and its relationship to the US).

11 'Berlin Plus' refers to the set of rules and procedures finalized in 2002 to govern EU access to NATO planning and military assets (see Cornish 2004).

12 One of the EU's top foreign policy officials has argued that soft power is only wielded by those who also possess hard power (see Cooper 2005).

13 James Lyon, 'EU's Bosnia police mission is "laughing stock"', *European Voice*, 15–21 September 2005, p. 16. The author is Serbia project director for the highly regarded International Crisis Group.

Further reading

The most comprehensive of recent works on the EU's international role is Hill and Smith (2005*b*). K. E. Smith (2003) offers a useful examination of how the EU pursues its foreign policy objectives. Specific EU policy actions are covered by Ginsberg (2001), Wiessala (2002), Peterson and Pollack (2003), Dannreuther (2004), and Youngs (2004). The European Security Strategy is analysed by Biscop (2005) and by Dannreuther and Peterson (2006). For a highly critical analysis of EU foreign policy, see Zielonka (1998). Some of the arguments in this chapter are drawn from M. E. Smith (2003).

Biscop, S. (2005), *The European Security Strategy: A Global Agenda for Positive Power* (Aldershot: Ashgate).

Dannreuther, R. (2004) (ed.), *European Union Foreign and Security Policy: Towards a Neighborhood Strategy* (London and New York: Routledge).

Dannreuther, R., and Peterson, J. (2006) (eds.), *Security Strategy and Transatlantic Relations* (London and New York: Routledge).

Ginsberg, R. (2001), *The European Union in International Politics: Baptism by Fire* (Lanham, MD and Oxford: Rowman & Littlefield).

Hill, C., and Smith, M. (2005) (eds.), *International Relations and the European Union* (Oxford and New York: Oxford University Press).

Peterson, J., and Pollack, M. A. (2003) (eds.), *Europe, America, Bush: Transatlantic Relations in the 21st Century* (London and New York: Routledge).

Smith, K. E. (2003), *European Union Foreign Policy in a Changing World* (Oxford and Malden, MA: Polity).

Smith, M. E. (2003), *Europe's Foreign and Security Policy: The Institutionalization of Cooperation* (Cambridge: Cambridge University Press).

Wiessala, G. (2002), *The European Union and Asian Countries* (Sheffield: Sheffield Academic Press).

Youngs, R. (2004), *Europe's Uncertain Pursuit of Middle East Reform* (Washington, DC: Carnegie Endowment for International Peace), available on *http://www.ceip.org/files/pdf/CP45.YOUNGS.final.PDF*

Zielonka, J. (1998), *Understanding Euro-Paralysis: Why Europe is Unable to Act in International Politics* (Basingstoke and New York: Macmillan/Palgrave).

Web links

All CFSP declarations and statements are archived in the *European Foreign Policy Bulletin*, available on: *http://www.iue.it/EFPB/Welcome.html*. The Council's own website is the best place to start a web search on the CFSP or ESDP (*http://ue.eu.int/cms3_of/showPage.asp?id=248&lang=en&mode=g*), although the general EU page (*http://www.europa.eu.int/pol/cfsp/index_en.htm*) runs a close second. The EU's own, internal, Paris-based think-tank, the Institute for Security Studies, produces high-quality analyses of foreign and security policy issues that are all available on-line: *www.iss-eu.org*. Finally, any student of European foreign policy should be aware of FORNET—a European foreign policy research network—which represents the first formal attempt to structure and coordinate a network of researchers across Europe focusing on foreign policy. More information at: *http://www.fornet.info/*

Chapter 14

National Interests

Coreper

Jeffrey Lewis

Contents

Summary

The Committee of Permanent Representatives (Coreper) originated as a diplomatic forum to meet regularly and prepare meetings of the Council of Ministers. It quickly and quietly evolved into a locus of continuous negotiation and *de facto* decision-making, gaining a reputation as 'the place to do the deal'. This reputation is based on insulation from domestic audiences and an unrivalled ability to make deals stick across a range of issue-areas and policy subjects. Most importantly, as this chapter will show, Coreper spotlights the process of integrating interests in a collective decision-making system with its own organizational culture, norms, and style of discourse. Coreper is an institutional environment where group-community standards create what neoinstitutionalists call a 'logic of appropriateness' which informs bargaining behaviour and influences everyday decision-making outcomes.

Introduction

This chapter addresses the role of the Committee of Permanent Representatives (Coreper) in the EU. According to one analyst, 'the caliber and effectiveness of permanent representative officials determines to a great extent how countries fare in the EU' (Dinan 1999: 260). Another claims that the members of Coreper are 'among the great unsung heroes' of European integration (Westlake 1999: xxiv). Both observations offer a useful entry-point to understanding Coreper and how it functions. First, it is a pivotal actor in everyday EU decision-making and for this reason, member-states consider Coreper one the most important postings in Brussels. Second, and what may seem counter-intuitive to the first point, Coreper is less visible than other institutional sites in the EU. As this chapter will clarify, Coreper's importance as an institutional actor is related to its ability over the years to avoid the limelight and to work behind the scenes at finding agreements and forging compromise.

Coreper is the site in EU decision-making where national interests and European solutions interact more frequently, more intensively, and across more issue-areas than any other. To work effectively, the committee relies on a culture of consensus-based decision making—an informal, intangible quality of the institutional environment and a critical component in the EU permanent representation's ability to 'find solutions'. Coreper is also something of a chimera. To some, it resembles a bastion of intergovernmentalism. To others, it appears less like interstate bargaining than a haven for Eurocrats to 'go native'. Neither view, in such stark terms, is accurate. Nor is either view entirely wrong. As Hayes-Renshaw and Wallace (1995: 563) found in their study of the Council's institutional form, 'it is both representative and collective'. From a theory perspective, successful negotiation in Coreper often requires subtle attention to both the 'logic of consequence' and the 'logic of appropriateness'.[1] Viewed with neoinstitutionalist lenses, it is precisely this tension that makes Coreper so interesting to study.

Coreper is 'responsible for preparing the work of the Council and for carrying out the tasks assigned to it by the Council' (Art. 207 TEU). From this austere mandate, Coreper has developed into a major player in the EU system. Among its 'assigned tasks' is the remit to 'coordinate the work of the various Council meetings and to endeavour to reach agreement at its level' (Council Guide 1996: 39). In essence, this means that Coreper holds responsibility for the performance of Council as a whole. In institutionalist language, there is an obligation of result which the permanent representatives find is an unwritten part of the job description. As one ambassador explained, 'there is a high collective interest in getting results and reaching solutions. This is in addition to representing the national interest'.[2] Another said 'if we have to take it to the Council, there is a sense that we have failed'. Signs of this responsibility and the mandate that it rests on can be traced back to the dog days of Eurosclerosis, and the heads of state and government who innovated European Council summitry. In particular, the communiqué of the 1974 Paris Summit holds: 'Greater latitude will be given to the Permanent Representatives so that only the most important political problems need be discussed in the Council'.[3] It was during this same period that integration researchers began to observe that Coreper resembled 'a Council of Ministers in permanent session' (Busch and Puchala 1976: 240).

In many ways, Coreper is the ideal institutional site to examine national interests in the context of everyday EU decision-making because Coreper is the needle's eye through which the legislative output of the Council flows. Because a defining trait of the Council is its sectoral differentiation, pursuing the 'national interest' across its operating formations requires complex national systems of interest intermediation and interministerial coordination. The permanent representatives have a cross-Council negotiating mandate which functions as an essential aggregation mechanism in everyday EU decision-making. The EU ambassadors and deputies are thus critical interlocutors in the ability of a member-state to pursue what Anderson (1999: 6) calls a 'milieu goal' in Brussels, or the ability to 'ensure that government policy objectives are consistent, both within Europe and across the national and supranational levels'.

The chapter proceeds as follows. In the next section, we examine how the permanent representatives acquired such a central position in the EU system. We then sketch out the structure of Coreper, including how it works and has changed over time. Next, the Committee's main powers, namely *de facto* decision-making and an institutional capacity for integrating interests, are examined. While still early days, with care and caution we will examine some preliminary findings regarding the addition of ten new members and how this affects the group's cohesiveness. A brief concluding section will follow, looking at the wider theory implications for an institutional body that so explicitly straddles *and blurs* the boundary between the national and European levels.

Coreper's origins

Although no mention was made in the Treaty of Paris for the creation of a preparatory body, it was less than six months after the Treaty entered into force in July 1952 that the need for such a body was apparent. At the first meeting of the Special Council of Ministers (September 1952), the ad hoc group on the organization of the Council's work was instructed to come up with a proposal for a preparatory committee. The Coordinating Commission, or Cocor (*Commission de Coordination du Conseil des Ministres*), was the result. The formal decision to create Cocor was taken by the Special Council of Ministers in February 1953. But it was only with the Treaty of Rome that the legal basis for a preparatory committee was established (Art. 151 EEC).

The first Cocor meeting was held in March 1953. Cocor began to meet monthly in Luxembourg, with representatives travelling back and forth from their national capitals. Cocor diplomacy was premised on mutual trust, a spirit of accommodation, and an equality of voice between big and small states. Ernst Haas, writing in the late 1950s, drew a sharp distinction between Cocor and the brand of diplomacy found at the Council of Europe for example, equating the former with the 'principle of a novel community-type organ' (1958: 491; 1960).

From the earliest proposals to set up a permanent preparatory body, the issue of delegating formal decision making authority was allowed to remain ambiguous. Such a non-debate is evident at the 1956 Intergovernmental Conference (IGC) where the design of a new permanent, Brussels-based committee was negotiated (see Exhibit 14.1). Over the course of discussions it became clear that there was agreement among the foreign ministers *not* to create a Brussels-body composed of deputy ministers. Instead, they agreed the permanent delegations should be headed by high-ranking diplomats. But there was little talk on what substantive form the permanent representatives' role should take and the issue was left open. Articles 151 EEC and 121 Euratom reflect this ambiguity. They allow simply for the Council's rules of procedure to 'provide for the establishment of a committee composed of representatives of member states. The Council shall determine the task and competence of that committee'.

Early on, the open-ended nature of Coreper's authority set off alarm bells at the Commission. Following the January 1958 decision to begin the work of the Committee without precisely defining its tasks and powers, the Commission asked for clarification of Coreper's role (de Zwaan 1995: 75). In March 1958, Belgian Foreign Minister Larock, acting as Council President, defended the Council's provisional rules of procedure and assured Commission President Hallstein they ruled out the possibility of delegating decisional authority to Coreper (Noël 1967: 228–9). There were similar questions raised in the European Parliament, with some MEPs concerned the

---

Exhibit 14.1 Constitutive politics and the Spaak Committee

The creation of a permanent Brussels-based body composed of high-ranking civil servants was based on a proposal from the Committee of the Heads of Delegations, chaired by the industrious Belgian Foreign Minister, Paul-Henri Spaak (more popularly known as the Spaak Committee). The Spaak Committee, set up by the foreign ministers at Messina (June 1955) to discuss future steps in European integration, began meeting intensively at the Château de Val Duchesse outside of Brussels in July 1955. Eight months of talks produced the Spaak Report (April 1956). The recommendations of the Spaak Report were approved by the foreign ministers' meeting in Venice (May 1956) and, after further IGC negotiations (again led by the Spaak Committee), culminated with the Treaty of Rome (March 1957). In one of the less well-known political coups in the history of the EU, it was the Spaak Committee that strongly endorsed a permanent negotiating body and, for the most part, were the same individuals who would become the first permanent representatives.

As Noël (1967: 219) recounts, Art 151 EEC became a 'means of prolonging and perpetuating . . . that rather extraordinary "club",' (that is, the Spaak Committee) which was 'both a meeting place of authorized and faithful spokesmen of the six Governments and a group of militants (even of 'accomplices') dedicated to a vast and noble political undertaking' (see also Lindberg and Scheingold 1970: 242). Noël hints at the novelty of this, whereby the Spaak Committee morphed into what would become Coreper, since the Interim Committee set up in March 1957 contained many of the same personnel and 'preserved the same atmosphere and spirit' (1966: 88). Except for France and Italy, the Interim Committee delegates would also become the first Permanent Representatives in early 1958. In short, the Spaak Committee and the creation of Coreper is a striking example of 'constitutive politics' in the institutional history of European integration.[4]

Committee could usurp the Commission's right of initiative (de Zwaan 1995: 75). Since these early years, the Commission, and in particular the Secretary-General's office, with Emile Noël at the helm from 1958 to 1987, would come to view the permanent representatives as potential allies in a common cause. As one Commission participant stated, 'We consider Coreper more as an ally than something we have to fight with'. Coreper is often the strategic point of inroad to the Council, since the Commission prefers to have detailed, substantive discussions with the permanent representatives who (unlike many ministers) are also well versed in the legal intricacies of the Treaty. Jacques Delors, while Commission President, often personally appeared in Coreper to explain and 'sell' key Single Market proposals to the permanent representatives before they were presented at the ministerial level.[5]

Since the late 1950s, Coreper, quietly and often unnoticed, acquired a reputation for forging compromise and finding solutions across an ever-growing range of issues. This was contrary to their reputation in academic circles, as integration researchers typically characterized Coreper as an embodiment of intergovernmentalism and hardball bargaining![6] As the EC deepened, Coreper acquired new responsibilities and general policy competencies (Noël and Étienne 1971). Agricultural policy was an exception to this because of the highly technical nature of administering the CAP, and in 1960 the Special Committee on Agriculture (SCA) was established to take over this specialized policy field.[7] The deepening process created exponential pressures for Coreper to develop *de facto* legislative competencies in order to minimize policy-making bottlenecks and impart coherence to the segmentation of the Council's work. The bifurcation of Coreper in 1962 into parts I and II (discussed below) was a realization of this burgeoning workload. But contrary to conventional accounts, such as Weiler's (1981: 285) claim that 'decisional supranationalism' was weakened by the addition of Coreper to the EC system, the committee institutionalized a deliberative, consensual style of decision making based on 'thick' bonds of trust, understanding, responsiveness and a willingness to compromise. The ability to serve as a gatekeeper for the Council's work was not simply about paving the way for ministers to find agreements, but increasingly, the ability to dispose of large quantities of business by forging consensus out of seemingly irreconcilable national positions.

Structure of the institution

In structural location, Coreper occupies a unique institutional vantage point in the EU system. Vertically placed between the experts and the ministers and horizontally situated with cross-Council policy responsibilities, the permanent representatives obtain a broad overview of the Council's work. Compared to the experts meeting in the working groups, they are political heavyweights; but unlike the ministers, they are policy generalists *and* experts in the substantive questions of a file. In his classic study of Coreper, Joseph Salmon referred to this unique perspective as the *vue d'ensemble* (1971: 642). The institutional perspective of the *vue d'ensemble* is a qualitative feature of Coreper, part of the organizational culture and a kind of cognitive map which newcomers must learn to read and navigate to be successful.

Defined narrowly, Coreper consists of fifty members, who are jointly referred to as the permanent representatives. This includes twenty-five EU permanent representatives (also known as the EU ambassadors) and twenty-five deputy permanent representatives. The Committee meets in two formats: I (deputies) and II (ambassadors). The Commission is always represented in both Committee formats. But such a narrow definition would miss how Coreper is embedded in a much more extensive network of national delegations in Brussels, known as the EU permanent representations 'Permreps'. At a glance, the Permreps look like embassies, but as the EU has deepened they have grown in size and coverage to become microcosms of the national governments and 'veritable administrative melting-pots' (Hayes-Renshaw *et al.* 1989: 128). Permreps also become the nerve centre to manage the duties of the EU Presidency, and delegations often swell by 25 per cent or more to handle the workload. This can be seen in Table 14.1, where the size of Luxembourg's Permrep grew from fourteen to seventy-six in preparation for the 2005 presidency.

Since 1975, a group of assistants to the ambassadors, known as the Antici counsellors, finalize and prepare the agendas for weekly Coreper II meetings. The

Table 14.1 Growth in the size of EU permanent representations

Year Member state	2005	2000	1995	1991	1986	1969	1965
Belgium	65	46	36	31	26	18	18
Czech Republic	58	—	—	—	—	—	—
Denmark	47	46	38	35	31	—	—
Germany	111	79	62	47	41	28	21
Estonia	41	—	—	—	—	—	—
Greece	86	55	66	62	48	—	—
Spain	76	58	54	50	31	—	—
France	94	70	50	41	29	19	18
Ireland	51	37	37	26	24	—	—
Italy	67	49	42	44	40	29	22
Cyprus	31	—	—	—	—	—	—
Latvia	36	—	—	—	—	—	—
Lithuania	35	—	—	—	—	—	—
Luxembourg	76	13	14	13	6	8	4
Hungary	57	—	—	—	—	—	—
Malta	31	—	—	—	—	—	—
Netherlands	89	47	45	30	24	21	19
Austria	72	68	65	—	—	—	—
Poland	56	—	—	—	—	—	—
Portugal	50	55	48	44	36	—	—
Slovenia	34	—	—	—	—	—	—
Slovakia	48	—	—	—	—	—	—
Finland	56	60	37	—	—	—	—
Sweden	61	50	52	—	—	—	—
United Kingdom	77	55	50	39	45	—	—

Source: For 2005 and 2000, IDEA online (*http://www.ue.eu.int*); Guide to the Council of the European Communities, various years.

Anticis also act as advisers to their ambassadors, minimizing the element of surprise by floating ideas and testing arguments before or at the margins of meetings, drafting reports to send back home, and attending European Council summits as note-takers. In 1993, the deputies formalized a similar group of assistants, known as the Mertens counsellors. With the addition of the ten new members, the Anticis and Mertens have taken on a more active role. One Antici portrayed the group as a 'full-fledged working group' for two sorts of issues: 'issues that should be dealt with close to the ambassadors, and ... issues that don't fit any other working group'. A good example of the latter is the Antici group's quiet handling of the fine print on how to implement a new language translation regime in the EU of twenty-five. The Antici and Mertens counsellors are also emblematic of a wider array of transgovernmental networking which takes place among national administrations through the Permreps. This includes CFSP and JHA counsellors, and now, even military types who work on ESDP matters. In general, the permanent representations are a mechanism for socialization to the EU, training new generations of diplomats and policy specialists, orchestrating presidencies, and educating national administrations to open their minds to a new EU reality (Lewis 2005).

Coreper I and II

Coreper is split into two formations based on a functional division of labour (see Table 14.2). Both meet weekly and each have their own Councils to prepare. Coreper II is composed of the ambassadors and responsible for the monthly General Affairs and External Relations Council (GAERC) as well as issues with horizontal, institutional, and financial implications. The lion's share of weekly Coreper II agendas deals with EU external relations (such as trade, aid, and foreign policy). What is more, discussions range widely, for example, shifting from canned tuna to relations with Russia. Coreper II is also closely implicated in multiannual budget negotiations (Delors I and II, Agenda 2000), and historically, with IGCs (often serving as a delegation's personal representative).[8]

Coreper I is made up of the deputies and is responsible for the misleadingly labelled 'technical' Councils such as Competitiveness, Environment, and Employment, Social Policy, Health and Consumer Affairs. While 'technical,' such as setting fish support prices every December for the Common Fisheries Policy, this work is also often intensely political. Coreper I is also responsible for representing the Council during codecision negotiations and conciliation committee meetings with the EP. It is estimated that as much as 50 per cent of the deputies' time is now devoted to codecision matters (Bostock 2002: 223). This places Coreper I at the heart of the Council's 'new legislative culture' with the EP (see Shackleton 2000).

As a general rule, the division of labour between Coreper I and II functions smoothly. Occasionally, a file that comes under Coreper I's remit is co-opted by the ambassadors. This occurred in 1997 with the EU embargo on fur imports from countries using leghold traps, which began as an animal rights issue for the Environmental Council and Coreper I, but was turned over to Coreper II when broader trade interests were entangled in a dispute with the United States. Finally, there are differences in status and ego between the ambassadors and deputies, with

Table 14.2 Responsibilities of Coreper I and II

Coreper II—Ambassadors
General affairs and external relations
Justice and home affairs
Multi-annual budget negotiations (Delors I and II, Agenda 2000)
Structural and cohesion funds
Institutional and horizontal questions
Association agreements and development
Accession
IGC personal representatives*
Coreper I—Deputies
Conciliation in areas of codecision
Single European Market
Environment
Employment, social policy, and consumer affairs
Competitiveness
Transport, telecommunications, and energy
Research
Culture Council
Education, youth affairs, and culture
Fisheries
Agriculture (veterinary and plant-health questions)

Note: * Varies by member state and IGC.

the former exuding almost limitless self-confidence to get the job done. 'We are mere mortals compared to the ambassadors', one deputy joked.

Who are the EU permanent representatives? Ambassadors are almost invariably senior ranking diplomats from the ministries of foreign affairs. For most member-states, the deputy is also recruited from foreign affairs; exceptions include Germany, where the deputy always comes from economic affairs, and the UK, where the deputy frequently comes from the Department of Trade and Industry (DTI). The EU permanent representatives are selected from the highest tier of career diplomats and senior civil servants, usually with a considerable background in European affairs. The member states control appointments, and there is no approval process in Brussels. Appointments are typically made after a recommendation or at least tacit approval from the head of state or government. Such high-level political selection contributes enormously to the credibility (and confidence) of the permanent representatives to negotiate in Brussels. 'We don't care if he wears a nice suit', one participant explained, 'we want to know: can he deliver?' In European diplomatic circles, Coreper is considered a top posting. EU permanent representatives rank the position on par or slightly above postings to Washington, New York, and Paris.

Coreper appointments are also noteworthy for the length of tenure and absence of partisan politics. The average appointment is five years, slightly longer than the typical three or four year diplomatic rotation. But some permanent representatives remain in Brussels for much longer, upwards of a decade or beyond. For example, since 1958, Belgium has had six ambassadors; Germany five deputies. Longer appointments provide 'continuity in the representation of interests' (de Zwaan 1995: 17). Permanent representatives even remain insulated from electoral politics and shifts in government (though with some exceptions such as Portugal and Greece; see Lewis 1998b: 109–113).

Contestation

Since 1958, Coreper has been the senior preparatory forum of the Council. The vertical channels of coordination placed the permanent representatives in clear command of how files were routed to the ministers. They were undisputed gatekeepers. While on paper all Treaty reforms have reconfirmed Coreper's senior preparatory status, two developments are gradually contesting this in practice.

Since the early 1990s, everyday EU decision-making has seen an intensification in rivalries between preparatory bodies (Lewis 2000). There are nagging turf battles over CFSP competences with the Political and Security Committee (PSC). However, the advent of the European security and defence policy (ESDP) (assisted by the new Military Committee and Military Staff) has more sharply delineated the boundaries of where Coreper does not wish to tread. (In interviews, Coreper officials claim the minutiae of military planning is as appealing to them as agricultural price schedules for wheat.) Some in Brussels see the coherence of EU foreign policy-making as limited by the fragmentation of preparatory authority.

In other policy areas, Coreper II has permanently conceded responsibility of the ECOFIN Council (and the 'Euro Group' of euro zone finance ministers) to the Economic and Finance Committee (EFC). EFC reports are not by rule even copied to the permanent representatives; they are sent directly to the finance ministers. Other, less serious, boundary disputes involve the Article 36 Committee (ex K-4) and JHA matters, and the Article 133 Committee (ex Art. 113) over administration of the common commercial policy (CCP). Over the last decade, Coreper has become more proactive in establishing boundaries for such turf battles and clarifying its senior preparatory status. The Council's rules of procedure are now more detailed in laying out Coreper's right to 'ensure consistency of the Union's policies and actions' (Art. 19(1)) with a footnote which holds 'in particular for matters where substantive preparation is undertaken in other fora' (Art. 19: footnote 2, statement (g)).

A second source of contestation is the relative decline of the General Affairs Council (redesigned as a 'bicameral' General Affairs and External Relations Council (GAERC) in 2002). For the first several decades of European integration, General Affairs was *primus inter pares*. But the process of deepening had the effect of raising the stature and importance of other sectoral Councils. By the 1990s, General Affairs had lost its claim to providing leadership or acting as an overall coordinator of EU affairs (Gomez and Peterson 2001). Today many in Brussels believe Ecofin has supplanted the GAC as the senior formation of the Council. For most member states, this is a reflection of the domestic inter-ministerial balance of power which has seen a relative eclipse of foreign affairs (Hocking 1999). The weakening of General Affairs (and in turn the foreign ministries' grip on Council leadership) is slowly having effects on Coreper as well. This is already evident in the EFC–Ecofin (and 'Euro Group') linkages which bypass Coreper. Another indicator is the Primenet system which connects prime ministers and their sherpas into a direct transgovernmental network.

In this case, links to Coreper are bypassed by horizontal linkages at the level of the prime ministers' offices. Some at the permanent representations perceive this general pattern of contestation as weakening Coreper's institutional role. Whether the new bifurcation of the GAERC into 'general affairs' and 'external relations' formats will remedy these dysfunctions remains to be seen (see Chapter 4).

Powers of the institution

By focusing on Coreper, we are essentially looking at what Peterson (1995) has termed the systemic level of 'policy-setting' decisions. But EU decision making is also 'heavily nuanced, constantly changing, and even kaleidoscopic' (Peterson and Bomberg 1999: 9) with significant variation by policy sector and issue-area. Within this complex and multidimensional setting, two formal and informal powers stand out at Coreper level: *de facto* decision-making and the institutional capacities to integrate interests.

De facto decision-makers

As a continuous negotiation chamber in the EU, Coreper is a place where, qualitatively speaking, many decisions are made. But the permanent representatives have no formal decision-making authority. Juridical decision-making authority is a power exclusively reserved for the ministers, and formal voting is expressly prohibited at any other level of the Council. But in practice, or *de facto*, Coreper has evolved into a veritable decision-making factory. There are ways around the formality of *de jure* voting, such as the 'indicative vote' of how a delegation would vote if the matter was put before the ministers. More common is the tactful packaging of a discussion by the Presidency, where the chair will ask 'I assume no one else requests the floor?' or state 'a sufficient majority exists'. No vote is taken. There is no raising of the hands. But many agreements are reached in this manner and many decisions are thus made.

Although we lack systematic empirical data, participants claim that the overwhelming bulk of decisions are made consensually (see Chapter 4). Even under conditions of QMV, permanent representatives regularly spend extra time to 'bring everyone on board'. Pushing for a vote is considered inappropriate in most cases, and the 'consensus assumption' is a reflexive habit. A clear example of this consensus-reflex can be seen in the legislative record of the 1992 Project. Out of the 260 single market measures subject to QMV, approximately 220 of them were adopted unanimously, without a vote at all (de Schoutheete 2000: 9–10). Spending extra time and not pushing for a vote is considered 'the right thing to do', offering a clear illustration of the logic of appropriateness in Coreper's institutional setting.

The most surprising finding here is not that civil servants have been delegated *de facto* decisional authority, but the density of this mechanism in maintaining the output and performance across so many policy fields of the Council's work. Whether this role can be sustained in an enlarged EU is an open question. On the one hand, there is the hypothesis that a bigger, less cohesive Council negotiating table will require increased reliance on Coreper's bottlenecking policy competencies and de facto decision making. On the other hand, there is a competing hypothesis that Coreper's culture cannot work the same in such a large and disparate group. The basic question—and one which many Brussels insiders privately wonder about—is whether Coreper's clubbiness and sense of mission to find consensual solutions can survive in an enlarged and much more heterogeneous group, a question returned to below.[9] We turn now to how Coreper is able to reach so many decisions, and what is potentially the group's most valuable contribution to EU decision-making, its capacity in integrating interests.

Integrating interests

Continuous negotiation

Coreper's structural placement imparts a coherence and continuity in the representation of interests which would otherwise be difficult to match. Not only is Coreper distinguishable by the intensity of negotiations, but the permanent representatives' involvement across the different domains of EU decision-making is pervasive as well. In addition to weekly meetings, the permanent representatives sit beside their ministers during Council sessions, briefing them beforehand and offering tactical suggestions. They attend European Council summits and can serve as behind-the-scenes consultants. They monitor the proceedings of the working groups and offer specific points of strategy or emphasis. The ambassadors are also closely involved in monitoring cooperation and association agreements, cooperation councils (including Euro-Med conferences and Euro–Asian summits), and accession negotiations. Finally, from the beginnings of the Lomé Convention with ACP states, the ambassadors have prepared ACP–EC Councils through the ACP–EC Committee of Ambassadors which precede each yearly meeting (Council Guide 1996: 53). And while the links between the EP and Coreper II remain weak, conciliation has created an intense negotiation network between MEPs and the deputies.

All this creates a dynamic of ongoingness in Coreper's work, reinforced through weekly meetings. Add to this the regular cycle of Coreper luncheons, held by Coreper II before the monthly GAC and sometimes on a more topical, *ad hoc* basis.[10] Lunches sometimes function as long-term strategic planning sessions, often with a European Commissioner invited as a guest. More frequently, and because attendance is so tightly restricted, lunches are used to tackle the thorniest of problems (Butler 1986: 30). Then there are the informal Coreper trips hosted by the Presidency which precede European Council summits.[11] Trips are long weekends of socializing 'rich in food and culture' used to reinforce interpersonal relations and the bonds of trust, a kind of 'oiling of the mechanism'. This ongoingness of negotiation builds an institutional memory in Coreper from which the permanent representatives learn to draw (Lewis 1999: 485).

Instruction and voice

Permanent representatives are under 'instruction' from their national capitals. In principle, for every agenda item there is an instruction, setting, at a minimum, what is and is not acceptable as an outcome. Again in principle, this instruction is arrived at after domestic coordination through the relevant line ministries and often through an interministerial coordination mechanism.[12] In practice, the instruction process is much more complex, especially in temporal sequence. For starters, most instructions have in-built flexibility. Of course, there are certain taboo areas (institutional reform, fiscal policy) and national sensitivities—but here permanent representatives claim to not even need instructions because they already know what positions to take.

Much more fundamental to this story is the degree to which permanent representatives have an institutionalized voice in the instruction process itself. Some generic patterns of this include, first, departing from instructions and making recommendations back to the capital for changes. The power of recommendations obviously varies by issue-area and the personal authority of a permanent representative, but they are most effective in areas where there is a risk of becoming isolated or, under the shadow of the vote, disregarded in a possible compromise. Second, the capitals often signal that a margin of manoeuvre exists. Sometimes, permanent representatives are told not to take an instruction seriously. Or that the position in the printed instruction can be disregarded. 'Instructions are a way for [the capital] to say they have done their job', one ambassador explained. Third, when there is a political need to avoid confrontation or politicization at the level of the ministers, permanent representatives (sometimes even told: 'avoid Council') will have a freer hand in making deals and selling success at home. Fourth, there are times when the capital does not know or cannot decide (or does not want to decide, see below). Here the permanent representatives are causally contributing to the definition of what national interests in the EU context are. As one Antici counsellor explained, 'Instructions already contain a big Brussels element in them, and sometimes they are Brussels instructions, because the first ten lines of our report imply an instruction ... sometimes they just copy our reports into instructions'. A different pattern emerges when the capital does not want to decide. According to a large member-state ambassador, 'Sometimes they don't give an instruction because sometimes the ministers don't want to be pinned down. The result of this is that we make policy often from here'.

The degree of voice which the permanent representatives can obtain is derivative of Coreper's basic mission: to find solutions. Finding collective solutions and 'getting on with it' is an unspoken job requirement which gives Coreper its reputation for being results-oriented. It can even happen that permanent representatives disregard their instructions. As one ambassador detailed:

> It [disregarding instructions] happens. The first time it feels like a big deal. The second time, its easy. The problem is to know what are the interests of your country ... Now sometimes the capital gets nervous, they have various lobbies behind it usually. We also have to keep in mind that what has been built up over the last forty years is important. That a file should go. That we should proceed forward. This is constantly a factor in what we do. Often we have much more at stake than the dossier.

While it is important to avoid an oversocialized view of the permanent represen-tatives, one should not underestimate the relative autonomy that Coreper as a col-lective decision making forum can obtain. The instruction process is often a two-way street, with permanent representatives able to insert a high degree of voice in their construction. And as a group, the Committee can engage in transgovernmental bar-gaining tactics such as the 'plotting' of a compromise in the collective interest of find-ing solutions (see below).

Insulation

One of the really distinctive features of Coreper diplomacy is the degree of insulation from the normal currents of domestic constituent pressures. The meetings them-selves are treated with an air of confidentiality, and many sensitive national positions are ironed out in restricted sessions where the permanent representatives can speak frankly and in confidence that what is said will not be reported to the capitals or the media. This can even include group discussion on how an agreement will be pack-aged and sold to the authorities back home. 'At our level, publicity does not exist', an ambassador explained, 'Our body is absolutely black; we can do deals'. Another stated, 'We are better placed than the capitals to know what are the real interests of our countries. We are less exposed to the pressures, the short term problems of the time. This affects us much less'.

A structural feature of Coreper that often goes unnoticed is that insulation affords member-states the capacity to reshape domestic constraints. As an ambassador put it, 'Coreper is the only forum in the EU where representatives don't have a domestic turf to defend'. Because of this, he went on to add, 'it is often politically necessary to present a position knowing it is unrealistic. My minister of finance needs certain arguments to be presented. He has certain pressures from his constituencies. We have to make it look like we fought for this even though we both know it will lead nowhere. I will present it, and if it receives no support, I will drop it'.

A dense normative environment

Coreper's institutional capacity to aggregate interests across such an array of issue-areas and under such a steady workload is facilitated by a dense normative environ-ment. While these norms are almost purely informal in character—meaning they are unwritten, not linked directly to any clauses in the Treaties, and are largely self-enforcing—the group-community standards in Coreper are highly institution-alized and engrained into the basic ethos of the Committee's work. Five mutually reinforcing norms in particular stand out. First, there is a norm of diffuse recipro-city, or the balancing of concessions over an extended shadow of the future. 'We do keep a sense in an unspecific way of obligations to another member-state', one ambassador remarked. Diffuse reciprocity can take many forms, including conces-sions and derogations, or 'going out on a limb' to persuade the capital for changes or a compromise. Dropping reserves or abstaining (rather than a 'no' vote) are also political gestures which can be filed away and later returned in kind.

Second, there is a norm of 'thick trust' and the ability to speak frankly, recon-firmed weekly through the normal cycle of meetings, trips, and lunches.[13] Thick trust is especially important during endgame negotiations and restricted sessions when the group collectively legitimates or rejects arguments based on deliberative processes such as principled reasoning, standards of fairness, or justifications for special consideration. Third, there is a norm of mutual responsiveness which is best described as a shared purpose to understand each other's problems. Mutual responsiveness is another form of collective legitimation, where arguments are accepted or rejected by the group. Mutual responsiveness works within broad normative parameters, on the one hand, recognizing that everyone has certain problems that require special consideration, but on the other hand, that no one can be a *demandeur* too often and expect anyone to listen. This is such a basic rule of the game in Coreper that several permanent representatives from the newest member states had already learned this after attending three or four meetings.

The fourth norm is a consensus-reflex. This is what Hayes-Renshaw and Wallace (1995: 465) refer to as 'the instinctive recourse to behave consensually'. Even under conditions of QMV, permanent representatives often spend extra time to 'bring everyone on board'. Finally, there is a culture of compromise which is premised on a basic willingness to accommodate divergent interests and is reinforced by the other norms listed above. The normative effects of this culture include a self-restraint in the calculations and defence of interests, seen for example when delegations quietly drop reserves after failing to convince the others of their arguments (Lewis 2005).

Norm socialization and enlargement

EU norms are internalized through a multilevelled process of socialization. At the microlevel, new participants in Coreper go through a process of adaptation and learning. One Mertens counsellor claimed that it takes newcomers at least six months to 'find their way,' since, 'They stick close to their instructions. They don't yet have all the technical knowledge of the dossiers. They cannot gauge what is whispered in their ears'. Early interviews point to steep learning curves for the ten new member states, with mixed evidence of how quickly the newcomers are acclimatizing to Brussels. One new ambassador said 'every Coreper, I take away a new lesson'. A small state deputy with a long tenure in Brussels summarized the newcomers as 'They have been very silent, they have been very careful. I am not sure the silence is from fascination; they may be flabbergasted at how things work in Coreper'.

Interviews with the Eastern newcomers reveal a degree of cynicism that was not apparent with the new Nordic members in the mid-1990s. One new ambassador stated, 'They are all polite, they are nice, but there is no sympathy. In my short time in Coreper I would say that it is a gathering of cynics condemned to compromise'. Another reached a similar conclusion: '[The group] can say no quite politely but equally strong, they can be sympathetically ungiving. And I'm not seeking sympathy! I'm assuming and view this as a tough, competitive environment and I may not enjoy it'.

Some interpret the new ten as a catalyst for deeper change in the EU's normative environment. A long-standing deputy noted, 'there is a marked change between 15 and 25, it will be very difficult to re-establish the club atmosphere of Coreper ... much has shifted to an informal circuit. I spend much more time on the telephone, "I have a point, can you support me?" [The newcomers] will have a problem doing this, the informal work'. An ambassador reached a similar conclusion, 'you do feel around the table you're not going to know them as well. In an EU of the future you will know your colleagues less well. It is inevitable that more will be done outside the meetings rather than in the room'.

Plotting

Plotting is a negotiation pattern found in Coreper that demonstrates how a collective rationality can reformulate individual, instrumental rationality. The basic function of plotting is using the group to redefine a national position or to reshape domestic constraints.[14] 'To get new instructions we have to show [the capital] we have a black eye,' an ambassador explained, 'We can ask Coreper for help with this; it is one of our standard practices'. According to another, 'Sometimes I will deal with impossible instructions, by saying, "Mr. Chairman, can I report back the fierce opposition to this?" And sometimes fierceness is exaggerated for effect'. An excellent illustration of plotting occurred with Coreper II negotiations to reduce the number of Council formations (following the conclusions of the December 1999 Helsinki Summit). In this case, as a participant explained:

> All fifteen [ambassadors] had negative instructions. They all had their own lists of what to keep, what to cut. This is because each has its own lobbies, you know, on gender questions, and so on. We all have our own [national] coordination problems. So we met in a luncheon. I told them, 'You understand this is pointless'. And I asked them, 'Will you report back that you were totally isolated?' So each has reported home that the other fourteen are more or less in agreement.

In general, plotting and underlining opposition is a tool to deal with recalcitrant bargaining positions. Exaggerating the fierceness of opposition is also a group strategy to collectively legitimate or reject arguments.

Style of discourse

Coreper has a shared discourse with its own key phrases, such as when a delegation is signalling a willingness to compromise. There is a style of presenting arguments. There is also the art of derogation, where permanent representatives ask for help or special consideration. Learning the discourse is an important socialization mechanism for newcomers who join the club. As Peterson and Jones (1999: 34) point out, new members to Coreper 'must learn to use the language (even rhetoric) of appeals to the "European project"'.

There is a discourse to reveal who is behind their instructions and who is not. 'I can tell', a deputy explained, 'when someone wants to distance themselves from their instructions'. One strategy is to just read them. 'They may say, "Mr. Chairman, I'd like to read you something which I myself do not understand," or "unfortunately I have to bore you with the following . . . "' Some claim to be able to tell if a colleague agrees with their instructions by body language alone.

Discourse is also key to signalling when something is important or to request mutual understanding. According to one ambassador:

> There is a Coreper language with its own code words and code phrases. When used, this language is clearly understood by everyone. For instance, if I have bad instructions that

I'm against, I can say, 'but of course the presidency has to take its responsibilities,' which
means put it to a vote and I'll lose, I accept this.

Most importantly, arguments matter. The power of a good argument can be as compelling as a blocking minority or the shadow of the veto. The possibility for persuasion and the norm of mutual responsiveness works as a great equalizer in Coreper
negotiations. As a result, smaller member-states who articulate clear, sound arguments can often punch above their weight. A financial counsellor from a large
member-state drew the following contrast: 'Sweden, who is always taking part in the
debate, has influence far beyond their votes. Germany, is the opposite; they have less
influence than votes.' An Antici echoed this sentiment, 'If you convince others, it's
with good arguments. Big or small makes no difference. In fact, the big member-
states often have higher burdens of proof in order to convince the others.'

Accountability

There is a common perception that decision making in Brussels is remote, opaque,
and even undemocratic. Given Coreper's role in everyday decision-making, it is
somewhat surprising that in all the discussions to address the EU's 'democratic
deficit' since the early 1990s, Coreper's name has been virtually unmentioned. But
given Coreper's workload and the need for insulation from politicization effects
discussed above, it is clear why member states are reluctant to tinker with such
finely-tuned mechanisms. There are occasional suggestions which emanate from a
capital that perhaps a new Coreper III of ministers or deputy prime ministers would
work to democratize the system, but support for this idea has never gained much
momentum.

   It is also easy to push the image of an all-powerful, unaccountable group of back-
room decision-makers too far. Committee members are accountable to their ministers for the positions taken in negotiations and it is always a possibility (though
specific examples are extremely hard to come by) that a minister can undo a deal
done at Coreper level. Permanent representatives who strayed too far or were over-
ruled by their ministers would quickly lose credibility in Coreper and in the home
capital.

   Whether such an indirect system of accountability is a sustainable form of governance is open to debate. Following Eastern enlargement, many believe the EU will
need to rely even more on the few but vitally important negotiation forums that
are based on a club-like and insulated atmosphere where collective norms guide acceptable behaviour and rule out a range of instrumentality (such as pushing for a
vote, making veto threats, and so on). Coreper is the exemplar of this, but they are
not alone. An intriguing analogue in macroeconomic and euro zone policy-making
is the Economic and Finance Committee which puts national central bank and finance officials together—in camera, with no note-takers, and under the long tradition of doing everything by consensus. Even with the veritable revolution we have
seen in the EU's legislative process—namely, the evolution of codecision into the 'ordinary' decision-making procedure—we see a very heavy reliance on informal and
more closed door settings, such as the trialogue methodology, to work out areas
of compromise between the Council and EP versions of a proposal. The insulated,
in camera, and club-like negotiation settings in the EU offer strong confirmation

for David Stasavage's (2004: 670) argument that states will often 'shun transparency' in international negotiations since openness can act as 'an incentive for representatives to "posture" by adopting uncompromising bargaining positions'. In the EU25+, the need for a mechanism like Coreper is greater than ever.

The institution in context

The 'Janus face' of Coreper

Coreper challenges the conventional dichotomy which sharply demarcates the national and European levels. Institutionally, Coreper embodies the claim that national and European levels of governance have become amalgamated in the EU system (H. Wallace 2000: 7; Wessels 1997). As state agents, the EU permanent representatives nicely illustrate how national and supranational roles and identifications can become nested and coexist. Coreper personnel offer empirical confirmation for Wendt's (1999: 242) hypothetical question 'whether the members of states can ever learn additional ... identities above and beyond the state, creating "concentric circles" of group identification'. Interviews with participants consistently confirm that permanent representatives obtain a distinct secondary allegiance to collective, EU decision-making. Although the 'nested' identity concept does not fully capture the quality of the identity configuration found here, because permanent representatives do not self-reflectively see these as competitive or contradictory to national allegiance. They are not 'different hats' worn at different times or held in juxtaposition to each other so much as a broadening of the cognitive boundaries of what counts as the 'self' and the 'national interest'. One deputy claimed, 'there is a confidence that I will deliver the goods at home and a confidence to deliver the goods collectively. I must find ways to synthesize the two'. The EU permanent representatives are

---

Exhibit 14.2 'Insider' reflections on Coreper

'Coreper works because there are no spotlights on it' (EU ambassador).

'Ambassadors themselves like to decide, not leave it to chance with the ministers' (Commission official).

'Arguments can play a role. We can be persuaded by them. It is one of the few places in the Union where this can happen' (EU ambassador).

'Tactically, delegations drop all stupid reservations at Coreper level' (EU ambassador).

'This is seen as the most important ambassador post abroad that we have' (EU ambassador from a new CEEC member state).

'We are very cautious not to become troublemakers' (EU ambassador from a new CEEC member state).

'If [the CEEC newcomers] stick to their instructions and don't put them aside from time to time, and cannot influence thinking back home, Coreper will be lost' (An 'original Six' deputy reflecting on enlargement).

examples of state agents who have found a way to operationalize what Laffan (2004: 90–4) describes as 'double hatting'.

Empirical findings from research on Coreper clearly shows national and supranational identities are not zero-sum commodities. Although some theorists still generally assume otherwise, such as Stone Sweet and Sandholtz (1998: 6) who claim, 'we leave as an open question the extent to which the loyalties and identities of actors will shift from the national to the European level. There is substantial room for supranational governance without an ultimate shift in identification'. Instead of limited conceptualizations of shifts and transfers in identity, what we see in Coreper is a blurring of the boundaries between the national and the European. Describing his own job description, one deputy claimed, 'I wear a Janus face'. The metaphor of the Janus face can be detected throughout the interview data in how permanent representatives perceive their institutional roles and multiple allegiances to represent national interests *and* participate in making collective decisions according to a deliberative process of negotiation. None of this implies that national identities and interests become marginalized or disappear; rather, what stands out is the infusion of the national with the European and *vice versa*. To be successful, EU permanent representatives develop a more complex identity configuration informing definitions of self and interest. From a Janus-faced perspective, they act as both, and simultaneously, state agents and supranational entrepreneurs. From an institutional design standpoint, this finding is highly significant to how the overall system of decision-making functions. As Weiler (1994: 31) so aptly summarized, the system 'replaces a kind of "liberal" premise of international society with a communitarian one: the Community as a transnational regime will not simply be a neutral area in which states seek to maximize their benefits but will create a tension between the national self and the collective self'. The implications of this tension for how we think of sovereignty in Europe is also significant. Waever (1995: 412) argues that the EU reconfigures conventional conceptions of national sovereignty because of the 'importance of Europe *in* national identities' where 'the European dimension is included in national self-conceptions'. The cognitive blurring of boundaries between the national and European layers also fits suggestively with what Risse (2004: 251–2) describes as a 'marble cake' concept of identity where 'identity components influence each other' and rather than being neatly compartmentalized, they 'mesh and blend'. As high-ranking national officials, the permanent representatives offer a striking empirical example of this at the everyday level of EU decision-making.

Conclusions

This chapter has focused on integrating interests in the context of the EU and in particular, the systemic, policy-setting level at which Coreper operates. Understanding Coreper negotiations requires being alert to the often subtle interplay of national and community perspectives. The EU permanent representatives are nation-state agents who represent national interests but have also internalized collective decision-making rules and norms which inform bargaining behaviour and shape legislative outcomes. The logic of action found in Coreper goes beyond cost–benefit, instrumental interest calculation and includes a distinctive 'appropriateness' logic based on group-community standards.

While the committee's normative environment is highly institutionalized it is also based almost exclusively on informal rules and norms, and, as such, it is subject to a much different change process than, say, revising the treaties or changing the formal voting rules. A major open question is whether Coreper's sense of mission to 'find solutions' within a consensus-based, deliberative style of negotiation can survive in an enlarged and much more heterogeneous EU. How easily the Council's decision-making system can consolidate its new members will depend on how they become socialized to the EU's normative environment. If for example, the new members are slow to internalize the established norms of mutual responsiveness and accommodation found in Coreper, the Council could develop a more rigid 'veto culture' or even divide into different voting blocks along geographic or gross domestic product lines. In such scenarios, the organizational culture and normative environment would change, and the 'double hatting' identity configuration of the EU permanent representatives could be altered as well. If Coreper developed into a body where voting weights and instrumental cost-benefit calculations ruled the day, rather than consensus-based deliberation and debate, we could see system-wide effects (and unintended consequences) on how effectively the Union can operate.

Notes

1 March and Olsen (1989) offer the classic distinction between logics of consequences and appropriateness. In the former, 'the only obligations recognized by individuals are those created through consent and contracts grounded in calculated consequential advantage'; while in the latter, individuals are 'acting in accordance with rules and practices that are socially constructed, publicly known, anticipated, and accepted' (March and Olsen 1998: 951, 952).

2 All interview quotes come from field research conducted by the author in Brussels.

3 *Bulletin of the EC*, 12–1974, point 1104.7.

4 Anderson (1997: 81) defines 'constitutive politics' as the 'processes and outcomes that establish or amend EU rules of the game,' as distinct from 'regulative politics' which are the 'processes and

outcomes that take place within established, routinized areas of EU activity'.

5 Interview, 15 May 2000.

6 See Webb (1977: 18–19), for instance.

7 Along the same lines, other partial exemptions from Coreper's remit involve macroeconomic policy coordination (the specialty of the Economic and Finance Committee), military planning (now managed by the Military Committee), and financial services (led by the Paris-based Committee of European Securities Regulators and a Securities Committee charged with 'fast-tracking' liberalization efforts). See the section on 'Contestation' for more.

8 Negotiations for the 2007–2013 budget certainly needed the input of the EU ambassadors to help keep the cauldron of issues—from the British rebate and relative size of Germany's contributions

to redistributive fairness between 'new' and 'old' members — off the boil.

9 I thank the editors for comments on this point.

10 Coreper I also convenes working lunches, usually two or three per Presidency.

11 Trips are restricted to the ambassadors, the Anticis, and spouses.

12 Such as the Cabinet Office in the UK or the SGCI (*Secrétariat général du Comité inter-ministériel pour les questions de*

coopération economique européenne) in France.

13 As Putnam (1993: 171) explains, thick trust is a key interpersonal ingredient of 'social capital' which tends to develop in 'small, close-knit communities' based on 'a belief that rests on intimate familiarity with *this* individual'.

14 This is known as 'COG collusion' in two-level games research. See Evans (1993: 406–7).

Further reading

For an excellent treatment of Coreper's role in EU decision-making, see Hayes-Renshaw and Wallace (2006). De Zwaan (1995) offers perhaps the most comprehensive study available in English, although it tends toward the descriptive and legalistic. Hayes-Renshaw *et al.* (1989) is a classic. See also Bostock (2002), Mentler (1996), and Westlake and Galloway (2004). For a testimonial of the EU system from the former *doyen* of Coreper, see de Schoutheete (2000). Finally, on the Spaak Committee, see Mayne (1962) and Willis (1965).

Bostock, D. (2002), 'Coreper Revisited,' *Journal of Common Market Studies*, 40/2: 215–34.

de Schoutheete, P. (2000), *The Case for Europe: Unity, Diversity, and Democracy in the European Union* (London and Boulder, CO: Lynne Rienner).

De Zwaan, J. (1995), *The Permanent Representatives Committee: Its Role in European Union Decision-Making* (Amsterdam: Elsevier).

Hayes-Renshaw, F., and Wallace, H. (2006), *The Council of Ministers*, 2nd edn. (Basingstoke and New York: Palgrave).

Hayes-Renshaw, F., Lequesne, C., and Mayor Lopez, P. (1989), 'The Permanent Representations of the member states to the European Communities', *Journal of Common Market Studies*, 28/2: 119–37.

Mayne, R. (1962), *The Community of Europe* (New York: W. W. Norton).

Mentler, M. (1996), *Der Auschuss der Standigen Vertreter bei den Europaischen Gemeinschaften* (Baden-Baden: Nomos).

Westlake, M., and Galloway, D. (2004), *The Council of the European Union*, 3rd edn. (London: John Harper Publishing).

Willis, F. R. (1965), *France, Germany, and the New Europe, 1945–1963* (Stanford, CA: Stanford University Press).

Web links

The best online resource to monitor Coreper's work is the Council's website (*http://ue.eu.int/en/summ.htm*) although details on meetings remain hard to come by. Links to the EU Presidency offer basic information such as dates, agendas, etc. For an online database of Coreper personnel (including valuable contact information for arranging interviews at the permanent representations), select 'Who's who in the Council' (and then choose the link 'Permanent Representatives Committee').

Chapter 15

Political Interests

The European Parliament's Party Groups

Tapio Raunio

Contents

Summary

The party system of the European Parliament (EP) is dominated by the two main party families: centre-right conservatives and Christian democrats on the one hand, and social democrats on the other. In the early 1950s, members of the EP (MEPs) decided to form ideological groups instead of national blocs to counterbalance the dominance of national interests in the Council. Since then the party groups have gradually but consistently consolidated their position in the Parliament, primarily through introducing procedural reforms that enable them to make effective use of EP's legislative powers. At the same time the shape of the party system has become more stable, at least as far as the main groups are concerned. Nevertheless, national parties remain influential within party groups, not least through their control of candidate selection.

Introduction

Compared with parties in EU member state legislatures, the party groups of the European Parliament operate in a very different institutional environment. There is no EU government accountable to the Parliament. There are no coherent and hierarchically organized European-level parties. Instead, MEPs are elected from lists drawn by national parties and on the basis of national electoral campaigns. The social and cultural heterogeneity of the EU is reflected in the internal diversity of the groups, with a total of 170 national parties from 25 member states winning seats in the Parliament in the 2004 elections. The party groups are thus structurally firmly embedded in the political systems of the EU member states. However, despite the existence of such factors, EP party groups have gradually over the decades consolidated their position in the Parliament, primarily through introducing procedural reforms that enable them to make effective use of EP's legislative powers. At the same time the shape of the party system has become more stable, at least as far as the main groups are concerned. One can thus talk of the 'institutionalization' of the EP party system.

The chapter begins by examining the shape of the EP party system. It then analyses the structure of the party groups and the role of national parties within them, before exploring the relationship between the groups and committees, arguing here that the delegation of authority downwards to committees and individual MEPs is essential to the Parliament's policy success. The EP party system has also become more competitive, with the left–right dimension constituting the main cleavage in the chamber. Next, it examines parties at the European level and argues that, without any executive office at stake in European elections, the vertical linkage function of the party groups—that of connecting voters to the EU policy process—will remain poorly developed. However, in horizontal terms, the EP party groups and the Europarties perform an important function by integrating political interests across the Union.

The shape of the EP party system

The Common Assembly of the European Coal and Steel Community (ECSC), the predecessor of the Parliament, held its inaugural session in September 1952. Already in the first important vote held in the Assembly, to elect its President, the members split along group lines instead of voting as national blocs. The decision to form party groups crossing national lines needs to be understood in the light of developments in the early 1950s. First, the creation of the High Authority (predecessor of the Commission) and the Assembly marked the emergence of truly supranational institutions, in contrast to those of the intergovernmental Council of Europe (particularly its Consultative Assembly). Second, national interests in the ECSC were already represented in the Council of Ministers, and the Assembly sought to counterbalance this through its ideologically based group structure.

Exhibit 15.1 Party groups in the 2004–09 European Parliament

European People's Party and European Democrats (EPP–ED, 268 seats)

The EPP–ED is a mix of Christian Democrats and Conservatives, joining together parties from all EU member states. The largest national party is the German Christian Democratic Union/Christian Social Union (CDU/CSU). The conservative wing of the group has strengthened over the years with the entry of the Spanish *Partido Popular*, *Forza Italia*, the French (Gaullist) *Rassemblement pour la République* and the British Conservatives. Despite the numerical growth of conservative forces in the group, the EPP has traditionally and consistently been strongly in favour of closer European integration.

Party of European Socialists (PES, 200 seats)

This group brings together social democratic and socialist parties from all EU countries. The largest party delegations are the French *Parti Socialiste*, the Spanish Socialist Workers' Party (PSOE), and the German Social Democrats (SPD). The PES supports further integration, primarily because with EMU the defence of traditional goals of the left—such as social and environmental legislation and employment policies—require European-level action to complement national measures.

Alliance of Liberals and Democrats for Europe (ALDE, 88 seats)

The liberal group consists of various liberal and centrist parties and has come to occupy a pivotal role between the two large groups. After the 2004 elections the group changed its name from European Liberal, Democrat and Reform Party (ELDR) to the Alliance of Liberals and Democrats for Europe (ALDE). The new group has 88 MEPs, the largest seat share held by the liberals since the 1979 elections.

Greens/European Free Alliance (G/EFA, 42 seats)

First formed after the 1999 elections, this group is an alliance between green parties and various regionalist parties. The regionalist parties of EFA—such as the Scottish National Party and the Catalan parties—did not win enough seats to form a group of their own and thus chose to sit with the Greens. The Greens have in recent years become strongly pro-EU, for similar reasons to the PES.

Confederal Group of the European United Left/Nordic Green Left (EUL–NGL, 41 seats)

The EUL–NGL brings together a variety of left-socialist and former communist parties. The title 'NGL' was added to the group name after the 1995 enlargement as the Finnish and Swedish left parties wanted to emphasize their separate identity within the then otherwise largely Mediterranean group. EUL is divided over the desirability of further integration.

Independence and Democracy (IND/DEM, 37 seats)

As a result of the electoral victories gained by Eurosceptical lists in several countries, the former Europe of Democracies and Diversities (EDD) group expanded its membership and changed its name to Independence and Democracy. The group is opposed to further integration and brings together Eurosceptics from ten countries, including Denmark, Italy (*Lega Nord*), and the UK (Independence Party).

continues

Exhibit 15.1 continued

Union for Europe of the Nations (UEN, 27 seats)

The UEN is an alliance between various conservative and Eurosceptic forces, with *Alleanza Nazionale* from Italy and the Polish Law and Justice as its leading national party delegations.

Note: The seat shares are from September 2004.

Throughout its history up to the present day (Exhibit 15.1 summarizes the parties in the EP after the 2004 elections) the EP party system has been based on the left–right dimension, the main cleavage in all European countries despite the gradual erosion of traditional class ties and the entry of new issues, such as environmental concerns, onto the political agenda (Huber and Inglehart 1995). The seating order in the chamber reflects this, with the social democrats and former communists on the left side of the hemicycle, the liberals in the middle, and Christian democrats and conservatives on the right. Table 15.1 shows the distribution of seats in the Parliament between 1979 (the date of the first direct elections to the EP) and 2004. Initially the party system consisted of only three groups: socialists/social democrats (PES), Christian democrats/conservatives (EPP), and liberals (ELDR), the three main party families in EU member states. The Christian Democratic group was the largest group until 1975 when the British Labour Party joined the Socialist group.[1] Since the first direct elections also the Greens and the group of the radical left parties, now titled the Confederal Group of the European United Left/Nordic Green Left (EUL–NGL), have become 'institutionalized' in the chamber. Moreover, Eurosceptical parties, parties whose main reason of existence is opposition to further integration, have formed a group under various labels since the 1994 elections.

The EP party system has throughout the history of the directly elected Parliament been effectively dominated by the centre-right EPP and the social democratic PES (Kreppel 2002). After the 2004 election, they retained control of approximately two-thirds of the seats. This duopoly is nicely illustrated by the system of electing the President of the Parliament. With the exception of the 1999–2004 Parliament, the PES and EPP have shared the Presidency from 1989 onwards. In the 1994–99 legislature, for example, the first President was Klaus Hänsch, a German SPD representative from the PES, with José María Gil-Robles Gil-Delgado, from the Spanish *Partido Popular* (EPP), replacing him at mid-term in January 1997. This cosy pact was temporarily suspended after the 1999 elections, when a centre-right coalition elected Nicole Fontaine (EPP) as the new President in July 1999. Imitating the deals between EPP and PES, the EPP and ELDR struck an agreement according to which the Liberals would support Fontaine and the EPP would in turn back the candidacy of ELDR group leader Pat Cox at mid-term in January 2002. The old alliance between EPP and PES was renewed after the 2004 elections, with the Presidency first held by the Spanish socialist Josep Borrell and then due to be replaced by a member of the EPP at mid-term in January 2007.

For the first time since the introduction of direct elections, the EPP became after the 1999 elections the largest group in the chamber. The EPP–ED continued after the 2004 elections as the largest group in the Parliament with 268 MEPs. EPP is also the only group that has representatives from all twenty-five member states. The

Table 15.1 Party groups in the European Parliament (1979–2004)						
Date group	1979	1984	1989	1994	1999	2004
PES	113	130	180	198	180	200
EPP	107	110	121	157	233	268
ELDR/ALDE	40	31	49	43	50	88
EDG	64	50	34			
EDA	22	29	20	26		
COM	44	41				
CDI	11					
RB		20	13			
ER		16	17			
Greens/EFA			30	23	48	42
EUL			28			
LU			14			
EUL–NGL				28	42	41
EN				19		
FE				27		
ERA				19		
UEN					21	27
TGI					20	
EDD					16	
IND/DEM						37
NA	9	7	12	27	16	29
Total	410	434	518	567	626	732

Note: Abbreviations: PES = Party of European Socialists; EPP = European People's Party, European People's Party and European Democrats (EPP-ED) since the 1999 elections; ELDR = European Liberal, Democrat and Reform Party, Alliance of Liberals and Democrats for Europe (ALDE) after the 2004 elections; EDG = European Democratic Group; EDA = European Democratic Alliance, European Progressive Democrats until the 1989 elections; COM = Communist and Allies Group; CDI = Technical Group of Co-ordination and Defence of Independent MEPs; RB = Rainbow Group; ER = European Right; Greens = The Green Group, Greens/European Free Alliance since the 1999 elections; EUL = European United Left; LU = Left Unity; EUL–NGL = Confederal Group of the European United Left, since 1995 the group has included the sub-group Nordic Green Left; EN = Europe of Nations; ERA = European Radical Alliance; FE = Forza Europa; UEN = Union for Europe of the Nations; TGI = Technical Group of Independent Members; EDD = Europe of Democracies and Diversities; IND/DEM = Independence and Democracy; NA = Non-attached. EDA and FE merged in July 1995 to form Union for Europe (55 MEPs). The UPE joined EPP in June 1998.
Date: 1979 = after the European elections (EE); 1984 = after the second EE; 1989 = after the third EE; 1994 = after the fourth EE; 1999 = after the fifth EE; 2004 = seat distribution in August 2004.

conservative wing of the group was strengthened during the 1990s, and the same trend continued in the 2004 elections, with particularly the Civic Democratic Party (ODS) from the Czech Republic displaying quite strong Eurosceptical tendencies.

The party that has had most difficulties to fit into the group has undoubtedly been the British Conservatives, whose views, particularly on European integration, are quite different from those of the group majority (Hix 2002b: 694). Indeed, the title 'European Democrats' was added to the EPP's group name after the 1999 elections so that the Tories could maintain their separate identity in the otherwise strongly pro-integrationist EPP group. Before the 2004 elections the group struck a deal with the Conservatives, who had threatened to leave the group and ally with other conservative parties that are critical of further integration. This deal caused a lot of controversy in the group—and in the end resulted in a section of MEPs defecting to the ELDR after the elections. According to the deal the Conservatives have a right to voice their own views on European constitutional and institutional matters, and have more favourable financing and staffing terms within the group, including the right to one of the group's Vice-Presidents.

The formation of the PES presents far fewer problems, as almost each member state has an electorally significant centre-left, social democratic party. PES was the largest party in the Parliament from 1979 until 1999. Latvia and Cyprus are the only countries that do not have representation in the PES group after the 2004 elections. The French *Parti Socialiste* is the largest national party in the group with 31 MEPs.

The Liberals played a key role in the early years of the Parliament, but between 1979 and 2004 their seat share remained below 10 per cent. After the 2004 elections, the Liberal group welcomed the Union for French Democracy (UDF) from France and the La Margherita list from Italy, among others, to its ranks. The new liberal group has 88 MEPs from 19 member states. The group also changed its name from 'ELDR' to the 'Alliance of Liberals and Democrats for Europe'. The group has a strong pro-European philosophy, and this may create problems between the group majority and the Centre parties from the Nordic countries that are considerably more Eurosceptical than the group majority.

The Greens achieved an electoral breakthrough in 1989, and have since then formed a group of their own in the Parliament. They benefit more than most groups from the second-order logic of Euro-elections, which favours small parties at the expense of larger mainstream parties (Reif and Schmitt 1980). The Green group is an alliance between representatives from green parties and from various regionalist parties, with the German Greens as the leading national party in the group. The regionalist parties of the European Free Alliance (EFA) have never mustered enough seats to form their own group, and their MEPs have instead sat as sub-groups in the Technical Group of Co-ordination and Defence of Independent MEPs (CDI) (1979–84), Rainbow Group (1984–94), ERA (1994–99), and in the Green group since 1999. As was expected, the 'eastern' enlargement did not profit the Greens as no Green MEPs were elected to the Parliament from the ten new member states.

Communists, or the radical left, have formed a group under various labels since 1973. The title 'Nordic Green Left' was added to the group name, 'Confederal Group of the European United Left' (EUL–NGL) after the 1995 enlargement. The group has traditionally been a quite loose alliance, and the group states in its own constituent declaration that EUL–NGL 'is a forum for cooperation between its different political components, each of which retains its own independent identity and commitment to its own positions.' After the 2004 elections the group has forty-one MEPs, among them seven MEPs of the German Party of Democratic Socialism (PDS) and six representatives of the Communist Party of the Czech Lands and Moravia.

The only truly Eurosceptical group in the Parliament—that is, a group whose *raison d'être* is opposition to further integration—is the Independence and Democracy group (IND/DEM). Eurosceptical lists achieved significant victories in several countries, including Poland, Sweden, and the UK, and this enabled the former Europe of Democracies and Diversities (EDD) group to expand its membership and change its name. The group has thirty-seven MEPs, and brings together Eurosceptics from the Czech Republic, Denmark, France, Greece, Italy, the Netherlands, Poland, Ireland, Sweden, and the UK. Eurosceptical MEPs continue therefore to be marginalized in the chamber. Conservative parties not included in the EPP–ED group belong to the Union for a Europe of Nations (UEN), the smallest group in the Parliament that has existed since the 1994 elections. It is an alliance between various conservative forces.

The extreme-right parties formed a group after the 1984 and 1989 elections. After the 2004 elections representatives of the extreme-right parties—such as Freedom Party from Austria, National Front from France, and Vlaams Belang[2] from Belgium—sit as non-attached MEPs.

Internal organization

In the context of national legislatures a parliamentary party group is defined as 'an organized group of members of a representative body who were elected either under the same party label or under the label of different parties that do not compete against each other in elections, and who do not explicitly create a group for technical reasons only' (Heidar and Koole 2000a: 249). Applying this definition to the Parliament, we note the features that distinguish the EP groups from national legislative parties. First, most—but not all—of the national parties in the EPP and PES groups were elected under the same label (EPP or PES), but these labels were hardly used in the campaigns and remain largely unknown among the voters.[3] Moreover, particularly the EPP, but also other groups, contain often more than one party per member state, and therefore these parties compete against each other in the elections.

The EP's Rules of Procedure, the standing orders of the Parliament, set numerical criteria for group formation. After the 2004 elections 'A political group shall comprise Members elected in at least one-fifth of the Member States. The minimum number of Members required to form a political group shall be nineteen' (Rule 29).[4] The availability of considerable material and procedural benefits explains the emergence of technical groups, such as CDI in 1979–84, the Rainbow Group in 1984–94, and the short-lived Technical Group of Independent Members (TGI) after the 1999 elections. While the money from the Parliament may appear inconsequential in absolute terms, it has nevertheless been crucial for certain smaller regionalist and green parties that have not enjoyed access to comparable resources at the national level. Material benefits include for example office space, staff, and money for distributing information.

The sum each group receives depends on the number of MEPs and working languages in the group.

Group staff perform a variety of duties, ranging from routine administration to drafting background memos, following developments in committees and drawing up whips in plenaries. In addition, each MEP has one to three personal assistants (financed from the EP budget) and both the committee and the EP staff assist groups and MEPs. Turning to procedural rights, appointments to committees and intra-parliamentary leadership positions, and the allocation of reports and plenary speaking time are based on the rule of proportionality between the groups. Certain plenary actions, such as tabling amendments or oral questions, require the backing of a committee, a party group or at least thirty-seven MEPs. Non-attached representatives are thus procedurally marginalized in the chamber.

Three factors work against cohesive party groups in the Parliament: the balance of power between the EU institutions, the rules for candidate selection, and the internal heterogeneity of the groups. A key element in producing unitary group action in national legislatures is the fact that governments depend on the support of the parliamentary majority. Especially when the government enjoys only a small majority, both it and the opposition have strong incentives to act cohesively. The EP party groups lack this motive. While the Commission has to be approved by the Parliament and can be brought down by it (as happened indirectly in 1999), the composition of the Commission is only partly based on the outcome of the Euro-elections. However, after the 2004 elections there is nonetheless a kind of government and opposition divide in the Parliament. As a result of the emergence of the EPP as the biggest group in the Parliament and the dominance of centre-right governments in the Council, the partisan composition of the Commission (including the President) leans towards centre-right, with fifteen out of twenty-five Commissioners representing either EPP or ELDR member parties. Therefore the PES, often backed by Greens and EUL–NGL, are more likely to criticize the Commission while the centre-right is supportive of it.

Second, 'centralized nomination procedures should lead to greater party cohesion' (Bowler *et al.* 1999: 8). National parties, and not EP groups or Europarties, control candidate selection. Therefore national parties possess the ultimate sanction against MEPs. This applies particularly to countries using closed lists (for example, France, Germany, UK, Greece, Portugal, Spain) or mixed systems, where parties present pre-ordered lists and the electors vote either for a party or an individual candidate (for instance, Austria, Belgium, The Netherlands, Sweden). In general national parties have so far adopted a somewhat lacklustre approach to their MEPs, leaving them relatively free in 'far away' Brussels (Raunio 2002). However, voting behaviour analysis indicates that (in those rare occasions) when MEPs receive conflicting voting instructions from national parties and their EP groups, they are more likely to side with their national party, particularly in parties where the leadership has better opportunities to punish and reward its MEPs (through controlling candidate selection):

> Despite the fact that the parliamentary principals in the EP control important benefits—such as committee assignments and speaking time—it is the principals that control candidate selection (the national parties) who ultimately determine how MEPs behave. When the national parties in the same parliamentary group decide to vote together, the EP parties look highly cohesive. But when these parties take opposing policy positions, the cohesion of the EP parties break down. (Hix 2002b: 696; Faas 2003; Hix 2004)

Table 15.2 Group cohesion in the European Parliament

Parliament Group	1979–84	1984–89	1989–94	1994–99	1999–01
PES	.76	.87	.90	.90	.90
EPP	.90	.93	.91	.90	.86
ELDR	.85	.85	.85	.86	.91
Gaullists and Allies (EDA, UFE, UEN)	.80	.84	.85	.79	.72
Radical left (COM, LU, EUL, EUL–NGL)	.81	.87	.86	.80	.76
Greens (RB, Greens, G/EFA)		.81	.85	.91	.91
Regionalists (RB (89-), ERA)			.87	.91	
EDG	.89	.92	.89		
ER		.93	.88		
Anti-EU groups (EDD)				.67	.54

Source: Hix *et al.* (2005: 218).

Note: The entries in the Table report group cohesion levels using an 'Agreement Index' (AI). The AI equals 1 when all group members vote together and it equals zero when the members of a group are equally divided between all three voting options ('yes', 'no', 'abstain'). For more information on how to compute the AI and its properties, see Hix *et al.* (2005: 215–216).

Hence we can expect particularly those MEPs that are seeking re-election to be very reluctant to ignore national party guidelines. Finally, of all the legislatures, the heterogeneity of the Parliament is probably matched only by that of the Indian Congress. No less than 170 national parties from 25 member states won seats in the 2004 elections. The largest group, EPP, consists of 44 national party delegations. Such a high level of heterogeneity, not to mention the problems involved in communicating in twenty official languages, presents a formidable challenge for the groups.

However, roll-call analyses (see Table 12.2) show that the groups do achieve rather high levels of cohesion (Attinà 1990; Raunio 1997: 79–124; Hix *et al.* 2005).[5] Reflecting its disagreements over European integration, the PES was prone to internal splits until the early 1990s, but has since become much more cohesive as the majority of European social democratic parties have adopted broadly similar views on both socio-economic matters and on the future of integration. The EPP, in turn, has become less cohesive since the mid-1990s as the group membership has been widened to include several conservative parties. Groups dominated by a single party have often reached very high levels of cohesion, while technical groups and the radical left groups have seldom made attempts to build common positions. In comparative terms, the EP groups are on average less cohesive than party groups in the EU member state legislatures, but have tended to be more cohesive than parties in the US Congress (Raunio 1997: 98–100; Hix 1998).

What accounts for this relatively unitary behaviour? Until the Maastricht and Amsterdam Treaties one could argue that as most votes in the Parliament had little if any impact, it did not really matter how MEPs voted. According to this line of reasoning the fragile foundations of group cohesion would be put to test once the Parliament acquired real legislative powers (Bardi 1994). However, in reality group cohesion has risen, not declined, as the EP has gained new powers.

The explanation advanced here for high cohesion levels focuses on policy influence and on how group organization is tailored to face the twin challenge of internal heterogeneity and the strong position of national parties. Decision-making within groups can be described as primarily consensual, with groups putting much effort into building positions that are acceptable to all or nearly all parties in the group. Unlike national party leaders, EP group chairs do not control or even influence candidate selection, nor can they promise lucrative ministerial portfolios or well-paid civil service jobs. Groups have whips, but they basically just remind MEPs of group positions and indicate which votes are important. While the groups have fairly similar organizational structures as their counterparts in national parliaments, with leaders, executive committees, and working parties, the groups can nevertheless be characterized as non-hierarchical and non-centralized.

At the start of the five-year legislative term the groups elect their leaders (chairperson/president), who usually occupy the post until the next elections or even longer. The chairs represent their group in the Conference of Presidents, the body responsible for setting the Parliament's agenda and for organizational decisions. The number of vice-chairs varies between the groups. The Green group uses two co-chairs, one of whom is a woman. The executive committee of the group is the Bureau, composed of the chairperson, vice-chairs, heads and possible additional members of national party delegations, and the treasurer. The Bureau is responsible for organizational and administrative issues, and prepares policy decisions for group meetings. It plays a key role in facilitating group consensus. In their discussion on factionalism within national parties, Bowler *et al.* (1999: 15) argue that

> there are reasons for thinking that factions can help rank-and-file members discipline their leadership, either by providing faction leaders to take part in policy discussions (reporting back to their members) or by making it clear to party leaders that a block of votes will desert if some policy line is crossed. In this sense, factions help party leaders understand where their support or opposition lies within the party and the levels of this support or opposition.

The same dynamic is at work in the EP groups. When one replaces factions with national party delegations, we see that by guaranteeing most national delegations representation in the executive committee, the group leadership learns about the positions of national parties and the intensity of their preferences. The groups convene regularly in Brussels prior to the plenary week as well as during plenaries. The meetings in Brussels constitute a 'Group week', usually lasting two to three days. When MEPs feel they cannot follow the group position, they are expected to make this clear in the group meetings. Party groups have also established working groups for examining specific policy areas and for coordinating group policy on those issues (Hix and Lord 1997: 77–166).

National party delegations are the cornerstones upon which the groups are based. Some groups are indeed no more than loose coalitions of national parties, while even in the oldest and most organized groups—EPP and PES—one can occasionally see divisions along national lines. Most national delegations have their own staff, elect their chairpersons, and convene prior to group meetings. However, the impact of national parties is mitigated by three factors. First, national parties are seldom unitary actors themselves. National parties throughout the Union are, to a varying extent, internally divided over integration, and these divisions are reproduced in the Parliament. Perhaps the best examples are the British Conservative and Labour delegations. Second, the EP is a committee-based legislature, with emphasis on building issue-specific majorities in the committees. Third, the majority of bills and resolutions do not produce divisions along national lines. Much of the Parliament's agenda is taken up by traditional socio–economic matters such as internal market legislation, not by constitutional matters or redistributive decisions like the allocation of structural funds.

But the most important reason why MEPs and national party delegations vote with their group most of the time is policy influence. After all, the main rationale for group formation in any decision-making body is that it helps like-minded legislators in achieving their policy goals. Cohesive group action is essential for achieving group's objectives, while co-operative behaviour within groups helps MEPs in pursuing their own policy goals. Moreover, given the huge number of amendments and final resolutions voted upon in each plenary, the voting cues provided by group whips are an essential source of guidance for MEPs. Considering that national parties control candidate selection, part of the answer lies also in the fact that national parties have by and large refrained from intervening in the EP's work. Were the party leaders to begin monitoring MEP behaviour on a more regular basis, through increased policy coordination or even voting instructions, group cohesion would be seriously threatened.[6]

To summarize, the desire to influence EU policy and the relatively non-hierarchical group structure, based on institutionalized interaction between the leadership, the committees (see the next section) and the national delegations, facilitates group cohesion. It is occasionally claimed that the accommodation of national viewpoints leads to lowest common denominator decisions. However, these policy compromises are a prerequisite for the Parliament to influence EU legislation. The next section examines coalition dynamics in the chamber, focusing on the role of party groups in the EP's committees.

Coalition politics and parliamentary committees

Committees are established to make parliaments more efficient. They facilitate specialization and thereby enhance parliaments' ability to influence legislation and to hold the government accountable. While there is much variation among European legislatures, most parliaments have strengthened the role of committees in order to reduce the informational advantage of the executive (Mattson and Strøm 1995;

Longley and Davidson 1998; Norton 1998). In a comparative study of European legislatures, Damgaard (1995) found that in twelve out of eighteen parliaments committee members had 'medium' or 'high' influence on party positions.

The same applies to the European Parliament (Mamadouh and Raunio 2003). Embedded in a separation-of-powers system, with executive functions divided between the Commission and the European Council (and also the Council), the main function of the Parliament is to influence the EU policy process. That is why the Parliament has delegated the scrutiny of legislation to its committees. Parliament's positions are in most cases in practice decided in the committees before the plenary stage. And, indeed the Parliament has proven successful in using its legislative and appointment powers. When explaining this success, scholars have emphasized the interaction between party groups and committees. More specifically, the rapporteurship system, with parliamentary resolutions and amendments based on reports drafted by individual members, is identified as crucial (Bowler and Farrell 1995; Wurzel 1999). As committees enjoy extensive procedural rights in processing legislation and in shaping the EP's agenda, the key question for the party groups is therefore how and to what extent they influence committee proceedings.

Representation on committees is roughly proportional to group size, with committee memberships and chairs reallocated at mid-term (after two-and-a-half years). Research on committee appointments by Bowler and Farrell (1995: 227) showed that 'the share of committee places is proportional by both nationality and ideological bloc. Within these limits, set by allocations along ideological or national lines, there is scope for the kinds of specialized membership and recruitment made in the US Congress'. Within committees are four positions of authority: chairperson, vice-chairs, party group co-ordinators, and *rapporteurs* (Neuhold 2001). Committee chairs are highly prestigious positions. Committees elect their own chairs, but in practice party groups decide the allocation of chairs and vice-chairs, with the d'Hondt method[7] used for distributing the chairs. Chair allocation is thus roughly proportional, again reflecting procedures used in most European parliaments (Mattson and Strøm 1995). Party group coordinators are responsible for coordinating the work of their groups in the committees. Together with the committee chair, the coordinators negotiate the distribution of rapporteurships between the groups.

Turning to the passage of legislation, when the Bill arrives in the Parliament from the Commission, a committee is designated as responsible for producing a report on the issue, with one or more committees assigned as opinion-giving committees.[8] Committees use an auction-like points system for distributing reports to the groups, with group coordinators making bids on behalf of their groups. The allocation of reports is also roughly proportional to group strength in the Parliament (but see Keading 2004). However, as the points total of each group is proportional to its seat share in the chamber, the most expensive reports (those that 'cost' the most points), such as those on the EU budget or on important pieces of co-decision legislation, are largely monopolized by EPP and PES (Mamadouh and Raunio 2003).

The *rapporteur* must be prepared to make compromises. Majority-building as early as the stage at which reports are drafted helps facilitate the smooth passage of the report in the committee and in the plenary. The draft report, together with amendments (tabled by any member), is voted upon in the committee. Before the plenary the groups decide their positions: what amendments to propose, and whether to support the report or not. National party delegations often hold their own meetings prior to the group meetings. Finally, the report and amendments (by the responsible committee, a party group, or at least thirty-seven members) are voted upon in the plenary.

Throughout the processing of the Bill, party groups monitor the proceedings in the committees, with group working parties and coordinators playing key roles (Whitaker 2001). However, the technicality of much EU legislation—for example, internal market or environmental legislation—strengthens the informational advantage and autonomy of the committees. With the exception of the assignment process, party group influence within committees is thus fairly modest, with groups having coordinating mechanisms for overseeing committee work instead of hierarchical structures for controlling MEP behaviour in the committees. The procedures for allocating committee chairs, seats, and reports can hence be interpreted as mechanisms for the party groups to control the committees in a situation where the former are relatively weak, at least when compared to European national parliaments (Bowler and Farrell 1995; Whitaker 2001; Mamadouh and Raunio 2003). Delegating authority to backbenchers through committee work and reports can also be understood as a key way of rewarding group members and tying them into the formation of group positions.

The 'partyness' of committee work may be relatively low, but coalition-building at the plenary stage is more clearly driven by partisan concerns. The EP party system is based on the left–right dimension, but the left–right cleavage is less important than in European national legislatures. This results from three factors: there is no government and opposition in the chamber, the Parliament (or the EU) does not have competence on many traditional left–right matters such as health care, taxation, or social policy, and the anti/pro-integration dimension constitutes the second main structure of competition in the Parliament (see Hix et al. 2005).

Coalition formation depends both on the issue voted upon and on the voting rules. While the primary decision rule is simple majority (50 per cent + 1 of those voting), for certain issues (mainly budget amendments and second reading legislative amendments adopted under the co-decision procedure) the Parliament needs to muster absolute majorities (50 per cent + 1 of all its members, 367/732 MEPs after the 2004 elections). The absolute majority requirement facilitates cooperation between EPP and PES, as the surest way of getting the required number of MEPs behind the Parliament's decision is when the two large groups agree on the issue. Co-operation between EPP and PES could also be regarded as a sign of 'maturity', as the Parliament needed to moderate its resolutions in order to get its amendments accepted by the Council and the Commission (Kreppel 2002). After all, the overwhelming majority of national ministers represented in the Council and members of the Commission are either social democrats or Christian democrats/conservatives.

However, after the 1999 elections this cooperation has played a lesser role than before, with EPP and PES opposing each other more often regardless of the voting rule. As a result of the increased left–right competition in the Parliament, the smaller groups have become more important in building winning coalitions. This applies particularly to the liberals, but also increasingly to the Greens. The Liberals, situated ideologically between EPP and PES, are often in a 'pivotal' position, that is, their inclusion can turn a losing coalition into a winning combination. The

Green group, which sits physically in the middle of the hemicycle between PES and ELDR, has become more pro-integrationist and market-friendly in recent years. Their ideological moderation facilitates cooperation with EPP and PES. So, the EP party system has become more competitive than before, but from the point of view of the elections this hardly matters, as is argued in the next section.

Electoral accountability

Voting decisions in Euro-elections are heavily influenced by domestic political allegiances and by the national party-political environment. The primacy of domestic factors results mainly from the strategies of national parties that control candidate selection and carry out electoral campaigns and from the institutional context in which EP elections are conducted.

Most national parties in most EU countries fight Euro-elections on domestic issues. National parties have good reason to avoid competing with each other on issues concerning the broad sweep of European integration. The overwhelming majority of the main national parties were established before European integration, and are therefore based on the traditional social cleavages recognized in political science literature. As the anti/pro-integration dimension cross-cuts these cleavages, parties tend to experience internal fragmentation on EU questions (Hix and Lord 1997: 21–53; Hix 1999; Ray 1999; Marks and Wilson 2000; Hooghe et al. 2002; Marks and Steenbergen 2004). Moreover, survey data show that both MEPs and MPs are on average more representative of their voters on traditional left–right matters than on issues related to European integration, with the elite far more supportive of further integration than the electorate (Thomassen and Schmitt 1999a; van der Eijk and Franklin 2004). Indeed, in most member states the main parties are in broad agreement over integration (Ray 1999, Thomassen and Schmitt 1999b). Parties classified as 'Eurosceptical' are normally either former communist parties or extreme right-wing parties (Taggart 1998). Hence established parties have an incentive in competing the elections along the familiar left–right dimension and downplaying contestation over European integration (Hix 1999; Hooghe et al. 2002).

Elections to the Parliament are therefore scarcely 'European'—they are held during the same week, and the candidates compete for seats in an EU institution, but there is no common electoral system, constituency boundaries do not cross national borders, and campaigning is conducted by national parties on the basis of largely national agendas.[9] So national politics is reproduced in EP elections, with the same set of actors and largely also the same set of issues. While it is true that the lack of discussion on the constitutional aspects of integration (more or less integration) is potentially very damaging, the current situation is arguably not without its merits (Mair 2000). By reproducing the ideological cleavages dividing party families at the national level, and by offering the electorates familiar faces and themes, national parties have probably facilitated electoral mobilization in EP elections. One could also argue that the focus on left–right issues in the campaigns is a positive factor in light of the EP's powers and the representation of citizens' opinions: the Parliament has no formal say over constitutional questions, the group structure of the EP is based on the left–right dimension, and the congruence of opinions between the representatives and the voters is higher on left–right matters than on integration issues.

Parties at the European level

With national parties in control of candidate selection, and with EP election campaigns dominated by national agendas, parties that operate at the European level, so-called 'Euro-parties', are largely unknown entities among European voters. The Maastricht Treaty assigned political parties a specific role to play in European integration (TEU 138a). That Party Article has now been included—in a somewhat shorter form but with a similar meaning—in the new Constitutional Treaty: 'Political parties at European level contribute to forming European political awareness and to expressing the will of citizens of the Union.'[10]

The constitutional recognition in the form of the Party Article in the Maastricht Treaty was directly linked to the subsequent development of Europarties (Johansson and Raunio 2005). With the exception of the European People's Party (EPP) that had already been founded in 1976, the (con)federations of national parties were quickly turned into Europarties. The Confederation of Socialist Parties of the European Community (CSP), founded in 1974, was transformed into the Party of European Socialists (PES) in November 1992. The Federation of European Liberal, Democrat and Reform Parties, founded in 1976, became the European Liberal, Democrat and Reform Party (ELDR) in December 1993. The European Greens took the name European Federation of Green Parties (EFGP) in June 1993, changing it to European Green Party (EGP) in 2004. A newcomer is the Democratic Party of the Peoples of Europe–European Free Alliance (DPPE–EFA), a regionalist party established in 1998.[11] Furthermore, plans both among radical left and right parties to form their own Europarties are likely to get further impetus from the decision to introduce public funding of parties at the European level.[12]

It is still more realistic to describe Europarties as federations of national parties or as party networks (for instance, Ladrech 2000; Bardi 2002), at least when comparing them with the often centralized and hierarchical parties found at the national level. At the same time, there can be no doubt that the constitutional and political changes that have taken place since the early 1990s have contributed to changes in the influence and organization of the Europarties. Internally, Europarties have introduced organizational reforms that reduce their dependence on individual member parties. In particular, (qualified) majority voting is now the standard decision rule in the main organs of the Europarties. The political environment in which the Europarties exist has also changed fundamentally. The empowerment of the Parliament, in terms of both legislative powers and of holding the Commission accountable, means that the Europarties' parliamentary groups are in a key position to influence the EU policy process. And finally, beginning from 2004 the Europarties were allocated funds from the EU's budget, introducing thus public funding of political parties at the European level akin to systems found in the member states of the Union.[13]

EP groups are represented in the party congresses and executive committees of the Europarties. The group chair reports to the congress on the work of the group, and sits in the Europarty's executive committee. The exact policy influence of Europarties is practically impossible to measure, and depends primarily on the willingness of national member parties to pursue and implement the agreed policy objectives. However, the Europarties serve as important arenas for the diffusion of ideas and policy co-ordination. Particularly the meetings of party leaders, held usually at the same venue as the summits of the European Council, enable national parties to coordinate their actions prior to the summits (Hix and Lord 1997; Ladrech 2000). Moreover, Europarties prepare the ground for future enlargements by integrating interests from the prospective member states. Through their membership in the Europarties, parties from the applicant countries engage in partisan cooperation that is important in nurturing wider, pan-European political allegiances.

Ideologically the Europarties have become increasingly similar, especially after social democrats (PES) and green parties (EGP) changed their attitudes to European integration (Hix 1999; Gabel and Hix 2002). Nevertheless, when examining both the issues that the Europarties prioritize and their positions on socio–economic issues, it is obvious that the parties have different objectives. For example, in the 2004 Euro-elections EPP and ELDR had quite typical centre-right programmes, with emphasis on economic competitiveness and eradicating remaining barriers to trade. The left-wing groups—PES, Greens, and also EFA—in turn placed more emphasis on solidarity, full employment, and social and environmental issues in general.

Considering the shape of the EU political system, the Europarties are likely to remain primarily as networks of national parties, even with public funding of Europarties from the EU budget. The Parliament has proposed a reform of the electoral process in EP elections, intended to take effect from the 2009 elections, which would strengthen the role of Europarties without changing the balance of power between the EU institutions. According to this proposal a share of MEPs would be elected from a single Union-wide constituency, with the remaining representatives elected from member states. This would probably mean that the Europarties were responsible for deciding the names and order of the candidates elected from the supranational EU-wide lists. If implemented, this reform might make the elections more 'European' through motivating national parties to connecting their own campaigns to those of their respective Europarties. However, as the right to control candidate selection is such an important instrument for national parties, this reform would also probably lead to frictions between them and Europarties.

Conclusions

The party groups in the European Parliament are often underestimated, or even ridiculed, by national media. To be sure, from the outside these transnational groups may appear as somewhat strange creatures, bringing together representatives from as many as twenty-five countries, with a plethora of languages spoken in the Parliament's meeting rooms and corridors.

However, such characterizations are quite simply not accurate. The Parliament as an institution has structured its internal organization so as to maximize its influence in the EU political system. The thrust of legislative work is done in the committees where individual rapporteurs draft reports that form the basis for parliamentary resolutions. In a similar fashion, the party groups have designed their rules of procedure and divided labour within them so as to make the most of Parliament's hard-won legislative powers. The relatively non-centralized group structure, with emphasis on building consensus among national party delegations, is essential in fostering group cohesion. And, research clearly shows that the EP groups have indeed mastered the art of both bargaining with other EU institutions and of achieving unitary group behaviour.

Another often aired claim is that MEPs and national parties live in different worlds, with lack of will and conflicting preferences over European integration preventing meaningful cooperation. While there is some truth to such arguments, with MEPs acting relatively independently of their parties, this does not mean that MEPs would be divorced from their national parties or constituencies. On the contrary, MEPs remain firmly connected to national politics through a variety of channels, with most of them holding simultaneously various offices in their parties (either at the local, district, or national level) and maintaining active links with their party organizations and voters. Moreover, it is interesting to note that overall the preferences of national MPs and MEPs over integration are quite similar, and that contrary to much accepted wisdom, MEPs do not 'go native' in Brussels, becoming considerably more pro-European than their party comrades back home (Scully 2005).

The biggest, and most demanding, challenge for the party groups is to command loyalty and support among EU citizens. This applies to both connecting vertically with the citizens in individual EU countries and to forging horizontal cross-national linkages. First, considering the lack of a common EU-wide identity, and the absence of any real European government, European elections are bound to remain 'second-order' contests in comparison with elections to national parliaments. This means that also the party groups in the Parliament will remain unknown to most Europeans. Second, while the Europarties and their EP groups undoubtedly perform an important role by integrating political interests across the Union, this integrative function takes exclusively place among national political elites, leaving thus the electorate to focus on national or local politics. In fact, the EU resembles in many ways the US pluralist political system, with multiple veto-players, power-sharing and policy coordination between state and federal levels, and strong interest groups—but also weak and internally divided parties (or party groups in the EU's case). While the EP's party groups may be more cohesive than the American Democrats and Republicans, the latter are certainly far better known to average citizens. To put it simply, Europeans do not yet know how and to what extent the EP party groups influence EU policies.

Notes

1 For analyses of party groups in the pre-1979 Parliament, see van Oudenhove (1965), Fitzmaurice (1975), and Pridham and Pridham (1981).

2 The party was previously known as Vlaams Blok, but adopted its new name following the verdict of the Belgian Supreme Court that had declared the Vlaams Blok a 'racist' organization.

3 In fact, Euro-party labels can be counter-productive for national parties. In their discussion on parties in the US House of Representatives, Cox and McCubbins (1993) argue that congressmen have an incentive to be loyal to their party groups, as the reputation of their groups is important in terms of re-election. Distancing oneself or the party from the Europarty can actually be a wise electoral strategy for MEPs, especially in member states whose publics are less supportive of European integration.

4 Groups comprising MEPs from only one country (such as Forza Europa in 1994–95) have not been permitted since the 1999 elections.

5 There is a growing body of research on voting behaviour in the Parliament. See Hix *et al.* (2005) for bibliographical information on these publications and their major findings.

6 For example, the British Labour Party has since the latter part of the 1990s introduced a mechanism for 'policy coordination' between London and the party's MEPs (Messmer 2003).

7 Named after its inventor, the Belgian mathematician Victor d'Hondt, the method is used for allocating seats in electoral systems based on proportional representation. The party group winning most seats in the Parliament gets the first committee chair, and the number of seats held by that group is then divided by two and compared with the seat shares of the other groups.

The group with most seats at this point receives the second committee chair. The process continues until all committee chairs have been allocated.

8 For detailed information on the processing of legislation in the Parliament, see Corbett *et al.* (2005: 120–148; 196–239).

9 For information on the campaigns in the 2004 elections, see the country chapters in Lodge (2005) and the election briefings at the homepage of the European Parties Elections & Referendums Network (EPERN) (*http://www.sussex.ac.uk/sei/1-4-2.html*).

10 Article I–46(4) in Title VI on the 'Democratic life' of the Union.

11 For comparative analyses of Euro-parties, see Hix and Lord (1997), Delwit *et al.* (2001), and Johansson and Zervakis (2002). For case studies of party families, see Ladrech (2000), Jansen (1998), and Dietz (2000).

12 The various Eurosceptical parties or movements may find it difficult to agree on a common programme, as the objectives of these parties range from opposing further integration (for example, the June List in Sweden) to demanding their country's withdrawal from the Union (for example, the Independence Party in the UK).

13 The appropriations are managed by the Parliament. To obtain funding, a Europarty must have gained seats in at least a quarter of member states in national or regional elections or it must have received at least 3 per cent of the votes at the most recent EP election in at least one quarter of the member states. The amount allocated to the Europarties in the second half of 2004 was 6.5 million euros, and in 2005 it was 8.4 million euros.

Further reading

The volume edited by van der Eijk and Franklin (1996) is an essential guide to understanding voter and party behaviour in Euroelections. Hix and Lord (1997) analyses the role of parties in the EU policy process, with chapters on national parties, EP party groups, and party federations. The Special Issue edited by Hix and Scully (2003) provides articles on various aspects of party groups, including voting behaviour and committee work. Kreppel (2002) provides a data-rich account of the development of the EP's party system. Scully (2005) examines the socialization of MEPs, showing that the often-heard claim of representatives 'going native' in Brussels needs to be re-evaluated.

Hix, S., and Lord, C. (1997), *Political Parties in the European Union* (Basingstoke: Palgrave).

Hix, S., and Scully, R. (eds.) (2003), 'The European Parliament at Fifty', Special Issue of *Journal of Common Market Studies*, 41/2.

Kreppel, A. (2002), *The European Parliament and the Supranational Party System: A Study of Institutional Development* (Cambridge: Cambridge University Press).

Scully, R. (2005), *Becoming Europeans? Attitudes, Behaviour and Socialization in the European Parliament* (Oxford: Oxford University Press).

van der Eijk, C., and Franklin, M. N. (eds.) (1996), *Choosing Europe? The European Electorate and National Politics in the Face of Union* (Ann Arbor, MA: University of Michigan Press).

Web links

- The European Parliament and its party groups (*www.europarl.eu.int/groups/*). The websites of the Parliament's party groups provide information on the members and national parties in the groups, the internal organization of the groups, together with policy statements, press releases and latest news regarding the groups.

- European People's Party: *www.epp-eu.org*

- Party of European Socialists: *www.pes.org*

- European Liberal, Democrat and Reform Party: *www.eldr.org*

- European Federation of Green Parties: *www.europeangreens.org*
  The homepages of the four Europarties provide a brief history of the parties, their election and policy programmes, and links to national member parties, the EP party group, and affiliated organizations.

- European Parliament Research Group: *www.lse.ac.uk/collections/EPRG/*
  Founded in 1998, EPRG brings together the leading scholars of the European Parliament from Europe and North America, with the homepage offering data and working papers for downloading.

Chapter 16

Social and Regional Interests

The Economic and Social Committee and Committee of the Regions

Charlie Jeffery

Contents

Summary

The Committee of the Regions (CoR) was established over thirty years later than the European Economic and Social Committee (Ecosoc) yet the two bodies have much in common. Both were established to bring in new expertise to European decision-making and given similar sets of consultative powers. Neither, though, has made an enduring impact. Ecosoc was rapidly marked down as an ineffectual body with weak powers and an unwieldy, disparate membership. And the CoR has followed in many ways an equivalent trajectory and has at best yet to prove itself. One outcome has been the growing tendency of social and regional interests to pursue their concerns through other, more effective channels of access to European decision-making.

Introduction

The European Economic and Social Committee is one of the founding institutions of the EU. It was created in the Treaty of Rome and launched in 1958 as a consultative body designed to bring in the advice of social and economic interests—above all business and labour—to European-level decision-making. The Committee of the Regions, a product of the Maastricht Treaty, had its inaugural meeting thirty-six years later in 1994. It too has an advisory role in EU decision-making and is comprised of representatives of local and regional authorities from all the member states.

For two institutions launched in such different eras Ecosoc and the CoR have a remarkable amount in common. Much of this was deliberate. Ecosoc was in most respects used as an institutional template for the CoR. The internal structures of the two bodies are similar, as are their advisory powers. They share administrative infrastructure. More fundamentally they had similar founding rationales: to mobilize additional input felt, at the time, to be valuable for the European decision-making process. In neither case, though, have observers been convinced that this rationale of added value has been delivered. The reason for this rests in a further commonality of the two committees: it has never been clear what *kind* of added value they should try to deliver. Are they primarily panels of experts there to help make better decisions? Or are they bodies which are genuinely representative of important interests in society which would otherwise be neglected in the routine course of interaction between member state governments and the core European-level institutions of Commission and European Parliament? If the latter, are they equipped to perform the classic role of democratic interest representation, that of building an interface between the political decision-making process and the citizens of the EU?

This 'role conflict' of technocratic expertise versus democratic representation forms a backdrop to this chapter. The chapter begins with an account of the factors which led to Ecosoc and CoR being set up. Though each is clearly a creature of a particular historical context—the post-war era of corporatist interventionism for Ecosoc, the more fluid dynamics of early 1990s 'multi-level governance' for the CoR—both were subject to competing technocratic and representative claims. Both were also set up in ways which limited the prospect of a genuinely *influential* role being developed, though arguably the debates on the future of Europe running through the first half of the 2000s have created at least for the CoR a more promising platform for developing that role. The limitations on the two committees' influence become evident in the chapter's discussion of the structure and composition of Ecosoc and CoR and the formal powers accorded to them by treaty. A look at the (changing) ways in which the two institutions have used their powers over time reveals the patterns of interaction they have had with the other key European institutions—Council, Commission, and Parliament.

A final section broadens the perspective. Ecosoc and CoR are not the only routes available for social and regional interests to bring their concerns to bear 'in Europe'. Both interest groups and regional and local authorities routinely use alternative routes to access EU decision-making. These alternative routes offer, for some at least, greater returns than working through Ecosoc or CoR and are logically given preference. To the extent that this happens, the credibility of Ecosoc and CoR just as logically suffers, creating a vicious circle. Ecosoc has, for most observers, never escaped this vicious circle. Whether the CoR can escape it still remains unclear.

The origins of Ecosoc and CoR

Ecosoc and CoR were each fashioned in treaty negotiations held at critical stages in the European integration process. The Treaty of Rome, which established Ecosoc, built out radically from the narrow foundations of the European Coal and Steel Community (ECSC) to inaugurate a much wider project of economic integration. The Maastricht Treaty of 1992 was an ambitious response to market deepening, new global economic pressures and, above all, the collapse of the Iron Curtain. At such critical moments as these, negotiating agendas are fluid and windows of opportunity for new, and often unanticipated initiatives can emerge. Ecosoc and the CoR both fall into this category.

The idea of establishing an Ecosoc as part of the new European Economic Community emerged only in September 1956 and was finally agreed just two months before the Rome Treaty was concluded in March 1957 (Smismans 2000: 4). It was brought onto the agenda by two of the smaller players in the negotiations, Belgium and The Netherlands. Their aim was to reproduce the corporatist models provided by their domestic Social–economic Councils—forums for consulting business and trade unions in economic policy-making—in the new EEC framework. The proposals fell on fertile ground, with all the other founding six except West Germany having similar domestic institutions (Lodge and Herman 1980: 267).

Two other factors argued for Ecosoc and led to its adoption against West German opposition. First, the idea of bringing in the expertise of the 'social partners' of business and labour to economic decision-making was consistent with both the predominantly economic logic of the early stages of the integration process and the prevailing climate of corporatist interest intermediation. 'Europe' could even lend its own example in the form of the Consultative Committee comprised of representatives of employers and workers (and also of traders and consumers) which had been established to support the work of the ECSC.

Second, the proposed EEC Assembly, the forerunner of the European Parliament, was to be indirectly elected, at least initially, and limited to a consultative role. As such it did not provide 'normal' parliamentary channels for bringing interest group influence to bear on European decision-making. In this sense some felt Ecosoc was needed as a supplementary *representative* body for the new Community, perhaps even 'as an incipient parliamentary-legislative assembly—the third organ in a tricameral legislature alongside the Council of Ministers and a European Parliament linked with the Commission' (Lodge and Herman 1980: 267).

A similar *mélange* of factors—with equivalent implications for establishing a clear sense of institutional purpose—lay behind the establishment of the CoR. The first was a change in the broad political context, heralded by the Single European Act of 1986 and sustained by the activist Commission Presidency of Jacques Delors. The implication of deepening integration for regional and local government was a much greater impact of European legislation in their fields of competence. In particular, regional and local governments across the Union were responsible for the on-the-ground implementation of many European policies. As the scope of these policies grew, regional and local governments were inevitably drawn in as desirable partners in policy-making. In certain fields, in particular structural policy after the reforms of 1988, this role became increasingly formalized, leading influential commentators to coin the term 'multi-level governance' (Marks 1993).

If regional and local governments were increasingly drawn in 'from above' into this multi-levelled European decision-making process, there were at the same time new trends which operated 'from the bottom up' (Jeffery 2000: 8). Patterns of governance within the member states were being recalibrated in ways which upgraded the significance of sub-state governments. Globalization processes were felt to make redundant traditional forms of economic policy intervention by central governments and to require more differentiated economic strategies tailored to local and regional strengths. In some member states movements for regional autonomy (re-)emerged to prominence. In each case the result was a growing capacity among regional and local governments to engage in policy-making processes, at both the domestic and the European levels. The new multi-level governance emerged, in other words, from the convergence of new trends of sub-state political mobilization launched from both 'above' and 'below'.

The institutional actors which supported the establishment of a Committee of the Regions at Maastricht can be distinguished by these 'top-down' and 'bottom-up' perspectives on the role of regional and local government. One key actor was the Commission. Its logic was impeccably 'top-down'. As the body responsible for the implementation of European legislation, but lacking its own implementation authorities on the ground, it needed partners for the implementation process. Sub-state governments fitted the bill, and as they became more heavily involved in European policy implementation there followed calls to regularize their input. The initial outcome was the creation by the Commission of its own Consultative Council of Regional and Local Authorities in 1988. The rationale behind the Consultative Council—'to improve the poor implementation of regional policy by member states by involving other stakeholders in its design and execution' (Warleigh 1999: 10)—was essentially the same technocratic impulse which had earlier argued for the inclusion of the economic expertise of interest groups, via Ecosoc, into economic integration policy.

In October 1990 the Commission went further and proposed that a body modelled on the Consultative Council be formalized in the treaty under negotiation in the pre-Maastricht Intergovernmental Conference (IGC) on Political Union. Just two months earlier, the German Länder had tabled a parallel proposal for a 'Regional Council'. This was not intended by the Länder (just) as a fount of expertise for the Commission to draw on but rather, quite explicitly, as a *representative* body which would 'ensure that representatives of all Europe's regions can bring in specific regional interests to the legislative process at the European level' (Kilpert and Lhotta 1996: 224). In some of the more ambitious versions, the Regional Council was even envisaged—*pace* early views of Ecosoc's role—as a prototype for a 'third chamber' which would come to take a place in the European legislative process alongside Council and Parliament (Hoppe and Schulz 1992).

The idea of the Regional Council was one of the responses the Länder had developed to meet the challenges of the accelerated European integration process. They were concerned that post-SEA integration was cutting increasingly deeply into the policy fields for which they were responsible under domestic law without giving them compensatory rights of involvement in European decision-making. Faced with this loss of power, they were naturally keen to 'strike back' (Jeffery 1996). The Regional Council was a key element of their thinking. The IGC on Political Union provided an opportunity to realize these aims. Unlike the parallel IGC on Economic and Monetary Union (EMU), the IGC on Political Union did not have a clear and settled agenda. It emerged as a kind of add-on to existing, relatively advanced debates about EMU, effectively as a *quid pro quo* for German agreement to the French-led EMU agenda. With many issues as a result left open until the very last stages of the negotiations at Maastricht, there was considerable scope for agenda-setting. The Länder took this opportunity with gusto.

They did this in part through a series of domestic policy papers designed to bind the German central government to their view in the IGC negotiations. Having established during the ratification of the SEA that they had a right of veto over the ratification of new European treaties, they had the wherewithal to make their views count. Judicious wielding of the possibility of veto helped ensure most Länder aims were adopted in the formal German position for the IGC.

The Länder also mobilised on a wider front. Their platform for the IGC resonated strongly with the aims of regional and (to a lesser extent) local governments elsewhere in the EU which had also been affected by growing European incursions into their fields of responsibility. Working closely with other 'strong' regions in Belgium and Spain, the Länder ensured that a range of other organizations including the Assembly of the European Regions, a Strasbourg-based lobby, and the European Parliament reiterated their demands during the IGC. These multiple pressures (Jeffery 1996: 256–7) coalesced with the Commission's proposals to force the Regional Council formally onto the IGC agenda in December 1990 and led, ultimately, to its adoption in the form of the Committee of the Regions in the European Summit at Maastricht one year later. What, of course, this odd alliance of 'top-down' *and* 'bottom-up', technocratic *and* representative agendas could not ensure was a clear sense of what the CoR was really for. Like Ecosoc it was launched into ambiguity.

The waters were muddied further by the structure and powers of the two bodies. In most respects the structure and powers of the CoR as decided at Maastricht were directly modelled on its elder sibling. This was no doubt in part a sheer administrative convenience adopted as a way of dealing quickly with one of the less important items on a crowded IGC agenda. It was also a clear political decision on the part of those outside the group of CoR advocates who did not wish to see the CoR, or the sub-state level more broadly, develop into genuinely influential policy actors. This, of course, was an implicit sideswipe at Ecosoc, which had been plodding along for over thirty years without wielding much influence on the course of European integration. The next two sections offer insights into why Ecosoc had failed to wield more influence, and, by implication, why the CoR was hampered from the outset.

The structure of Ecosoc and CoR

Membership

Ecosoc has what can at best be called a diffuse membership. The vision of the Belgian and Dutch proponents of Ecosoc—a coherent forum of the 'social partners' of business and labour—was diluted at West German insistence. The result was a more broadly based body representing 'the various categories of economic and social activity, in particular, representatives of producers, farmers, carriers, workers, dealers, craftsmen, professional occupations, consumers and the general interest' (Art. 257 TEC).[1] These 'various categories' are combined in Ecosoc in three groups: I—Employers; II—Workers; and III—Various Interests', a residual category which mops up the rest of the interest group spectrum.

The number of members has grown from an initial 102 as a result of periodic enlargements, and currently stands—like the CoR membership—at 317, with each member state sending a delegation whose size is loosely linked with population size.

Table 16.1	National delegations to Ecosoc and CoR
France	24
Germany	24
Italy	24
United Kingdom	24
Poland	21
Spain	21
Austria	12
Belgium	12
Czech Republic	12
Greece	12
Hungary	12
Portugal	12
Netherlands	12
Sweden	12
Denmark	9
Finland	9
Ireland	9
Lithuania	9
Slovakia	9
Estonia	7
Latvia	7
Slovenia	7
Cyprus	6
Luxembourg	6
Malta	5
Total	**317**

Ecosoc members are proposed by the member state governments and are appointed by the Council of Ministers (since the Treaty of Nice by qualified-majority vote, beforehand unanimously) to serve four-year terms. They are not mandated, so are not expected directly to represent the interests of the interest group they belong to 'at home' (though, of course, many do see this as their role). However—not least because members states have different ways of selecting their Ecosoc members—some members do not hold office in, or even belong to, interest groups (Smismans 2000: 8). The membership of the Committee therefore provides only patchy coverage of the possible spectrum of 'economic and social activity' across the EU. It also looks, at the start of the twenty-first century, a little anachronistic. Its categories of membership are those of the 1950s and have not kept pace well either with changes in economic structure across the Union or with a picture of interest group politics which has been radically changed by new kinds of organization and activity, for example in the field of environmental protection or equal opportunities. The notion of Ecosoc as a *representative* body is therefore difficult to sustain.

Again there are parallels with the CoR. Its membership was also 'diluted'. The Länder vision had been for a body restricted to regional governments (notwithstanding the fact that this would have left a number of member states, including pre-devolution UK, unrepresented). With its interest in improving policy implementation, the Commission was interested in drawing the wider palette of sub-state government, both regional and local. The Commission view won out. The result has been a very diverse body bringing together representatives of sub-state governments in fully fledged federal states (from Germany, Belgium and Austria), through to English district councillors and pretty much everything in-between (Schöbel 1995: 30).

CoR members are also unmandated, and appointed by the Council (also, since Nice, by QMV) to four-year terms on the basis of proposals by member state governments. The latter choose their CoR delegations in as many different ways as there are member states. Until the Treaty of Nice, CoR members did not have to be electorally accountable. Unlike Ecosoc an equal number of 'Alternate Members' is appointed who can deputize when full members are unavailable.

Organization

Ecosoc and CoR have much the same form of internal organization. Presidents are elected for two-year periods along with Vice-Presidents (VPs). There are two VPs in Ecosoc to ensure that all three Groups are represented in the presidency, and twenty-six (!) in the CoR, including a 'chief' VP who is in effect the designate for the next Presidency, and another VP from each of the twenty-five member states. Supported by other officers, the President and VPs form a Presidium (Ecosoc)/Bureau (CoR) which organizes their institution's business. This is carried out at two levels: in committee and in Plenary. Ecosoc currently has six standing committees, or sections plus a Consultative Committee on Industrial Change which took over the business of the equivalent ECSC committee when that institution was wound up in 2002. The CoR calls its committees Commissions, and currently has six policy-focused Commissions, plus a Commission for Financial and Administrative Affairs. Standing committee membership is structured to reflect the wider composition of Ecosoc/CoR, balanced across

Table 16.2 Standing committees of Ecosoc and CoR			
Ecosoc Sections		**CoR Commissions**	
Section NAT	Agriculture, rural development and the environment	COTER	Territorial cohesion policy
Section ECO	Economic and monetary union and economic and social cohesion	ECOS	Economic and social policy
Section SOC	Employment, social affairs, and citizenship	DEVE	Sustainable development
Section INT	The single market, production and consumption	EDUC	Culture and education
Section TEN	Transport, energy, infrastructure, and the information society	CONST	Constitutional affairs and European governance
Section REX	External relations	RELEX	External relations
CCMI	Industrial change (coal and steel industries)	CAFA	Administrative and financial affairs

the three Groups in the case of Ecosoc and across national delegations and political groups in the CoR. Both Ecosoc and CoR members belong to at least one but (with minor exceptions) no more than two standing committees.

Whenever Ecosoc or CoR has the task of drawing up an opinion, the Presidium/Bureau assigns the task to the most appropriate standing committee. The latter in turn appoints a study group (effectively a sub-committee) in Ecosoc and a *rapporteur* in CoR to draft the opinion. The ensuing draft is discussed and amended in the standing committee, then referred to the Presidium/Bureau for presentation to the Plenary. Ecosoc Plenary normally convenes ten times per year, that of the CoR five times. The main business is to discuss and—if there is a majority—adopt opinions, though more general debates on other important issues within the Committees' remits are also held.

A 'civil service' headed by a Secretary-General supports the work of committees, Plenary and Presidium/Bureau in Ecosoc/CoR. For the period between the CoR's foundation and the Amsterdam Treaty of 1997, Ecosoc and CoR shared common support services, such as translation, printing, postroom and so on. Since 1997 each has had separate core staff. In 2005 over 500 staff worked jointly for the two organizations, with each committee having over 100 of its own staff. The budget for running Ecosoc in 2004 was €93 million and CoR €55 million. By comparison—and a clear indicator of relative importance—the European Parliament had a budget of €1.15 billion.

Coalition-building

Both Ecosoc and CoR have a diffuse and disparate membership, though both bodies have a highly consensual style, issuing most of their opinions unanimously or at least with large majorities. Achieving such consensus requires mechanisms or, more informally, coalition-building processes which coordinate and trade off the different interests and positions held by members. Consensus-building in Ecosoc is perhaps the more straightforward process (Nugent 1994: 237). It revolves around the three Groups: Employers, Workers, and Various Interests. These are organized in Ecosoc as quasi-political parties. The three Groups have their own secretariats and as noted above Section membership always reflects the balance between them. The Groups meet collectively on a regular basis to discuss their take on Ecosoc business, including voting intentions on opinions as they are being drafted in the Sections and before they are presented to the Plenary. Groups I and II are, predictably, more cohesive and therefore more capable of generating a clear view.

This Group-based concertation of opinion limits the number of competing voices in the Committee and makes it easier to achieve impressively high levels of consensus. Van der Voort (1997: 212 in Smismans 2000: 7) calculated that between 1978 and 1990 72.6 per cent of opinions were issued unanimously and a further 18.2 per cent with overwhelming majorities. Cases where no agreement can be found between Groups and Ecosoc is unable to issue an opinion are rare.

The situation in the CoR is rather more complex. The basic units for concerting opinion at the launch of the CoR were the national delegations which, like Ecosoc Groups, are resourced by the CoR to meet regularly to discuss the Committee's work programme (Schwaiger 1997: 13). An alternative forum for concerting opinion has since emerged in the form of political parties. Four party groupings equivalent to (some of) those in the European Parliament began to meet consistently before plenary sessions during 1998: the Party of European Socialists (PSE), the European People's Party (EPP), the Alliance of Liberals and Democrats for Europe (ALDE) and the Union of Europe of the Nations–European Alliance (UEN–EA). Revised rules of procedure adopted by the CoR in 1999 formalized this development by giving the party groups status and resources equivalent to national delegations (Switalska 1999: 93–5).

There are not just national and party-political cleavage structures in the CoR though. A number of loose regional groupings exist providing for cross-national exchange of views in the Mediterranean, the Nordic and Alpine regions (Schwaiger 1997: 15). These periodically appear more generally as a 'north-south' divide focused on issues of structural funding and cohesion policy. A more enduring cleavage is that which exists between the different kinds of sub-state entity represented on the Committee, specifically regional versus local or, perhaps more precisely 'strong' regions with legislative powers versus the rest (see Christiansen 1997). This division of interest has clearly become more important in the context of the European constitutional debate since 2000, with the 'strong' regions forming their own pressure group (Regions with Legislative Power, or RegLeg) outside of the CoR and expressing reservations about the utility of the committee as a forum for representing their particular concerns (Wiedmann 2002). This is an issue taken up further below.

An interim conclusion is that the CoR is a body with a diverse internal structure in which coalition-building is a complex, multidimensional enterprise. As it is also an enterprise which has sought the same kind of consensual spirit as Ecosoc, decisions often need to be pitched at the lowest common denominator of cross-CoR acceptability (Farrows and McCarthy 1997: 31). And inherent in this is the danger of producing such anodyne opinions that the CoR's influence is minimal. The discussion in the next section of Ecosoc and CoR powers and the way they are exercised will explore this issue further.

The powers of Ecosoc and CoR

This section first sets out the formal powers given to Ecosoc and CoR by treaty, before turning to an account of how those powers 'play' in practice in interaction with the other main EU institutions.

Formal powers

Ecosoc was not generously endowed at the outset. The Rome Treaty provided for mandatory consultation of Ecosoc by Council and Commission in certain specified fields and optional consultation in others. The Amsterdam Treaty also opened up the possibility for Ecosoc to be consulted by the European Parliament, though this happens only rarely. The list of areas where consultation is mandatory has expanded over time, in particular since the SEA. It includes agriculture, the free movement of labour, internal market issues, economic and social cohesion, social policy, regional policy, the environment, research and technological development, employment policy, equal opportunities, and public health policy. Optional consultation where Council, Commission or Parliament 'consider it appropriate' can cover any other aspect of the treaties. Initial aims on the part of the Dutch sponsors of Ecosoc to give the Committee a right of initiative, i.e. the right to give opinions on issues not specified by treaty or selected by Council or Commission were not fulfilled until 1974 (and not confirmed by treaty until Maastricht). In recent years around 180 opinions have been issued annually with 30–40 per cent of them arising from optional referrals, the same again from mandatory referrals and the remainder from own initiative. The right to give opinions did and does not extend to a right to have those opinions heard. Neither Commission nor Council (nor Parliament) is obliged to give feedback on Ecosoc opinions, let alone take them into account.

The CoR was initially given more or less the same set of powers. Mandatory referrals naturally covered a rather different group of fields, reflecting the CoR's regional/local remit while the possibility of optional referral and of own initiative were the same as for the post-Maastricht Ecosoc. The CoR presents significantly fewer opinions than Ecosoc—around 50-60 per year—with around 10 per cent arising from its own initiative. The initial fields for mandatory referral comprised education, training and youth, economic and social cohesion, the Structural Funds, trans-European networks, public health and culture. These were extended in the Amsterdam Treaty to cover also aspects of employment policy, social policy, the environment and vocational training. Amsterdam also allowed Parliament to consult the CoR, though in practice it has rarely ever done so.

Ecosoc in practice

Despite the limited powers it had been given, there were confident expectations in Ecosoc both that 'its accumulated expertise would be valued and exploited by the EC's institutions' and that it would be able to develop a representative role as a 'mediator on behalf of national economic and social interests vis-à-vis the Commission and the Council of Ministers' (Lodge and Herman 1980: 269). Neither expectation was fulfilled.

The impact of the 'accumulated expertise' of Ecosoc was limited in the early years of the EEC in part by the nature of the early integration process, in part by the nature of its powers. Early EEC integration was typically a matter of detailed regulation of a gradual economic harmonization process in fairly narrow policy sectors. Though Ecosoc input here may well have been valuable, it tended to be more or less invisible—not least because Commission and Council were not obliged to give any evaluation of what they thought of Ecosoc opinions. Ecosoc also suffered from the tight timetable—sometimes just ten days—between referral of an issue and the due date of an opinion. The Council in particular gave little scope for Ecosoc to undertake detailed consideration of issues. A more general problem was the point in the legislative process at which Ecosoc was consulted—generally at a relatively late stage when the main policy choices and directions were already well established and any debate was at the level of detail only.

In these circumstances Ecosoc was naturally keen to establish its own right of initiative. This would allow the Committee itself to set the timetable for deliberation and approach issues as they emerged onto the agenda rather than after their key points had already been set out. A first attempt to establish a right of initiative to draw up opinions on any matter of European competence at any time failed in the mid-1960s. A second was accepted by the member states in 1972 and incorporated into Ecosoc rules of procedure in 1974. The right of own initiative has typically been used to widen the focus of Ecosoc deliberations away from matters of technical detail and towards more general agenda-setting. It has not, though, done much to change the wider pattern of Ecosoc's interactions with the other European institutions. To put it bluntly, there is little evidence to suggest that Council has ever taken the slightest notice of Ecosoc's opinion. At times it has been overtly hostile, most notably when a UK-led initiative in 1982 demanded a full-scale review of a body held to produce opinions too late, to express them too generally, and to be given too many optional referrals (Brüske: 1983, 91). One reason for the Council's scepticism was no doubt because Ecosoc has generally tended to support the supranational agenda of the Commission and has therefore been prone to run up against the buffers of member state intergovernmentalism. The fact that Ecosoc members carry no formal mandate—and therefore no guarantee of 'delivering' the interest group they hail from—may also play a role.

Ecosoc's support for a supranational agenda does not mean, though, that the Commission has been much more open to Ecosoc opinions. For Lodge and Herman (1980: 276–7) the Commission viewed Ecosoc as 'an unimportant and at times an irritating source of work because papers must be routed to it and because it is another body whose voice insists on it being heard'. There is little evidence that the Commission has become any less wearied by Ecosoc since, no matter how much Ecosoc's own reports trumpet how great an impact it has had. As Desmond Dinan wrote more recently (2000: 153), though Ecosoc's 'output is a valuable and generally underused source of EU policy analysis', 'Council and Commission rarely heed its advice'. Former Commissioner Bruce Millan (1997: 9) echoed this evaluation (in a speech warning the CoR not to fall into the same trap): 'The Economic and Social Committee ... produces a lot of admirable reports, but again most of my fellow Commissioners, as far as I could see, paid no attention to what the Economic and Social Committee said. They did not consider it to be of any importance.'

There are of course periodic exceptions to this rule of Ecosoc non-influence. Occasionally it does bring something onto the agenda which then 'flies'. The most important example concerns what became the Social Charter adopted by all except the UK at Maastricht and later fully incorporated in the Amsterdam Treaty. An Ecosoc report on a 'Community Charter of Basic Social Rights' formed the basis of the Commission proposals on the Social Charter which were accepted at the Strasbourg European Summit in 1989. 'In this case Ecosoc set the agenda decisively, before the usual decision-making process began, for the first time in its history' (Brüske 1994: 345).

The fields covered by the Social Charter—*inter alia* pay, working conditions, freedom of association, health and safety at work and workplace co-determination—might well be considered the 'natural' terrain of a body which had emerged as a European-level equivalent of national councils of business and labour organizations. Strikingly, though, Ecosoc itself has not been used as the forum for organizing 'Euro-corporatist' initiatives. A number of Tripartite Conferences were held during the 1970s which brought together European and national-level representatives of business and labour together with national and European officials to discuss matters of macroeconomic and social policy. Ecosoc had no role then, or in similar, shorter-lived discussions in the mid-1980s. Schmitter and Streeck (1994: 177) put this down to the composition of Ecosoc which, diluted by the amorphous 'Group III—Various Interests', was simply 'too cumbersome and insufficiently *paritaire* to bear the burden of leading the Community into the brave new world of social partnership'.

The fact that 'Euro-corporatism' effectively ignored Europe's corporatist institution is instructive and points to a wider reason for Ecosoc's marginal influence: interest groups had and have other channels at their disposal for influencing EU decision-making. Much more attention and resources are devoted by most interest groups—business, labour and beyond—to influencing the positions their national governments take to the Council of Ministers, to lobbying the Commission and Parliament directly, or to working through the European-level peak organizations which also have direct routes into Commission and Parliament. Equally if Commission or Parliament want to mobilize technical expertise or policy implementation capacity, direct links to national or European peak organizations can provide them quickly and efficiently. If both interest groups and the key European institutions have these routes at its disposal, the potential added value of Ecosoc as a channel for influence is inherently limited.

This question mark over Ecosoc's value raises questions not just about Ecosoc as a forum for bringing specialist expertise to the EU, but about the notion of Ecosoc as a representative body. The absence of mandate and the patchy membership of Ecosoc always undermined its claims to 'supply' representativeness. Nor is there any clear 'demand' for a representative body among the interest group community and the other European institutions. Put simply the idea of corporatist interest representation—despite the tripartite experiments of the 1970s and 1980s—was never one universally accepted across the EU and is now deeply anachronistic. It is all the more surprising, therefore, that Ecosoc has in recent years sought to relaunch itself with a (reformulated) representative rationale.

This reformulated rationale focuses on the concept of 'civil society' and is hung on the hook provided by the widely perceived democratic deficit which faces the EU. In the words of Ecosoc (2001: 2), the aim is 'to promote a greater commit-ment/contribution from civil society to the European venture, and to build and strengthen a Europe that is close to its public'. To this end Ecosoc has made greater use of open 'hearings intended to deepen contacts between the public and EU institu-tions' in developing its opinions. It has also developed a more explicit self-image as 'the representative of civil society organisations' (Smismans 2000: 6, 14). It has also tried to hook onto the debates on subsidiarity and more systematic pre-legislative consultation on EU policy which accompanied the constitutional debate in the early 2000s and the parallel debate on governance process opened up by the Commis-sion's 2001 White Paper on Governance. Ecosoc sought to stretch the conventional definition of subsidiarity—attached to tiers of government—to incorporate 'func-tional' criteria that would also bring in 'organised civil society' (Ecosoc 2001: 7). By its own admission though Ecosoc's aims in this direction were 'fully overlooked' in the European Convention and the Constitutional Treaty (Grosse-Hüttmann 2004: 111). Moreover Ecosoc was not seen as the primary route of input for organized civil soci-ety into the Convention, which was organized instead through seven 'contact groups' (social sector, environment, academia/think-tanks, citizen's groups, local authori-ties, human rights, development and culture) and developed largely through elec-tronic media (Bertelsmann Stiftung 2002). The contrast between the subject-matter and working method of those working groups and the way Ecosoc works and is struc-tured is striking. It reinforces the impression that Ecosoc is an anachronism. It is hard to escape the conclusion that the recent emphasis on civil society is just another throw of the dice by an organization still searching for a role almost half a century on from its launch.

CoR in practice

This image of Ecosoc searching in vain for a significant role is one which has dogged the CoR through its short life. The parallels in structure, function and powers it shared with Ecosoc meant that CoR's initial priority in developing its work was to demonstrate that it would not become an Ecosoc mark two. Repeated warnings from friends of the CoR in the Commission—such as Bruce Millan (below)—who had helped bring the CoR into being urged the CoR to develop a clear sense of purpose and a reputation for producing focused and useful opinions.

> You should spend your time coming together, uniting your views … rather than squab-bling among yourselves. It would give great pleasure to member states that are not en-thusiastic about the Committee, and to the Council and even to the Parliament to some extent, if you spent time quarrelling among yourselves rather than putting forward views which you expect to be taken seriously by the Council and the Commission … The real danger for the Committee is that if it does not do its work well, it will not be taken seriously.[2]

In some respects the starting position for the CoR was a favourable one. Unlike Ecosoc, it did not have to fight for years to be able to set its own priorities through the right of own initiative. It also had a broad and vocal coalition of early backers, including senior Commissioners but also the most powerful regional governments in the EU, the German Länder. The Länder had styled themselves as the architects of a new 'third', regional level in EU decision-making and envisaged the CoR as the key route in making this third level count (Jeffery 1996).

These favourable conditions allowed the CoR to hit the ground running. It issued over seventy opinions (including twenty-nine on CoR own initiative) in the first ten plenary sessions from March 1994 to January 1996. The main policy areas covered were regional policy, social policy, health and education, with the CoR responding within the consultative timetable to referrals from Council and Commission (typically involving detailed policy questions), and using own initiative as a mechanism to set more general priorities for action (Farrows and McCarthy 1997: 32–6).

Impact is difficult to measure. It was significant, though, that the then Commissioner for Regional Policy, Monika Wulf-Mathies, committed the Commission in April 1995—just eleven months after the CoR's launch—to extending the range of referrals beyond the mandatory areas required by treaty. She also unveiled a code of conduct for Commission/CoR relations modelled on that between Commission and Parliament which lifted the relationship with the CoR to a level above that enjoyed by Ecosoc. A succession of appearances at CoR meetings by a series of Commissioners also indicated a positive relationship with the Commission was emerging (Jeffery 1995: 249). The most comprehensive academic analysis of the CoR's impact on the Commission by Switalska (1999: 53–61) confirms this picture: the Commission takes the CoR seriously, quickly got into the habit of giving feedback on CoR opinions, and frequently takes CoR views on board.

A similar picture does not apply to the Council of Ministers, which has treated the CoR with 'benign indifference' (Warleigh 1999: 28), refusing to give feedback on CoR opinions and allowing the CoR little more than infrequent access to informal meetings. The relationship with the European Parliament is a little more nuanced. Though there is frequent cooperation between CoR *rapporteurs* and their counterparts in EP Committees dealing with the same issues, there has been an underlying rivalry. This rivalry can be traced at one level to a policy turf battle, with the EP's Regional Affairs Committee covering much the same ground as the CoR. There is a deeper dimension, though, which can be traced back to some of the visions surrounding the creation of the CoR. In particular, the German Länder notion of a 'third level' had an implicit representative claim which was confirmed in the CoR's discussions on the 1996–97 IGC which commenced soon after its launch. The Länder, with some support from Spanish and Belgian regions, revived the idea of the CoR as a potential 'third chamber' in the EU legislative process and called in the early IGC debates for the CoR to be given an explicit legislative role. They also proposed that the CoR itself be divided into two 'chambers', one for regional and one for local representatives, with the implication that the 'regional chamber' might take on that legislative role alongside Parliament and Council (Jeffery 1995: 254).

Unsurprisingly, such proposals soured relations with the EP, which was not keen on the idea of a competitor legislative organ undermining its hard-won authority (Millan 1997: 10), and created a legacy of suspicion which has been slow to clear, despite a rhetoric of cooperation and close relations. Significantly, the EP had by the end of 2004 only once made use of the possibility, established at Amsterdam, to refer matters to the CoR. This has to do in part with timetable issues, but more with an 'absence of imagination' and, ultimately, interest on the part of the EP (Blanke 2002: 22–4).

The reluctance of the other EU institutions — the Commission in part excepted — to take the CoR seriously suggests a repetition of the path Ecosoc followed. There has been one important difference however. The EU has been in institutional ferment for the whole period of the CoR's life. Successive IGCs since Maastricht have tried to prepare the EU for the enlargement which increased the number of member states from fifteen to twenty-five in 2004, while also addressing the 'democratic deficit' revealed in the early 1990s in the widespread disinterest in, and in some places hostility to, the Maastricht Treaty. The Convention and the IGC that followed in 2003–4 were likewise focused on the dual challenges of institutional adaptation to a bigger and more complex Union and of democratic legitimation.

The CoR was in other words born into a fluid context in which it had opportunities to prove its relevance, bed down and extend its powers, and avoid following the Ecosoc path. In doing so it had to confront the 'role-conflict' its original sponsors had thrust it into: was it to be a representative body as the German Länder had hoped, or was it to be an expert body to be consulted wherever its expertise counted and could improve EU policy, as the Commission had envisaged (see Christiansen: 1997: 51, 61–3)? This issue of role has exposed clear differences between the local and regional 'wings' of the CoR from the Amsterdam IGC through into the constitutional debate of the early 2000s. The local wing has proposed limited and incremental adjustments to the CoR's consultative powers, while the regional wing has sought a fuller legislative-representative role. These differences were papered over in what the coordinator of a CoR Special Commission on the Amsterdam IGC called a 'compromise without consensus' (Kalbfleisch-Kottsieper 1995: 13).

The notion of 'compromise without consensus' points to a paradox inherent in the CoR's creation. While on the one hand its establishment was a triumph for the third level, its subsequent operation has provided a platform not just for those, like the German Länder, which were keen for better third-level representation, but also for all the other, and very different perspectives and priorities which exist among the highly differentiated units of sub-state government across the EU. The danger — and in practice the tendency — has been that the CoR's most powerful members, the strong regions in Germany, Belgium, Spain, Austria and elsewhere, would turn their back on the CoR and pursue their interests in different ways. The creation of the RegLeg grouping in 2000, with a central focus on securing special status for legislative regions outside the framework of the CoR in the forthcoming Constitutional Treaty, was a clear signal of intent. The point was made in a statement in November 2000:

> The mode of operation and the composition of the Committee of the Regions do not fully match the expectations of regions with legislative power, in so far as it is not a special forum for them and the regions sit alongside local authorities which may well have quite different concerns. As a result the regions with legislative power have the impression that their work in an institution like this has so far not delivered the desired results. These regions therefore need to move ahead in a coordinated way so that they can present greater political weight and establish ad hoc frameworks able effectively to represent them at European level (cited in Wiedmann 2002: 546).

During the Convention the RegLeg regions met regularly, issuing a number of demands, but also developing and exchanging strategies for influencing their respective member state's central governments, whose role was central in the later stages of the Convention and in the IGC that followed. RegLeg also coordinated its work with the CoR, which was able to send a delegation of observers with (limited) speaking rights to the Convention, though these had no discernible impact on the Convention's deliberations. What emerged from the Convention (and was endorsed in the IGC) was highly significant. Unexpectedly far-reaching new powers were awarded to the CoR in monitoring a subsidiarity principle for the first time formally extended in the core treaty text to the regional level, including a right of the CoR to appeal to the European Court of Justice if it felt that EU institutions had failed to take due account of subsidiarity. More generally the Constitutional Treaty made explicit the need for the EU to respect the structures and roles of sub-state tiers of government within the member states, reflecting the concern in the constitutional debate to establish for the EU greater 'proximity' to citizens' concerns.

These powers clearly demarcated the CoR as a body of greater political weight in the EU than Ecosoc, whose pleas for equal rights under the notion of 'functional subsidiarity' had fallen on deaf ears. There is a catch though. The RegLeg regions did not win the advances they had sought concerning recognition of a special status for themselves. There was also good cause to think that the new powers of the CoR and the more general sensitization of the Constitutional Treaty (whatever its fate) to sub-state tiers of government were outcomes of RegLeg members lobbying their central governments rather than anything the CoR did. In other words the case for greater recognition of regions in EU decision-making was recognized, but there was no appetite for further institutional innovation beyond the CoR. That is a paradoxical and rather galling outcome for the legislative regions (Jeffery 2005). It is also a major challenge for the CoR. If it is to make the most of its new powers it will need to find ways of (re-)engaging the RegLeg regions in its work. That task does not promise to be easy, not least because, as the next section suggests, legislative regions have other ways of securing their concerns.

Ecosoc and CoR in context

It is clear enough from the discussion above that Ecosoc has never found itself a lasting niche in European decision-making, and that the CoR is still having trouble establishing one. The combination of weak, consultative powers, the lack of a clear role, and highly diverse membership establishes an unenviable set of barriers which have to be hurdled if Ecosoc's interest groups or the CoR's regional and local authorities are to be able to exert any genuine collective influence—whether generated through technical expertise or a plausible claim to representativeness. The higher barriers to influence are the more likely it is that social and regional interests will choose to use any alternative channels of influence open to them. The European decision-making process is both highly sectorized and multi-levelled. There are as a result many different access points available for particular interests to press and realize their concerns.

The attractiveness of alternative access points has long been noted in the case of the interest groups gathered in Ecosoc (see, for example, Feld 1966; Mazey and Richardson 1989; Platzer 1999). Many interest groups—or even individual members of those groups—are well enough placed to exert influence over national government and, indirectly, the Council of Ministers. And, as the scope of EU policies has grown, a vast range of transnational Euro-groups and Brussels-based Euro-lobbyists has emerged which seeks to exert direct influence over Commission, Parliament and Council (usually via its working groups). For most groups the choice between un-diluted and direct access to some of the key nodes of the EU decision-making process and the consensual working style and (at best) diffuse impact of Ecosoc is fairly clear cut. And, of course, the more that interest groups favour alternative routes, the harder it is for Ecosoc to establish itself as a plausible channel for influence.

This is not a new conclusion. It has been standard fare in assessments of Ecosoc for decades (see Brüske 1982: 107–8; 1994: 345; Wallace and Wallace 2000: 25). What is striking, though, is how a similar situation has begun to emerge regarding the pursuit of regional interests in EU decision-making. Put starkly, the CoR quickly became a low priority for some regional interests because there are better ways of getting things done. A number of EU member states now have domestic policy formulation processes for EU matters which formally include sub-state governments in determining the member state position. These include Belgium, Germany, Austria, the UK (for Scotland, Northern Ireland, and Wales), and, to lesser extents, Spain and Italy. In the first four of these cases, regional governments have the right in some fields of policy to speak for the national delegation in the Council of Ministers. These national channels offer, needless to say, rather fuller opportunities for influencing EU decision-making than those of the CoR. Significantly, new opportunities for legislative regions to call EU institutions to account on subsidiarity were not just awarded to the CoR, but also to regional parliaments acting through the new 'early warning system' for national parliaments on subsidiarity matters agreed by Convention and IGC.

Moreover, alongside this kind of 'national' route into European policy, there are also channels of sub-state influence which act directly on 'Brussels'. Well over 200 sub-state authorities maintain representative offices in Brussels designed to garner intelligence from, and communicate ideas to, Commission and Parliament. A vast range of transnational organizations bring together regions with shared sectoral or territorial interests to exert collective influence on the Commission in particular (Schmitt-Egner 2000). These transnational alliances are organised in part around the cleavage structures also evident in the CoR—but of course can present their shared concerns more directly, without having to negotiate a common denominator with other sets of regional interests as is the case in the CoR.

Conclusion

At best, the Committee of the Regions is one of a large number of channels open for regional interests to make a mark on Europe. A highly complex pattern of multi-level governance has emerged in which sub-state governments pursue their interests in a range of arenas: national, transnational, Brussels-focused, sometimes the CoR where it is expedient. The new powers the Constitutional Treaty (should it ever be ratified) proposed to give the CoR might offer an opportunity to claim a fuller share of this interest representation—but regardless it will have to find a way of satisfying different groupings of interest rather more adequately than the 'lowest common denominator' approach hitherto. There are signs that it is focusing its efforts precisely on this as it takes steps to streamline its procedures and establish its credibility as a subsidiarity monitor.[3] In all this Ecosoc stands as an admonition. Interest groups too have multiple channels of access to the EU and they too devise particular strategies to achieve their specific sectional interests. These strategies may be directed at national governments or at the main European-level institutions, though Ecosoc will typically not figure very high on the Euro-institution list. In this sense Ecosoc is a frozen legacy of a constellation of factors which, in 1957, in an era of corporatist interest intermediation, seemed an appropriate way forward but which rapidly became anachronistic and is now more or less irrelevant. Fifteen years or so on from its conception at Maastricht, the CoR needs to take care not to follow the same path to anachronism and irrelevance. The constitutional debate has given it an opportunity—one last opportunity?—for relevance. Whether it takes it or not remains to be seen.

Notes

1 Prior to the Treaty of Nice, the phrase 'representatives of the general public' was used instead of 'consumers and the general interest'. Otherwise, the constituencies of Ecosoc have remained unchanged since 1958.

2 Address at Queen's University, Belfast, November 1995.

3 At the time of writing the CoR is planning an electronic subsidiarity monitoring and exchange network alongside new procedures to enable swift decision-making on subsidiarity matters that make explicit overtures to the legislative regions. Unsurprisingly the latter are proving controversial for other interest groupings in the CoR.

Further reading

Little has been published on Ecosoc. The best paper on the foundation and initial development of Ecosoc is Lodge and Hermann (1980). Smismans (2000) and Sherington and Warleigh (2002) provide solid updates on more recent developments. Much more attention has been given to the CoR. Warleigh (1999; 2002) provides solid overviews. The special issue of *Regional and Federal Studies* (Vol. 7/1, Spring 1997) is less comprehensive but more incisive on the early years. A good wider analysis of EU interest-group politics is Greenwood, Grote, and Ronit (1992); for a wider discussion of multi-level governance see the special issue of *Regional and Federal Studies* on 'The Regional Dimension of the European Union' (Vol. 6/2, Summer 1996) and Marks and Hooghe (2001).

Web links

Ecosoc's website at *http://www.esc.eu.int* is well organized, with a reasonable archive of Ecosoc papers and publications. The CoR equivalent at *http://europa.cor.eu.int* has a less comprehensive archive but contains useful general information. Useful facts and figures on the work of the two bodies can be found in the Commission's annual General Report at *http://europa.eu.int/abc/doc/off/rg/en/2000* (and/1999,/1998, etc).

Chapter 17
Conclusion

John Peterson and Michael Shackleton

Contents

Summary

Uncertainty about the future of the EU should not be allowed to obscure the enduring character of its institutions and the persistence of the difficulties they face. They remain irrevocably interdependent, obliged to work together to deliver collective governance even as they compete to maintain or extend their prerogatives. Their capacity to govern collectively is increasingly called into question, especially given their acute problems of leadership, management, and accountability. These problems are becoming ever more complex with governments constantly looking for new ways of governing collectively without necessarily accepting 'communitarization'. Analytically, no one can understand the European Union, or wider debates about legitimising international institutions, without understanding the EU's institutions.

Introduction

We conclude at a time of unparalleled uncertainty. The 2005 referenda in France and The Netherlands generated a year-long 'pause for reflection', with few very clear about how the EU's institutional system could or should develop. The ideas of creating new institutions, such as a standing President of the European Council, or reinforcing existing ones, such as increasing the powers of the Parliament by extending co-decision, seemed to have been set aside for the time being. There were widely differing views about the possibility of retrieving the contents of the Constitutional Treaty. Some believed the Treaty could still be ratified in all member states, with one leading MEP predicting the Parliament's 'steely determination' to revive the Constitutional Treaty would only strengthen over time.[1] Others considered that parts of the Treaty could be brought into effect without a new treaty, with interest focusing in particular on moving forward towards an EU External Action Service on the grounds that it would one day exist in any case (see Cameron 2005). Still others considered that the Union could live with the existing structure established by the 2000 Treaty of Nice. The Commission President, José Manuel Barroso, urged that the EU should 'get things done that ordinary people can see and appreciate. We should not focus our efforts exclusively on devising institutional scenarios', pointedly adding that during the first months of the 'pause', there anyway 'ha[d]n't been much reflection'.[2]

This chapter contains no crystal ball gazing. Instead, it looks back over the rest of the book to identify what is *enduring* about the character of the EU's institutions. Chapter 1 began by stressing how unique they are, and how the fundamental, overriding goal of the Union—managing the enormous interdependence which links European states—gave rise to the need for collective (or 'post-sovereign') governance (W. Wallace 2005). Collective governance logically requires institutions that work *collectively* to offer leadership, manage diverse tasks and integrate interests in the pursuit of common goals.

The EU's institutional system may seem more complex and arcane than its counterparts at the national level. Truly 'common' goals may seem to be a thing of the past now that the EU is a Union of twenty-five or more. Yet, it would be difficult to argue that states in Europe were ever more interdependent than they are today, and it is easy to forget how diverse Europe is. It comprises a tremendous range of densely populated states, many of them small, whose histories are closely intertwined but marked above all by conflict. More than most regions in the world, Europe must co-operate to prosper, or even survive (Dogan 1994). Collectively governing Europe is neither easy nor optional.

The historical focus of this volume's contributions reminds us that European integration began with what, in retrospect, seem to be strikingly narrow and overwhelmingly economic objectives: first, to manage jointly the production of coal and steel, and then, to develop a common market. Yet, the earliest moves to institutionalize European cooperation were never seen as final. They represented something new and unspecified, but which definitely went beyond the intergovernmental cooperation of (say) the Council of Europe, with its limited agenda and resources and non-binding decision-making. From the beginning, EU institution-building had a decidedly political purpose: to create a structure of interdependence among European states which would oblige them to develop common solutions to common problems. Then as now, this aim generates tensions between those who wish to reinforce the central institutions in a federalist direction and those who see them as instrumental vehicles for maximizing state interests. As Dehousse and Magnette argue (see Chapter 2), this tension—reminiscent of eighteenth-century debates in the United States between 'federalists' and 'anti-federalists'—has defined European integration but not prevented the growth and acceptance of ever greater interdependence.

Over the last half-century, the EU has expanded to take on an enormous number of new tasks. As it has done so, it has expanded its membership to include a far more diverse collection of states than anyone could have imagined at the beginning. One crucial by-product is that it now has far more and far more disparate members than its institutional system was ever intended or expected to accommodate. Institutional-izing collective governance has become a steadily more politicized process that domi-nates the calculations of European governments and increasingly touches the lives of European citizens.

Moves to extend the EU's remit to matters of monetary, foreign, defence, and in-ternal security policies have led to more diverse institutional choices. Rather than simply framing the question as a straight black or white one—'do we want to *com-munitarize* this policy sector or not?'—member governments have created a wider set of options for themselves. Deciding to make policy in the EU context is only a first step which leads to a set of further choices: 'do we communitarize, *or* do we orga-nize new cooperation using one of the existing alternative institutional mechanisms *or* do we create an entirely new institutional solution'?

The stakes surrounding such choices are much higher now than they were in the 1950s. There are more players—more governments and affected interests, plus the EU's increasingly assertive institutions themselves—making compromises more difficult to strike. The 'permissive consensus' that allowed bold steps forward in European integration without much public attention during most of the history of the EU is now gone. Citizens' sense of loyalty to the EU institutions is generally weak, even if there is a somewhat stronger attachment to 'Europe' as a focus for collective action, especially in foreign policy (see Chapter 13). Weak loyalties cannot be separated from increased institutional complexity. Most average citizens cannot help but be befuddled by the arcane language that has characterised the Treaty changes of the last decade. The idea that the rejection by Irish voters of the Treaty of Nice in the June 2001 referendum was a rare aberration was firmly knocked down in 2005. Much needs to be done before EU citizens truly identify with the institutions of the Union as 'their own'.

This volume has tried to cut through the complexity by approaching each insti-tution in a roughly similar way. Four basic themes have emerged. First, the EU's institutions are intensely and irrevocably interdependent. Regardless of how much they compete for power and influence among themselves, and how divided they are about where the EU is going, they are doomed to succeed or fail together. Second, the capacity of the EU's institutions to continue to provide collective direction for the EU is being increasingly called into question. The prospect of a constant pro-cess of enlargement raises doubts about the ability of the system to generate policies that work. Third, the process of embedding what is 'national' into what is 'European' has become far more complicated than it was when, say, the decision was taken in the 1960s to create a common agricultural policy to replace national agricultural policies. One result is that member governments have experimented with new forms of decision-making, such as the 'Schengen *acquis*' and the 'CFSP *acquis*,' to achieve collective governance. But in doing so they have added to the EU's dizzying com-plexity. Fourth, without discounting the insights that arise from the application of alternative theoretical models, this volume has shown that neoinstitutionalism has a lot to tell us about the EU. In particular, it reveals that an essential first step to understanding the politics of European integration is to understand the EU's often mystifying institutions.

We develop each of these themes below, and conclude by grappling with perhaps the most urgent question facing students of the EU's institutional system: can it be reformed to be made more accountable and more legitimate in the eyes of European citizens? Put another way, can it become a more accepted, respected pivot of political life in Europe, or must it inevitably become a target of the same range of populist doubts, pressures and protests that have affected other international organizations, such as the WTO or IMF? Our essential argument is that, regardless of the answers to these questions, the EU's institutions remain at the vanguard of efforts to legitimise international institutions that have become increasingly powerful regulators of economic and political life globally.

Institutional interdependence

A constant theme of this book has been that none of the institutions of the European Union is free to act autonomously. All are interlinked and interdependent. Every contribution to this volume has focused on the relationship between the institution(s) in question and its EU counterparts. The effect has been to highlight the *collective* responsibility that the Union's institutions assume for EU policies. All components in the EU's institutional system are cogs in a network of mutually reliant actors (see Keohane and Hoffmann 1991: 13–15).

Even bodies that appear to be independent—and are assured a very large measure of independence in their statutes, such as the ECB (see Chapter 9)—need links with the rest of the EU institutional system, and moreover the outside world, to prosper. To deny this need is to invite the opprobrium of other institutional actors and popular disillusion with what the EU does more generally. Witness the damaging (not least to the value of the Euro) and now notorious statement of the ECB President, Wim Duisenberg, to pleas for lower interest rates to spur economic growth in 2001: 'I hear but I do not listen'. The comment met with the ire of (particularly) the EP as well as many beyond Brussels.

In fact, the EU's institutional system virtually *demands* that actors within each institution both hear and listen to actors in the other institutions. Even the ECJ, whose deliberations remain shrouded in secrecy and which fosters an image of distant independence, ultimately depends on the good will of the member states and the readiness of their courts to implement its judgments (see Chapter 7). Whatever talk there may be of the decline of the Commission, it is hard to see how the Council could prosper without a Commission strong enough to make suggestions, broker deals, and sometimes accept criticism for the results. In particular, the need to assert the Union's economic clout internationally is sometimes so clear that EU member governments are essentially obliged to defend the institutional system they have created, warts and all, when its basic authority is questioned. A good example was the quotas agreed on the import into the EU of Chinese textiles after the decades-old international Multi-Fibre Agreement was discontinued at the end of 2004. All EU member governments publicly supported the Commission's attempt to protect against a flood of Chinese imports (or at least did not condemn it) when the quotas were initially agreed, despite the preference of several member states for a more liberal approach. Later the Commission and especially the Trade Commissioner, Peter Mandelson, were blamed by EU governments when the quotas were filled far faster than projected by mid-2005, leaving many European retailers howling that they could not satisfy consumer demand. Yet, it was the governments that had effectively mandated the Commission to negotiate the quotas and were themselves integral parts of the Brussels system that was attacked by most of the European press and public for the chaos of the 'bra war'.

Of course, collective responsibility does not mean that turf-battling is not a primary feature of the EU's institutional system. It is surely one of its most harmful pathologies. At times, the EU's institutions can seem more concerned with expanding their own remits than with ensuring that the EU turns out effective policies. Yet, the Union's institutions also compete for credit for policies (such as the single market) that *do* prove to be effective, thus revealing how the fortunes of the EU's institutions have become more closely linked over time.

Moreover, the EU's institutions have become collectively *accountable* for the work of the Union. Within Council working groups, as Hayes-Renshaw points out (see Chapter 4), as well as in Coreper—as shown by Lewis (see Chapter 14)—national views are merged into an agreed position. Afterwards, national actors are staunchly reluctant to reveal to others the range of views that preceded decision. The Council often collectively and stubbornly defends its common position in co-decision with the EP, even if it has been accepted with difficulty by some member states.[3] But after conciliation produces agreement, it becomes very hard to separate out who was responsible for what. As one of us has argued (see Chapter 6), co-decision has not only become something like the EU's 'template' decision rule. It also has firmly established that most legislative decisions are made more or less collectively by the EU's three main legislative institutions—Commission, Council, and Parliament. All are obliged to defend legislative outcomes in the Court of Justice in the case of a legal challenge. The more general point is that the future of the European project, to create a more prosperous and unified Europe, depends as never before on the ability of the EU's institutions to work together to offer collective governance.

Capacity—decline or renewal?

A second underlying theme of the book has been the emergence of new questions about whether the EU's institutions are up to the job. Even before the Union's membership expanded to twenty-five member states, it had become tempting to ask whether the EU's institutional system had worked about as effectively as it ever *could* in the past, and in a way it never *would* in the future. Even if it once fostered and consolidated international cooperation of a kind unprecedented in modern history, need we accept that it could never work as well again? Are *immobilisme* and decline now inevitable in a radically enlarged EU of twenty-five plus? It is worth reviewing the arguments presented in this volume that give rise to such stark questions.

The leadership problem

This book has highlighted the pluralistic, non-hierarchical character of the EU, and its lack of both government and opposition. No political party or coalition of parties can really claim to govern the Union. There is no Cabinet, no true executive.[4] As de Schoutheete (Chapter 3) argues, the European Council may seem to sit at the top of a pyramid structure, acting as a sort of board of directors. Yet, its capacity to give strong political impulse to the Union's affairs may well be declining.

The EU often seems woefully short on political leadership. Leadership is a contested commodity in the EU, as we can see if we look at the various institutional candidates to provide it: the Commission, the Council Presidency, the European Council, even (to a lesser degree) the EP. The Commission looks more and more like an international bureaucracy and less and less like a proto-government. The Council Presidency can only act within a limited mandate and cannot go further than the other states will let it, as Tony Blair found during the 2005 UK Presidency when he found himself compromising on his liberal economic policy agenda and backing the Commission's proposed 'global adjustment fund' to help workers retrain if they lost their jobs from a corporate restructuring. The European Council only meets occasionally and for the equivalent of less than one working week per year. The EP continues to struggle both to attract the loyalties of European citizens and to offer leadership.

It might be argued that it is up to the EU's member governments, individually or in alliances with one another, to provide political direction. If we take this view, we inevitably end up asking whether past sources of leadership—such as the Franco–German alliance—can be resurrected. Two of the fundamental lessons of this volume help us to frame, if not answer, this question. First, we have seen that powers are now more widely shared, making it more difficult for one member state or any group of them to give political impulses that resonate across the Union's institutional system. Second, strong, decisive action at the EU level requires political agency from multiple sources: a strong Council requires a strong Commission. The evolution of the EU's institutional system casts new doubts about whether the EU of the future can rely on past sources of political leadership.

The management problem

The EU's lack of hierarchy has undoubted benefits. It sustains participation by many parties because the policy agenda seems (in appearance, at least) remarkably open. No one wins all the time, and even losers can often become winners by shifting the agenda towards new policies that are more favourable to them. Ultimately, collective governance is unsustainable in the absence of compromise: we can expect all to be willing to compromise today only if all can hope for better results tomorrow.

Yet, the lack of hierarchy creates problems of management as well as political drift. At earlier stages in its evolution, the EU's business might have been managed relatively effectively by the Hallstein and Delors Commissions, or by its largest and most committed member governments (especially the French and German) when they held the Council Presidency (although many of the most successful Presidencies were run by small states; see Hayes-Renshaw and Wallace 2006). In any case, the reality is now different: no genuine hierarchy of policy goals exists and there is no body or institution able to impose one. It often seems that too many voices must be accommodated, and everyone has a say without anyone being able to get the final word. The American delegation headed by George W. Bush that visited Brussels in early 2005 was reportedly bemused by the approximately seventy different speeches they were subjected to by various EU representatives in the course of only a few days of meetings.

The severity of the management costs arising from the EU's hyperpluralism has been highlighted perceptively by Metcalfe (2000). Put simply, the EU's institutional system—whatever its virtues—is also a recipe for *undermanagement*. Regardless of how high and mighty the European Council looks to the untrained eye, much EU governance occurs in practice within horizontally structured and often highly autonomous and technocratic policy networks which preside over individual policy sectors (see Peterson and Bomberg 1999; Peterson 2004). The EU's main institutions are well represented in most of them (especially since co-decision marked a substantial upgrade in the EP's powers), and inter-institutional politics can be lively: agents of the Commission, EP, and Council can be relied upon to defend their institutions' prerogatives and priorities staunchly.

Yet, responsibility is shared widely both for policy outputs and outcomes. As such, none of the EU's individual institutions have strong incentives to invest in the capacity of policy networks to *manage* the policy agenda—that is, to set priorities, follow up past initiatives, ensure effective implementation, and so on. Moreover, even leaving aside the effects of enlargement, the Union's management problem almost naturally gets worse over time since:

> a combination of factors operating within the EU's institutional framework creates political incentives to take on more tasks while imposing constraints on the acquisition and development of capacities for managing them effectively. In the Council, political decision-makers too readily assume the existence of management capacities and governance structures to implement policies or dodge the difficult issues about who should provide them (Metcalfe 2000: 824).

The wide 'spread' of the roots of the EU's management deficit means that all of the Commission's recent efforts to make itself more organizationally efficient (see Chapters 5 and 8) cannot, by themselves, produce more effective EU governance.

Weak management means poor coordination and a lack of clear priorities. Witness Hayes-Renshaw's (Chapter 4) discussion of the General Affairs Council and its increasing inability to impose direction on or set priorities for EU policy-making. Perhaps some kind of permanent Council of European Affairs Ministers could help close the management deficit. Yet, it remains difficult to imagine EU governments collectively biting the bullet and single-tasking senior, heavyweight cabinet ministers with the job of making the EU work better. They would have to defy a system of incentives that encourages all actors in EU decision-making to focus on winning today's policy argument, as opposed to ensuring that the policy agenda does not become too crowded or that yesterday's decisions are implemented properly. And when they had the opportunity to pursue this idea in the 2003–4 European Convention, and the IGC that followed, they did not take it.

The problem of integrating interests

Until the 1980s, the task of integrating interests was a relatively simple one of integrating the *national* interests of its member states. The then European Community only dealt with narrowly circumscribed areas of policy marked out for collective governance, such as the CAP and external trade. Policy-making was an elite-driven exercise, more or less monopolized by national executives working with the Commission and a very limited range of 'insider' pressure groups. The EP was an assembly of seconded national parliamentarians, with limited power and resources. The Economic and Social Committee was a pseudo-corporatist talking shop. Both were easily ignorable by the Council. The Commission was always less ignorable, and took pains to ingratiate itself with broad socio–economic interests while trying to integrate them into Europe-wide associations. But not until the Delors era did the Commission manage very often to integrate pan-European interests into its work to the point where it was able to 'use' them to challenge the Council or encourage member governments to accept its own policy agenda.

Now, of course, the problem of integrating interests is far more acute. The EU's policy agenda has expanded enormously, and continues to do so. More societal interests both have a stake in EU policy-making and demand a voice in the process. One of us noted in the 1990s that the EU had (at the time) only recently been transformed from 'a system concerned with the *administration of things* to one concerned with the *governance of people*' (Shackleton 1997: 70; emphasis in original). The speed of developments is such that this moment now seems a very long time ago. The EU has become a far more important purveyor of public goods. Yet, the Union has made far fewer and shorter strides towards integrating societal interests compared to the steps it has taken to subject policies to collective governance.

Two caveats must be offered here. First, as we have seen, the EU system does a remarkably proficient job of integrating the *institutional* interests of its main institutional players. No important EU policy can be agreed—outside of very few sectors such as competition or agriculture—without a very large measure of consensus spanning the institutions. Even the EU's more recent or planned institutions, which privilege national interests and are overwhelmingly staffed by national officials, provide the central institutions with channels for input. A good example is The Hague Programme on justice and home affairs (JHA), and its plans to bring together both national foreign affairs and JHA officials to assess terrorist threats from particular countries, but with annual assessments of whether liaison on counter-terrorism with foreign governments is effective to be carried out by the Commission.[5] Collective institutional responsibility for EU policy, a central goal of any effective system of collective governance, is something the EU does rather well.

Second, the EU has become increasingly innovative in the task of integrating different *sectoral* interests. One of the central features of the shift to so-called 'post-sovereign' political structures in response to globalization is the 'sectoral unbundling of territoriality in various functional regimes' (Ruggie 1998: 27); that is, the emergence of various kinds of policy-specialized transgovernmental networks, populated by actors who have more in common with each other than with officials who specialize in *other* policy areas in their own nation-states. The implication for the EU is that it now must aggregate and adjudicate between a far wider diversity of more differentially concerned 'national interests' than was the case for most of its history. On this test, the EU again scores quite well. Lewis (Chapter 14) portrays Coreper as a remarkably effective integrator of the interests of increasingly divided and less single-minded national civil services. Coreper is widely viewed as an effective broker of 'political' and 'technical' interests, although (as is the case with all EU institutions) its ability to continue to work so well following enlargement is less clear. Meanwhile, Majone (Chapter 10) argues that the growing popularity of strong, independent agencies offers a potential mechanism for the effective integration of functional interests in an era of 'sectoral unbundling'.

At the same time, Part III of this volume also contains plenty of proof of the EU's failure to integrate many wider societal interests very effectively. Raunio (Chapter 15) starkly suggests that pan-European party groups in the EP are very far from commanding the loyalty and support of European citizens, who in large part do not understand the influence the groups can have on EU policies. Jeffery (Chapter 16) strains to conclude that Ecosoc is even worth having. At best, the Committee of the Regions is one of a number of channels open for regional interests to make their mark, and by no means obviously the most important one.

The problem of the EU's limited capacity to integrate societal interests can easily be overstated. Those who view it as a major pathology of the Union sometimes neglect the essential distinction between input and output legitimacy (see, for example, McNamara's Chapter 9 on the ECB). Input legitimacy comes from ensuring that a large number of voices are heard in the policy process; output legitimacy comes from ensuring that policies work, in the sense of bringing the greatest good to the greatest number of citizens. If the EU manages to produce policies that work, then it may not matter that much *how* they are made (see Scharpf 1999). Advocates of this view contend that however much the EU's policy remit has expanded, its competences remain tiny compared to those of its member states. What is less often stated, although clearly implied by such arguments, is that integrating more interests into EU policy-making could well be counter-productive to the goal of producing effective policies, since the Union is already so fundamentally reliant on compromise.

The prospects for renewal

Reform of the EU's institutional system to address problems of leadership, management and representation is likely to remain on the Union's agenda, in spite of (or perhaps because of) the deadlock over the Constitutional Treaty. Even the UK, one of the least enthusiastic states for pressing ahead with ratification after the French and Dutch no votes, publicly conceded during its 2005 Presidency that the Constitutional Treaty remained 'formally on the table'.[6] Regardless of its formal fate, the Constitutional Treaty's provisions may well foreshadow what the EU's institutions end up looking like in the long term.

The near-term prospects for institutional reform look bleak. Still, there are good reasons to believe that European integration is not permanently stalled, the EU is not moribund, and that its institutions are not doomed to atrophy. One reason is the EU's proven capacity for improvisation (see Peterson and Bomberg 2001: 58–9). Traditionally, only when faced with a crisis has the Union been able to innovate.

Another good reason is the wide variety of new methods for embedding the 'national in the European' that have been embraced, some quite successfully, since the late 1990s. Most have eschewed the traditional Community method of decision-making and thus circumscribed the powers of the Commission, EP, and others in new areas of policy-making, much to the chagrin of admirers of that method. But these methods at least have signalled that EU member governments remain willing to extend collective governance to the point of institutionalizing new policy cooperation, even if new institutions are often strange and awkward creatures. The section that follows confronts these new methods of policy coordination and assesses their implications for the EU's institutional system.

Embedding the national in the European

One of the central themes of this book is how much more varied and complex the institutionalization of collective governance has become in Europe over time. The eclecticism of recent responses to demands for the extension of collective governance is striking. Take, for example, the arrangements for enforcing the Stability and Growth Pact (Chapter 9), the 'dirty Communitarization' of justice and home affairs policy (Chapter 12), the 'Lisbon process' for the pursuit of economic reform (Chapter 5), or the mounting of a European Security and Defence Policy (Chapter 13). Of course, we must not blithely lump together these and other non-traditional modes of collective governance, as significant differences exist between them (see H. Wallace 2005). Yet, what most have in common is that they preserve a role for individual member states which is stronger and less challengeable by the EU's institutions than is the case under the 'Community method' of decision-making (applied when policy is truly Communitarized, and according to which the Commission—exclusively—proposes, the EP and Council amend and dispose).

In retrospect, we can see that the Community method, in its pure form, has been under threat since the early 1990s (see Devuyst 2005). Moreover, there is nothing new about the EU being used for narrow and ostensibly 'national' purposes 'to extend the policy resources available to the member states' (H. Wallace 2005: 77). But the increasingly frequent institutionalization of collective governance in ways that preserve national prerogatives and priorities more explicitly has been a spur to a burgeoning new literature on 'Europeanization' (see Goetz and Hix 2000; Featherstone and Radaelli 2003; Börzel 2005; Bulmer and Lequesne 2005; Wong 2005). Contributors to this literature have struggled to come up with a definition of Europeanization (much as institutionalists strain to define 'institution'[7]) that is broad enough to convey the eclecticism of the process yet specific enough to be meaningful. Ladrech (1994: 69) does as good a job as any, defining Europeanization as a 'process reorienting the direction and shape of politics to the degree that E[U] political and economic dynamics become part of the organizational logic of national politics and policy-making'.

The point for any student of the EU's institutions is simple. To privilege or preserve national practices and goals when reorienting national policy processes to the European level—especially in sensitive areas such as policing, defence, and fiscal policy—could be viewed less as a *barrier* to the success of the EU than an essential *precondition* of its success. Here, we come to grips with the relationship between the new, post-Maastricht politics of European integration and the recent institutionaliz-ation of new forms of policy cooperation. In an abstract sense (as well as, we suspect, an empirical one), it would be difficult to imagine cases in which any set of demo-cratically elected governments would choose to transfer powers, in a straight and linear way, from themselves to an international organization during a period when the secular trend is towards declining public support for the latter. As such, it should not surprise us that we have not witnessed a straightforward communitarization of newly 'Europeanized' policy areas, such as the ESDP, justice and home affairs, or em-ployment policy. What is perhaps more surprising is that the trend towards *more* collective governance in Europe—albeit via methods that were unfamiliar until re-cently—has been effectively unbroken despite the disappearance of the 'permissive consensus'. Understanding why EU member governments have chosen to embed the national in the European in such a dizzyingly diverse number of ways starts with acknowledging that unless European governments can see their own practices and goals in some way reflected in Brussels policy-making, and can convince their cit-izens that this 'reflection' is genuine, they are unlikely to accept new shifts of com-petence to Brussels.

The power of the general imperative to retain national levers of control even as new policies are Europeanized is abundant in this volume. Perhaps the prime illu-stration is the increasingly ubiquitous role of the European Council in the full range of what the EU does, even if de Schoutheete's (Chapter 3) analysis casts doubt as to how much it really controls (or even effectively monitors). Another is the debate about the role of national parliaments in EU decision-making, which refuses to go away. To these could be added the way that Coreper has retained such an essential role at the interface between what is Europeanized and what is Communitarized, and incidentally has gone from being a collection of 'bad guys' to one of 'good guys' in the eyes of those who are most enthusiastic about European integration. Even the most ardent of European federalists realize that sustaining the project requires em-bedding the national in the European, because replacing the former with the latter simply does not happen any more.

Even where Europeanization has, over time, produced genuine Communitariza-tion, levers for national influence have been retained and guarded very jealously. Monetary policy, as McNamara (Chapter 9) shows, is one such area. There is now a single currency but the structures of the ECB reflect the imperative to preserve chan-nels for national influence, and even some measure of control for national central banks. Even the development of Community law reveals a similar pattern. It can be argued that the EU has achieved such strength as a legal system *only* because national courts are so intimately involved in interpreting and enforcing EU law, and because no democratic state can resist the injunctions of its own courts (see Weiler 1999).

Analytically, some suggest that 'Europeanisation' has become an alternative to 'Communitarization' as a response to pressures for collective governance (see Laffan *et al.* 2000: 84–90). According to this view, European integration no longer has any clear teleology (if it ever had one at all). The EU is likely to become an increasingly complex, differentiated, and polycentric institutional system over time.

Others portray Europeanization as a step on the path towards Communitariza-tion, as in the cases of JHA, environmental, and research policies. Advocates of this view argue that the emergence of new methods of embedding the national in the European does not imply that European integration has lost its purpose in institutional terms. They predict that 'the basic EU/EC set-up will remain and evolve as the major channel for dealing with an increasing number of public policies .... [because] no real alternative is available' (Wessels 2001: 215).

We cannot predict with any certainty where the EU is headed in institutional terms. But it is clear that the EU has reached a crossroads in its institutional development (see Devuyst 2005). We hope that this volume helps its readers to make up their own mind about whether Europeanization is replacing Communitarization, or merely signalling the inevitability of the latter over time.

EU institutions and the new institutionalism

If this book has grappled with one theoretical question above all others, it is: do institutions matter? In line with the teachings of the new institutionalist literature, we have seen that institutions—how they are constructed, how they work, and how they interact—are a powerful determinant of EU politics. A close reading of this volume yields one heuristic point above all others: the process of collective governance in Europe cannot be understood without intimate knowledge of the EU's institutions, and how they work both individually and together as a system. Moreover, the main themes that emerge from a careful scan across the full landscape of the EU's institutions are all, we would submit, central to the study of the EU more generally. They include:

- the considerable scope for institutional *agency* in EU politics, which inevitably makes inter-institutional competition a primary feature of EU policy-making. We have seen that new mechanisms, such as trialogues and inter-institutional agreements, have had to be constructed to channel and control conflict between the EU's institutions. In one sense, fiercer inter-institutional competition is the product of the empowerment of the Commission and the EP after the 1980s (and the Court before and after that) to the point where the Council can agree relatively little of importance without the consent of one or the other or both. As such, the main cleavages in EU policy debates have become as much inter-institutional as intergovernmental;

- the EU's institutional system generates *multiple identities*, the importance of which cannot be discounted in EU policy debates. Virtually all actors in EU policy-making must balance or at least reconcile different identities. Consider a few random, imagined examples. What motivates a Socialist minister from the Spanish Foreign Office who hails from Catalonia when the Council debates a move to centralise decision-making on the structural funds? What advice does an German *cabinet* official give to her Commissioner (for monetary policy) on a proposal to reprimand the German government for breaching the Stability and Growth Pact targets for budget deficit, and which incidentally sets a precedent for rapping future *coupables* on the knuckles? Recent attempts to develop accounts of EU policy-making which draw on constructivist theory and ascribe causal importance to questions of identity, have met with some (modest) success (see Christiansen *et al.* 2001; Jupille *et al.* 2003; Pollack 2005; Sedelmeier 2005). Such accounts leave open the question of which out of various multiple identities motivates key actors in the policy process at any given time and insist that identities, and thus interests, are 'constructed' as part of the process of repeated interactions between actors in Brussels. Regardless of how accurately (or not) they portray the EU policy process, there is no doubting that the EU's institutions are a crucial, additional source of identity—along with nationality, party affiliation, and so on—for actors in EU policy-making, who often go to considerable lengths to defend the prerogatives and dignity of 'their' institution in policy debates. One upshot is that the Council (in all of its forms) is a far from purely intergovernmental institution, *and* there exists plenty of scope for the defence of national interests within the Union's ostensibly 'supranational' institutions;

- *path dependence* is so powerful in the EU's institutional system as to make it hard not to be rather pessimistic about the system's ability to cope with the Union's enlargement. The EU's institutions—and, equally if not more so, their national counterparts—often resemble generals meticulously prepared to fight the last war (see Peters 1999: 40). Witness the tendency of the Economic and Social Committee (see Chapter 16) to defend a corporatist model of state–society relations that was never accepted across Europe even in its heyday. Or take the (initial, at least) resistance of national justice and home affairs ministries (see Chapter 12) to the obvious need to Europeanize cooperation in JHA policy. Path dependency is especially acute in a system that remains quite 'young' and thus relies heavily on past precedents, political and above all legal, to define the scope for future action. More generally, the EU provides plenty of grist for the institutionalist mill in the way it has embraced the values of openness, transparency and democratic accountability only slowly and often reluctantly. This volume has uncovered much to validate the basic institutionalist assumption that 'an inconsistency in cultures is likely to develop across time as an institution recreates an internal value system that is incompatible with a changed environment' (Peters 1999: 40);

- a crucial implication of the strength of path dependence in the EU is that *principal–agent relationships* are often troubled and contested, with inevitable policy costs. Majone (Chapter 10) shows how member states have been unwilling to give new European agencies the degree of autonomy necessary to enable the system to prosper, not least because they remain stuck with a doctrine that severely circumscribes the autonomy of European regulatory bodies from the Commission. As Majone suggests, the burgeoning of new European agencies might be taken as evidence that both the Commission and EU member governments are slowly coming to grips with the mismatch between regulatory needs and old, anachronistic doctrines about delegating powers. But it remains possible to cite a lengthy list of policy areas—food safety, JHA policy, financial control and the CFSP among them—where half-hearted or disorderly delegation from member states to the EU's institutions (principals to agents) has produced confused and/or ineffective policy.

This survey of the EU's institutions, like the new institutionalist literature itself, might seem to paint a generally sombre, downbeat, pessimistic picture of modern politics. Prominent themes include inertia, pathology, inconsistency, turf battles, and so on. Yet, as is suggested by work that applies institutionalist theory to international organizations (see Keohane 1998; Peters 1999: 126–40; Ikenberry 2001), it is possible to view international institutions—including those of the European Union—as *the* leading purveyors of innovative solutions to the problems of modern governance. While they may be trapped by path dependency in important respects, the EU's institutions are usually better able than European governments to develop, embrace and promote long-term solutions to problems such as global warming or the fostering of civil society in Central Asia. It is in the nature of politics that governments, whose calculations are governed by four-to five-year electoral cycles, have great difficulty in thinking beyond short-term time horizons and investing in policies which will only pay off long after the next election. To illustrate the point, it is difficult to imagine that there would have been a Kyoto agreement if the EU had not acted together to make the necessary deals required with states such as Japan, Canada and Russia that were reluctant to act without the United States.

Moreover, an important insight of the institutionalist literature is that different institutional traditions in different polities reflect the values held most dear by the societies in question. In the continental (west) European tradition, which remains the basic *leitmotiv* for the EU, an abiding principle is that 'the State is linked organically with society and society is significantly influenced by the nature of the State' (Peters 1999: 6). Whatever the inadequacies of the EU's institutions, which are often laid bare by the application of institutionalist theory, this principle offers at least a set of aspirations to guide institutional reform. One hopes that it also motivates governments to think about how the relationship between the EU and its citizens can be made more organic.

Conclusion

If there is one single burning question that arises from studying the EU's institutions, it is the vexed one of accountability: how can the Union's institutions, in the absence of a truly European polity, become more accountable to European citizens and thus a more legitimate level of governance? In our view, it is difficult to imagine that the problem can be solved simply with a dose of 'direct democracy', such as by instituting the direct election of the President of the Commission, empowering national parliaments in EU decision-making, or spending more to foster truly pan-European political parties. It might be rather easier to envisage the future election of governments able and willing to do a better job of selling the EU's institutions to average citizens as both necessary and competent agents in the tasks of governing Europe and defending its interests in a new, modern, and increasingly globalized world. So far, however, the post-Kohl and Mitterrand generation has shown little inclination to invest in the building of Europe. It is difficult to think of any occasion in the twenty-first century when any large state European government has taken even the slightest domestic political risk to defend the EU.

The EU's accountability problem might be seen as a conundrum. Member governments accept the need to pool sovereignty at the EU level to achieve collective governance. But they refuse to create clear, straight, simple lines of accountability of the sort that allow citizens in democratic systems to throw out a government they themselves have elected and substitute an opposition (see Peterson 1997). It is a conundrum that could lead to the conclusion that the EU's institutional system is on the verge of breakdown, given enlargement to include generally poorer states whose citizens are hungry for rapid economic development, combined with declining enthusiasm for the EU in Europe's older democracies. Incredibly, for many Europeans, at this fragile moment in the EU's development the Union has even committed itself to the eventual membership of Turkey, which contributed to large numbers of French and Dutch voters rejecting the Constitutional Treaty (even if it itself had no link to Turkish accession). Little-noticed amid all the political angst about Turkey was the view, made plain in a leading article in a leading EU-dedicated newspaper, that:

> Institutionally, the EU is not prepared to digest Turkey's entry—and not just because there is no approved scheme to squeeze more members of the European Parliament into the hemicycle or more ministers round the Council table … The EU's institutions are likely to be bypassed by member states if they fear that their political interests are not well defended in a Union where Turkey wields such power.[8]

The collective action problems of all successful international organizations (IOs) grow as their membership increases. But no IO is as powerful as the EU and thus none faces such demands for accountability according to democratic standards. The problem of 'scaling up' democracy to suit a more integrated and globalized world is by no means unique to Europe. Rather, the problem of subjecting global governance to democratic controls is one of the most vexing problems facing governments everywhere. Robert Dahl (1994), a shrewd student of democracy, has posed the problem as an essentially generic one. To simplify only slightly, the closer that governments work to the citizen, the more they must respond to the needs and preferences of average people. However, small-scale governments cannot hope to cope with problems such as international terrorism, nuclear proliferation, or humanitarian tragedies that are only solvable—if they are solvable at all—through the collective efforts of states working through international organizations. Above all, the problem of governing the global economy in a political world where the overwhelming majority of governments believe in the virtues of open commerce requires global rules and adjudication of conflicting interests. In this context, the European Union may be seen as an essential, driving force behind the freeing of international trade, however much it frustrates its trading partners with its tendency to back-slide towards protectionism, but also a staunch defender of values that are easily trammelled by free trade, such as environmental protection or core labour standards. The European economy could be seen as a prototype for the global economy of the future, in which the main factors of production become basically borderless, but remain subject to supranational regulation.

Taking the analogy further, the EU's institutions could be viewed as prototypes for global institutions that might one day govern something like a 'single' global market. It is easy to stretch this analogy too far, and to be seduced by the same naïve,

Wilsonian vision of world government that was widely embraced in the inter-war period, only to be exposed by realist international relations theorists in the 1950s as intellectually bankrupt. Yet, it was precisely then that the EU embarked on its extraordinary mission of institution-building in the pursuit of collective governance. One long-term effect, certainly foreseen by *none* of the EU's founding fathers, has been to mark out the EU's institutions as models suitable for emulation by other IOs that need to be made more accountable and subject to democratic controls. The view of Keohane (1998), perhaps the most influential of all international relations scholars, is that the task of democratizing IOs is not that much more challenging than was the task of creating and institutionalising democracy at the domestic level during the passing of the era of the 'divine right of kings' in the seventeenth and eighteenth centuries. This view might be dismissed as overly naïive (and peculiarly American), but its existence shows us both that there is much about the EU's institutional system that is admired internationally, *and* that the Union's democratic conundrum reflects wider problems of democratizing global governance.

Meanwhile, there exists no consensus about the severity of the democratic deficit (see Moravcsik 2003). When compared to other IOs, the EU even appears to be a relatively 'democratic' one. It over-represents its smaller member states in a way that, say, the United Nations or WTO never could. It does not discriminate against poorer states, as the IMF is frequently accused of doing. All of its constituent political units, at least for now, are entitled to representation in the college of Commissioners in a way that, say, the individual American states are not in the US Cabinet. Maybe its most distinguishing feature is that it is subject to increasingly close and powerful scrutiny by the world's only democratically elected multinational parliament.

In this context, it is worth recalling the view of the so-called 'new governance' perspective (see Majone 1996, 2005; Eberlein and Kerwer 2004). According to this view, the EU's democratic deficit is overblown by its critics, who fail both to recognize that the Union's competence is relatively narrow compared to that of its member states, *and* that the EU's core tasks of regulating economic activity are rarely subject to majoritarian democratic controls in national polities. Some of the collective goods provided by the EU—free trade, fair competition, healthy food, a stable currency—could not be provided without insulating policy-makers from short-term political pressures (see also Moravcsik 2003). The EU's *real* problem, according to Majone (2005), is that 'integration by stealth' has produced sub-optimal policies and thus the EU's institutions have suffered a loss of legitimacy.

Even if we conclude that the new governance school is too complacent about the democratic deficit, there is at least some evidence to suggest that the problem of fragmented accountability alongside collective responsibility is beginning to be tackled by new and creative solutions. One is to subject all EU institutions to standard sets of rules or procedures, or scrutiny by agents who are both 'dedicated' to a single task but responsible for applying it across the entire EU institutional system. A good example is the European Ombudsman, who has figured little in this book but has begun to appear as an important figure in forcing the institutions to march to the sound of a single drum on a range of issues of (mal)administration.[9] Or, as Laffan (Chapter 11) suggests, the empowerment of the Court of Auditors, and the creation of OLAF could be taken as evidence that, from a rather modest beginning, the EU has adopted a much tighter and uniform regime of financial control in recent years.

None of this is to deny that the EU's institutions do not suffer from severe problems of the same kind that plague IOs generally. Especially given the EU's enlargement to twenty-five and soon twenty-seven members or more, the Union's institutions often appear ill suited to the modern tasks of European governance and more likely to stifle innovation than to encourage it. There is a clear need for analysts of the EU's institutions to embrace more sophisticated normative thinking about how the Union's institutional system could work better.

However, there is another side to the ledger. As we have seen, the EU's institutions—regardless of their problems, both collective and individual—often facilitate collective governance on divisive issues such as migration, market liberalization, and the EU's relations with its near abroad in a way that is often just short of miraculous. When the EU's institutions work well together, the Union's policy process takes on a sort of idiosyncratic charm, much like good jazz music, blending European traditions, languages, and experiences. We cannot tell yet, but it may happen far less often in an enlarged EU than it did in the past. Still, historically it has happened often enough to ensure that (so far, anyway) the European Union remains the champion of those who wish and hope for more and more effective collective governance internationally.

Notes

1 Andrew Duff MEP, quoted in *Euractiv*, 'MEPs criticise Barroso's lack of leadership on the Constitution', 18 October 2005, available on *http://www.euractiv.com*

2 Quoted in BBC News World Edition, 'EU admits Constitution on ice', 21 September 2005, available on *http://news.bbc.co.uk/2/hi/europe/4268094.stm*

3 The importance of this rule in the Council was underlined in the Spring of 2001 when Germany withdrew its support from the common position that had been agreed unanimously one year earlier on the Takeovers Directive. This was the first time in the history of the EU that a member state had acted in this way and the incident caused enormous consternation, particularly when the European Parliament rejected the Directive in July 2001. One member state had been able to overcome the opposition of the (then) other fourteen.

4 As Weiler has argued tirelessly, the tiny share of EU policy for which the Commission is responsible for implementing, and the almost as small percentage of the EU budget which it spends, means that is far from being a true 'executive'. According to this view, the Council has more right to be termed the executive of the Union than does the Commission (Weiler 1999; see also Metcalfe 2000: 825).

5 See 'The Hague Programme: Ten Priorities for the Next Five Years', available on *http://europa.eu.int/comm/justice_home/news/information_dossiers/the_hague_priorities/index_en.htm*. See also *European Voice*, 13–19 October 2005, pp. 18–19.

6 Address by John Grant, UK Ambassador to the EU, 'The UK EU Council Presidency', University of Edinburgh, 20 October 2005.

7 Note, for example, that almost every chapter in Peters' (1999) survey of

different variants of institutionalism includes a section entitled 'what is an institution?', and manages to limit rational choice theorists alone to no less than four different, alternative definitions! (Peters 1999: 53).

8 See 'Dual Challenge of Turkey's Entry Effort', *European Voice*, 6–12 October 2005, p. 8.

9 The Ombudsman has assumed extensive powers under Art. 195 TEC to examine cases of maladministration, and more generally, has felt free to criticize the way in which the institutions operate. The institutions have in turn felt obliged to respond and to improve their working methods, such as recruitment procedures or the response to requests for information from the general public.

References

Allen, D. (1998), 'Who speaks for Europe?', in J. Peterson and H. Sjursen (eds.), *A Common Foreign Policy for Europe* (London: Routledge).

Allen, D. (2000), *The Common Foreign and Security Policy of the European Union* (New York: Addison-Wesley).

Allison, G. T., and Zelikow, P. (1999), *Essence of Decision: Explaining the Cuban Missile Crisis*, 2nd edn. (London: Longman).

Alter, K. (2001), *Establishing the Supremacy of European Law* (Oxford and New York: Oxford University Press).

Alter, K., and Meunier-Aitsahalia, S. (1994), 'Who are the Masters of the Treaty? European Governments and the European Court of Justice', *International Organization*, 52/1: 121–4.

Anderson, J. (1997), 'Hard Interests, Soft Power, and Germany's Changing Role in Europe', in P. J. Katzenstein (ed.), *Tame Power: Germany in Europe* (Ithaca: Cornell University Press), 80–107.

Anderson, J. (1999), *German Unification and the Union of Europe: The Domestic Politics of Integration Policy* (Oxford: Oxford University Press).

Armstrong, K., and Bulmer, S. (1998), *The Governance of the Single European Market* (Manchester: Manchester University Press).

Arnull, A. (1999), *The European Union and its Court of Justice* (Oxford: Oxford University Press).

Arnull, A. (2006), *The European Union and its Court of Justice*, 2nd edn. (Oxford: Oxford University Press).

Attinà, F. (1990), 'The voting behaviour of the European Parliament members and the problem of the Europarties', *European Journal of Political Research*, 18/4: 557–79.

Baldwin, R., and McCrudden, C. (1987), *Regulation and Public Law* (London: Weidenfeld & Nicolson).

Bardi, L. (1994), 'Transnational Party Federations, European Parliamentary Party Groups, and the Building of Europarties', in R. S. Katz and P. Mair (eds.), *How Parties Organize: Change and Adaptation in Western Democracies* (London: Sage), 357–72.

Bardi, L. (2002), 'Parties and Party Systems in the European Union', in K. R. Luther, and F. Müller-Rommel (eds.), *Political Parties in the New Europe: Political and Analytical Challenges* (Oxford: Oxford University Press), 293–321.

Barnett, M. A., and Finnemore, M. (1999), 'The Politics, Power and Pathologies of International Organizations', *International Organization*, 53/4: 699–732.

Barrett, G. (1997) (ed.), *Justice Cooperation in the European Union* (Dublin: Institute of European Affairs).

Bauer, M. W. (2002), 'Reforming the European Commission: a (Missed?) Academic Opportunity', *European Integration Online Papers*, 6/18, available on *http://eiop.or.at/eiop/texte/2002–008.htm*

Berman, S., and McNamara, K. R. (1999), 'Bank on Democracy: Why Central Banks Need Public Oversight', *Foreign Affairs*, 78 (March/April) : 2–8.

Bertelsmann, Stiftung (2002), 'Zivilgesellschaft und Konvent. Wege zur Stärkung der öffentlichen Resonanz', *Konvent-Spotlight*, 06/2002.

Better Regulation Task Force (2004), *Make it Simple, Make it Better: Simplifying EU Law*, available on *http://www.brtf.gov.uk/*

Bieber, R., and Monar, J. (1995) (eds.), *Justice and Home Affairs in the European Union: The Development of the Third Pillar* (Brussels: European Interuniversity Press).

Bieber, R., Dehousse, R., Pinder, J., and Weiler, J. H. H. (1988) (eds.), *1992: One European Market? — A Critical Analysis of the Commission's Internal Market Strategy* (Baden-Baden: Nomos).

Bigo, D., and Leveau, R. (1992), *L'Europe de la Sécurité Intérieure* (Paris: Institute des Hautes Etudes de Sécurité Intérieure).

Bildt, C. (1998), *Peace Journey: the Struggle for Peace in Bosnia* (London: Weidenfeld & Nicolson).

Biscop, S. (2005), *The European Security Strategy: A Global Agenda for Positive Power* (Aldershot: Ashgate).

Blanke, H.-J. (2002), *Der Ausschuss der Regionen. Normative Ausgestaltung, politische Rolle und verwaltungstechnische Infrastruktur* (Tübingen: EZFF).

Borràs, S., and Jacobsson, K. (2004), 'The Open Method of Coordination and new governance patterns in the EU', *Journal of European Public Policy*, 11/2: 185–208.

Börzel, T. A. (2005a), 'The Disparity of European Integration: Revisiting Neofunctionalism in Honour of Ernst Haas', *Journal of European Public Policy*, 12/2: 217–36.

Börzel, T. A. (2005b), 'Europeanization: How the European Union Interacts with its Member States', in S. Bulmer and C. Lequesne (eds.), *The Member States of the European Union* (Oxford and New York: Oxford University Press).*

Bostock, D. (2002), 'Coreper Revisited', *Journal of Common Market Studies*, 40/2: 215–34.

Bowler, S., and Farrell, D. M. (1995), 'The Organizing of the European Parliament: Committees, Specialisation and Co-ordination', *British Journal of Political Science*, 25/2: 219–43.

Bowler, S., Farrell, D. M., and Katz, R. S. (1999), 'Party Cohesion, Party Discipline, and Parliaments', in S. Bowler, D. M. Farrell and R. S. Katz (eds.), *Party Discipline and Parliamentary Government* (Columbus: Ohio State University Press).

Brittan, L. (2000), *A Diet of Brussels: the Changing Face of Europe* (London: Little, Brown and Company).

Brüske, E. (1982), 'Der Wirtschafts- und Sozialausschuss', in W. Weidenfeld and W. Wessels (eds.), *Jahrbuch der Europäischen Integration 1981* (Bonn: Europa Union Verlag), 107–19.

Brüske, E. (1983), 'Der Wirtschafts - und Sozialausschuss', in W. Weidenfeld and W. Wessels (eds.), *Jahrbuch der Europäischen Integration 1982* (Bonn: Europa Union Verlag), 91–7.

Brüske, E. (1994), 'Wirtschafts - und Sozialausschuss', in W. Weidenfeld and W. Wessels (eds.), *Europa von A–Z* (Bonn: Bundeszentrale für politische Bildung), 343–45.

Buiter, Willem H. (1999), 'Alice in Euroland', *Journal of Common Market Studies*, 37/2: 181–209.

Bulmer, S. (1994), 'The Governance of the European Union: a New Institutionalist Approach', *Journal of Public Policy*, 13/1: 351–80.

Bulmer, S., and Lequesne, C. (2005) (eds.), *The Member States of the European Union* (Oxford and New York: Oxford University Press).

Bulmer, S., and Wessels, W. (1987), *The European Council* (London: Macmillan).

Bunyan, T. (1991), 'Towards an authoritarian European state', *Race and Class*, 32(3): 179–88.

Burley, A.-M., and Mattli, W. (1993), 'Europe Before the Court: A Political Theory of Legal Integration', *International Organization*, 47/1, Winter: 41–76.

Busch, P., and Puchala, D. (1976), 'Interests, Influence, and Integration: Political Structure in the European Communities', *Comparative Political Studies*, 9/3: 235–54.

Butler, M. (1986), *Europe: More Than a Continent* (London: William Heinemann).

Cain, B. E. (2000), 'Is The Democratic Deficit A Deficiency?: The Case Of Immigration Policy In The US And EU', available on http://www.igs.berkeley.edu/reports/democraticDeficit.html

Cameron, D. (1998), 'EMU After 1999: the Implications and Dilemmas of the Third Stage', Columbia Journal of International Law, 4, Spring: 425–46.

Cameron, F. (2005), 'Making the EU a Global Actor', European Voice, 1–7 September: 16.

Campbell, J. (1983), Roy Jenkins: a Biography (London: Weidenfeld & Nicolson).

Cappelletti, M. (1987), 'Is the European Court Running Wild?', European Law Review, 12/1: 3–17.

Carlsnaes, W., Sjursen, H., and White, B. (2004) (eds.), Contemporary European Foreign Policy (London and Thousand Oaks, CA: Sage).

Checkel, J. (1999), 'Social construction and integration', Journal of European Public Policy, 6/4: 545–60.

Christiansen, T. (1997), 'The Committee of the Regions at the 1996 IGC Conference: Institutional Reform', Regional and Federal Studies, 7/1: 50–69.

Christiansen, T., Jørgensen, K. E., and Wiener, A. (2001) (eds.), The Social Construction of Europe (London and Thousand Oaks, CA: Sage).

Cini, M. (1996), The European Commission: Leadership, Organisation and Culture in the EU Administration (Manchester: Manchester University Press).

Citrin, J., and Sides, J. (2004), 'Can There be Europe without Europeans? Problems of Identity in a Multinational Community', in R. Herrmann, M. Brewer and T. Risse (eds.), Transnational Identities: Becoming European in the EU (Lanham, MD: Rowman and Littlefield), 161–85.

Clark, W. K. (2001), Waging Modern War (New York: Public Affairs).

Clegg, N., and van Hulten, M. (2003), Reforming the European Parliament (London: Foreign Policy Centre).

Cockfield, A. (1994), The European Union: Creating the Single Market (Chichester: Chancery Law Publishing).

Cohen, Benjamin J. (1998), The Geography of Money (Ithaca: Cornell University Press).

Commission (1994), Press Release, 39/94, 21/11/1994.

Commission (1998), Area of Freedom, Security and Justice—Action Plan, COM (1998) 459.3.

Commission (2000), Reforming the Commission: A White Paper, 1 March, available on http://europa.eu.int/comm/off/white/index_en.htm

Commission (2001), European Governance (Luxembourg: Office for Official Publications of the European Communities).

Commission (2002a), Reforming the Commission: Recruitment of Senior Managers to the Commission Staff, available on http://europa.eu.int/comm/reform/2002/selection/index_en.html

Commission (2002b), Reforming the Commission: Other Commission Staff, available on http://europa.eu.int/comm/reform/2002/chapter04_en.htm

Commission (2002c), The Operating Framework for the European Regulatory Agencies (Brussels), COM (2002) 718 final.

Commission (2004), Reforming the Commission: Reform of Europe's Public Services, available on http://europa.eu.int/comm/reform/index_en.htm

Commission (2005), Staff Regulations of Officials of the European Communities. Conditions of Employment of Others Servants of the European Communities. Consolidated version of 1/1/2005 based on 'The Staff Regulations of officials and the conditions of employment of other servants of the European Communities applicable from 5 March 1968, as laid down by Articles 2 and 3 of Council Regulation' (EEC, Euratom, ECSC) No 259/68 of 29 February 1968 (Official Journal of the European Communities L 56, 4.3.1968—Special Edition 1968, 1 December

1972), and subsequent 98 Regulations amending that Regulation. I-124pp + II-40pp, available on *http://europa.eu.int/comm/dgs/personnel_administration/statut/tocen100.pdf*

Committee of Independent Experts (1999a), *First Report on Allegations Regarding Fraud, Mismanagement and Nepotism in the European Commission*, Brussels: European Parliament, 15/3/1999.

Committee of Independent Experts (1999b), *Second Report on Reform of the Commission: Analysis of Current Practice and Proposals for Tackling Mismanagement, Irregularities and Fraud*, 2 vols. (Brussels: European Parliament), 10/9/1999.

Committee for the Study of Economic and Monetary Union (1989), *Report on Economic and Monetary Union in the European Community* (Brussels: European Community).

Coombes, D. (1970), *Politics and Bureaucracy in the European Community: A Portrait of the Commission of the EEC* (London: Allen & Unwin).

Cooper, R. (2004), 'Hard Power, Soft Power and the Goals of Diplomacy', in D. Held and M. Koenig-Archibugi (eds.), *American Power in the 21st Century* (Oxford: Polity).

Corbett, R. (1993), *The Treaty of Maastricht* (Harlow: Longman).

Corbett, R. (1998), *The European Parliament's Role in Closer Integration* (Basingstoke: Palgrave).

Corbett, R., Jacobs, F., and Shackleton, M. (2000), *The European Parliament*, 4th edn. (London: John Harper).

Corbett, R., Jacobs, F., and Shackleton, M. (2005), *The European Parliament*, 6th edn. (London: John Harper).

Cornish, P. (2004), 'NATO: the practice and politics of transformation', *International Affairs*, 80/1: 63–74.

Costa, O. (2001), *Le Parlement européen, assemblée délibérante* (Brussels: Editions de l'Université de Bruxelles).

Costa, O., and Magnette, P. (2003), 'Idéologies et changement institutionnel dans l'Union Européenne. Pourquoi les Gouvernements ont-ils constamment renforcé le Parlement européen', *Politique européenne*, no.9, hiver 2003: 49–75.

Council and European Commission (1998), *Action Plan on how best to implement the provisions of the Treaty of Amsterdam establishing an area of freedom, security and justice*, 12/7/1998, available on *http://ue.eu.int/jai/article.asp?lang=en&id=39813844*

Council of the European Union (1996), *Council Guide, Volume II: Comments on the Council's Rules of Procedure*, Council General Secretariat, DG F—Information Policy.

Council of the European Union (1998), Special Report on UCLAF, OJC 230, 22/7/1998.

Council Guide (1996), *Volume II: Comments on the Council's Rules of Procedure* (Council General Secretariat, DG F—Information Policy).

Court of Auditors (2004) *Annual Report Concerning the Financial Year 2003*, C293, 30/11/2004.

Cowles, M. G., and Curtis, S. (2004), 'Developments in European Integration theory: the EU as "Other"', in M. G. Cowles, and D. Dinan (eds.), *Developments in the European Union II* (Basingstoke and New York: Palgrave).

Cox, G., and McCubbins, M. (1993), *Legislative Leviathan: Party Government in the House* (Berkeley: University of California Press).

Craig, P., and De Búrca, G. (2003), *EU Law: Text, Cases and Material* (Oxford: Oxford University Press).

Cram, L. (1999), 'The Commission' in L. Cram, D. Dinan, and N. Nugent (eds.), *Developments in the European Union* (Basingstoke and New York: Palgrave), 44–61.

Cram, L., Dinan, D., and Nugent, N. (1999) (eds.), *Developments in the European Union* (Basingstoke and New York: Palgrave).

Crowe, B. (2005), *Foreign Minister of Europe* (London: The Foreign Policy Centre).

Dahl, R. A. (1994), 'A Democratic Dilemma: System Effectiveness versus Citizen Participation', *Political Science Quarterly*, 109/1: 23–34.

Damgaard, E. (1995), 'How Parties Control Committee Members', in H. Döring (ed.), *Parliaments and Majority Rule in Western Europe* (Frankfurt and New York: Campus and St. Martin's Press), 308–25.

Dannreuther, R. (2004) (ed.), *European Union Foreign and Security Policy: Towards a Neighborhood Strategy* (London and New York: Routledge).

Dannreuther, R., and Peterson, J. (2006), *Security Strategy and Transatlantic Relations* (London and New York: Routledge).

Dashwood, A., and Johnston, A. (2001), *The Future of the Judicial System of the European Union* (Oxford and Portland, OR: Hart Publishing).

De Búrca, G., and Weiler, J. H. H. (2001) (eds.), *The European Court of Justice* (Oxford: Oxford University Press).

De Gaulle, C. (1970), *Discours et messages: Tome IV: Pour l'effort* (Paris: Plon).

De Haan, J., Amtenbrink, F., and Waller, S. (2004), 'The Transparency and Credibility of the European Central Bank', *Journal of Common Market Studies*, 42/4: 775–94.

De Ruyt, J. (1987), *L'Acte Unique Européen* (Brussels: Editions de l'Université Libre de Bruxelles).

de Schoutheete, P. (2000), *The Case for Europe: Unity, Diversity, and Democracy in the European Union* (London and Boulder, CO: Lynne Rienner).

de Schoutheete, P. (2003), *Die Debatte des Konvents über den Europäischen Rat* (Berlin: Integration, Nr 4/03).

de Schoutheete, P. and Wallace, H. (2002), *The European Council* (Paris: Notre Europe—Research and European Issues, Nr 19).

de Zwaan, J. (1995), *The Permanent Representatives Committee: Its Role in European Union Decision-Making* (Amsterdam: Elsevier).

Dehaene, J.-L., von Wiezsäcker, R., and Simon, D. (1999), *The Institutional Implications of Enlargement: Report to the European Commission* (Brussels: European Commission), 18/10/1999.

Dehousse, R. (1988), 'Completing the Single Market: Institutional constraints and Challenges', in R. Bieber, R. Dehousse. J. Pinder, and J. H. H. Weiler (eds.), *1992: One European Market?—A Critical Analysis of the Commission's Internal Market Strategy* (Baden-Baden: Nomos): 311–36.

Dehousse, R. (1995), 'Constitutional Reform in the European Community: Are there Alternatives to the Majoritarian Avenue?', *West European Politics*, 18/1: 118–36.

Dehousse, R. (1998), *The European Court of Justice: the Politics of Judicial Integration* (Basingstoke and New York: Palgrave).

Dehousse, R. (2004), *La Stratégie de Lisbonne et la méthode ouverte de coordination: 12 recommandations pour une stratégie à plusieurs niveaux plus efficace* (Paris: Notre Europe), 28/2/2004, available on *http://www.notre-europe.asso.fr/sommaire.php3?lang=fr*

Dehousse, R., and Majone, G. (1994), 'The Dynamics of European Integration: From the Single European Act to the Maastricht Treaty', in S. Martin (ed.), *The Construction of Europe, Essays in Honour of Emile Noël* (Dordrecht: Kluwer), 91–112.

Delors, J. (2004), *Mémoires* (Paris: Plon).

Delwit, P., Külachi, E., and Van De Walle, C. (2001) (eds.), *Les federations européennes de parties: Organisation et influence* (Brussels: Editions de l'Université de Bruxelles).

den Boer, M., and Wallace, W. (2000), 'Justice and Home Affairs: Integration through Incrementalism', in H. Wallace and W. Wallace (eds.), *Policy-Making in the European Union*, 4th edn. (Oxford and New York: Oxford University Press).

Devuyst, Y. (1999), 'The Community Method After Amsterdam', *Journal of Common Market Studies*, 37/1: 109–20.

Devuyst, Y. (2005), *The European Union Transformed: Community Method and Institutional Evolution from the Schuman Plan to the Constitution for Europe* (Brussels: P.I.E.—Peter Lang).

Dietz, T. (2000), 'Similar but Different? The European Greens Compared to Other Transnational Party Federations in Europe', *Party Politics*, 6/2: 199–210.

Dimitrakopoulos, D. G. (2004) (ed.), *The Changing European Commission* (Manchester and New York: Manchester University Press).

Dinan, D. (1999), *Ever Closer Union? An Introduction to the European Community*, 2nd edn. (Boulder, CO: Lynne Rienner).

Dinan, D. (2000) (ed.), *Encyclopaedia of the European Union* (London: Macmillan).

Dogan, M. (1994), 'The Decline of nationalisms within Western Europe', *Comparative Politics*, April 1994, 26/3: 281–305.

Doutriaux, Y., and Lequesne, C. (2002), *Les Institutions de l'Union Européenne*, 4th edn. (Paris: La Documentation Française, collection Réflexe Europe).

Duchêne, F. (1994), *Jean Monnet: the First Statesman of Interdependence* (London and New York: Norton).

Duhamel, O. (2000), *Report on the Constitutionalisation of the Treaties* (Brussels: European Parliament), 12/2000 (A5-0289/2000).

Duisenberg, W. (1998a), 'EMU: the Building of One Monetary System in the European Union', speech delivered in Tokyo, Japan, 16 January.

Duisenberg, W. (1998b), 'The ECB: Independent, Transparent and Communicative', speech delivered at Bankers' Club Annual Banquet, London, England, 16 February.

Dyson, K., and Featherstone, K. (1999), *The Road to Maastricht* (Oxford: Oxford University Press).

Easton, D. (1971), *The Political System: an Inquiry into the State of Political Science*, 2nd edn. (New York: Alfred A. Knopf).

Eberlein, B., and Kerwer, D. (2004), 'New governance in the European Union: a theoretical perspective', *Journal of Common Market Studies*, 42/1: 121–42.

Economic and Social Committee (2001), *Opinion on the Organised Civil Society and European Governance: the Committee's Contribution to the White Paper*, CES 535/2001.

Economist (2005), 'Those Ozymandian Moments', 11 June.

Edward, D. A. O. E. (1996), 'Judicial Activism—Myth or Reality?', in A. I. L. Campbell and M. Voyatzi (eds.) *Legal reasoning and Judicial Interpretation of European law—Essays in honour of Lord Mackenzie Stuart* (London: Trenton).

Eichengreen, B. (1996), 'How to Avoid a Maastricht Catastrophe', *International Economy*, (May/June): 16–20.

Eichengreen, B., and Frieden, J. (1995) (eds.), *Politics and Institutions in an Integrated Europe* (New York: Springer Verlag).

Elster, J. (1998), 'Deliberation and Constitution-Making', in J. Elster (ed.), *Deliberative Democracy* (Oxford: Oxford University Press).

Emerson, M., Gros, D., and Italianer, A. and others (1992), *One Market, One Money* (Oxford: Oxford University Press).

European Parliament (2004), *Activity report 1 May 1999–30 April 2004 of the delegations to the Conciliation Committee*, PE 287.644.

European Union (2003), *A Secure Europe in a Better World: European Security Strategy* (Brussels) December, available on *http://ue.eu.int/cms3_fo/showPage.ASP?id=266&lang=EN&mode=g*

European Union (2004), *Facing the Challenge: the Lisbon strategy for growth and employment* (Brussels: High Level Group chaired by Wim Kok) November, available on *http://europa.eu.int/growthandjobs/pdf/kok_report_en.pdf*

Evans, P. (1993), 'Building an Integrative Approach to International and Domestic Politics: Reflections and Projections', in P. Evans, H. Jacobson and R. Putnam (1993) (eds.), *Double-Edged Diplomacy: International Bargaining and Domestic Politics* (Berkeley: University of California Press), 397–430.

Evans, P., Jacobson, H., and Putnam, R. (1993) (eds.), *Double-Edged Diplomacy: International Bargaining and Domestic Politics* (Berkeley: University of California Press).

Everts, S., and Keohane, D. (2003), 'The European Convention and EU foreign policy: learning from failure', *Survival*, 45/3: 167–86.

Faas, T. (2003), 'To Defect or Not to Defect? National, institutional and party group pressures on MEPs and their consequences for party group cohesion in the EP', *European Journal of Political Research*, 42/5: 841–66.

Farrell, H., and Heritier, A. (2005) 'A rationalist–institutionalist explanation of endogenous regional integration', *Journal of European Public Policy*, 12/2: 273–90.

Farrows, M., and McCarthy, R. (1997), 'Opinion Formulation and Impact in the Committee of the Regions', *Regional and Federal Studies*, 7/1: 23–49.

Featherstone, K., and Radaelli, C. (2003) (eds.), *The Politics of Europeanization* (Oxford and New York: Oxford University Press).

Feld, W. (1966), 'National Economic Interest Groups and Policy Formulation in the EEC', *Political Science Quarterly*, 81/3: 392–411.

Fitzmaurice, J. (1975), *The Party Groups in the European Parliament* (Farnborough: Saxon House).

Fligstein, N. (1997), 'Social skill and institutional theory', *American Behavioral Scientist*, 40/4: 397–405.

Fligstein, N., and Brantley, P. (1995), 'The 1992 single market program and the interests of business' in B. Eichengreen and J. Frieden (eds.), *Politics and Institutions in an Integrated Europe* (New York: Springer Verlag).

Fligstein, N., and McNichol, J. (1998), 'The institutional terrain of the European Union', in W. Sandholtz and A. Stone Sweet (eds.), *Supranational Governance: the Institutionalisation of the European Union* (Oxford and New York: Oxford University Press).

Freedman, O. (1978), *Crisis and Legitimacy* (Cambridge: Cambridge University Press).

Frieden, J. (1991), 'Invested Interests: the Politics of National Economic Policies in a World of Global Finance', *International Organization*, 45/4: 425–51.

Gabel, M. J., and Hix, S. (2002), 'Defining the EU Political Space: An Empirical Study of the European Elections Manifestos, 1979–1999', *Comparative Political Studies*, 35/8: 934–64.

Gali, J., Gerlach, S., Rotenberg, J., Uhlig, H., and Woodford, M. (2004), 'The Monetary Policy Strategy of the ECB Reconsidered', *Monitoring the European Central Bank* (London: Centre for Economic Reform).

Garrett, G. (1995), 'The Politics of Legal Integration in the European Union', *International Organization*, 49/1 Winter: 171–81.

Garrett, G., Keleman, D., and Schulz, H. (1998), 'Legal Politics in the European Union', *International Organization*, 52/1 Winter 1998: 149–76.

Gatsios, K., and Seabright, P. (1989), 'Regulation in the European Community', *Oxford Review of Economic Policy*, 5: 37–60.

Gerardin, D., Munoz, R., and Petit, N. (2005) (eds.), *Regulation through Agencies: A New Paradigm of European Governance* (Cheltenham: Edward Elgar).

Ginsberg, R. H. (1989), *Foreign Policy Actions of the European Community: the Politics of Scale* (London and Boulder, CO: Lynne Rienner).

Ginsberg, R. H. (2001), *The European Union in International politics: Baptism by Fire* (Lanham MD and Oxford: Rowman & Littlefield).

Giscard d'Estaing, V. (1988), *Le Pouvoir et la Vie*, 2nd vol. (Paris: Compagnie 12).

Giscard d'Estaing, V. (2002), 'Introductory Speech by President V. Giscard d'Estaing to the Convention on the Future of Europe', 26 February, available on *http://european-convention.eu.int/docs/speeches/1.pdf*

Glarbo, K. (2001), 'Reconstructing a common European foreign policy', in T. Christiansen, K. E. Jørgensen, and A. Wiener (eds.), *The Social Construction of Europe* (London and Thousand Oaks, CA: Sage).

Goetz, K., and Hix, S. (2000), *Europeanized Politics? European Integration and National Political Systems* (London: Frank Cass).

Golub, J. (1999), 'In the Shadow of the Vote? Decision-Making in the European Community', *International Organization*, 53/4: 733–64.

Gomez, R., and Peterson, J. (2001), 'The EU's Impossibly Busy Foreign Ministers: "No One is in Control" ', *European Foreign Affairs Review*, 6/1: 53–74.

Gouldner, A. W. (1957–58), 'Cosmopolitans and Locals: Towards an Analysis of Latent Social Roles', I and II, *Administrative Science Quarterly*, 2: 281–306; 444–80.

Grant, C. (2002), 'Restoring leadership to the European Council', *Bulletin of the Centre for European Reform*, 15 April, available on *http://www.cer.org.uk/pdf/policybrief_eucouncil.pdf*

Gray, M., and Stubb, A. (2001), 'Keynote article: The Treaty of Nice: negotiating a poisoned chalice?', *The European Union: Annual Review of the EU 2000/2001 (Journal of Common Market Studies)* 39: 5–23.

Greenwood, J., Grote, J., and Ronit, K. (1992), *Organized Interests and the European Community* (London: Sage).

Grieco, J. M. (1995), 'The Maastricht Treaty, Economic and Monetary Union and the Neo-realist Research Programme', *Review of International Studies*, 21/1: 21–40.

Griffith, Richard T. (2001), *Europe's First Constitution* (London: I. B. Tauris).

Gronbech-Jensen, C. (1998), 'The Scandinavian tradition of open government and the European Union: problems of compatibility?', *Journal of European Public Policy*, 5/1: 185–99.

Grosse-Hüttmann, M. (2004), 'Wirtschafts- und Sozialausschuss', in W. Weidenfeld and W. Wessels (eds.), *Jahrbuch der Europäischen Integration 2003/2004* (Bonn: Europa Union Verlag), 109–12.

Haas, E. B. (1958), *The Uniting of Europe: Political, Social, and Economic Forces, 1950–1957* (Stanford: Stanford University Press).

Haas E. B. (1960), *Consensus Formation in the Council of Europe* (Berkeley, CA: University of California Press).

Hall, P., and Franzese, R. (1998), 'Mixed Signals: Central Bank Independence, Coordinated Wage-Bargaining, and European Monetary Union', *International Organization*, 52/3: 505–35.

Hall, P. A. (1997), 'The Role of Interests, Institutions and Ideas in the Comparative Political Economy of the Industrial Nations', in Mark Lichbach and Alan Zuckerman (eds.), *Comparative Politics: Rationality, Culture and Structure* (Cambridge: Cambridge University Press), 174–207.

Hall, P. A., and Taylor, R. C. R. (1996), 'Political Science and the Three New Institutionalisms', *Political Studies*, 44/5: 936–57.

Halliday, F. (1983), *The Making of the Second Cold War* (London: Verso).

Haseler, S. (2004), *Super-State: the New Europe and its Challenge to America* (London: H.B. Tauris).

Hayes-Renshaw, F. (1999), 'The European Council and the Council of Ministers', in L. Cram, D. Dinan, and N. Nugent (eds.), *Developments in the European Union* (Basingstoke and New York: Palgrave), 23–43.

Hayes-Renshaw, F., and Wallace, H. (1995), 'Executive Power in the European Union: The Functions and Limits of the Council of Ministers', *Journal of European Public Policy*, 2/4 December: 559–82.

Hayes-Renshaw, F., and Wallace, H. (1997), *The Council of Ministers* (Basingstoke and New York: Macmillan).

Hayes-Renshaw, F., and Wallace, H. (2006), *The Council of Ministers*, 2nd edn. (Basingstoke and New York: Palgrave).

Hayes-Renshaw, F., Lequesne, C., and Mayor Lopez, P. (1989), 'The Permanent Representations of the Member States to the European Communities', *Journal of Common Market Studies*, 28/2: 119–37.

Heidar, K., and Koole, R. (2000*a*), 'Parliamentary party groups compared', in K. Heidar and R. Koole (eds.), *Parliamentary Party Groups in European Democracies: Political parties behind closed doors* (London: Routledge), 248–70.

Heidar, K., and Koole, R. (2000*b*) (eds.), *Parliamentary Party Groups in European Democracies: Political parties behind closed doors* (London: Routledge).

Held, D., and Koenig-Archibugi, M. (2004) (eds.), *American Power in the 21st Century* (Oxford: Polity).

Helleiner, E. (1998), 'National Currencies and National Identities', *American Behavioral Scientist*, 41 (August): 1409–36.

Henning, C. R. (1997), *Cooperating with Europe's Monetary Union* (Washington: Institute for International Economics).

Héritier, A. (1999), *Policy-Making and Diversity in Europe: Escape from Deadlock* (Cambridge: Cambridge University Press).

Herrmann, R., Brewer, M., and Risse, T. (2004) (eds.), *Transnational Identities: Becoming European in the EU* (Lanham, MD: Rowman and Littlefield).

Hill, C. (1993), 'The Capability-Expectations Gap, or Conceptualizing Europe's International Role', *Journal of Common Market Studies*, 31/3: 305–28.

Hill, C. (1996) (ed.), *The Actors in Europe's Foreign Policy* (London: Routledge).

Hill, C. (1998), 'Closing the capabilities-expectations gap?', in J. Peterson and H. Sjursen (eds.), *A Common Foreign Policy for Europe?* (London and New York: Routledge).

Hill, C. (2003), *The Changing Politics of Foreign Policy* (Basingstoke and New York: Palgrave).

Hill, C. (2004), 'Renationalizing or regrouping? EU foreign policy since 11 September 2004', *Journal of Common Market Studies*, 42/1: 143–63.

Hill, C., and Smith, M. (2005*a*), 'Acting for Europe: Reassessing International Relations and the European Union', in C. Hill and M. Smith (eds.), *The International Relations of the European Union* (Oxford and New York: Oxford University Press).

Hill, C., and Smith, M. (2005*b*) (eds.), *International Relations and the European Union* (Oxford and New York: Oxford University Press).

Hill, C., and Wallace, W. (1996), 'Introduction: actors and actions', in C. Hill (ed.), *The Actors in Europe's Foreign Policy* (London: Routledge).

Hill Knowlton (2000), *The European Commission 2000–2005: One Year On* (Brusssels: Hill and Knowlton).

Hix, S. (1998), 'Elections, Parties and Institutional Design: A Comparative Perspective on European Union Democracy', *West European Politics*, 21/3: 19–52.

Hix, S. (1999), 'Dimensions and alignments in European Union politics: Cognitive constraints and partisan responses', *European Journal of Political Research*, 35/1: 69–106.

Hix, S. (2002a), 'Constitutional Agenda-Setting Through Discretion in Rule Interpretation: Why the European Parliament Won at Amsterdam', *British Journal of Political Science*, 32/3: 259–80.

Hix, S. (2002b), 'Parliamentary Behavior with Two Principals: Preferences, Parties, and Voting in the European Parliament', *American Journal of Political Science*, 46/3: 688–98.

Hix, S. (2004), 'Electoral Institutions and Legislative Behavior: Explaining Voting-Defection in the European Parliament' *World Politics*, 56/1: 194–223.

Hix, S., and Lord, C. (1997), *Political Parties in the European Union* (Basingstoke: Macmillan).

Hix, S., Noury, A., and Roland, G. (2002), *How MEPs Vote* (Brighton: ESRC and Weber Shandwick Adamson).

Hix, S., Noury, A., and Roland, G. (2005), 'Power to the Parties: Cohesion and Competition in the European Parliament, 1979–2001', *British Journal of Political Science*, 35/2: 209–34.

Hix, S., and Scully, R. (2003) (eds.), 'The European Parliament at Fifty', Special Issue of *Journal of Common Market Studies*, 41/2.

Hocking, B. (1999) (ed.), *Foreign Ministries: Change and Adaptation* (New York: St. Martin's Press).

Hocking, B., and Spence, D. (2002) (eds.), *Foreign Ministries in the European Union* (Basingstoke and New York: Palgrave).

Hoffmann, S. (1966), 'Obstinate or Obsolete: The Fate of the Nation-State in Europe', *Daedalus*, 95/3: 862–915.

Holbrooke, R. (1999), *To End a War* (New York: The Modern Library).

Hooghe, L. (2002), *The European Commission and The Integration of Europe: Images of Governance* (Cambridge: Cambridge University Press).

Hooghe, L. (2005), 'Several Roads Lead To International Norms, But Few Via International Socialization. A Case Study of the European Commission', *International Organization*, 59/4: 861–98.

Hooghe, L., and Marks, G. (2001), *Multi-level Governance and European Integration* (Boulder, CO: Rowman & Littlefield).

Hooghe, L., Marks, G., and Wilson, C. J. (2002), 'Does Left/Right Structure Party Positions on European Integration?', *Comparative Political Studies*, 35/8: 965–89.

Hoppe, U., and Schulz, G. (1992), 'Der Ausschuss der Regionen', in F.-U. Borkenhagen, C. Bruns-Kloss, G. Memminger, and O. Stein (eds.), *Die deutschen Länder in Europa* (Baden-Baden: Nomos).

House of Commons (1990), *Session 1989–90, Home Affairs Committee Seventh Report Practical Police Co-operation in the European Community, Volume 1* (London: HMSO).

House of Lords (2001), *The European Court of Auditors: The Case for Reform*, 12th Report, 3 April, available on *www.publications.pariamen98/99/Idselect/Ideucom/63/6302.htm*

House of Lords (2004), *Strengthening OLAF, the European Anti-Fraud Office*, 24th Report, 13 July.

Howorth, J. (2004), 'The European Draft Constitutional Treaty and the Future of the European Defence Initiative: A Question of Flexibility', *European Foreign Affairs Review*, 9/4: 483–508.

Huber, J., and Inglehart, R. (1995), 'Expert Interpretations of Party Space and Party Locations in 42 Societies', *Party Politics*, 1/1: 73–111.

Hurd, D. (1981), 'Political Cooperation', *International Affairs*, 57/3: 383–93.

Huysmans, J. (2000), 'The European Union and the Securitisation of Migration', *Journal of Common Market Studies*, 38/5: 751–77.

Ikenberry, G. J. (2001), *After Victory: Institutions, Strategic Restraint, and the Rebuilding of Order After Major War* (Princeton, NJ: Princeton University Press).

Ikenberry, G. J. (2002) (ed.), *America Unrivaled: the Future of the Balance of Power* (Ithaca, NY and London: Cornell University Press).

Issing, O. (1999), 'The Eurosystem: Transparent and Accountable or Willem in Euroland', *Journal of Common Market Studies*, 37/3: 503–20.

Jacqué, J. P. (1991), 'Cours Général de Droit Communautaire', in A. Clapham (ed.), *Collected Courses of the Academy of European Law*, Vol. 1, Book 1 (Dordrecht: Martinus Nijhoff Publishers): 247–360.

Jacqué, J. P. (2004), 'Les principes constitutionnels fondamentaux dans le projet de traité établissant la constitution européenne', in L. S. Rossi (ed.), *Vers une nouvelle architecture de l'Union européenne* (Brussels: Bruylant).

Jansen, T. (1998), *The European People's Party: Origins and Development* (Basingstoke: Macmillan).

Jeffery, C. (1995), 'Whither the Committee of the Regions?', *Regional and Federal Studies*, 5/2: 247–57.

Jeffery, C. (1996), 'Towards a Third Level in Europe? The German Länder in the European Union', *Political Studies*, 44/2: 253–66.

Jeffery, C. (2000), 'Sub-National Mobilization and European Integration: Does it Make any Difference?, *Journal of Common Market Studies*, 38/1: 1–23.

Jeffery, C. (2005), 'Regions and the European Union: Letting them in, and leaving them alone', in S. Weatherill and U. Bernitz (eds.), *The Role of Regions and Sub-National Actors in Europe* (Oxford: Hart).

Jenkins, R. (1989), *European Diary: 1977–1981* (London: Collins).

Joana, J., and Smith, A. (2002), *Les Commissaires Européens: technocrates, diplomates or politiques?* (Paris: Presses des Sciences Po).

Joerges, C., and Vos, E. (1998), *EU Committees: Social Regulation, Law and Politics* (Oxford: Hart Publishing).

Johansson, K. M., and Raunio, T. (2005), 'Regulating Europarties: Cross-Party Coalitions Capitalizing on Incomplete Contracts', *Party Politics*, 11/5: 515–34.

Johansson, K. M., and Zervakis, P. (2001) (eds.), *European Political Parties between Cooperation and Integration* (Baden-Baden: Nomos).

Jordana, J., and Levy-Faur, D. (2004) (eds.), *The Politics of Regulation* (Cheltenham: Edward Elgar).

Jørgensen, K. E. (2000), 'Continental IR Theory: the Best Kept Secret', *European Journal of International Relations*, 6/1: 9–42.

Josselin, D., and Wallace, W. (2001) (eds.), *Non-State Actors in World Politics* (Basingstoke and New York: Palgrave).

Judge, D., and Earnshaw, D. (2003), *The European Parliament* (London: Palgrave Macmillan).

Jupille, J., Caporaso, J., and Checkel, J. T. (2003), 'Integrating Institutions: Rationalism, Constructivism, and the Study of the European Union', *Comparative Political Studies*, 36/1–2: 7–40.

Kalbfleisch-Kottsieper, U. (1995), 'Kompromiss ohne Konsens?', *EU-Magazin*, No. 6.

Kassim, H. (2004), 'A historic accomplishment: the Prodi Commission and Administrative Reform', in D. G. Dimitrakopoulos (ed.), *The Changing European Commission* (Manchester and New York: Manchester University Press).

Kassim, H., and Menon, A. (2001) (eds.), *The National Co-ordination of EU Policy: The European Level* (Oxford: Oxford University Press).

Kassim, H., and Menon, A. (2004), 'EU member states and the Prodi Commission', in
D. G. Dimitrakopoulos (ed.), *The Changing European Commission* (Manchester and New York:
Manchester University Press).

Keading, M. (2004), 'Rapporteurship Allocation in the European Parliament: Information or
Distribution?', *European Union Politics*, 5/3: 353–71.

Kenen, P. B. (1969), 'The Theory of Optimal Currency Areas: An Eclectic View', in
R. A. Mundell and A. K. Swoboda (eds.), *Monetary Problems of the International Economy*
(Chicago: University of Chicago Press).

Keohane, R. O. (1998), 'International Institutions: Can Interdependence Work?', *Foreign Policy*,
110 (Spring): 82–96.

Keohane, R. O., and Hoffmann, S. (1991) (eds.), *The New European Community: Decisionmaking and
Institutional Change* (Boulder, CO: Westview Press).

Kilpert, H., and Lhotta, R. (1996), *Föderalismus in der Bundesrepublik Deutschland* (Opladen: Leske
+ Budrich).

Kingdon, J. W. (1984), *Agendas, alternatives, and public policies* (New York: Harper Collins).

Kohler-Koch, B. (2000), ' "Framing": the bottleneck of constructing legitimate institutions',
Journal of European Public Policy, 7/4: 513–31.

Kohler-Koch, B., and Eising. R. (1999) (eds.), *The Transformation of Government in the European
Union* (London and New York: Routledge).

Kostakopoulou, T. (2000), 'The "Protective Union": Change and Continuity in Migration Law
and Policy in Post-Amsterdam Europe', *Journal of Common Market Studies*, 38/3: 497–518.

Kreppel, A. (2002), *The European Parliament and the Supranational Party System: A Study of
Institutional Development* (Oxford: Oxford University Press).

Kupchan, C. A. (2003), *The End of the American Era: US Foreign Policy and the Geopolitics of the
Twenty-First Century* (New York: Knopf).

Ladrech, R. (1994), 'Europeanization of Domestic Politics and Institutions: The Case of France',
Journal of Common Market Studies, 32/1: 69–88.

Ladrech, R. (2000), *Social Democracy and the Challenge of European Union* (Boulder, CO: Lynne
Rienner).

Laffan, B. (1997*a*), *The Finances of the Union* (London: Macmillan).

Laffan, B. (1997*b*), 'From Policy Entrepreneur to Policy Manager: the challenge facing the
European Commission', *Journal of European Public Policy*, 4/3: 422–38.

Laffan, B. (1999), 'Becoming a 'Living Institution': The Evolution of the European Court of
Auditors', *Journal of Common Market Studies*, 37/2: 251–68.

Laffan, B. (2000), 'The big budgetary bargains: from negotiation to authority', *Journal of
European Public Policy*, 7/5: 725–43.

Laffan, B. (2003), 'Auditing and Accountability in the European Union', *Journal of European
Public Policy*, 10/5: 762–77.

Laffan, B. (2004), 'The European Union and Its Institutions as 'Identity Builders'', in
R. Hermann, T. Risse, and M. Brewer (eds.), *Transnational Identities: Becoming European in the
EU* (Lanham, MD: Rowman and Littlefield), 75–96.

Laffan, B., O'Donnell, R., and Smith, M. (2000), *Europe's Experimental Union: Rethinking Integration*
(London and New York: Routledge).

Lavenex, S., and Wallace, W. (2005), 'Justice and Home Affairs', in H. Wallace, W. Wallace,
and M. Pollack (eds.), *Policy-Making in the European Union*, 5th edn. (Oxford and New York:
Oxford University Press), 429–56.

Leonard, M. (2005), *Why Europe Will Run the 21st Century* (London and New York: Harper Collins).

Lequesne, C. (1993), *Paris-Bruxelles: Comment se fait la politique européene de la France* (Paris: Presses Universitaires de la Fondation Nationale des Sciences Politiques).

Lequesne, C. (1996), 'La Commission Européenne entre autonomie et dépendance', *Revue Française de Science Politique*, 46/3: 389–408.

Levy R. (1996), 'Managing Value for Money Audit in the European Union: The Challenge of Diversity', *Journal of Common Market Studies*, 43/4: 509–29.

Levy, R. (2000), *Implementing European Union Public Policy* (Cheltenham: Edward Elgar).

Levy, R. (2003), 'Critical Success Factors in Public Management Reform: The Case of the European Commission', *International Review of Administrative Sciences*, 69: 553–66.

Lewis, J. (1998a), 'Is the 'Hard Bargaining' Image of the Council Misleading? The Committee of Permanent Representatives and the Local Elections Directive', *Journal of Common Market Studies*, 36/4: 479–504.

Lewis, J. (1998b), 'Constructing Interests: The Committee of Permanent Representatives and Decision-Making in the European Union' unpublished dissertation, University of Wisconsin–Madison.

Lewis, J. (2000), 'The Methods of Community in EU Decision-Making and Administrative Rivalry in the Council's Infrastructure', *Journal of European Public Policy*, 7/2: 261–89.

Lewis, J. (2005), 'The Janus Face of Brussels: Socialization and Everyday Decision Making in the European Union', *International Organization*, 59/4: 937–91.

Lindberg, L. N. (1963), *The Political Dynamics of European Integration* (Stanford: Stanford University Press).

Lindberg, L. N., and Scheingold, S. A. (1970), *Europe's Would-Be Polity. Patterns of Change in the European Community* (Englewood Cliffs, NJ: Prentice-Hall).

Lindner, J., and Rittberger, B. (2003), 'The creation, interpretation and contestation of institutions: revisiting historical institutionalism', *Journal of Common Market Studies*, 41/3: 445–73.

Linz, J. J. (1998), 'Democracy's Time Constraints', *International Political Science Review*, 19: 19–37.

Lodge, J. (2005) (ed.), *The 2004 Elections to the European Parliament* (London: Palgrave).

Lodge, J., and Herman, V. (1980), 'The Economic and Social Committee in EEC Decision-Making', *International Organization*, 34/2: 265–84.

Lohmann, Suzanne (1999), 'The Dark Side of Monetary Union', in E. Meade (ed.), *The European Central Bank: How Decentralized? How Accountable? Lessons from the Bundesbank and the Federal Reserve System* (Washington, DC: American Institute for Contemporary German Studies).

Longley, L. D., and Davidson, R. H. (1998) (eds.), *The New Roles of Parliamentary Committees* (London: Frank Cass).

Lord, C., and Magnette, P. (2004), 'E pluribus unum? Creative disagreement about legitimacy in the EU', *Journal of Common Market Studies*, 42/1: 183–202.

Loth, W. (1998), Wallace, W. and Wessels, W. (1998b) (eds.), *Walter Hallstein: the Forgotten European?* (Basingstoke and New York: Macmillan and St. Martin's Press).

Lowe, D. (1996), 'The Development Policy of the EU and the Mid-Term Review of the Lomé Partnership', *The European Union 1995: Annual Review of Activities (Journal of Common Market Studies)*, 33: 15–28.

Ludlow, P. (1992), 'Europe's Institutions: Europe's Politics', in G. F. Treverton (ed.), *The Shape of the New Europe* (New York: Council on Foreign Relations Press).

Ludlow, P. (2000), *A View from Brussels. (Nr 8) July 2000* (Brussels: CEPS).

Ludlow, P. (2001), *The European Council at Nice: Neither Triumph nor Disaster*, Background Paper, CEPS International Advisory Council, 1–2 February, Brussels.

Ludlow, P. (2002), *The Laeken Council* (Brussels: EuroComment).

Ludlow, P. (2004), *The Making of the New Europe: The European Councils in Brussels and Copenhagen 2002* (Brussels: EuroComment).

McKinnon, R. I. (1963), 'Optimum Currency Areas', *American Economic Review*, 53/September: 717-25.

MacMullen, A. (1999) 'Fraud, mismanagement and nepotism: the Committee of Independent Experts and the Fall of the European Commission', *Crime, Law and Social Change*, 31/4: 193-208.

MacMullen, A. (2000), 'European Commissioners 1952-1999: National Routes to a European Elite', in N. Nugent (ed.), *At the Heart of the Union*, 2nd edn. (Basingstoke and New York: Palgrave).

McNamara, K. R. (1998), *The Currency of Ideas: Monetary Politics in the European Union* (Ithaca: Cornell University Press).

McNamara, K. R., and Jones, E. (1996), 'The Clash of Institutions: Germany in European Monetary Affairs', *German Politics and Society*, 14/3: 5-31.

Mace, C. (2003), 'Operation Artemis: mission improbable?', *European Security Review*, 18 (July), available on *http://www.isis-europe.org*

Magnette, P. (2001), 'Appointing and Censuring the Commission: the Adaptation of Parliamentary Institutions to the Community Context', *European Law Journal*, 1/3: 289-307.

Magnette, P. (2005a), *What is the European Union?* (Basingstoke: Palgrave).

Magnette, P. (2005b), 'In the Name of Simplification, Coping with Constitutional Conflicts in the Convention on the Future of Europe', *European Law Journal*, 11/4: 434-53.

Magnette, P., and Nicolaïdis, K. (2004), 'The European Convention: Bargaining under the shadow of rhetoric', *West European Politics*, 27/3: 381-404.

Maher, I. (2004) Economic policy coordination and the European Court: excessive deficits and ECOFIN discretion, *European Law Review*, 29/6: 831-41.

Mair, P. (2000), 'The Limited Impact of Europe on National Party Systems', *West European Politics*, 23/4: 27-51.

Majone, G. (1996), *Regulating Europe* (London: Routledge).

Majone, G. (2000), 'The Credibility Crisis of Community Regulation', *Journal of Common Market Studies*, 38/2: 273-302.

Majone, G. (2003) (ed.), *Risk Regulation in the European Union: Between Enlargement and Internationalization* (Florence: European University Institute).

Majone, G. (2005), *Dilemmas of European Integration — The Ambiguities and Pitfalls of Integration by Stealth* (Oxford: Oxford University Press).

Mamadouh, V., and Raunio, T. (2003), 'The Committee System: Powers, Appointments and Report Allocation', *Journal of Common Market Studies*, 41/2: 333-51.

Manners I., and Whitman, R. (2000) (eds.), *The Foreign Policy of the EU Member States* (Manchester: Manchester University Press).

March, J. G., and Olsen, J. P. (1989), *Rediscovering Institutions: The Organizational Basis of Politics* (New York: The Free Press).

March, J. G., and Olsen, J. P. (1998), 'The Institutional Dynamics of International Political Orders', *International Organization*, 52/4: 943-69.

Marks, G. (1993), 'Structural Policy and Multi-Level Governance in the EC', in A. Cafruny and G. Rosenthal (eds.), *The State of the European Community* Vol. 2. *The Maastricht Debates and Beyond* (Boulder, CO: Lynne Rienner).

Marks, G. (1996) 'An Actor-Centred Approach to Multilevel Governance', *Regional & Federal Studies*, 6/2: 21–36.

Marks, G., and Hooghe, L. (2001), *Multi-level Governance and European Integration* (Boulder, CO: Rowman & Littlefield).

Marks, G., Hooghe, L., and Blank, K. (1996), 'European Integration from the 1980s: State-Centric v. Multi-Level Governance', *Journal of Common Market Studies*, 34/3: 341–78.

Marks, G., and Steenbergen, M. R. (2004) (eds.), *European Integration and Political Conflict* (Cambridge: Cambridge University Press).

Marks, G., and Wilson, C. (2000), 'The Past in the Present: A Cleavage Theory of Party Response to European Integration', *British Journal of Political Science*, 30/3: 433–59.

Mattson, I., and Strøm, K. (1995), 'Parliamentary Committees', in H. Döring (ed.), *Parliaments and Majority Rule in Western Europe* (Frankfurt and New York: Campus and St. Martin's Press): 249–307.

Mayne, R. (1962), *The Community of Europe* (New York: W. W. Norton).

Mazey, S., and Richardson, J. (1989), 'Pressure Groups and Lobbying in the EC', in J. Lodge (ed.), *The European Community and the Challenge of the Future* (London: Pinter), 37–47.

Mentler, M. (1996), *Der Auschuss der Stindigen Vertreter bei den Europäischen Germeinschaften* (Baden-Baden: Nomos).

Messmer, W. B. (2003), 'Taming Labour's MEPs', *Party Politics*, 9/2: 201–18.

Metcalfe, L. (2000), 'Reforming the Commission: Will Organisational Efficiency Produce Effective Governance?', *Journal of Common Market Studies*, 38/5: 817–41.

Millan, B. (1997), 'The Committee of the Regions: In at the Birth', *Regional and Federal Studies*, 7/1: 5–10.

Milton, G., and Keller-Noëllet, J. (2005), *The European Constitution: its origins, negotiation and meaning* (London: John Harper)

Milward, A. (1992), *The European Rescue of the Nation-State* (London: Routledge).

Moe, T. M. (1990), 'Political Institutions: the Neglected Side of the Story', *Journal of Law, Economics and Organization*, 6/2: 213–53.

Monar, J. (2001), 'The Dynamics of Justice and Home Affairs: Laboratories, Driving Factors and Costs', *Journal of Common Market Studies*, 39/4: 747–64.

Monar, J. (2002) 'Institutionalising Freedom, Security and Justice', in J. Peterson and M. Shackleton (eds.), *The Institutions of the European Union* (Oxford and New York: Oxford University Press).

Monnet, J. (1978), *Memoirs* (New York: Doubleday and London: Collins).

Moravcsik, A. (1991), 'Negotiating the Single European Act: National Interests and Conventional Statecraft in the European Community', *International Organization*, 45/1: 19–56.

Moravcsik, A. (1993), 'Preferences and Power in the European Community: A Liberal Intergovernmentalist Approach', *Journal of Common Market Studies*, 31/4: 473–524.

Moravcsik, A. (1998), *The Choice for Europe: Social Purpose and State Power from Messina to Maastricht* (London and Ithaca, NY: UCL Press and Cornell University Press).

Moravcsik, A. (2003), 'Reassessing Legitimacy in the European Union', in J. H. H. Weiler, I. Begg, and J. Peterson (eds.), *Integration in an Expanding European Union* (Oxford and Malden, MA: Blackwell).

Moravcsik, A. (2005), 'The European Constitutional Compromise and the neofunctionalist legacy', *Journal of European Public Policy*, 12/2: 349–86.

Moravcsik, A. and Nicolaïdis, K. (1999), 'Explaining the Treaty of Amsterdam: Interests, Influence, Institutions', *Journal of Common Market Studies*, 37/1: 59–85.

Morgenthau, H. J. (1948), *Politics Among Nations* (Chicago: Chicago University Press).

Munchau, W. (2005), 'Barroso's Misguided Priorities', *Financial Times*, 7 February, p. 17.

Mundell, R. A. (1961), 'The Theory of Optimum Currency Areas', *American Economic Review*, 51/2: 509–17.

Narjes, K.-H. (1998), 'Walter Hallstein and the Early Phase of the EEC', in W. Loth, W. Wallace, and W. Wessels (eds.), *Walter Hallstein: the Forgotten European?* (Basingstoke and New York: Macmillan and St. Martin's Press).

Nelsen, B. F., and Stubb, A. (1998) (eds.), *European Union: Readings on the Theory and Practice of European Integration*, 2nd edn. (Basingstoke and Boulder, CO: Palgrave and Lynne Rienner).

Neuhold, C. (2001), 'The "Legislative Backbone" keeping the Institution upright? The Role of European Parliament Committees in the EU Policy-Making Process', *European Integration Online Papers*, 5/10, available on *http://eiop.or.at/eiop/texte/2001-010a.htm*

Noël, E. (1966), 'The Permanent Representatives Committee', lecture to the Institute of European Studies, Université Libre de Bruxelles, 19 and 21 April 1966. Reprinted in: *A Tribute to Emile Noel: Secretary-General of the European Commission from 1958 to 1987* (Luxembourg: Office for Official Publications of the European Communities), 87–124.

Noël, E. (1967), 'The Committee of Permanent Representatives', *Journal of Common Market Studies*, 5/3: 219–51.

Noël, E., and Étienne, H. (1971), 'The Permanent Representatives Committee and the 'Deepening' of the Communities', *Government and Opposition*, 6/4, Autumn: 422–47.

Norman, P. (2003), *The Accidental Constitution: the Story of the European Convention* (Brussels: Eurocomment).

Norman, P. (2005), *The Accidental Constitution*, 2nd edn. (Brussels: Eurocomment)

Norton, P. (1998) (ed.), *Parliaments and Governments in Western Europe* (London: Frank Cass).

Nugent, N. (1994), *The Government and Politics of the European Union*, 3rd edn. (Basingstoke and New York: Macmillan and St Martin's Press).

Nugent, N. (1999), *The Government and Politics of the European Union*, 4th edn. (Basingstoke and New York: Palgrave).

Nugent, N. (2000) (ed.), *At the Heart of the Union*, 2nd edn. (Basingstoke and New York: Palgrave).

Nugent, N. (2001), *The European Commission* (Basingstoke and New York: Palgrave).

Nugent, N. (2002), 'The Commission's Services', in J. Peterson and M. Shackleton (eds.) *The Institutions of the European Union* (Oxford: Oxford University Press), 141–63.

Nugent, N. (2006), *The Government and Politics of the European Union*, 6th edn. (Basingstoke and New York: Palgrave).

Nuttall, S. (2000), *European Foreign Policy* (Oxford: Oxford University Press).

Nye Jr, J. (2004), 'Europe's Soft Power', *Globalist*, 3 May, available on *http://www.globalpolicy.org/empire/analysis/2004/0503softpower.htm*

Oatley, T. (1997), *Monetary Politics: Exchange Rate Cooperation in the European Union* (Ann Arbor, MA: University of Michigan Press).

OLAF (2000), *First Report of the European Anti-Fraud Office (OLAF) on Operational Activities*, available on *europa.eu.int/commdgs/anti-fraud/index en.htm*

OLAF (2004) *Fifth Activity Report for the Year Ending June 2004*, available on *europa.eu.int/commdgs/anti-fraud/index en.htm*

Olsen, J. P. (2002), 'Reforming European Institutions of Governance', *Journal of Common Market Studies*, 40/4: 581–602.

Olsen, J. P. (2003), 'Reforming European Institutions of Governance', in J. H. H Weiler, I. Begg, and J. Peterson (eds.), *Integration in an Expanding European Union: Reassessing the Fundamentals* (Oxford and Malden, MA: Blackwell).

Padoa-Schioppa, T. (1987), *Efficiency, Stability, and Equity: A Strategy for the Evolution of the Economic System of the European Community* (Oxford: Oxford University Press).

Page, E. (1997), *People Who Run Europe* (Oxford: Clarendon Press).

Palmer, J. (2005), 'After the Dutch referendum', *Political Europe*, (Brussels: European Policy Centre), available on *www.theepc.be*

Parsons, C. (2003), *A Certain Idea of Europe* (Ithaca, NY and London: Cornell University Press).

Pedler, R., and Schaeffer, G. F. (1996) (eds.), *Shaping European Law and Policy, The Role of Committees and Comitology in the Political Process* (Maastricht: EIPA).

Peers, S. (2000), *EU Justice and Home Affairs* (Harlow: Longman).

Peers, S. (2004), 'Mutual recognition and Criminal Law in the European Union: Has the Council Got it Wrong?', *Common Market Law Review*, 41/1: 5–36.

Persons, C. (2002), 'Sharing ideas as causes: the origins of the European Union', *International Organization*, 56/1: 47–84.

Pescatore, P. (1987), 'Some critical remarks on the 'Single European Act', *Common Market Law Review*, XXIV/1: 9–18.

Pescatore, P. (1994), 'Jusqu'oú le juge peut-il aller trop loin?', *Festskrift til Ole Due* (Copenhagen), 299–338, in T. Kennedy (1998), *Learning European Law* (London: Sweet & Maxwell), 271.

Peters, B. G. (1999), *Institutional Theory in Political Science* (London and New York: Continuum).

Peters, B. G., and Wright, V. (2000) (eds.), *The National Coordination of EU Policy: The Domestic Level* (Oxford: Oxford University Press).

Peterson, J. (1995), 'Decision-making in the European Union: Towards a Framework for Analysis', *Journal of European Public Policy*, 2/1: 69–93.

Peterson, J. (1997), 'The European Union: Pooled Sovereignty, Divided Accountability', *Political Studies*, 45/3: 559–78.

Peterson, J. (1999), 'The Santer Era: the European Commission in Normative, Historical and Theoretical Perspective', *Journal of European Public Policy*, 6/1: 46–65.

Peterson, J. (2001), 'The Choice for EU Theorists: Establishing a Common Framework for Analysis', *European Journal of Political Research*, 37/1: 1–30.

Peterson, J. (2002), 'The College of Commissioners', in J. Peterson, and M. Shackleton (eds.), *The Institutions of the European Union* (Oxford and New York: Oxford University Press).

Peterson, J. (2004a), 'The Prodi Commission: fresh start or free fall?', in D. G. Dimitrakopoulos (ed.), *The Changing European Commission* (Manchester and New York: Manchester University Press).

Peterson, J. (2004b), 'The 'Enlarged' European Commission', (Mimeo: University of Edinburgh).

Peterson, J. (2004c), 'Policy Networks', in A. Wiener and T. Diez (eds.), *European Integration Theory* (Oxford: Oxford University Press).

Peterson, J. (2005), *The 'enlarged' European Commission* (Paris: Notre Europe), October, available on *http://www.notre-europe.asso.fr*

Peterson, J. (2006), 'Where does the Commission stand today?', in D. Spence (ed.), *The European Commission* (London: John Harper).

Peterson, J., and Bomberg, E. (1999), *Decision-Making in the European Union* (Basingstoke and New York: Palgrave).

Peterson, J., and Bomberg, E. (2001) 'The EU After the 1990s: Explaining Continuity and Change', in M. G. Cowles and M. Smith (eds.) *The State of the European Union Vol. V: Risks, Reform, Resistance or Revival?* (Oxford and New York: Oxford University Press).

Peterson, J., and Jones, E. (1999), 'Decision Making in an Enlarging European Union', in J. Sperling (ed.), *Two Tiers or Two Speeds? The European Security Order and the Enlargement of the European Union and NATO* (Manchester: Manchester University Press), 25–45.

Peterson, J., and Pollack, M. A. (2003) (eds.), *Europe, America, Bush: Transatlantic Relations in the 21st Century* (London and New York: Routledge).

Peterson, J., and Sjursen, H. (1998) (eds.), *A Common Foreign Policy for Europe?* (London: Routledge).

Phinnemore, D. (2004), *The Treaty establishing a Constitution for Europe: an overview* (London: Royal Institute for International Affairs).

Pierson, P. (1996), 'The Path to European Integration: A Historical Institutionalist Analysis', *Comparative Political Studies*, 29/2: 123–63.

Pierson, P. (2004), *Politics in Time: History, Institutions, and Social Analysis* (Princeton, NJ and Oxford: Princeton University Press).

Platzer, H. (1999), 'Interessenverbände und europäischer Lobbyismus', in W. Weidenfeld (ed.), *Europa-Handbuch* (Gütersloh: Verlag Bertelsmann Stiftung): 410–23.

Polanyi, M. (1951), *The Logic of Liberty: Reflections and Rejoinders* (London: Routledge and Kegan Paul).

Pollack, M. (1997), 'Delegation, Agency and Agenda-Setting in the European Union', *International Organization*, 51/1: 99–134.

Pollack, M. (1998), 'The Engines of Integration? Supranational Autonomy and influence in the European Union', in A. Stone Sweet and W. Sandholz (eds.), *European Integration and Supranational Governance* (Oxford: Oxford University Press).

Pollack, M. (2000), 'The End of Creeping Competence? EU Policy-Making Since Maastricht', *Journal of Common Market Studies*, 38/3: 519–38.

Pollack, M. (2003), *The Engines of European Integration: Delegation, Agency, and Agenda Setting in the EU* (Oxford and New York: Oxford University Press).

Pollack, M. (2004), 'The new institutionalisms and European integration', in A. Wiener and T. Diez (eds.), *European Integration Theory* (Oxford and New York: Oxford University Press).

Pollack, M. (2005), 'Theorizing the European Union: International organization, domestic polity, or experiment in new governance?', *Annual Review of Political Science*, 8: 357–98.

Pridham, G., and Pridham, P. (1981), *Transnational Party Co-operation and European Integration: The process towards direct elections* (London: Allen & Unwin).

Prodi, R. (1999), speech to the European Parliament, 4 May, available on *http://europa.eu.int/comm/commissioners/prodi/speeches/040599_en.htm*

Pujas, V. (2003), 'The European Anti-Fraud Office (OLAF): A European policy to fight against economic and financial fraud?', *Journal of European Public Policy*, 10/5: 778–97.

Putnam, R. (1993), *Making Democracy Work: Civic Traditions in Modern Italy* (Princeton, NJ: Princeton University Press).

Quermonne, J.-L. (1999), *The European Union in pursuit of legitimate and effective institutions* (Paris: Commissariat général du plan).

Rasmussen, H. (1986), *On Law and policy in the European Court of Justice* (Leiden: Nijhoff).

Rasmussen, H. (1988), Between self restraint and activism: A judicial policy for the European Court, *European Law Review*, 13: 28–38.

Raunio, T. (1997), *The European Perspective: Transnational Party Groups in the 1989–94 European Parliament* (Aldershot: Ashgate).

Raunio, T. (2002), 'Beneficial Cooperation or Mutual Ignorance? Contacts Between MEPs and National Parties', in B. Steunenberg and J. Thomassen (eds.), *The European Parliament: Moving toward Democracy in the EU* (Lanham, MD: Rowman & Littlefield): 87–111.

Ray, L. (1999), 'Measuring party orientation towards European integration: Results from an expert survey', *European Journal of Political Research*, 36/2: 283–306.

Raz, J. (2002), 'On the Authority and Interpretation of Constitutions: Some Preliminaries', in L. Alexander (ed.), *Constitutionalism, Philosophical Foundations* (Cambridge: Cambridge University Press).

Rees, W. R. (1998), *The Western European Union at the Crossroads* (Oxford and Boulder, CO: Westview Press).

Reid, T. R. (2004), *The United States of Europe: the New Superpower and the end of American Supremacy* (New York and London: The Penguin Press).

Reif, K., and Schmitt, H. (1980), 'Nine second-order national elections: A conceptual framework for the analysis of European election results', *European Journal of Political Research*, 8/1: 3–44.

Rhodes, R. A. W. (1995), 'The Institutional Approach', in D. Marsh and G. Stoker (eds.), *Theory and Methods in Political Science* (Basingstoke and New York: Palgrave).

Rifkind, J. (2004), *The European Dream* (Cambridge: Polity Press).

Rittberger, B. (2001), 'Which institutions for post-war Europe? Explaining the institutional design of Europe's first community', *Journal of European Public Policy*, 8/5: 673–708.

Rittberger, B. (2005) *Building Europe's Parliament: Democratic Representation beyond the Nation State* (Oxford: Oxford University Press).

Risse, T. (2004), 'European Institutions and Identity Change: What Have We learned?', in R. Hermann, T. Risse, and M. Brewer (eds.), *Transnational Identities: Becoming European in the EU* (Lanham, MD: Rowman & Littlefield): 247–71.

Ross, G. (1995), *Jacques Delors and European Integration* (New York and London: Polity Press).

Ruggie, J. G. (1998), *Constructing the World Polity: Essays on International Institutionalization* (London and New York: Routledge).

Salmon, J. (1971), 'Les Représentations et Missions Permanentes Auprès de la CEE et de l'EURATOM', in M. Virally *et al.* (eds.), *Les Missions Permanentes Auprès des Organisations Internationales. Tome* 1 (Brussels: Dotation Carnegie pour la Paix Internationale): 561–831.

Sanders, D. (1995), 'Behavioural Analysis' Approach', in D. Marsh and G. Stoker (eds.), *Theory and Methods in Political Science* (Basingstoke and New York: Palgrave).

Sandholtz, W. (1993), 'Choosing Union: Monetary Politics and Maastricht', *International Organization*, 46/1: 1–39.

Sandholtz, W., and Stone Sweet, A. (1998a) (eds.), 'Integration, Supranational Governance, and the Institutionalization of the European Polity', in W. Sandholtz and A. Stone Sweet (eds), *European Integration and Supranational Governance* (Oxford: Oxford University Press), 1–26.

Sandholtz, W., and Stone Sweet, A. (1998b) (eds.), *European Integration and Supranational Governance* (Oxford: Oxford University Press).

Sbragia, A. (1991) (ed.), *Europolitics* (Washington: Brookings Institution).

Sbragia, A. (1993), 'The European Community: A Balancing Act', *Publius*, 23/3: 23–38.

Scharpf, F. (1994), 'Community and Autonomy: Multilevel Policy Making in the European Union', *Journal of European Public Policy*, 1/2: 219–42.

Scharpf, F. (1999), *Governing in Europe: Effective and Democratic?* (Oxford and New York: Oxford University Press).

Schermers, H. G., Flinterman, C., Kellerman, A. E., van Haersotte, J., and van de Meent, G.-W. (1993) (eds.), *Free Movement of Persons in Europe* (Dordrecht: Martinus Nijhoff).

Schmitt-Egner, P. (2000), *Handbuch der Europäischen Regionalorganisationen* (Baden-Baden: Nomos).

Schmitter, P. (1970), 'A Revised Theory of Regional Integration', *International Organization*, 24/autumn: 836–68.

Schmitter, P., and Streeck, W. (1994), 'Organized Interests and the Europe of 1992', in N. Ornstein and W. Streeck (eds.), *Political Power and Social Change* (Washington: AEI Press).

Schöbel, N. (1995), 'Der Ausschuss der Regionen—eine erste Bilanz', *Europäisches Zentrum für Föderalismus-Forschung Tübingen, Occasional Papers, Nr 4*.

Schwaiger, P. (1997), 'The European Union's Committee of the Regions: A Progress Report', *Regional and Federal Studies*, 7/1: 12–22.

Scully, R. M. (2005), *Becoming Europeans? Attitudes, Behaviour and Socialization in the European Parliament* (Oxford: Oxford University Press).

Sedelmeier, U. (2005), *Constructing the Path to Eastern Enlargement* (Manchester and New York: Manchester University Press).

Shackleton, M. (1997), 'The Internal Legitimacy Crisis of the European Union', in A. W. Cafruny and C. Lankowski (eds.), *Europe's Ambiguous Unity* (Boulder, CO and London: Lynne Rienner).

Shackleton, M. (2000), 'The Politics of Co-decision', *Journal of Common Market Studies*, 38/2: 325–42.

Shackleton, M. (2005), 'Parliamentary Government or Division of Powers: Is the Destination Still Unknown?', in C. Parsons and N. Jabko (eds) *The State of the European Union: With US or Against US* (Oxford and New York: Oxford University Press), 123–41.

Shackleton, M., and Raunio, T. (2003), 'Codecision since Amsterdam: a laboratory for institutional innovation and change', *Journal of European Public Policy*, 10/2: 171–87.

Shermers, H. (1993) (ed.), *Free Movement of Persons in Europe* (Dordrecht: Martinus Nijhoff).

Sherrington, P. (2000), *The Council of Ministers: Political Authority in the European Union* (London: Pinter).

Sherrington, P., and Warleigh, A. (2002), 'The Economic and Social Committee', in A. Warleigh (ed.) *Understanding European Institutions* (London: Routledge).

Sherrington, P., and Waelbroek, D. (2004), *Judicial Protection in the European Communities*, 6th edn. (Deventer: Kluwer).

Shore, C. (2000), *Building Europe: The Cultural Politics of European Integration* (London: Routledge).

Sie Dhian Ho, M., and Van Keulen, M. (2004), *The Dutch at the Helm—Navigating on a Rough Sea: The Netherlands 2004 presidency of the European Union* (Paris: Notre Europe).

Siedentop, L. (2000), *Democracy in Europe* (Harmondsworth: Penguin).

Skach, C. (2005), 'We, the Peoples? Constitutionalizing the European Union', *Journal of Common Market Studies*, 43/1: 149–70.

Skocpol, T. (1985), 'Bringing the State Back In: Strategies of Analysis in Current Research', in P. B. Evans, D. Rieschemeyer, and T. Skocpol (eds.), *Bringing the State Back In* (Cambridge: Cambridge University Press).

Slaughter, A.-M. (2004), *The Real New World Order* (Princeton, NJ: Princeton University Press).

Slaughter, A.-M., Stone Sweet, A, and Weiler, J. H. H. (1998) (eds.), *The European Court and National Courts–Doctrine and Jurisprudence: Legal Change in its Social Context* (Oxford: Hart Publishing).

Sloan, S. (2003), *NATO, the European Union and the Atlantic Community* (Oxford and Boulder, CO: Rowman & Littlefield).

Smismans, S. (2000), 'The European Economic and Social Committee: Towards Deliberative Democracy via a Functional Assembly', *European Integration Online Papers*, 4/12, available on *http://eiop.or.at/eiop/texte/2000-012a.htm*

Smith, J. (1999), *Europe's Elected Parliament* (Sheffield: Sheffield University Press).

Smith, K. E. (2003), *European Union Foreign Policy in a Changing World* (Oxford and Malden, MA: Polity).

Smith, M. E. (2003), *Europe's Foreign and Security Policy: The Institutionalization of Cooperation* (Cambridge: Cambridge University Press).

Spaak, P. H. (1969), *Combats Inachevés*, 2 Vols. (Paris: Fayard).

Spence, D. (1991), 'Enlargement without Accession: the EC's Response to German Unification', RIIA Discussion Paper, 36 (London: Royal Institute of International Affairs).

Spence, D. (2000), 'Plus ça change, plus c'est la même chose? Attempting to reform the European Commission', *Journal of European Public Policy*, 7/1: 1–25.

Spence, D. (2002), 'The evolving role of foreign ministries in the conduct of European Union affairs', in B. Hocking and D. Spence (eds.), *Foreign Ministries in the European Union* (Basingstoke and New York: Palgrave).

Spence, D. (2005) (ed.), *The European Commission*, 3rd edn. (London: John Harper).

Stacey, J. (2003), 'Displacement of the Council via informal dynamics? Comparing the Commission and Parliament', *Journal of European Public Policy*, 10/6: 936–55.

Stasavage, D. (2004), 'Open-Door or Closed Door? Transparency in Domestic and International Bargaining', *International Organization*, 58/2: 667–703.

Stein, J. (1981), 'Lawyers, Judges and the Making of a Transnational Constitution', *American Journal of International Law*, 75/1: 1–27.

Steinmo, S. (2004), 'Néo-Institutionnalismes', in L. Boussaguet, S. Jacquot, and P. Ravinet (eds.), *Dictionnaire des politiques publiques* (Paris: Presses de Sciences Po).

Stevens, A. (2001), *Brussels Bureaucrats: The Administration of the European Union* (Basingstoke: Palgrave).

Stewart, R. (1975), 'The Reformation of American Administrative Law', *Harvard Law Review*, 88: 1667–813.

Stone Sweet, A. (2000), *Governing with Judges* (Oxford and New York: Oxford University Press).

Stone Sweet, A., and Sandholtz, W. (1998), 'Integration, Supranational Governance, and the Institutionalization of the European Polity', in W. Sandholtz and A. Stone Sweet (eds), *European Integration and Supranational Governance* (Oxford: Oxford University Press), 1–26.

Strasser, D. (1992), *The Finances of Europe*, 7th edn. (Luxembourg: EC Official Publications).

Suleiman, E. (2003), *Dismantling Democratic States* (Princeton, NJ: Princeton University Press).

Switalska, J. (1999), *The Quest for Political Identity in the Committee of the Regions: Symbolism and Pragmatism*, MA dissertation, South Bank University, London.

Szymanski, M., and Smith, M. E. (2005), 'Coherence and Conditionality in European Foreign Policy', *Journal of Common Market Studies*, 43/1: 171–92.

Taggart, P. (1998), 'A touchstone of dissent: Euroscepticism in contemporary Western European party systems', *European Journal of Political Research*, 33/3: 363–88.

Tallberg. J. (2003), 'The Agenda-Shaping Powers of the EU Council Presidency', *Journal of European Public Policy*, 10/1: 1–19

Tallberg, J. (2004), 'The Power of the Presidency: Brokerage, Efficiency and Distribution in EU Negotiations', *Journal of Common Market Studies*, 42/5: 999–1024.

Taulègne, B. (1993), *Le Conseil Européen* (Paris: PUF).

Thelen, K., and Steinmo, S. (1992), *Structuring Politics: Historical Institutionalism in Comparative Analysis* (Cambridge: Cambridge University Press).

Thomassen, J., and Schmitt, H. (1999a), 'Issue Congruence', in H. Schmitt and J. Thomassen (eds.), *Political Representation and Legitimacy in the European Union* (Oxford: Oxford University Press), 186–208.

Thomassen, J., and Schmitt, H. (1999b), 'Partisan Structures in the European Parliament', in R. S. Katz and B. Wessels (eds.), *The European Parliament, the National Parliaments, and European Integration* (Oxford: Oxford University Press), 129–48.

Tsakatika, M. (2005), 'The European Commission between continuity and change', *Journal of Common Market Studies*, 43/1: 193–220.

van Buitenen, P. (2000), *Blowing the Whistle: One Man's Fight Against Fraud in the European Commission* (London: Politico's Publishing).

van der Eijk, C., and Franklin, M. N. (1996) (eds.), *Choosing Europe? The European Electorate and National Politics in the Face of Union* (Ann Arbor, MI University of Michigan Press).

van der Eijk, C., and Franklin, M. N. (2004), 'Potential for contestation on European matters at national elections in Europe', in G. Marks and M. R. Steenbergen (eds.), *European Integration and Political Conflict* (Cambridge: Cambridge University Press), 32–50.

van Oudenhove, G. (1965), *The Political Parties in the European Parliament: The First Ten Years (September 1952—September 1962)* (Leyden: A. W. Sijthoff).

Vedel, G. (1972), *Report of the Working Party examining the problem of the Enlargement of the Powers of the European Parliament* ('Vedel Report') (Brussels: Bulletin of the European Communities, Supplement 4/72).

Waever, O. (1995), 'Identity, Integration and Security: Solving the Sovereignty Puzzle in EU Studies', *Journal of International Affairs*, 48/2: 389–431.

Walker, N. (2004) (ed.), *Europe's Area of Freedom, Security and Justice* (Oxford: Oxford University Press).

Wallace H. (1980), *Budgetary Politics: The Finances of the European Union* (London: Allen & Unwin).

Wallace, H. (2000), 'The Institutional Setting: Five Variations on a Theme', in H. Wallace and W. Wallace (eds.), *Policy Making in the European Union*, 4th edn. (Oxford and New York: Oxford University Press), 3–38.

Wallace, H. (2002), 'The Council: an institutional chameleon', *Governance*, 15/3 (2002): 325–44.

Wallace, H. (2005), 'An Institutional Anatomy and Five Policy Modes', in H. Wallace, W. Wallace, and M. Pollack (eds.), *Policy-Making in the European Union*, 5th edn. (Oxford and New York: Oxford University Press), 49–90.

Wallace, H., and Wallace, W. (1996) (eds.), *Policy Making in the European Union*, 3rd edn. (Oxford and New York: Oxford University Press).

Wallace, H., and Wallace, W. (2000) (eds.), *Policy Making in the European Union*, 4th edn. (Oxford and New York: Oxford University Press).

Wallace, W. (1977), 'Less than a federation, more than a regime: the Community as a political system', in H. Wallace, W. Wallace, and C. Webb (eds.) *Policy-Making in the European Community* (Chichester: Wiley).

Wallace, W. (2005), 'Post-sovereign Governance: the EU as a Partial Polity', in H. Wallace, W. Wallace, and M. A. Pollack (eds.), *Policy-Making in the European Union*, 5th edn. (Oxford and New York: Oxford University Press), 483–503.

Waltz, K. (1979), *Theory of International Politics* (Reading, MA: Addison-Wesley).

Warleigh, A. (1999), *The Committee of the Regions: Institutionalising Multi-Level Governance* (London: Kogan Page).

Warleigh, A. (2002*a*), 'The Committee of the Regions', in A. Warleigh (ed.), *Understanding European Institutions* (London: Routledge).

Warleigh, A. (2002*b*) (ed.), *Understanding European Institutions* (London: Routledge).

Weatherill, S. (2005), *Cases and Materials on EU Law*, 7th edn. (Oxford and New York: Oxford University Press).

Webb, C. (1977), 'Introduction: Variations on a Theoretical Theme', in H. Wallace, W. Wallace and C. Webb (eds.), *Policy-Making in the European Community* (Chichester: Wiley), 1–31.

Weidenfeld, W., and Wessels, W. (1982) (eds.), *Jahrbuch der Europäischen Integration 1981* (Bonn: Europa Union Verlag).

Weidenfeld, W., and Wessels, W. (1983) (eds.), *Jahrbuch der Europäischen Integration 1982* (Bonn: Europa Union Verlag).

Weidenfeld, W., and Wessels, W. (1994) (eds.), *Europa von A–Z* (Bonn: Bundeszentrale für politische Bildung)

Weigall, D., and Stirk, P. (1992) (eds.), *The Origins and Development of the European Community* (Leicester: Leicester University Press).

Weiler, J. H. H. (1981), 'The Community System: The Dual Character of Supranationalism', *Yearbook of European Law*, 1: 268–306.

Weiler, J. H. H. (1994), 'Fin-de-siècle Europe: On Ideals and Ideology in Post-Maastricht Europe', in D. Curtin and T. Heukels (eds.), *Institutional Dynamics of European Integration: Essays in Honour of Henry G. Schermers* (Dordrecht: Martinus Nijhoff Publishers), 23–41.

Weiler, J. H. H. (1999), *The Constitution of Europe* (Cambridge: Cambridge University Press).

Weiler, J. H. H. (2003), 'A Constitution for Europe? Some hard choices' in J. H. H. Weiler, J. Begg and J. Peterson (eds.), *Integration in an Expanding European Union* (Oxford and Malden MA: Blackwell).

Weiler, J. H. H., Begg, I., and Peterson, J. (2003) (eds.), *Integration in an Expanding European Union* (Oxford and Malden MA: Blackwell).

Wendt, A. (1999), *Social Theory of International Politics* (Cambridge: Cambridge University Press)

Werts, J. (1992), *The European Council* (The Hague: TMC Asser Instituut).

Wessels, W. (1997), 'An Ever Closer Fusion? A Dynamic Macropolitical View on Integration Processes', *Journal of Common Market Studies*, 35/2: 267–99.

Wessels, W. (2001), 'Nice Results: the Millennium IGC in the EU's Evolution', *Journal of Common Market Studies*, 39/2: 197–219.

Westlake, M. (1999), *The Council of the European Union* (London: Cartermill International Ltd.).

Westlake, M., and Galloway, D. (2004), *The Council of the European Union*, 3rd edn. (London: John Harper Publishing).

Whitaker, R. (2001), 'Party control in a committee-based legislature? The case of the European Parliament', *Journal of Legislative Studies*, 7/4: 63–88.

White, B. (2001), *Understanding European Foreign Policy* (Basingstoke: Palgrave).

Wiedmann, T. (2002), 'Abschied der Regionen vom AdR—Der Ausschuss der Regionen vor der Zerreissprobe', *Jahrbuch des Föderalismus 2002* (Baden-Baden: Nomos), 541–51.

Wiessala, G. (2002), *The European Union and Asian Countries* (Sheffield: Sheffield Academic Press).

Willis, F. R. (1965), *France, Germany, and the New Europe, 1945–1963* (Stanford, CA: Stanford University Press).

Wong, R. (2005), 'The Europeanization of foreign policy', in C. Hill and M. Smith (eds.), *International Relations and the European Union* (Oxford and New York: Oxford University Press).

Wurzel, R. (1999), 'The Role of the European Parliament: Interview with Ken Collins MEP', *Journal of Legislative Studies*, 5/2: 1–23.

Youngs, R. (2004), *Europe's Uncertain Pursuit of Middle East Reform* (Washington, DC: Carnegie Endowment for International Peace), available on *http://www.ceip.org/files/pdf/CP45.YOUNGS.final.PDF*

Zielonka, J. (1998), *Understanding Euro-Paralysis: Why Europe is Unable to Act in International Politics* (Basingstoke and New York: Macmillan/Palgrave).

Zwart, T., and Verhey, L. (2003) (eds.), *Agencies in European and Comparative Law* (Antwerp: Intersentia).

Index

Fligstein, N. 6
fonctionnaires 159
Fontaine, Nicole 296
Fontainebleau European Council, 1984 50
Foreign Minister *see* Minister for Foreign Affairs
foreign ministers 38, 40, 42, 53, 72
  see also European Council
foreign policy 24, 253–4
  accountability 266
  Coreper 280
  Council of Ministers 72
  EU record 264–5
  European Council 51–2, 53
  origins of institutions 254–5
  see also common foreign and security policy
Fouchet Plan 20–1, 255
Framework Decision on Freezing of Assets and
  Evidence 243
Framework Decision on the European Arrest
  Warrant 243–4
Framework Decision on the European Evidence
  Warrant 243, 244
framework decisions 239
Framework Directive on Combating
  Terrorism 245–6
France
  agencies 191
  Barroso Commission 93
  Commission 83
  Constitutional Treaty 2, 10, 12, 13, 29, 89, 118,
    155, 185, 260, 261, 269, 345
  Contact Group 262
  Council of Ministers Presidency 70
  EDC Treaty 19
  empty chair crisis 21, 83
  ESDP 264
  Eurogroup 183
  European Convention 28
  European Council 31–2, 40
  European integration 57
  Europol 236
  exchange rate policy 184
  foreign policy 255, 256, 257
  Fouchet Plan 20–1
  High Authority 82
  and Iran 262
  Maastricht Treaty 154
  national interests 29
  President 38
  Schengen Agreement 233
  single currency 172, 173
  Stability and Growth Pact 140, 182
  UN 267
Frankfurt 170, 179
Franklin, M. N. 306
Fratini, Franco 93

fraud *see* Court of Auditors; OLAF
free movement of goods 137–8
Freedman, O. 205
Frieden, J. 172
functionalism 19–20, 31–2, 33

Gabel, M. J. 308
Galloway, D. 67
Garrett, G. 6, 132
Gatsios, K. 193
General Affairs and External Relations Council
  (GAERC) 63, 72, 278, 280, 281
General Affairs Council (GAC) 43, 51, 71, 72,
  235, 258, 280, 337
General Agreement on Tariffs and Trade 5
General Electric 7
Geoghegan-Quinn, Maire 227n
Germany
  Barroso Commission 93
  Bundesbank 179
  CFSP 254
  Committee of the Regions 315–16, 318, 325,
    326
  Constitutional Court 132
  Contact Group 262
  Coreper 279, 287
  Eurogroup 183
  European Convention 28
  European integration 57
  European Parliament 109
  infringement proceedings 135
  and Iran 262
  justice and home affairs 233, 236
  national interests 29
  parliamentarization 31
  qualified majority voting 68
  regional government 328
  Stability and Growth Pact 140, 182
  Tobacco Advertising case 123n, 139
  unification 23, 85
  see also West Germany
Ghent European Council, 2001 46
Giavazzi, Francesco 177
Gil-Robles Gil-Delgado, José Maria 296
Ginsberg, R. H. 254, 264
Giscard d'Estaing, Valéry 4, 15n, 27, 40, 85, 108,
  140
Glarbo, K. 267
global governance 345–6
Goetz, K. 340
Golub, J. 6
Gomez, R. 280
Gouldner, Alvin 203
governance 332, 346
  global 345–6